The Linguistics Student's Handbook

'Laurie Bauer's *Handbook* is a truly unique, as well as a wonderfully original resource for students coming to grips with the ins and outs of modern linguistics. Bauer does what few linguists are able to do well: write in a down-to-earth way about the subject matter. The *Handbook* is not just about linguistics and its leading ideas, however. It is brimming with all kinds of useful information to help students understand the very practical side of doing linguistics, such as how to spell *diphthong*, gloss examples, write assignments in linguistics, and make sense of linguistic notation. The *Handbook* helps the student of linguistics with all the things that the instructor doesn't quite get round to.'

Professor John Newman, University of Alberta

THE LINGUISTICS STUDENT'S HANDBOOK

Laurie Bauer

EDINBURGH UNIVERSITY PRESS

© Laurie Bauer, 2007

Transferred to digital print 2013

Edinburgh University Press Ltd
22 George Square, Edinburgh

Typeset in 11/13 Ehrhardt MT and Gill Sans
by Servis Filmsetting Ltd, Manchester, and
printed and bound by CPI Group (UK) Ltd
Croydon, CR0 4YY

A CIP record for this book is available from the British Library

ISBN 978 0 7486 2758 5 (hardback)
ISBN 978 0 7486 2759 2 (paperback)

The right of Laurie Bauer
to be identified as author of this work
has been asserted in accordance with
the Copyright, Designs and Patents Act 1988.

£20.99

Contents

Part III Reading linguistics

Part IV Writing and presenting linguistics

Part V Bibliographies

Part VI Language file

Preface

'Handbook' seems to be a fashionable title, where once the Latinate label 'manual' might have held sway. But in the case of this book, it also seems an inevitable title. This book is not a dictionary of linguistics, not an encyclopedia of linguistics, not a textbook of linguistics but contains elements which might be found in all or any of these. It is a book which the tertiary student of linguistics will need at hand for continual reference while they are studying.

This handbook is intended as the kind of reference work which can be valuable at any stage in the career of a tertiary linguistics student, and which can fill in the gaps that are often left in lectures and the like. Its main focus is not the nitty-gritty of syntactic theory or the ethics of doing sociolinguistic research: these topics are likely to be covered in detail in lectures, and the opinions of your teachers on these topics may be very different from the opinions of the author of this work. Rather, its focus is the kind of general material that may be of interest to any linguistics student, whatever the kind of linguistics they are doing.

The organisation of the material is vaguely thematic. In the first part, some of the fundamentals of linguistics are considered: what linguistics is, what a language is, the fundamental distinctions in structuralist linguistics. These things could be found in many other textbooks and specialised works on linguistics and languages, but very often these fundamental points are rather glossed over in early lectures on linguistics (because they are not easy to deal with) and then ignored in later lectures, or they are dealt with early on in linguistics courses and then often forgotten by students by the time they become central to the problems the students are working with. Although this part is called 'Some fundamentals of linguistics' and deals with topics which are vital to the understanding of linguistic topics, the sections here are seen less as introductions to these topics than as sources of clarification and revision when the topics have already been met.

The second part deals with matters of notation and terminology.

The third part, called 'Reading linguistics' is concerned with the student's ability to understand the technical aspects of the linguistics texts they are likely to be faced with.

Although you cannot write any linguistics without having read some, there are other areas which become much more important when it comes to presenting material, in essays, assignments or theses. These points appear in the fourth part, 'Writing and presenting linguistics'.

The fifth part deals specifically with the problems raised by writing and understanding reference lists and bibliographies.

The sixth and largest part, called the 'Language file', attempts to present structural and social information on a large number of languages in a consistent format so that students can gain a very brief overview of many of the languages they will hear about in their linguistics courses.

It must be admitted that this handbook presents its author's view, and there are many sections where the author's perception of what is required may not meet the user's. Which names students will not know how to pronounce, for example, is probably an impossible question to answer, and any list will both state some things which seem obvious and miss others which are less obvious (or more common) than the author realised. Similarly, some of the areas covered may seem obvious and unnecessary, while others which might have been of value may have been missed. At the risk of being swamped with responses, I would encourage readers and reviewers to let me know where I have failed. If the book finds a wide enough and enthusiastic enough audience, Edinburgh University Press may be persuaded to provide an updated edition which can take such points into account.

Finally, I should like to thank all those who have helped by answering questions that arose in the writing of this book, and also my teachers who first fed my interest in linguistics and taught me such fundamentals as I know. Specific thanks go to Richard Arnold, Winifred Bauer, Louise Bourchier, Alana Dickson, Jen Hay, Janet Holmes, Kate Kearns, Marianna Kennedy, Jim Miller, Liz Pearce, Tony Quinn, Emily Rainsford, Theresa Sawicka, Agnes Terraschke, Paul Warren and the anonymous referees for Edinburgh University Press. The IPA chart on p. 129 is reprinted with the permission of the International Phonetic Association, which can be contacted through its website, www.arts.gla.ac.uk/IPA/ipa.html.

Laurie Bauer
Wellington, August 2006

Abbreviations and conventions used in the text

<...>	Enclose spellings
/.../	Enclose phonemic transcriptions
[...]	Enclose phonetic transcriptions
italics	Forms cited in the text (see p. 98), titles of books etc.
SMALL CAPITALS	Technical terms introduced; emphasis
*	Indicates a string which is not grammatical

Transcriptions

Transcriptions of English are presented in a Standard Southern British pronunciation, with symbols for the vowels as set out below. The transcriptions for the consonants are standard International Phonetic Alphabet symbols (see p. 129), as are transcriptions of other languages.

FLEECE	iː	FACE	eɪ
KIT	ɪ	PRICE	aɪ
DRESS	e	CHOICE	ɔɪ
TRAP	æ	MOUTH	aʊ
STRUT	ʌ	GOAT	əʊ
PALM, START	ɑː	NEAR	ɪə
LOT	ɒ	SQUARE	eə
NURSE	ɜː	CURE	ʊə
THOUGHT, FORCE	ɔː	COMM*A*	ə
FOOT	ʊ	HAPP*Y*	i
GOOSE	uː		

Part I: Some fundamentals of linguistics

1

Language

Because we have a word *language*, we assume that there must be some corresponding entity for the word to denote (see section 32). However, the linguist Saussure (1969 [1916]: 19) points out to us that 'language is not an entity'.[1] Defining something like 'The English Language' turns out to be a difficult task.

Part of the problem is that the language has so many different aspects. We can view it as a social fact, as a psychological state, as a set of structures, or as a collection of outputs.

A language is a social fact, a kind of social contract. It exists not in an individual, but in a community.

> It is a treasure buried by the practice of speech in people belonging to the same community, a grammatical system which has virtual existence in each brain, or more exactly in the brains of a collection of individuals; because language is not complete in any individual, but exists only in the collectivity. (Saussure 1969 [1916]: 30, my translation, see the footnote for the original French[2])

A language can also be viewed as a mental reality. It exists in the heads of people who speak it, and we assume its existence because of people's ability to learn languages in general and their practice in dealing with at least one

---

[1] 'La langue n'est pas une entité.'

[2] 'C'est un trésor déposé par la pratique de la parole dans les sujets appartenant à une même communauté, un système grammatical existant virtuellement dans chaque cerveau, ou plus exactement dans les cervaux d'un ensemble d'individus; car la langue n'est complète dans aucun, elle n'existe parfaitement que dans la masse.'

particular language. '[A] grammar is a mental entity, represented in the mind/brain of an individual and characterising that individual's linguistic capacity' (Lightfoot 2000: 231). Note that Lightfoot here talks of a *grammar* rather than of a *language*, but one possible definition of a language is precisely that it is the grammatical system which allows speakers to produce appropriate utterances. 'Grammar' has as many meanings as 'language' (see section 4).

In this sense, we might see a language as a set of choices, a set of contrasts. We can say *Kim kissed the crocodile* or *The crocodile kissed Kim*, but we cannot choose to say, as a meaningful sentence of English, *Kissed crocodile Kim the*. There is a system to what orders the words have to come in if they are to make sense. We choose, in English, whether to say *towel* or *cowl*, but we cannot choose, in English, to say something with a consonant half-way between the /t/ of *towel* and the /k/ of *cowl* to mean something which is part towel and part cowl (or, indeed, to mean anything else). There is a system to what sounds we use in English. So a language can be viewed as a system of systems. This view is usually attributed to Meillet: 'Every language forms a system in which everything is interconnected' (Meillet 1903: 407 [my translation][3]). But he has forerunners who make the same point in similar terms, e.g.: 'Every language is a system all of whose parts interrelate and interact organically' (von der Gabelentz 1901: 481, as cited and translated by Matthews 2001: 6; see the footnote for the original German[4]).

Another alternative way of considering language is to ignore the way in which speakers go about constructing utterances, and consider instead their output, an actual set of utterances or (in a more idealised form) a set of sentences. A language can be defined as a set of sentences:

> the totality of utterances that can be made in a speech community is the language of that speech community. (Bloomfield 1957 [1926]: 26)

> [A] language [is] a set (finite or infinite) of sentences, each finite in length and constructed out of a finite set of elements. (Chomsky 1957: 13)

The question of whether we should be dealing with utterances (things produced, whether in speech of in writing, by speakers) or sentences raises another potential distinction. Chomsky (1986) introduces the notion of a distinction between E-language and I-language. Smith (1994) already talks of this distinction as a 'customary' one, which may be an overstatement of the case, but he draws the distinction very clearly:

---

[3] 'chaque langue forme un système où tout se tient.'
[4] 'Jede Sprache is ein System, dessen sämmtliche Theile organisch zusammenhängen und zusammenwirken.'

> E-language is the 'external' manifestation of the 'internally' (i.e. men-
> tally) represented grammars (or I-languages) of many individuals.
> E-languages are the appropriate domain for social, political, mathe-
> matical or logical statements; I-languages are the appropriate domain
> for statements about individual knowledge. That this apparently nar-
> rower domain is worth considering follows from the fact that, as a
> species, humans appear to be essentially identical in their linguistic
> abilities. . . . [E]very child brings the same intellectual apparatus
> (known as 'universal grammar') to bear on the task of acquiring his or
> her first language. (Smith 1994: 646)

So the utterances are E-language, while the sentences may well belong to I-
language, that hypothesised rather less error-prone system which we have in
our heads. But the 'intellectual apparatus' which allows children to construct a
language like English for themselves is also, it is suggested, language in a rather
different sense. The language capacity, the feature which distinguishes humans
from other animals, is sometimes also simply called 'language'.

There are so many complexities here that we might argue that it would be
better for linguists to give up attempting even to describe particular languages,
let alone 'language' in the abstract. What are they to describe? Are they to
describe the social structure which is complete only in the collectivity, or the
mental structure which speakers of that language must be assumed to carry in
their heads, or the set of systems which are presumed to allow speakers to create
new utterances for themselves, or the actually produced utterances? All of these
have been tried. But note that there are logical inconsistencies between these
various potential objects of description. If language as a social fact exists only in
the collectivity, no individual speaks 'the language'; any individual must have
only a partial knowledge of the language. This isn't hard to prove: open any large
dictionary of English at random, and read the first fifty headwords you come to.
You did not know all of these words before you started reading (you probably
don't after you've finished), but somebody (or, more likely, a set of individuals)
knows them and has used them or they wouldn't be in the dictionary. So the
description of what is in any person's head can never provide a full description
of a language in the sense that English is a language. Many linguists prefer to use
the term IDIOLECT for the language of an individual. So you don't speak English,
you speak your idiolect. That seems simple enough until we ask what 'English'
consists of. Presumably it consists of the sum of all the idiolects of people who
we agree are speaking English. But some of these people have conflicting ideas
about what is part of their language. To take a simple example, there are millions
of people speaking what we would call 'English', for whom the past tense of the
verb *dive* is *dove*. For these speakers *dived* sounds like baby-talk, as *writed* would
instead of *wrote*. There are also millions of speakers for whom *dived* is the only

possible past tense of *dive*, and *dove* sounds like the kind of joke you make when you say that the past tense of *think* must be *thank* or *thunk*. The example is trivial, but it means that we must allow for a lot of different answers to what is English, even mutually incompatible ones. So it must be true that there is no clear–cut line where English stops and something else begins (and it is frequently not clear what that something else is). The language 'English' is not well–defined (and the same will be true for any other language which is given a name in this way).

Neither is language in the sense 'language faculty' well–defined. A lot of work has gone into trying to understand Universal Grammar (or UG as it is usually termed) within Chomskyan approaches to linguistics (see section 8), and we do not yet understand what it must look like or how it must function. There is even dispute as to whether it is a specifically linguistic set of functions, or whether it is a general set of cognitive abilities which together allow human beings to be language users.

If neither a language nor language (the language faculty) is easily definable, we have to ask what it is that linguists deal with. Linguists have to define language for their own purposes. They do not have an external definition of language or of a particular language which is clearly sufficient for their needs. This is not necessarily a bad thing, but it does mean that care is required.

References

Bloomfield, Leonard (1957 [1926]). A set of postulates for the science of language. *Language* 2: 153–64. Reprinted in Martin Joos (ed.), *Readings in Linguistics*. Chicago and London: University of Chicago Press, 26–31.

Chomsky, Noam (1957). *Syntactic Structures*. The Hague and Paris: Mouton.

Chomsky, Noam (1986). *Knowledge of Language*. New York: Praeger.

Chomsky, Noam (2000). *New Horizons in the Study of Language and Mind*. Cambridge: Cambridge University Press.

Gabelentz, Georg von der (1901 [1891]). *Die Sprachwissenschaft*. 2nd edn. Leipzig: Tauchnitz.

Lightfoot, David (2000). The spandrels of the linguistic genotype. In Chris Knight, Michael Studdert-Kennedy & James R. Hurford (eds), *The Evolutionary Emergence of Language*. Cambridge: Cambridge University Press, 231–47.

Matthews, Peter (2001). *A Short History of Structural Linguistics*. Cambridge: Cambridge University Press.

Meillet, Antoine (1903). *Introduction à l'étude comparative des langues indo-européennes*. Paris: Hachette.

Saussure, Ferdinand de (1969 [1916]). *Cours de linguistique générale*. Paris: Payot.

Smith, N[eil] V. (1994). Competence and performance. In R. E. Asher (ed.), *Encyclopedia of Language and Linguistics*. Oxford: Pergamon, Vol. 2, 645–8.

2

Accent, dialect, variety

Since the term 'language' is hard to define (see section 1), it virtually follows that all other terms referring to the linguistic systems of groups of individuals will be equally hard to define. That is certainly the case, though the major mis-understandings with terms like *accent* and *dialect* arise from the fact that lay people and linguists use them rather differently.

Accent

The term *accent* has a number of different senses in discussions about language. It can refer to a graphological mark (e.g. the acute accent on the last letter of <passé> – see section 23). It can refer to some form of phonetic prominence (e.g. in *an accented syllable*). But the meaning that is to be discussed here is the one used in, for instance, *a regional accent*.

There are two things to note about the term *accent* as used technically by linguists in this sense. The first is that it involves only pronunciation, and the second is that it is universal: everybody speaks with an accent.

The Oxford English Dictionary defines *accent* (in the relevant sense) as 'The mode of utterance peculiar to an individual, locality, or nation'. The phrase 'mode of utterance' could be understood to include the words used or the way in which words are strung together. For linguists, these are not counted as part of accent. An accent is purely a matter of pronunciation. So it is possible to take any sentence in this book and read it in an Edinburgh, New York or New Zealand accent (although in each of those cases it would probably be more accurate to say 'in one of the accents of Edinburgh . . . '). Conversely, you can use Australian words and phrases like *kangaroo* or *stone the crows* without using an Australian accent.

It appears that the term *accent* was once used specifically for intonation or voice-quality (probably reflecting the origin of the word). *The Oxford English Dictionary* quotes the eighteenth-century essayist Addison as saying 'By the Tone or Accent I do not mean the Pronunciation of each particular Word, but the Sound of the whole Sentence.' In modern usage, the vowel in a word like *home* or the quality of the /r/ sound in a word like *merry* are potential distinctive characteristics of one's accent.

The second point above is the more important of the two. In common parlance, especially in England, if you say that somebody 'has an accent' you mean that they have a regional accent and not a standard one (see again, *The Oxford English Dictionary*). Ellis phrases this, in a note in *The Oxford English Dictionary*'s entry, by saying that an accent 'may include mispronunciation of vowels or consonants, misplacing of stress', which clearly indicates by the use of the prefix *mis-* that an accent is undesirable. The converse of this is that people are sometimes said 'to speak without an accent' or 'not to have an accent'. This can mean one of three things.

1. A person X may say that another person Y does not have an accent if they judge that Y's accent is, in relevant respects, the same as their own.
2. A person may be said not to have an accent if they speak with a standard accent.
3. A person who is known not to use English as their first language but who nevertheless sounds like a native English speaker may be said not to have an accent.

None of these notions would be accepted by linguists. Linguists would say that nobody can speak without an accent. Everybody who speaks has particular features of pronunciation, and these form the accent. Even people who speak Received Pronunciation (RP, the standard accent of England) give themselves away as being British the moment they go to the United States or Canada. So everyone has an accent, and the fact that your accent sounds like mine does not make it less true that we both have an accent.

Furthermore, while linguists acknowledge that different accents convey different social messages, and that some may be valued more highly than others in particular social situations, they would claim that no accent is linguistically superior to any other. All accents allow the economical transfer of information between people who use them.

Dialect

The problem with *dialect* is similar to that with *accent*. First of all we need to recognise that for linguists the word *dialect* is more encompassing than *accent*, including syntactic and lexical features. So although I have an English accent, I might be said to have New Zealand dialect features, since I talk of eating *chippies* and *lollies* rather than *crisps* and *sweets*. I do not speak pure New Zealand dialect because I do not have a New Zealand accent and do not use all the typical New Zealand syntactic structures. Similarly, because it differs in grammar and vocabulary from the standard *Hadn't you all finished giving Christmas presents?*, *Hadn't y'all done gave Christmas gifts* (Feagin 1991: 178) is clearly not written in the same standard dialect.

But, as with accents, linguists would agree that *Hadn't y'all done gave Christmas gifts*, while not part of the standard dialect in which books like this are written, is not wrong: it is different. It makes no more sense to say that this sentence is wrong than it makes to ask whether saying *quarter to three* or *quarter of three* is 'right'. They are just different ways in which different dialects of English express the same thought. *Hadn't y'all done gave Christmas gifts?* is no more wrong than *Hattet Ihr nicht schon alle Weihnachtsgeschenke gegeben?* (the German equivalent). Neither fits with the kind of language otherwise used in this book, but each is correct in its own terms.

One of the definitions of *dialect* in *The Oxford English Dictionary* is 'A variety of speech differing from the standard or literary "language"; a provincial method of speech, as in "speakers of dialect"'. Again, linguists would say that even the standard form of a language is a dialect of that language – one which is given some special status within the community, but a dialect none the less. Thus in the same way that everybody speaks with an accent, as far as linguists are concerned, everybody speaks a dialect. There is no contradiction in speaking of the 'standard dialect' of a particular language, or even, in the case of English, of 'standard dialects'. Moreover, despite the definition from *The Oxford English Dictionary* cited above, we would say that it is perfectly possible to write a dialect as well as speak it: many people write in the dialect of the standard English of England.

One of the problems of linguistics is drawing a distinction between *language* and *dialect*. It might seem that people who cannot understand each other speak different languages, while those who can understand each other but who show consistent differences in their speech speak different dialects of the same language. Matters are not that simple, though. On the basis of examples like Cantonese and Mandarin, which may not be mutually comprehensible but which are commonly termed 'dialects', and Danish and Swedish, which (with some good will) are mutually comprehensible but are usually termed different 'languages', it is often pointed out that the distinction between language and dialect is more a political division than a linguistic one. Serbian and Croatian have gone from being viewed as dialects of Serbo-Croat to being viewed as independent languages as the political situation has changed. Tyneside English and Texan English may be mutually incomprehensible. Max Weinreich (1945) is credited with the encapsulating aphorism that a language is a dialect with an army and a navy.

Variety

There are other terms used by linguists for the language of particular groups within society. They are not all used particularly consistently. For example, we have *idiolect* for the dialect of a single individual. *Register* is another technical term, but has several definitions. The term *patois* is used in French linguistics, but not consistently in English linguistics. *Jargon* and *slang* tend to be used specifically of vocabulary.

The term *variety* is employed by linguists as a neutral term to cover any coherent language system typical of a set of people (even if the set contains only one member). So *variety* is a cover term for *idiolect, register, dialect, accent, language* and possibly *patois* as well. This term is currently preferred among linguists because it avoids taking decisions about whether, for example, the two varieties under discussions are dialects of the same language or different languages, or in the case of languages, whether they are pidgins or creoles or not. Using the term *variety* is an attempt to avoid giving offence by the use of a term which may be semantically or emotionally loaded because of its ordinary language use. Talking about a *standard variety* also has the advantage that it does not cause any semantic clash in the way that *standard dialect* may for speakers unaware of the way in which the term is used by linguists.

References

Feagin, Crawford (1991). Preverbal *done* in Southern States English. In Peter Trudgill & J. K. Chambers (eds), *Dialects of English*. London and New York: Longman, 161–89.

Oxford English Dictionary (2006). Oxford: Oxford University Press. On-line edition http://dictionary.oed.com/, accessed July 2006.

Weinreich, Max (1945). Der *YIVO* un di problemen fun undzer tsayt. *YIVO Bletter* 25 (1): 3–18. [In this article, Weinreich quotes an unnamed source for the aphorism cited in this section. The point is, of course, since the original is in Yiddish, that by this definition Yiddish would not be classified as a language.]

3

Linguistics

A typical dictionary definition of linguistics is something like 'the science of language'. Unfortunately, such a definition is not always helpful, for a number of reasons:

- Such a definition does not make clear in what respects linguistics is scientific, or what is meant by *science* in this context.
- Such a definition masks the fact that it is, for some linguists, controversial to term their subject a science.
- Such a definition fails to distinguish linguistics from related fields such as philology.
- The word 'science' may carry with some misleading connotations.

A rather looser definition, such as 'linguistics is the study of all the phenomena involved with language: its structure, its use and the implications of these', might be more helpful, even if it seems vaguer.

What does linguistics cover?

Linguistics deals with human language. This includes deaf sign-languages, but usually excludes what is often termed BODY-LANGUAGE (a term which itself covers a number of different aspects of the conscious and unconscious ways in which physiological actions and reactions display emotions and attitudes). Human language is just one way in which people communicate with each other, or gather information about the world around them. The wider study of informative signs is called SEMIOTICS, and many linguists have made contributions to this wider field.

One obvious way of studying language is to consider what its elements are, how they are combined to make larger bits, and how these bits help us to convey messages. The first part of this, discovering what the elements are, is sometimes rather dismissively termed TAXONOMIC or classificatory linguistics. But given how much argument there is about what the categories involved in linguistic description are, this is clearly an important part of linguistics, and is certainly a prerequisite for any deeper study of language.

The study of the elements of language and their function is usually split up into a number of different subfields.

1. PHONETICS deals with the sounds of spoken language: how they are made, how they are classified, how they are combined with each other and how they interact with each other when they are combined, how they are perceived. It is sometimes suggested that phonetics is not really a part of linguistics proper, but a sub-part of physics, physiology, psychology or engineering (as in attempts to mimic human speech using computers). Accordingly, the label LINGUISTIC PHONETICS is sometimes used to specify that part of phonetics which is directly relevant for the study of human language.

2. PHONOLOGY also deals with speech sounds, but at a rather more abstract level. While phonetics deals with individual speech sounds, phonology deals with the systems which incorporate the sounds. It also considers the structures the sounds can enter into (for example, syllables and intonational phrases), and the generalisations that can be made about sound structures in individual languages or across languages.

3. MORPHOLOGY deals with the internal structure of words – not with their structure in terms of the sounds that make them up, but their structure where form and meaning seem inextricably entwined. So the word *cover* is morphologically simple, and its only structure is phonological, while *lover* contains the smaller element *love* and some extra meaning which is related to the final <r> in the spelling. Another way of talking about this is to say that morphology deals with words and their meaningful parts.

4. SYNTAX is currently often seen as the core of any language, although such a prioritising of syntax is relatively new. Syntax is concerned with the ways in which words can be organised into sentences and the ways in which sentences are understood. Why do apparently parallel sentences such as *Pat is easy to please* and *Pat is eager to please* have such different interpretations (think about who gets pleased in each case)?

5. SEMANTICS deals with the meaning of language. This is divided into two parts, LEXICAL SEMANTICS, which is concerned with the relationships

between words, and SENTENCE SEMANTICS, which is concerned with the way in which the meanings of sentences can be built up from the meanings of their constituent words. Sentence semantics often makes use of the tools and notions developed by philosophers; for example, logical notation and notions of implication and denotation.

6. PRAGMATICS deals with the way the meaning of an utterance may be influenced by its speakers or hearers interpret it in context. For example, if someone asked you *Could you close the window?*, you would be thought to be uncooperative if you simply answered *Yes*. Yet if someone asked *When you first went to France, could you speak French? Yes* would be considered a perfectly helpful response, but doing something like talking back to them in French would not be considered useful. Pragmatics also deals with matters such as what the difference is between a set of isolated sentences and a text, how a word like *this* is interpreted in context, and how a conversation is managed so that the participants feel comfortable with the interaction.

7. LEXICOLOGY deals with the established words of a language and the fixed expressions whose meanings cannot be derived from their components: idioms, clichés, proverbs, etc. Lexicology is sometimes dealt with as part of semantics, since in both cases word-like objects are studied.

In principle, any one of these levels of linguistic analysis can be studied in a number of different ways.

- They can be studied as facets of a particular language, or they can be studied across languages, looking for generalisations which apply ideally to all languages, but more often to a large section of languages. The latter type of study is usually called the study of LANGUAGE UNIVERSALS, or LANGUAGE TYPOLOGY if the focus is on particular patterns of recurrence of features across languages.

- They can be studied as they exist at some particular time in history (e.g. the study of the morphology of fifteenth-century French, the study of the syntax of American English in 2006, the phonetics of the languages of the Indian subcontinent in the eighteenth century) or they can be studied looking at the way the patterns change and develop over time. The first approach is called the SYNCHRONIC approach, the second the DIACHRONIC or historical approach (see section 7).

- They can be studied with the aim of giving a description of the system of a particular language or set of languages, or they can be studied with the aim of developing a theory of how languages are most efficiently described or how languages are produced by speakers. The first of these approaches is usually called DESCRIPTIVE LINGUISTICS, the second is often called THEORETICAL LINGUISTICS.

- They can be treated as isolated systems, at though all speakers talk in the same way as each other at all times, or they can be treated as systems with built-in variability, variability which can be exploited by the language user to mark in-group versus out-group, or to show power relations, or to show things as diverse as different styles and personality traits of the speaker. The latter types are dealt with as part of SOCIOLINGUISTICS, including matters such as DIALECTOLOGY.

- We can study these topics as they present in the adult human, or we can study the way they develop in children, in which case we will study LANGUAGE ACQUISITION. Perhaps more generally, we can view the development of any of these in the individual human, that is we can take the ONTOGENETIC point of view, or we can consider the way each has developed for the species, taking the PHYLOGENETIC point of view.

- Finally, most of these facets of linguistics can be studied as formal systems (how elements of different classes interact with each other, and how the system must be arranged to provide the outputs that we find in everyday language use). Alternatively, they can be studied in terms of how the use to which language is put in communication and the cognitive functions of the human mind shape the way in which language works (iconicity, the notion that language form follows from meaning to a certain extent, is thus a relevant principle in such studies). This is the difference between FORMAL and FUNCTIONAL approaches to language.

In principle, each of these choices is independent, giving a huge range of possible approaches to the subject matter of linguistics.

Many people are less interested in the precise workings of, say, phonology than they are in solving problems which language produces for humans. This study of language problems can be called APPLIED LINGUISTICS, though a word of warning about this label is required. Although there are people who use the term *applied linguistics* this broadly, for others it almost exclusively means dealing with the problems of language learning and teaching. Language learning (as opposed to language acquisition by infants) and teaching is clearly something which intimately involves language, but often it seems to deal with matters of educational psychology and pedagogical practice which are independent of the particular skill being taught. Other applications of linguistics may seem more centrally relevant. These include:

- ARTIFICIAL INTELLIGENCE: Turing (1950) suggested that a machine should be termed intelligent when humans could interact with it without realising they were not interacting with another human. Among many other problems, this involves the machine being able to produce something akin to human language.

- FORENSIC LINGUISTICS: this deals with the use of language in legal contexts, including matters such as the linguistic techniques of cross-examination, the identification of speakers from tape-recordings, and the identification of authorship of disputed documents.
- LANGUAGE POLICY: some large organisations and nations have language policies to provide guidelines on how to deal with multilingualism within the organisation.
- LEXICOGRAPHY: the creation of dictionaries; although some people claim that this is not specifically to do with linguistics, it is a linguistic study in that it creates vocabulary lists for individual languages, including lists of things like idioms, and in translating dictionaries provides equivalents in another language.
- MACHINE TRANSLATION: the use of computers to translate a written text from one language to another.
- SPEECH AND LANGUAGE THERAPY: speech and language therapists deal with people who, for some reason, have not acquired their first language in such a way that they can speak it clearly, or with the re-education of speakers who have lost language skills, e.g. as the result of a stroke. The linguistic aspects of this are sometimes called CLINICAL LINGUISTICS.
- SPEECH RECOGNITION: the use of computers to decode spoken language in some way; this may include computers which can write texts from dictation, phone systems which can make airline bookings for you without the presence of any human, or computers which can accept commands in the form of human language. More specifically, VOICE RECOGNITION can be used for security purposes so that only recognised individuals can access particular areas.
- SPEECH SYNTHESIS: the use of computers to produce sound waves which can be interpreted as speech.
- TEACHING: it is clear that second- and foreign-language teaching involve, among other things, linguistic skills, but so does much mother-language teaching, including imparting the ability to read and to write. At more advanced levels, teaching students to write clearly and effectively may involve some linguistic analysis.

Another way of looking at what linguistics covers is by taking the list of topics given at the head of this section as being some kind of core, and then thinking of all the types of 'hyphenated' linguistics that are found.

- AREAL LINGUISTICS deals with the features of linguistic structure that tend to characterise a particular geographical area, such as the use of retroflex consonants in unrelated languages of the Indian subcontinent.
- COMPARATIVE LINGUISTICS deals with the reconstruction of earlier stages of a language by comparing the languages which have derived from that earlier stage.
- COMPUTATIONAL LINGUISTICS deals with the replication of linguistic behaviour by computers, and the use of computers in the analysis of linguistic behaviour. This may include CORPUS LINGUISTICS, the use of large bodies of representative text as a tool for language description.
- EDUCATIONAL LINGUISTICS investigates how children deal with the language required to cope with the educational system.
- ETHNOLINGUISTICS deals with the study of language in its cultural context. It can also be called ANTHROPOLOGICAL LINGUISTICS.
- MATHEMATICAL LINGUISTICS deals with the mathematical properties of languages or the grammars used to describe those languages.
- NEUROLINGUISTICS deals with the way in which linguistic structures and processes are dealt with in the brain.
- PSYCHOLINGUISTICS deals with they way in which the mind deals with language, including matters such as how language is stored in the mind, how language is understood and produced in real time, how children acquire their first language, and so on.
- SOCIOLINGUISTICS deals with the way in which societies exploit the linguistic choices open to them, and the ways in which language reflects social factors, including social context.

We can finish by pointing out that the history of linguistic thought is itself a fascinating area of study, since ideas about language are closely related to the philosophical fashions at different periods of history, and often reflect other things that were occurring in society at the time.

Even this overview is not complete. It indicates, though, just how broad a subject linguistics is.

Is linguistics a science?

In the 1950s and 1960s there was a lot of money for scientific research, but very little for research in the humanities. There was thus more than just a political point to be made by terming linguistics a science. A great deal of linguistic research was funded through the American National Science Foundation, for example. Today things are not greatly different, and a great deal of linguistic research gets funded as applications of computer-related work. But calling linguistics a science was not simply a political stance aimed at gaining prestige and funding for the subject. There are good reasons for calling linguistics a science.

Like the biological sciences, linguistics is concerned with observing and classifying naturally occurring phenomena. The phenomena to be classified are speech sounds, words, languages and ways of using language to interact rather than organs, mating behaviours and plant species, but the general principles of classification do not change.

Because language is manifested in human behaviour, it can be studied in the same way that other human behaviour is studied in psychology and medical science.

As in many sciences, the argument in linguistics runs from the observed data to the potentially explanatory theories to provide an account of the data. In physics you move from the observation of falling objects through to theories of gravity; in linguistics you move from the observation of particular kinds of linguistic behaviour through to theories on how linguistic behaviour is constrained.

Like many scientists, linguists construct hypotheses about the structure of language and then test those hypotheses by experimentation (the experimentation taking a number of different forms, of course).

These days most linguists would agree that linguistics is a science, and very few would wish to query such a suggestion. Those that do query the suggestion tend to view linguistics as a branch of philosophy, a metaphysics (see e.g. Lass 1976: 213–20). It is not clear how important any such distinction is. What we call *physics* today was once called *natural philosophy*, and philosophers construct hypotheses, carry out thought experiments and base their conclusions on arguing from what can be observed as well.

For the beginning linguist, saying that linguistics is a science can be interpreted as implying careful observation of the relevant real-world phenomena, classification of those phenomena, and the search for useful patterns in the phenomena observed and classified. For the more advanced linguist, saying that linguistics is a science is a matter of seeking explanations for the phenomena of language and building theories which will help explain why observed phenomena occur while phenomena which are not observed should not occur.

What is not linguistics?

Are there aspects of the study of language which are not encompassed within linguistics? To a certain extent this is a matter of definition. It is perfectly possible to define linguistics very narrowly (usually to include only phonology, morphology, syntax and perhaps semantics) and to exclude all the rest by that act of definition. But while this is clearly the core of linguistic study in the sense that any other facet of language that is studied will make reference to some of this material, this very narrow definition would not be widely accepted.

Perhaps the most general exclusion from linguistics is the study of the literary use of language in order to provide emotional effect. While linguists are frequently happy to study particular figures of speech such as metaphors or metonymy, they do not do this to relate it to the building up of an atmosphere or the development of characterisation. Such matters are left to literary scholars. So although linguistics and literature may both deal with language production as their basic material, there is often little if any overlap between the two fields.

Similarly, although linguists deal with matters of formality and informality in language use, and matters of what language is appropriate in what circumstances, there is an area of literary stylistics which seems to be beyond what most linguists see as being the proper domain of linguistics.

The difference between linguistics and philology is either a matter of history or a matter of method. What we would now call historical or diachronic linguistics was in the nineteenth and early twentieth centuries (and to a certain extent still) covered under the title of PHILOLOGY. Philology was usually based on the close reading of older texts (often, but not exclusively, literary texts). Linguists use such texts as evidence, but are more concerned with giving a systematic account of the language system: the focus is on the language description rather than on the texts from which the system is deduced.

References

Lass, Roger (1976). *English Phonology and Phonological Theory*. Cambridge: Cambridge University Press.
Turing, Alan M. (1950). Computing machinery and intelligence. *Mind* 59: 433–60.

4

Grammar

Like so many fundamental words in any field of study, the word *grammar* has come to mean a number of different things, some of its uses being more general among linguists, others more general among lay people. An attempt will be made below to sort out some of these disparate meanings.

Grammar books

A search of the catalogue of any well-endowed university library should turn up any number of books with titles like *A Grammar of* . . . , *A Descriptive Grammar of* . . . , *A Reference Grammar of* . . . , *A Comprehensive Grammar of* . . . . So here is a first meaning for *grammar*: 'a book which provides a description of a language'. But what do such books contain? Self-evidently, they contain information on the grammar of the language described. Note that we have now changed the meaning considerably. *Grammar* in the book sense is countable: *I found three grammars of Japanese on the shelves. Grammar* in the content sense is not: *These books describe the grammars of Japanese* is odd, though perhaps interpretable in some other sense of *grammar* (see below).

Grammars were introduced in western Europe primarily for the teaching of Greek and later of Latin, the language of literacy and culture in Europe long after the fall of the Roman Empire. Following Roman models, such works laid out the PARADIGMS of nouns, adjectives, verbs, etc., models for the learner to imitate. Generations of users grew up learning to recite these paradigms, such as that in (1) for the present tense of a first conjugation verb:

(1) amo   'I love'
     amas   'you (singular) love'

amat	'he *or* she *or* it loves'
amāmus	'we love'
amātis	'you (plural) love'
amant	'they love'

The amount of space given over to other matters was comparatively constrained. This experience gave rise to the idea that grammar was a matter of such paradigms. Thus the idea arose that Latin had a lot of grammar, while English hardly had any (because there is very little to put in equivalent paradigms, as people discovered when they started trying to write English grammars on the model of the Latin ones they knew). So we have a meaning of *grammar*, perhaps now no longer encountered, according to which grammar dealt with the shapes of the words (i.e. what we would now call MORPHOLOGY, specifically inflectional morphology) and the uses to which those words could be put (typically in sections with titles like 'The uses of the ablative' or 'The uses of the subjunctive'). This latter part, relatively undeveloped in most grammar books from before the twentieth century, deals with putting words together to make sentences, i.e. with SYNTAX. So grammar meant (and still means for some) 'morphology and syntax', specifically here excluding anything to do with the sound structure of language or the vocabulary of the language.

Traditional grammar

This picture of what grammar is and what grammar does, deriving from the classical Greek and Latin traditions, was handed down in Western society for generations, and remained virtually intact for language-teaching purposes well into the twentieth century. Each word is assigned to a part of speech (noun, verb, adjective, adverb, etc.), of which there are often said to be eight. These are assumed as given categories (see the section 5). School students traditionally showed their mastery of the system by considering each word in a text in turn, and explaining what cell in the paradigm it came from. This is called parsing, and involves looking at a word like *amāmus* and saying that it is the first person plural of the present tense indicative of the verb *amo* 'I love', for example. Students were also expected to write on the basis of the classical models provided. We can call this picture of what grammar is and does 'traditional grammar'. The extent to which such methods encouraged good writing, which was clearly the aim, is perhaps best left unexplored, although it should be recalled that until the nineteenth century, most of the people being taught to read and write were those who had the leisure and frequently the desire to learn the skills well.

Prescriptive and descriptive grammar

When we consider grammar as providing a set of skills which we need to be able to write Latin (or any other foreign language), it is clear that there is a set of correct answers to any given problem. There is only one answer to what the form of the first person plural of the present tense indicative of the verb *amo* 'I love' is, and any other form is wrong. This leads people to expect that any language is a fixed system, where there is on any occasion a correct answer as to what form should be used. For all but the best learners, that was virtually true in Latin, a language which existed for many centuries mainly in a written form and without native speakers, but the expectation gets carried forward to modern languages like English. By the same logic, people expect there to be a single right answer to questions of usage in English. However, consideration of examples like those below will show that things are not so simple.

(2) a.   I have no money.
     b.   I haven't any money.
     c.   I don't have any money.
     d.   I haven't got any money.
     e.   I've not got any money.
     f.   I've got no money.
     g.   I ain't got no money.

(3) a.   I want you to start to write immediately.
     b.   I want you to start writing immediately.

(4) a.   This is the woman about whom I spoke to you.
     b.   This is the woman whom I spoke to you about.
     c.   This is the woman who I spoke to you about.
     d.   This is the woman that I spoke to you about.
     e.   This is the woman as I spoke to you about.
     f.   This is the woman I spoke to you about.

A number of different factors contribute to the variations shown in these examples. There are matters of style, matters of change (albeit extremely slow change) and matters of dialect. The end result is that there may not be any single correct answer on questions of usage. Nevertheless, it is clear that some of these versions give very clear social messages. (4e), for example, not only provides evidence of geographical origin, but is unlikely to be said by a highly educated person talking on a formal occasion. This leads some people to believe that it is 'wrong', and that there must be a correct version to replace it.

Accordingly there is an industry playing on people's inferiority complexes by telling them what the 'right' answer is. Linguists call this PRESCRIPTIVE

GRAMMAR: it prescribes the correct form (and proscribes forms it considers 'wrong'). Prescriptive grammar has two typical features:

1. It presents an oversimplification: a particular form is right or wrong.
2. It considers a very small part of the grammatical structure of English (or any other language with a similar prescriptive tradition); in (4e) it might comment on the use of *as*, but would ignore the fact that the word *this* agrees with *the woman* in being singular, or that the verb *speak* requires a preposition *to*, or that the implicit meaning here is that 'I spoke to you about the woman.'

The result of prescriptive grammar is that although all of the forms in (2) are heard from real speakers, the standard, formal, written language has less variation available within it than spoken English. (2e) sounds perfectly normal to many people, particularly in Scotland, but it is probably not part of standard, formal, written English.

Models of grammar

The alternative to prescriptive grammar is DESCRIPTIVE GRAMMAR, the study of language structures in order to describe them thoroughly rather than in order to tell someone else what they should be saying. The line between the two is probably less secure than this might imply: many a descriptive grammarian has seen their work used (or abused) by prescriptivists. The difference between saying that a certain class of people tend to say *x* and saying that you should say *x* is a thin one.

Descriptive grammarians (or descriptive linguists; the two are synonymous) attempt not only to describe a particular language or a set of languages, but to explain why they should be the way they are. They often have a theoretical structure, a MODEL of grammar, which they are testing against particular data from a given language. Many of the names of these models contain the word *grammar*: case grammar, cognitive grammar, construction grammar, functional grammar, phrase-structure grammar, role and reference grammar, scale and category grammar, transformational grammar, word grammar and so on.

Perhaps the major difference between ideas of grammar in the nineteenth and early twentieth centuries and later ones is the introduction of the idea of a generative grammar.

Generative grammar

The notion of a generative grammar was made central in linguistics by Chomsky in his book *Syntactic Structures* (1957). According to Chomsky, linguists should not merely describe a particular set of sentences or utterances they have observed, they should explain how it is that humans can produce an infinite number of sentences with finite resources.

> Any grammar of a language will *project* the finite and somewhat accidental corpus of observed utterances to a set (presumably infinite) of grammatical utterances. (Chomsky 1957: 15) [italics in original]

> The grammar of [any language] L will thus be a device that generates all the grammatical sequences of L and none of the ungrammatical ones. (Chomsky 1957: 13)

That is, grammar has to be concerned with every detail of the most mundane sentences and the ways in which humans can make these more complex and produce and understand sentences which they have never produced or even heard before. Like that last sentence, for instance. Grammar has a finite number of rules (we all hold a grammar in some sense in our heads) which it can use to produce, enumerate or generate an infinite number of sentences. It has to be able to go beyond the set of sentences previously heard, and provide the ability to produce novel sentences on demand. This view of grammar has often been termed the Chomskyan revolution in linguistics (see section 8). Grammar goes from being a study of texts and the analysis of given sentences to being the study of how we can cope with the complexity represented by human language.

At this stage, grammar is often taken to include not only morphology and syntax, but also phonology, since that is part of the facility humans have for dealing with language.

> Adapting a traditional term to a new framework, we call the theory of Peter's language the 'grammar' of his language. Peter's language determines an infinite array of expressions, each with its sound and meaning. In technical terms, Peter's language 'generates' the expressions of his language. (Chomsky 2000: 5)

Universal Grammar

If we all have our own grammars in our heads, how do they get there during childhood? We know that we are not born with the grammar of a particular language in our heads, we have to learn the language which surrounds us, and if we are moved in early childhood to a place where a different language surrounds us, we will acquire that. Yet we are never instructed in language, we acquire it from listening to a very small sample of possible messages. Chomsky and his colleagues claim that the stimulus that children are provided with is nowhere near sufficient to allow the acquisition of such a complex system if they were not in some way predisposed towards it. They postulate that humans are born with a hard-wired predisposition which tells them, somehow, how to make appropriate generalisations from the input they receive. They call this predisposition UNIVERSAL GRAMMAR (or UG), universal in the sense that it is available to all humans, grammar in the sense that it helps people acquire the specific grammar of the language they are to learn.

Conclusion

We now have a number of meanings for the word *grammar*: it can be (a volume containing) a physical description of some part of a language; it can be the subject matter of such descriptions (usually restricted to morphology and syntax); it can be a set of rules for good behaviour in polite society constructed by fallible humans for other fallible humans; it can be the mental ability we have to produce language (including the sounds of language); it can be a model of that mental ability; it can be the predisposing mental prerequisite to acquiring such a mental ability. Perhaps the most surprising thing about this plethora of distinctions is how often the context makes clear what is meant by *grammar*.

References

Chomsky, Noam (1957). *Syntactic Structures*. The Hague and Paris: Mouton.
Chomsky, Noam (2000). *New Horizons in the Study of Language and Mind*. Cambridge: Cambridge University Press.

5

Parts of speech

If you were taught any grammar at school, it is almost certainly the idea that a noun is a naming word and a verb is a doing word. If you meet the same terminology of noun and verb in university study, your teachers are quite likely to pour scorn on definitions of this kind, and provide in their place definitions in terms of the environments in which the various parts of speech (which they may now call WORD CLASSES or FORM CLASSES) are found. The trouble with the high-school definitions is that it is rarely made clear precisely how they work. Students could emerge from that kind of teaching unable to find a verb in the sentence *People are usually kind to each other*, even though there is a verb there. Students who did manage to absorb the categorisation implicit in the terminology were likely to get confused that *up* was sometimes an adverb and sometimes a preposition, and not to know what to call *excess* in *He wiped the excess glue off the label*. All of this suggests something rotten in the state of grammar teaching, and it is worth considering what is going on.

Some history

It is often assumed (at least by those who have not been trained in such matters) that it is blindingly obvious which part of speech a given word belongs to. Note that the very fact that *which* is judged to be appropriate in that last sentence implies that there is (or is believed to be) a fixed number of such categories, and it is simply a matter of putting the right token in the right box. The slow development of the notion of parts of speech in itself shows that this is far from being the entire story.

Plato (d. 347 BCE) worked with two major parts of speech (the label was used then) which today we would probably gloss as 'subject' and 'predicate', though to some extent the distinction between these and 'noun' and 'verb' was not secure. His student Aristotle (d. 322 BCE) added a third class made up of conjunctions (and possibly some other grammatical word types; Robins 1967: 26). The Stoics distinguished five parts of speech: the proper noun, the common noun, the verb, the conjunction and the article (Matthews 1994 [1990]: 33–4). This developed until in the later Greek grammars, such as that attributed to Dionysius Thrax, we find noun, verb, participle, article, pronoun, preposition, adverb and conjunction (Robins 1967: 33–4; Matthews 1994: 38). This is the system that was carried forward into Latin grammatical study, although by the time we get to Priscian (sixth century CE) interjection has been added to the list (Law 2003: 89). Note that adjective is missing from the list. Since the adjective in Greek and Latin took the same endings as the noun, and could, indeed, be used nominally, there was no need to separate it from the noun. The participle, on the other hand, needed to be treated separately from the verb since it was marked for categories like past, present or future like the verb but also for categories such as possessive like the noun: it thus participated in both nominal and verbal qualities (hence the label).

Nouns and verbs were distinguished from the earliest times by being marked for these categories, called CASE on the noun and TENSE on the verb, so that there was in origin a formal distinction here. By the period of Priscian, the notional definitions had made an appearance, nouns being said to indicate substances, verbs to indicate actions, etc. (Robins 1967: 57).

It took until the early Middle Ages for adjectives to get added to the list of parts of speech, probably in the light of languages in which they were more formally distinct from nouns than they were in Latin and Greek.

What is basically the Greek tradition lasted into the twentieth century, at least in school grammar. Among most linguists, however, it was overtaken by the structuralist tradition. Mixed up with this is the tradition characterised by Joos (1957: 96) as the Boas tradition, which implies that 'languages [can] differ from each other without limit and in unpredictable ways'. If that is the case, we should not expect every language to fit neatly into a Greek model or to show the same parts of speech as European languages.

The structuralist backlash

There are innumerable reasons why the notional definitions of the parts of speech run into problems. Verbs are termed 'doing words' but verbs which denote states (STATIVE VERBS) do not denote action. The sentences in (1) are very odd at best.

(1) a. What the vase did was cost ten dollars.
    b. What John did was resemble his father.

    c.   What Sally did was be sensible.
    d.   What the answer did was seem unlikely.
    e.   What I did was know the answer.

There is a clash here between the *did*, which implies an action, and the stative verb (*cost, resemble, be, seem, know*) which does not imply any action at all. Not all verbs are doing words. Conversely, not all doing words are necessarily verbs. Words like *action, criticism, response* are, or can be, doing words in the right context.

   (2) a.   Their action saved the day (= 'the thing that they did saved the day').
        b.   Their criticism of my book wounded my self-esteem (= 'they criticised my book, and the fact that they did that – or the way that they did it – wounded my self-esteem').
        c.   Their rapid response was not enough to stop the house burning down (= 'they did something rapidly, but despite that the house burnt down').

We can make similar cases for nouns and adjectives not fitting the definitions they were given in this tradition, although the case from verbs is perhaps the strongest.

    Under such circumstances, it seems folly to stick with these notional definitions, and structuralists looked on parts of speech as substitution classes (see section 9). Thus we get definition by slot and filler or paradigmatic structure. For example, we might say that for English a verb is anything which fits all the slots: __*s*, __*ed*, __*ing* (of course, we need to have special cases for irregular verbs, and for many languages we would have to be more accurate and say that what occurs in such slots is a verb stem rather than 'a verb', but the general principle is clear enough). When we get to adjectives in English, we have to start pushing this rather more and use syntactic frames as well as morphological frames. Thus we might say that an adjective can end in *-able, -al, -an, -ar, -ic, -ish, -ous, -y* (and so on), and can be found in all the frames given in (3).

   (3) a.   The ___ thing/person/event
        b.   The thing/person/event is ___
        c.   The very ____ thing/person/event

The trouble with such definitions is that we do not know how to treat words like *former* and *awash*. *Former* will arise in places like (3a), but not in places like (3b), while the reverse is true of *awash*. Neither arises in (3c). Since these do not end in any of the endings we have listed, we might wonder whether they are really adjectives at all. Or, if we are unwilling to accept such a conclusion, we need a bigger set of substitution frames to solve the problem – though such frames are not necessarily easy to produce.

Then we have the problem that substitution classes frequently produce strange bed-fellows. If we take a substitution frame such as *The ___ man*, we might end up with *the walk man, the remittance man, the fancy man, the lady's man*; we should at least be worried by calling all of these things 'adjectives'.

The problem for the structuralists is that there are too many possible substitution frames, some rather specific, some very general, and they all delimit different classes. Thus, in effect, we end up with a vast set of possible parts of speech, with little reason to believe that some are more important than others. Fortunately, linguists were saved from this quagmire by psychologists, or more specifically by one psychologist, Eleanor Rosch.

Psychology to the rescue

Rosch (e.g. 1978) argued that people do not view natural categories in terms of necessary and sufficient conditions. Rather, in many cases, they have a mental image of some kind of ideal, and members of the class which resemble the ideal closely are more quickly recognised than members which are distant from the ideal. Thus a robin (not the same bird in North America as in the United Kingdom or as in Australasia) is more easily recognised as a bird than an ostrich or a penguin, for example. These ideals Rosch unfortunately termed PROTO-TYPES (this is quite out of keeping with earlier meanings of *prototype*; *archetype* or *stereotype* would have been a much better label, but it is too late to change that now). But however unfortunate the label, the idea is powerful and helpful. For now we can return to the notional theory of the parts of speech and give it a far firmer theoretical anchor than it used to have. Although traditional grammarians may have treated concepts like noun as prototypes, we had no way to theorise what they were doing, and it seemed that they were simply wrong. Now we have a theoretical framework within which to describe what is going on, and a more subtle idea of what a category might look like.

Now we can say that the prototypical noun denotes some concrete individual object. We might be able to go further and suggest that the best examples of nouns (compare robins as the best examples of birds) denote humans. So *woman* is a really good noun, close to the prototype, while *criticism* is a noun because our language happens to deal with it grammatically in much the same way as it deals with *woman*, but it is nevertheless further from the prototype. Similarly, a verb like *kill* is probably fairly close to the prototype for a verb, while *seem* is a lot further away. They belong to the same category because the language inflects them in the same way (*kills, killed; seems, seemed*). A prototypical adjective may fit all the frames in (3), but things can be adjectives and yet fit less well into our picture of what an adjective is. Note that this does not necessarily make it any easier to determine where the class of adjectives stops, but it does lead us to expect that not all adjectives will be equally clear members of the set.

The view from typology

It seems that all languages distinguish a class of words like *woman* from a class of words like *kill*, and thus all languages can be said to have nouns and verbs. Sometimes the same forms can be used in both ways (much as with English *murder*), but there are always differences in constructions between words of the two types. Thus nouns and verbs are usually taken to be universal classes. Whether all languages distinguish a class of adjectives is a matter of some controversy. Certainly, if they do all have adjectives, the class of adjectives is sometimes extremely small. In many instances things which we, from our Eurocentric point of view, think of as adjectives turn out to behave more like intransitive verbs or like some other class of words. It is dangerous to make assumptions beyond that, though usually languages will have a class or several classes of grammatical forms in addition. These forms are usually finite in number and so said to belong to CLOSED CLASSES, because speakers cannot freely add to their number; nouns and verbs by contrast are OPEN CLASSES. Since the words in these closed classes frequently derive from nouns and verbs historically (by the process called GRAMMATICALISATION or GRAMMATICISATION), in principle it should be possible to find a language with only open-class words, though this seems extremely unlikely. The closed-class words include prepositions, auxiliary verbs, pronouns, etc.

Some minor parts of speech

Most of the descriptions of languages you look at will provide discussion of nouns, verbs and adjectives. We have already seen that defining an adjective can be difficult for English, though this does not imply that it is equally difficult in all languages. Because so many other parts of speech are possible (especially if we consider subcategories of verb), it is not practicable to attempt an exhaustive listing. Some of the common labels are explained briefly below.

> Adjunct: An ADJUNCT is an optional element of sentence structure. Probably the most common adjuncts are adverbial in nature.
> Adposition: ADPOSITION is the cover term for PREPOSITIONS, which precede the noun phrase they accompany (as English *to* in *to the concert*, for example), and POSTPOSITIONS, which follow their noun phrase (as *ni* in Japanese *konsaato ni* 'to the concert').

Adverb: While an adverb is literally something which modifies a verb, like *quickly* in *She ran quickly*, adverbs have a much wider usage than that. They frequently modify adjectives, like *particularly* in *a particularly intelligent person*, or whole sentences, like *unfortunately* in *Unfortunately they could not come*. Adverb tends to be a ragbag category in traditional grammar, with many words which do not fit obviously into other categories being classified as adverbs. Adverbs are not always marked morphologically: *not* in *She did not look up* is classified as an adverb, and the *up* may also be classified as an adverb in some sources (see below under particle).

Article: In English there are two articles, *the* and *a(n)*, the so-called definite and indefinite articles respectively. Articles are one type of determiner.

Conjunction: Conjunctions link elements together. They are usually divided into COORDINATING CONJUNCTIONS (like English *and, but, or*), which link units of equivalent status, and SUBORDINATING CONJUNCTIONS (like English *because, if, when*, etc.), which mark something as being a constituent element within a larger construction (so in *I wonder if he will come*, *if* shows that *if he will come* is an element, in this case acting as the direct object of the verb, in the larger sentence).

Determiner: Determiners are closely associated with nouns and express notions such as quantity, definiteness and possession. The phrases *the house, this house, my house, every house, Kim's house* contain the noun *house* and determiners of different kinds. Note that although the word *this* is a determiner in this construction, it is not always a determiner.

Interjection: An interjection is something like *Ow!* or *Gosh!*, words which do not have relations with the other words in the sentence but stand alone.

Participle: Participles were introduced earlier. They have verbal features and nominal or adjectival features. In English, forms in *-ing* and in *-ed* such as *loving* and *desired* are participles, though other languages may have more participles, relating to different tenses. An *-ing* participle (or the equivalent in other languages) used nominally may be termed a GERUND.

Particle: Particles are usually short, uninflected, grammatical words. What counts as a particle may vary from language to language, or even from author to author. In English, things called particles include the *up* in *She looked her sister up* (which may also be termed an adverb or an adposition – see above), the *to* in *We wanted to leave*, the *like* in *Kim's like really cross with me*, or *innit* (derived from *isn't it*) used as a tag question.

Pronoun: A pronoun is usually said to be something which stands for a noun, though it would be better to say it stands for a complete phrase centred on a noun. Thus the pronoun *it* in *It is beautiful* could stand for *music*, for *Kim's cat* or for *the diamond necklace which I saw at the jeweller's last Saturday*. Various kinds of pronoun are distinguished, including personal pronouns (*I, you, us, them*, etc. or equivalent words in other languages), possessive pronouns (*my, your, our, their*, etc.; note that these are one type of determiner), relative pronouns (*which, whom, that*, etc.), reflexive pronouns (*myself, yourselves, ourselves*, etc.), demonstrative pronouns (*this, those*, etc.) and interrogative pronouns (*which?, who?*, etc.). Despite the general definition given above, it is very difficult to make a word like *who* replace a noun: *Pat came?* is likely to be a disbelieving echo of an earlier statement rather than a genuine request for information like *Who came?*

Pro-sentence: Things like *yes* and *no* can be seen as standing for complete sentences, and thus separate from other parts of speech. They are sometimes classified as adverbs.

Quantifier: Some linguists separate out quantifiers such as *each, all, every* and numerals from the set of determiners, and treat them as a different class.

Conclusion

This does not lead us to a neat list of possible parts of speech. Neither does it answer what parts of speech we may have in English. Such questions are theoretical questions, and different theories may provide different answers for them. There are some things which might be explained by this discussion, though.

- When you read a discussion of the grammar of some language which is unknown to you, you cannot assume that you understand what belongs in any particular part of speech just on the basis of the name which the part of speech is given.
- The invention of new parts of speech for the description of particular languages, while not necessarily particularly helpful, may be well-motivated and may allow an author to draw parallels in behaviour which are not otherwise clear.
- There is no definitive answer to how many parts of speech there are in any particular language, even less to how many there might be in 'language' in general. Neither is there any finite list of parts of speech.

References

Joos, Martin (ed.) (1957). *Readings in Linguistics 1*. Chicago and London: Chicago University Press.

Law, Vivien (2003). *The History of Linguistics in Europe*. Cambridge: Cambridge University Press.

Matthews, Peter (1994 [1990]). Greek and Latin linguistics. In Giulio Lepschy (ed.), *History of Linguistics. Vol. II: Classical and Medieval Linguistics*. London and New York: Longman, 1–133.

Robins, R. H. (1967). *A Short History of Linguistics*. London: Longman.

Rosch, Eleanor (1978). Principles of categorization. In Eleanor Rosch & Barbara B. Lloyd (eds), *Cognition and Categorization*. Hillsdale NJ: Erlbaum, 27–48.

6

Rules

The usual meaning of 'rule' in everyday language is some statement which is intended to constrain behaviour in some way. For example, there might be a school rule which says that students should not run in the school corridors. The intention behind such a rule is that it should prevent the undesirable behaviour (and often there will be sanctions if the rule is broken).

There are other kinds of rules, too, though we sometimes call them *laws* in everyday speech. You might say 'It seems to be a rule that the car in front of me gets the last parking space', for example, and this is a rule describing what actually happens rather than a rule saying what should happen. Murphy's Law (also known as Sod's Law) is a rule of this second kind, though perhaps an overly cynical one.

Rules in modern linguistics are like this second kind. Linguistic rules are statements of observed regularity in behaviour. If the linguistic notion of rule were applied to the running-in-the-corridor scenario mentioned above, the statement of observed behaviour might be that students run only when no person in authority is visible to them. This is a statement about what actually happens on a regular basis (note the etymology of *regular*, which is related to *rule*), whether it is officially sanctioned or not.

Consider a linguistic example. Small children learn to say *cats* when they want to talk about more than one cat, and to say *feet* when they want to talk about more than one foot. They do not distinguish between these two cases. There comes a time, though, when they notice the regularity of the *cats* form, and start to overgeneralise. At this point they continue to say *cats*, but may say *foots* (sometimes *feets*). At this point, the linguist says that the children have acquired the rule for making nouns plural by the addition of an appropriate segment containing a sibilant. This rule will give *cats*, which follows the same rule as the adult community norms, and *foots*, which does not follow the same rule as the adult community norms. In linguistic terms, though, both show the application of the rule, because the rule is the observation that a particular piece of behaviour is taking place. To say that something is a rule is not to pass judgement on the social effect of the behaviour that is described by the rule in any way at all.

Another way to formulate this is to say that modern linguistic rules are descriptive and not prescriptive: they describe a situation, but do not tell you what ought to be done (see section 4). Of course, it is perfectly possible to have prescriptive statements about language, but modern linguists do not call these *rules*.

In fact, linguistic rules usually give you only a small part of the information that you need to understand a particular piece of behaviour: they tell you what happens in structural linguistic terms, but do not tell you what group of speakers this particular structural equivalence is valid for. Consider, for example, a statement of a diachronic change whereby /r/ becomes pronounced [z]. We need to know what language this change occurs in, or what dialect(s) of that particular language are affected. We need to know at what period the change took place. We might need to know what social group the change affected, or whether the change is observed only in child language, only in pathological speech, only in the speech of a particular individual, and so on. The particular change I have in mind is one which affected the popular French of Paris in the sixteenth century, having been found in other varieties of French since before the fourteenth century (von Wartburg 1967: 156). Similar changes seem to have affected other languages at other periods (consider the alternation between <s> and <r> in Latin *honos / honorem* and in English *was / were*). The rule itself would not tell us which of these (or other similar) changes was involved, only that a particular change is observed. In order to understand the rule fully, the reader has to be able to put it into its appropriate context. It would normally be expected that this context can be deduced from the text accompanying the statement of the rule.

Rule format

A linguistic rule generally takes the form in (1) below in which the capital letters represent linguistic elements or strings of linguistic elements, which may be zero.

(1) A → B / C ___ D

This rule is to be read as 'A becomes B when it is surrounded by C and D.'

The first element on the left is the element which is changed or expanded by the rule. Only a single element should be in position A, never a sequence of elements. Where A changes only when in a particular sequence, this will be covered by the addition of an environment at the right-hand edge of the rule. Where A is zero, the rule will act as a rule of insertion.

The arrow indicates that the rule is interpreted as a dynamic statement (see section 13). Depending on the context it can be read as 'becomes, is changed into, is further specified as, is expanded into'. Some scholars use different arrows for synchronic and diachronic rules, but the conventions are not fixed. The other potential readings of the arrow are not distinguished in general practice.

The element or elements in B are the output of the rule. Depending on the content of the rule the effect of what is in B may be subtly different, as is illustrated by the partial rules in (2) and their explanations in (3).

(2) a.   r   →   z
    b.   [+ voice]   →   [− voice]
    c.   [+ voice]   →   [+ nasal]
    d.   S   →   NP + VP
    e.   r   →   Ø

(3) a.   [r] changes into [z] (see above)
    b.   Anything which is voiced becomes voiceless instead (e.g. [b] becomes [p] and [v] becomes [f]).
    c.   Anything which is voiced is further specified as being nasal as well (e.g. [d] becomes [n]).
    d.   S is expanded as NP + VP so that where we previously had just S, we now work with the concatenation of two categories, NP and VP.
    e.   [r] is replaced by zero, i.e. is deleted.

There are some conventions involved in the interpretation of these rules. For example, where features are used as in the (b) example in (2) and (3), those features not mentioned in the rule retain their original values. Equivalently, where features retain their values, they do not need to be specified in the rule. It is usually assumed that rules apply to every possible input available in the structure simultaneously, so that if there are several [r]s, they will be changed by (a) or deleted by (e) (the two are incompatible, and could not apply simultaneously to the same description).

The slash '/' is to be read as 'in the following environment'. Not all rules need an environment. If none of the rules in a grammar has an environment, the grammar is said to be a CONTEXT-FREE phrase-structure grammar, and if there are rules with environments, it is said to be a CONTEXT-SENSITIVE phrase-structure grammar. If a particular rule has no environment stated, it applies on every occasion when the input condition is met. Thus (2a) as stated says that every [r] becomes [z].

The underscore, often termed the ENVIRONMENT BAR, shows the position in which the affected element has to be for the change described by the rule to take place. Consider the examples in (4), where, as is customary, C indicates 'any consonant', V indicates 'any vowel' and # indicates a boundary (the precise nature of the boundary need not concern us in detail just yet).

$$(4) \quad a. \quad d \rightarrow ð \, / \, V \underline{\quad} V$$

$$b. \quad r \rightarrow \emptyset \, / \, \underline{\quad} \begin{Bmatrix} C \\ \# \end{Bmatrix}$$

$$c. \quad [+ \text{voice}] \rightarrow [- \text{voice}] \, / \, \begin{bmatrix} + \text{obstruent} \\ \underline{\quad} \end{bmatrix} \#$$

(4a) is a rule with the full environment specified. It states that [d] (presumably a dental [d], though this is not stated explicitly in the rule and must be deduced from what else we know about the language in which this rule applies) becomes a fricative when it is immediately preceded by a vowel and immediately followed by a vowel. In other words, sequences of [ado], [ida] will be affected by the rule, and the stop will be replaced by a fricative, while sequences of [nda], [#da], [adr], [ad#] will not be affected, and the plosive articulation will be retained. This rule could be seen as a first approximation to a rule of allophony in Spanish. Note that when we use phonetic symbols in rules of this kind we do not enclose them in phonemic slashes or phonetic brackets. This is partly to prevent the rule statement from becoming too cluttered, but it is also theoretically motivated in that we may not wish to take a stance on whether the sounds involved are or are not contrastive units.

In (4b) no environment is specified to the left of the environment bar, and this indicates that nothing in the environment in this position is relevant to the operation of the rule. The braces to the right of the environment bar indicate options: the rule will apply equally well if there is a C here or if there is a #-boundary in this position. Thus this rule states that [r] will be deleted from sequences such as [ər#], [ərd], [trt], [lr#] and even [#r#], but will not be deleted from [trə]. Of course, not all of these strings will necessarily exist in the input. If we take it that (4b) is a first approximation to a rule for the deletion of [r] in non-rhotic varieties of English, for example, there will never be a [trt] input because this can never arise in the phonology of English. This does not make (4b) a poor rule. The important thing is that (4b) should cover the data for which it is intended to provide an account. A rule will sometimes make predictions about data which has not been included, and if so the generality of the rule can be tested against new data.

In (4c) the environment bar is within a particular phonological segment. The square brackets in (4c) enclose a single phonological segment, and do not imply anything about its phonological status. (4c) is to be read as 'anything which is voiced becomes voiceless if it is an obstruent occurring immediately before a boundary'. This could be written equivalently as (5), and with a simple example like this one, (5) might be a better formulation; there are, however, instances where the kind of formulation shown in (4c) is valuable.

(5) $\begin{bmatrix} +\,\text{obstruent} \\ +\,\text{voice} \end{bmatrix} \rightarrow [-\,\text{voice}]\ /\ \underline{\quad}\ \#$

(4c), or, equivalently, (5), could be seen as a first approximation to the rule of final consonant devoicing in Dutch.

Since boundaries sometimes cause problems for beginners, it is worth pointing out how they are presumed to work. Some linguistic models avoid the use of boundaries by the ordering of sets of rules, and this is seen as a benefit of such models. However, they are used frequently enough for an understanding of their functioning to be important. In this presentation only one boundary, the #-boundary, will be used, but others are current in the literature and work in similar ways (see section 16 for some examples). In general, boundaries enclose the item bounded by them. Thus the word *word* is enclosed by boundaries to give #word#, and similarly for all other words. Thus the notation '___#' meaning 'immediately before a boundary' can also be read as 'word-finally': in #word#, the <d> occurs in the environment ___#. Similarly, '#___' indicates 'immediately following a boundary' or 'word-initially': in #word#, <w> occurs in the environment #___. Where words are strung together, each carries its own boundaries with it, so that the phrase *in other words* has the boundaries #in##other##words#. Chomsky & Halle (1968: 13) also put boundaries round larger constituents, including round sentences, corresponding to a bracketing of constituent structure (see section 12), so that boundaries proliferate as in (6), but such complexities are rarely referred to in phonological rules.

(6)

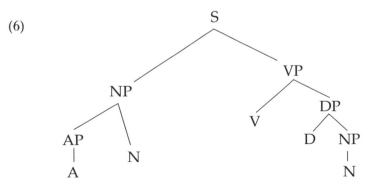

Fine # # words # # # # butter # # # no # # parsnips # # #

The one place where the principle of enclosing elements in boundaries fails to hold is with affixes. Affixes are separated from their bases by a single boundary, but are not enclosed in boundaries. So that if we include affixal boundaries in the phrase *fine words*, we get ##fine##word#s##. Sometimes this difference is supposed to hold only with those affixes (as in the example just cited) which might be assumed to have no word-class marking. In a language like English this means with inflectional suffixes and with prefixes. Suffixes like the *-ness* in *happiness* are said to have their own word class (they always create nouns), and thus to work like words in terms of the tree structure. (See e.g. Lieber 1992: 35-7, but contrast with Jensen 1990: 35.) This is controversial.

Before we move on to consider alternative ways of writing environments, two more abbreviatory conventions need to be considered. The first of these is the use of parentheses to enclose optional material. Where an item is enclosed in parentheses at any point in the rule, the rule works equally well with or without the parenthesised material. However, if you are applying the rule to potential input data, you should always try to apply the rule with all the optional elements present, and only if the rule cannot be applied that way should you apply it without the optional elements. That is, you apply the longest expansion first. The options presented by the use of parentheses in this way are alternatives: if one option applies the other does not; the two options cannot both apply. This is called DISJUNCTIVE ordering. For example, the stress in French words spoken in isolation can be stated by rule (7).

(7) V → [+ stress] / ___ (C) (C) (ə) #

Given a form like /pətitə/ the final /ə/ has to be seen as matching the /ə/ in (7), otherwise, if it was ignored and the rule was applied without the optional elements first, we would get the stress on the final vowel, i.e. on the /ə/. Since the stress in this word falls on the /i/, we need to consider the longest applicable version first, and then stop applying the rule. Anything else will give the wrong output.

The other abbreviatory convention to mention briefly is the rather informal use of the asterisk after an element to show that it may be repeated. This is found most often in syntactic rules, where a given NP may include an indefinite number of adjectives, or where a given sentence may include an indefinite number of prepositional phrases. A rule such as (8) illustrates both these conventions.

(8) NP → (Num) (AP*) N (PP)

(8) states that an NP must contain an N and may also contain a number, one or more adjective phrases and, following the noun, a prepositional phrase.

(Note, incidentally, that for the sake of the example, (8) does not presuppose a binary structure for syntactic rules, which many scholars would wish to impose as a requirement: see section 11.) The rule in (8) is compatible with the various examples in (9).

(9) sheep
     three sheep
     big sheep
     three big white fleecy sheep
     three sheep of mine
     big white sheep from Sussex
     etc.

Alternative environments

Although the format in (1) is a standard way of expressing environments, there is an alternative, especially in phonology, of expressing an environment in terms of the structure in which the change occurs. For example, consider (4b) above. This can be expressed, perhaps more insightfully and certainly more economically, by saying that the [r]s which are deleted are those which occur in coda position in the syllable. This can then be shown using the notation in (10), where the relevant portion of the tree is reproduced in the environment to indicate where the change occurs.

(10)   Coda
                          |
       r → Ø / ____

Even such notational conventions sometimes end up looking like the linear ones in (4), however. For example, in some varieties of English, voiceless plosives are aspirated in just those cases where they occur initially in a prosodic foot. Using the Greek letter φ as the notational symbol for a foot, we might write this as in (11), which uses the same kind of prosodic structure that is used in (10), with a notation which looks more like that in (1) or (4).

(11) $\begin{bmatrix} + \text{ plosive} \\ - \text{ voice} \end{bmatrix}$ → [+ aspirated] / [$_\varphi$ ____

Greek letter variables (or alpha-notation)

Agreement in features is marked in phonological rules by the use of Greek letter variables. A Greek letter such as $<\alpha>$ is used as the value for a feature when the precise value is not important, but matching of values is. With binary features, the α stands in place of a + or a –, so that we can get rules like (12); where features have a wider range of potential values, the alpha-notation can cover those as well, as in (13).

(12) [+ nasal] → [α back] / ___ [α back]
(13) [+ nasal] → [α place] / ___ [α place]

The important point in (12) and (13) is that the α must have the same value everywhere it occurs on any given application of the rule. So (12) means that the nasal is further specified as [+ back] before something which is [+ back] and as [– back] before something which is [– back]. Similarly (13) means that whatever value for [place] the following segment has (e.g. labial, coronal, dorsal, etc.), the nasal will take the same value.

Refinements

Only the basics of rule notation have been dealt with here, and there are a number of conventions for writing and interpreting rules which are not mentioned here. For example, alpha-notation can be used for marking disagreement as well as agreement, and can become more complex than was illustrated in (12) and (13). Such complexities have not been mentioned partly because they may not be required (at some particular level of study, in a particular model), partly because, being more complicated than those facets which have been mentioned here, they require more assumptions about the form of the grammar. Many phonology textbooks will provide more elaborate discussions of rule writing and rule interpretation.

References

Chomsky, Noam & Morris Halle (1968). *The Sound Pattern of English*. New York: Harper & Row.

Jensen, John T. (1990). *Morphology*. Amsterdam and Philadelphia: Benjamins.

Lieber, Rochelle (1992). *Deconstructing Morphology*. Chicago and London: University of Chicago Press.

Wartburg, Walther von (1967). *Évolution et structure de la langue française*. 8th edn. Berne: Francke.

7

The Saussurean dichotomies

The Swiss linguist Ferdinand de Saussure is sometimes thought of as the father of modern linguistics. Although Saussure was well known in his lifetime for his work in the history of Indo-European, his most influential work was not published until after his death, when some of his students got together and, on the basis of their lecture notes, reconstructed the course in linguistics that he had taught in Geneva. The *Cours de linguistique générale* (Saussure 1969 [1916]) became one of the key texts in linguistics, and ushered in the era of structuralism which we might argue continues today.

In the *Cours*, among a number of important statements and illuminating comparisons, Saussure made a number of fundamental distinctions which are still basic to linguistic thinking. These are outlined below.

Langue versus *parole*

Saussure says there are two sides to language: *langue* and *parole*. While the French terms are generally used in English, they are sometimes translated as 'language' and 'speech' respectively, though not without some danger of ambiguity. LANGUE is that part of language which 'is not complete in any individual, but exists only in the collectivity' (Saussure 1969 [1916]: 30, my translation, see the footnote for the original French[1]). PAROLE, on the other hand, is observable in the behaviour of the individual. According to Saussure, it is not homogeneous.

Saussure believes that linguistics is fundamentally the study of *langue*, although some later scholars have suggested that there might also be a

---

[1] 'n'est complète dans aucun, elle n'existe parfaitement que dans la masse'.

linguistics of *parole*. Had corpus linguistics been a concept with which Saussure was familiar, he would no doubt have dismissed it as dealing with *parole* rather than with *langue*. In one of his celebrated images (Saussure 1969 [1916]: 36), he suggests that when an orchestra plays a symphony, the symphony exists externally to the way in which it is performed: that existence is comparable to *langue* in language study. The actual performance, which may contain idiosyncrasies or errors, is to be compared to *parole*.

The distinction between *langue* and *parole* has suffered two major changes in subsequent scholarship. First, a third level has been added, that of the NORM (see especially Coseriu 1962 [1952]). Our *langue* would allow us to say what the time is by saying *It is ten minutes before four o'clock*, or *It wants ten minutes to be four o'clock*, or *In ten minutes it will be four o'clock*, or *It is five minutes after a quarter to four*. We do not find such utterances attested in *parole*. Rather, we find multiple utterances of *It is ten (minutes) to four*. This cannot be related to vagaries of *parole*, because it is extremely homogeneous within relevant speech communities. Neither can it be a matter of *langue*, because *langue* allows us to say the same thing in many different ways. It is a matter of norm that we say *It is ten to four* rather than one of the alternatives. Note that different dialects may have different norms. There are also varieties of English in which the expression is *It is ten of four*.

The second thing that has happened to the *langue/parole* distinction is that it has been overtaken by other, similar distinctions. Chomsky (1965: 4) introduces the distinction between competence and performance. PERFORMANCE is very like Saussure's *parole*. It is prone to error, to memory lapse and the like. COMPETENCE, however, is unlike Saussure's *langue* in that it has no social side to it; it is a mental construct in the individual. Although Saussure concedes that 'It [*langue*] is something which exists in each individual', he also adds 'yet is common to all of them'[2] (Saussure 1969 [1916]: 38).

Chomsky (1965: 4) also points out that for Saussure *langue* is 'a system of signs' (Saussure 1969 [1916]: 32), while for Chomsky competence is a generative system. This is an accurate description of *langue*, but does not seem to be fundamental to the notion of it in the way that its social aspect is.

In more recent work (Chomsky 1986), competence and performance have given way to a third distinction, that between I-language and E-language (where I and E are to be interpreted as 'internalised' and 'externalised' – see section 8). For Saussure, linguistics deals with *langue*; for Chomsky linguistics deals with I-language. Thus, for Saussure, linguistics involves studying the language of the community, while for Chomsky it involves studying the language potential of the individual. Yet both agree that if we use an analogy with a game

---

[2] 'C'est donc quelque chose qui est dans chacun d'eux [les individus], tout en étant commun à tous'.

of chess, the particular moves made in any given game are not what is to be studied; rather it is the rules of the game which allow for an infinite number of different actual games. For Saussure the rules correspond to *langue*; for Chomsky they correspond to I-language (Saussure 1969 [1916]: 43; Chomsky 1986: 31).

Synchrony versus diachrony

We can study a given language in two ways, Saussure maintains. The first is that we can look at the language as it is (or was) at any particular point in time. Thus we might study the syntax of American English in the early twenty-first century, or the phonology of seventeenth-century French or the patterns of compounding in Classical Chinese. These are all SYNCHRONIC studies (*syn-* 'alike', *chronos* 'time').

The alternative is to look at the way in which a language develops or changes over time. In this way we might consider the development of the English verb system, or changes in Arabic phonology from the classical period until today. These are DIACHRONIC studies (*dia-* 'through', *chronos* 'time').

Saussure was reacting to an environment in which the only linguistic study that was seen as being scientific was the study of the development of languages. By putting the synchronic side of language studies back on the linguistic map, he expanded the scope of linguistics. Yet by the late twentieth century, there were some linguists complaining that this strict distinction between synchronic and diachronic linguistics had become a major problem in dealing with language.

All living languages are in a continuous state of change. Much of the complaint tradition, which is a social factor affecting many languages including English, is a reaction to recent changes. For example, people who complain that some speakers do not distinguish between *imply* and *infer* are caught up in a change whereby the two used to mean different things and now are less likely to be semantically distinct, especially in less formal contexts. This is evidence that aspects of language change are reflected in the synchronic structure of any given language or variety. This is the subject matter of variationist linguistics, as developed by William Labov. Any linguistic change progresses gradually through a speech community. Some speakers adopt the change more quickly than others, and some speakers use both the conservative and the innovative form for some period during the change. Thus any synchronic description of a variety, if it is detailed enough, can make sense only if aspects of diachrony are taken into account. Furthermore, language change leaves relics behind whose structure can be understood only with reference to their history. Why is blackmail called *blackmail*, for example? Why is it black and why is it mail? The synchronic structure of twenty-first-century English does not provide an answer for this. *Blackmail* has become an unmotivated word, even though we can see the elements *black* and *mail* within it.

Despite such problems, the distinction between synchronic and diachronic studies is generally maintained today.

Paradigmatic versus syntagmatic

When we speak, language is produced in time, so that some bits of our utterance precede or follow other bits. When we write, this temporal aspect of language is replaced by a spatial aspect: the words are set out on the page in a conventional way such that linear order corresponds to the temporal order in speech. Thus English is written from left to right, with elements further to the left corresponding to elements produced earlier than elements further to the right. So in (1) *cat* precedes *mat* in linear order, corresponding to temporal structure in speech: we would say *cat* before we would say *mat*.

   (1) The   cat   sat   on   the   mat

The elements in (1) are said to be related to each other syntagmatically. Together they form a SYNTAGM (/ˈsɪntæm/) or construction. We can say that the verb *sit* (or *sat* in this particular sentence) determines what it will be related to syntagmatically in that it demands something in the position of the cat in (1) and allows, but does not demand, an equivalent phrase after it (as in *They sat the dog on the mat*).

However, language is also structured in terms of the words (or other elements) which are not there but which could have been. Each of the words in (1) could have been replaced by a number of other possible words. Some examples are given in (2).

(2) The	cat	sat	on	the	mat
This	girl	sits	across	your	bed
That	student	walked	over	her	car
My	frog	ran	by	their	lap

The words in each of the columns in (2) are related to each other paradigmatically. They are related by being alternative possible choices at a position in the syntagm. While elements which are related syntagmatically are all present, elements which are related paradigmatically are mostly absent: they are relationships of potential.

Each of the columns in (2) can be called a PARADIGM (/ˈpærədaɪm/), although that name is more usually reserved for a particular type of paradigmatic relationships, those holding between different forms of the same word (or, more technically, lexeme). Thus (3) illustrates a Latin noun paradigm.

(3) 'lord'   *singular*   *plural*
    nominative   dominus   dominī
    vocative   domine   dominī
    accusative   dominum   dominōs
    genitive   dominī   dominōrum
    dative   dominō   dominīs
    ablative   dominō   dominīs

In (3) we see a number of suffixes, each of which has a syntagmatic relationship with the stem *domin-*. The endings themselves are in a paradigmatic relationship.

Note that elements in paradigmatic relationships share common features. All the words in the first column in (2) are determiners, all those in the second column are nouns and so on. Word classes can be thought of as being derived from sets of paradigmatic relationships. Very specific syntagms can also show semantically related words in relevant paradigms. Thus, consider (4), where the verb – except in figurative uses – demands the word *cat* or a closely related word.

(4) The   cat   miaowed.
         kitten
         tom
         moggy

Signifier (*signifiant*) and signified (*signifié*)

Saussure insisted that the linguistic sign has two aspects to it: a sound side and a meaning side. The two are tightly linked within a speech community, and can be seen as being the two sides of the same playing card, but we must nevertheless keep these two aspects of the sign separate from each other in our technical understanding of the way in which language functions. The concept of a pig may be carried by the sounds /pɪg/, but that concept is not to be equated with that series of sounds. The sign unites the physical set of sounds (the signifier, or *signifiant*) with a particular mental image (the signified or *signifié*). Note that real-world pigs do not feature here. The sign links our mental image of a pig with a particular set of sounds, not a real pig. The real pig has a very indirect relationship with the sound sequence /pɪg/. The same argument could be repeated for the series of hand-shapes and gestures in sign-languages and their link to a particular meaning.

Saussure makes a number of other points about linguistic signs which have become accepted, although they had not always been seen as obvious prior to Saussure. Perhaps the most important of these is the fact that the linguistic sign is arbitrary. There is no natural link between the sound sequence /pɪg/ and particular animals. If there were, how could the same or very similar animals be easily associated with the word *pig* in English, *cochon* in French, *gris* in Danish, *Schwein* in German, and so on? Even onomatopoeic signs are to a large extent conventional. We only have to think about the words we use to represent animal noises in a number of languages to see that. Without knowing, it is hard to guess what animal says *gav-gav* in Russian, or what animal says *chu-chu* in Japanese. While the signs of sign-languages are often said to be iconic and resemble some feature of what is denoted, it can be difficult there to guess what a particular sign means if it has not been explained.

References

Chomsky, Noam (1965). *Aspects of the Theory of Syntax*. Cambridge MA: MIT Press.
Chomsky, Noam (1986). *Knowledge of Language*. New York: Praeger.
Coseriu, Eugenio (1962 [1952]). Sistema, norma y habla. In Eugenio Coseriu, *Teoria del lenguaje y linguistica general*. Madrid: Gredos, 11–113.
Saussure, Ferdinand de (1969 [1916]). *Cours de linguistique générale*. Paris: Payot.

8

Chomsky's influence

Noam Chomsky is the world's most influential linguist. His influence can be seen in many ways, from the expansion of linguistics as an academic subject in the wake of his early work on the nature of grammars to the way in which even linguists who do not agree with him define their position in relation to his. His ideas have attracted many brilliant people to take up linguistics and contribute to the study of language. It has become common to talk of a 'Chomskyan revolution' in linguistics beginning in the late 1950s or early 1960s as the influence of his teaching permeated the way in which language was viewed and was discussed. If the term 'revolution' may be a little over-dramatic, linguistics certainly took what Kasher (1991: viii) calls a 'Chomskyan Turn' at that point. In this section we look at some of the major features of Chomskyan linguistics which distinguish it from earlier approaches.

Chomsky is also a renowned political philosopher and activist, but while his views in the political field have been argued to be congruent with his views about language, this part of his work will not be considered here (this is covered in works such as McGilvray 2005; Smith 1999). Furthermore, since Chomsky's ideas about language have implications for the workings of the human mind, Chomsky's work is also regularly cited by psychologists. Again, that aspect of his work will receive very little attention here.

The centrality of syntax

Traditional European grammar usually gives syntax a rather minor role. To a certain extent, of course, this depends on the language being described, with descriptions of more analytic languages perforce devoting more space to syntactic matters. But descriptions of highly inflecting European languages typically have a brief section on the phonology of the language concerned, a lot of information on the inflectional morphology of the language concerned, and some relatively brief sections with headings such as 'Uses of the dative' or 'Sequence of tenses' which considered the interface between morphology and syntax.

For Chomsky, this is entirely back to front. A language is a set of sentences, and what allows a speaker to produce and a hearer to understand these sentences is the ability to manipulate syntactic structure. Chomsky focuses on that part of grammar which most previous commentators had simply presupposed or ignored: the ability to produce and understand sentences such as (1) (Chomsky 1965: ch. 2), to understand the ambiguity of sentences like (2) (Chomsky 1957: 88), to understand sentences like (3) even though some information is missing from them (Chomsky 1957: 66), and to preceive the relatedness of pairs of sentences like those in (4).

(1) Sincerity may frighten the boy.
(2) The shooting of the hunters frightened the boy.
(3) John has arrived and so have I.
(4) The girl has eaten the peach.
     The peach has been eaten by the girl.

For Chomsky, phonology and semantics are dependent on syntax, and these other components of the grammar take the output of the syntactic component and turn it into a spoken utterance or a semantic representation. In early work, morphology is dealt with as part of the syntax, in later work it is dealt with as part of the lexicon, but in neither case is it central to the workings of the grammar.

In many ways this is Chomsky's most successful innovation, and is now taken as axiomatic by many linguists.

Idealisation of data

Chomsky points out that researchers in the hard sciences such as chemistry and physics standardly discount factors which might confound their experimental results: the effect of air resistance on the effect of gravity on falling bodies, for example. The kinds of factors that Chomsky wants to exclude in the study of language are those that divert attention from the underlying generalisations, just as would be the case in chemistry or physics. These factors are not well defined, but in principle the idea of idealisation of data seems uncontroversial, and has probably always been part of the business of a linguist or grammarian, who would otherwise be faced with too much variability to be able to produce a coherent description. What is different about Chomsky, in this regard, is that he is quite open about his procedure.

The ideal speaker-listener

Perhaps the most important statement about the idealisation of data is made in a passage which has become famous or infamous (depending on one's point of view):

> Linguistic theory is concerned primarily with an ideal speaker-listener, in a completely homogeneous speech-community, who knows its language perfectly and is unaffected by such grammatically irrelevant conditions as memory limitations, distractions, shifts of attention and interest, and errors (random or characteristic) in applying his knowledge of the language in actual performance. (Chomsky 1965: 3)

This statement has been attacked on many sides, not least by variationist sociolinguists who have pointed out the unnaturalness of a homogeneous speech-community, and who have a built a whole branch of linguistics devoted to examining precisely the lack of homogeneity in speech-communities. While it would be preposterous to deny the value of the variationist programme, the success of this branch of linguistics is not a criticism of Chomsky's proposal in the passage cited. Any syntactician who tried to write a grammar of standard English so that it would account for the sentence *How come is the Wellington gas twice the price of the Hutt Valley's?* (heard on the radio) would be mocked as much as a lexicographer who tried to list a word *anenome* meaning 'anemone' on the grounds that many people are heard to say that. We all make errors in our production from time to time, and we would not expect any linguist to use them as primary data for creating a theory of language. (Of course, speech errors are sometimes used as evidence to support theories of how the mind accesses stored material and manipulates linguistic strings, but that is a separate matter.)

Competence and performance, I-language and E-language

Chomsky also distinguishes between the speakers' actual knowledge of the language, which is termed COMPETENCE, and the use of that knowledge, which is termed PERFORMANCE. The errors listed above are presumably performance errors. Any piece of text (spoken or written) represents a performance of language, which will match the speaker's competence more or less inaccurately. Thus performance is often taken as a poor guide to competence, but competence is the object of study for the linguist.

   As with so many of the claims Chomsky makes, this one has been the subject of criticism, some focusing on the structured nature of variation within performance and the correspondingly variable nature of competence, some focusing on the performance as a body of evidence whose close analysis can lead to a more sophisticated appreciation of how the speaker-listener's competence might be structured (the first of these criticisms comes from sociolinguists, the second from corpus linguists and psycholinguists). It also seems that it can be difficult to tell whether a particular phenomenon is best seen as a matter of competence or a matter of performance, despite the apparently clear-cut division between the two (see e.g. Bauer 2001: 29-32).

In later versions of Chomsky's theory, the distinction between competence and performance is replaced by the distinction between I-language and E-language. I-LANGUAGE (and the *I* is deliberately ambiguous between 'internalised' and 'intensional' – and others add 'individual' and 'idiolectal' as well, e.g. Lyons 1991: 170) corresponds more or less to the old competence. It is what is held in the head of a single individual speaker-listener. E-language (where the *E* stands for 'externalised' and 'extensional') is not like performance, though. E-LANGUAGE includes languages viewed as a set of sentences, it includes the material actually produced by a speaker, it includes 'languages' like French and Mandarin, and it includes the objects of study of sociolinguistics and corpus linguistics. Lyons (1991: 170, 193) calls this concept 'ill-defined and confusing', and Chomsky himself (1991: 9) says that 'it is doubtful that there is such an entity'.

Generativism and transformationalism

Chomskyan grammar in the early days was regularly termed 'generative-transformational', and while the label is less used today, the principles remain unchanged.

The term 'generate' in *generative* is to be understood in a mathematical sense, whereby the number one and the notion of addition can be used to generate the set of integers or where 2^n can be used to generate the sequence 2, 4, 8, 16.... In linguistics a generative grammar is one which contains a series of rules (see section 6) which simultaneously (a) confirm (or otherwise) that a particular string of elements belongs to the set of strings compatible with the grammar and (b) provide at least one grammatical description of the string (if there is more than one description, the string is ambiguous) (see Lyons 1968: 156).

The first thing to notice about this is that a generative grammar is a FORMAL grammar. It is explicit about what is compatible with it. This is in direct contrast to most pedagogical grammars, which leave a great deal of what is and is not possible up to the intuition of the learner. In practice, this often leads to disputes about how much the grammar is expected to account for. To use a famous example of Chomsky's (1957: 15), is *Colourless green ideas sleep furiously* to be accepted as a sentence generated by the grammar, on a par with *Fearless red foxes attack furiously* (and, significantly, different from *Furiously sleep ideas green colourless*, which the grammar should not generate)? If so, its oddness must be due to some semantic or pragmatic compatibility problems which are not part of the syntax. Alternatively, should the grammar specify that *sleep* is not compatible with *furiously* and that abstract nouns cannot be modified by colour adjectives (although, having said that, I have seen the expression *green ideas* in use, where *green* meant 'ecologically sound')? In 1957 Chomsky was clear that the grammar would and should generate this sentence, despite its superficial oddity. McCawley (1971: 219) supports this view, claiming that 'A person who utters [*My toothbrush is alive and is trying to kill me*] should be referred to a psychiatric clinic, not to a remedial English course.' Despite such problems, the explicitness of Chomskyan grammar is one of its great strengths. It has led to computational approaches to linguistics in which (partial) grammars are tested by implementing them on computer, and such approaches have implications for the eventual use of natural languages by computer systems.

The second thing to notice is that although the rules in linguistics are usually stated as operations which look as though they are instructions to produce a particular string, in principle they are neutral between the speaker and the listener, merely stating that the string in question does or does not have a coherent parse.

Grammaticality and acceptability

In principle, something is GRAMMATICAL if it is generated by the grammar, and ungrammatical if it is not. Since we do not have complete generative grammars of English (or any other language) easily available, this is generally interpreted as meaning that a string is grammatical if some linguist believes it should be generated by the grammar, and ungrammatical otherwise. Given what was said above, it should be clear that there is a distinction to be drawn between strings which are grammatical and those which are ACCEPTABLE, that is, judged by native speakers to be part of their language. *Colourless green ideas sleep furiously* is possibly grammatical, but may not be acceptable in English (though poems have been written using the string). *There's lots of people here today* is certainly acceptable, but it might not be grammatical if the grammar in question requires the verb to agree with the *lots* (compare *Lots of people are/*is here today*). Although the asterisk is conventionally used to mark ungrammatical sequences (this generalises on its meaning in historical linguistics, where it indicates 'unattested'), it is sometimes used to mark unacceptable ones.

Deep structure and surface structure

Chomsky (1957) argues that context-free phrase structure rules (see section 6) are not sufficient to generate natural languages. This claim has been vigorously refuted, e.g. by Gazdar et al. (1985), but was generally accepted for many years. It seemed, however, that separate rules would be required to move constituents in pairs like (5) and (6) if the relationships holding between these pairs was to be recognised by the grammar. These movement rules are different in type from the phrase-structure rules (also known as rewrite rules), and are called TRANSFORMATIONAL RULES. The form and nature of movement rules have changed considerably over the various versions of Chomskyan grammar, but we still have an underlying order of elements created by phrase-structure rules, and transformational or movement rules which produce the actually occurring sentence structure. The underlying order of elements was originally called DEEP STRUCTURE, and the observable output of the full set of rules was called the SURFACE STRUCTURE. The term *deep structure* was often used informally to mean any level more abstract than the actually occurring surface form. In later versions this was reformulated in terms of D-structure and S-structure, where D-STRUCTURE is equivalent to deep structure, but S-structure differs from surface structure. Surface structure is the immediate input into the rules which provide a pronunciation of the sentence under consideration, while S-STRUCTURE is the input to the semantic component, and still contains some empty elements such as traces, which are not pronounced at all.

(5) a. I can put up Kim
    b. I can put Kim up.
(6) a. I can't stand olives.
    b. Olives, I can't stand.

The evaluation of grammars

According to Chomsky (1964), grammars can hope to achieve one of three levels of adequacy. A grammar that is OBSERVATIONALLY ADEQUATE contains sufficient information to reproduce just the data on which it is based. A grammar is DESCRIPTIVELY ADEQUATE if it contains sufficient information not only to account for the input data, but to assign a structure which reflects precisely those patterns in the data that are captured by the intuitions of the native speaker. Finally, a grammar is EXPLANATORILY ADEQUATE if it derives from a linguistic theory which allows the selection of the best possible descriptively adequate grammar from those which are compatible with the data. Chomsky has consistently sought explanatory adequacy. However we may phrase this requirement, what it translates as is a push to find out why particular patterns should occur in individual languages, why languages should differ in the observed patterns, and what fundamental principles govern the kinds of pattern that are observed. Examples are provided by the pairs in (7) and (8), where one language allows a pattern which a neighbouring language does not allow, and Chomsyan grammar seeks the principles by which these languages differ that will predict that precisely these differences will emerge.

(7) a. English:
Jean speaks French fluently.
*Jean speaks fluently French.
b. French:
Jean parle le français courament.
Jean parle courament le français.
(8) a. German:
Ich glaube, daß der Lehrer ein Buch gesehen hat.
I believe that the teacher a book seen has.
b. Dutch:
Ik geloof dat de leraar een boek heeft gezien.
I believe that the teacher a book has seen.
[Note the contrasting order of the words meaning 'has' and 'seen'.]

Realism and mentalism

A particularly strong formulation of the realist (sometimes called God's Truth: Householder 1966) position in linguistics is given by Lightner (1983: 276): 'In linguistics, there is an overriding principle – an arbiter – to judge correctness or incorrectness of theoretical constructs: if the construct corresponds to the human brain's treatment of language, it is correct; if not, incorrect'. Even with such a strong statement, it can be difficult to say whether some construct is, as the jargon has it, psychologically real. Does it mean that the human mind deals with the data in a manner which is essentially parallel to the way in which it is treated in the linguistic theory, or does it mean that the individual constructs of the theory (for example, the individual rules, movements, components) have counterparts in the human mind?

Language as a mental 'organ'

Chomsky and his followers talk about language as a mental organ, a figure which makes one think about gall-bladders and hearts, and which is misleading in the sense that the language 'organ' does not appear to have any locational unity which would differentiate it from the brain: the functions of language appear to be distributed through the brain (see Everett 2006). The reasons for calling it an 'organ' are thus of some interest. They include (see Smith 2005: 84-5) the following:

- Except in pathological cases it is universally present in humans.
- Faults in the language faculty may be inherited.

- It is present only in humans.
- Language is learned extraordinarily quickly, and probably with critical periods (i.e. the faculty stops operating properly if not employed at the right period of maturation).
- We appear to learn far more than we have evidence for in our linguistic surroundings – this is often referred to, following Chomsky, as PLATO'S PROBLEM or as the problem of the POVERTY OF THE STIMULUS.
- Despite different inputs, speakers of the same variety seem to end up with very closely matching grammars.

These factors, it is suggested, make the language faculty seem much more like something with which we are biologically endowed, like the facility for sight, than like something which we learn, like the ability to do arithmetic.

It should be said that many of these reasons have been challenged, with a greater or lesser degree of success. There is, for example, a large literature devoted to the idea that some animals other than humans have linguistic abilities. My personal judgement about this literature is that it is ultimately not convincing, and that the astonishing abilities demonstrated by some of the animals that have been studied still do not approach the even more astonishing abilities demonstrated by human children. Similarly, the notion of critical period has been questioned, as has the notion of the poverty of the stimulus, that is, the idea that we are presented with insufficient data from which to deduce the form of a linguistic system. In the end, though, the crunch question here is to what extent humans are specifically pre-programmed for language, and how far language is a by-product of other things for which humans are hard-wired. The Chomskyan answer is that there is a specific language faculty. Yet when we look at the evidence from the FOXP2 gene, fancifully dubbed by the popular press a 'gene of speech', and important because it is the first time it has been shown that a fault in an individual gene can cause lack of ability to use language fully, it turns out that the gene affects, among other things, the ability to articulate smoothly. While this may be a necessary facility for the efficient exploitation of spoken language, in itself it does not provide any evidence for the hard-wiring of anything as specific as language.

Universal Grammar

If we accept that the language faculty is hard-wired into humans in an organ-like way, we must nevertheless accept that what humans have is a facility to acquire language, rather than the facility to acquire a particular language. Orphans whose parents spoke one language and who are adopted at an early age by speakers of a different language in a different country end up speaking the language of their adoptive community, and do not have any built-in benefit if, at some later stage, they wish to learn the language of their biological parents. So what is universal to humans is the ability, in the appropriate conditions, to learn a language, any language. If we accept the points made in the last section, though, children will not be given enough input to allow them to construct the linguistic system of English or Sierra Miwok for themselves. Thus, the argument runs, they must have, at birth, certain specifically linguistic expectations in order for them to develop a language from the impoverished data they will actually be provided with. This set of expectations or pre-programmed knowledge is Universal Grammar (often abbreviated as UG). If linguists knew the contents of UG, they would be able to work out how children learn languages so quickly, and how languages must pattern in order to fulfil the requirements of UG, and thus why a particular descriptively adequate grammar might be better than another descriptively adequate grammar of the same language. Unfortunately, UG is not available for perusal, and its form must be deduced from the actual languages we can observe. We can see the main thrust of the Chomskyan research enterprise as being the uncovering of UG on the basis of data from natural languages.

References

Bauer, Laurie (2001). *Morphological Productivity*. Cambridge: Cambridge University Press.

Chomsky, Noam (1957). *Syntactic Structures*. The Hague and Paris: Mouton.

Chomsky, Noam (1964). *Current Issues in Linguistic Theory*. The Hague and Paris: Mouton.

Chomsky, Noam (1965). *Aspects of the Theory of Syntax*. Cambridge MA: MIT Press.

Chomsky, Noam (1991). Linguistics and adjacent fields: a personal view. In Kasher (ed.), 3–25.

Everett, Daniel L. (2006). Biology and language. *Journal of Linguistics* 42: 385–93.

Gazdar, Gerald, Ewan Klein, Geoffrey Pullum & Ivan Sag (1985). *Generalized Phrase Structure Grammar*. Oxford: Blackwell.

Householder, F. W. (1966). Phonological theory: a brief comment. *Journal of Linguistics* 2: 99–100.

Kasher, Asa (ed.) (1991). *The Chomskyan Turn*. Cambridge MA and Oxford: Blackwell.

Lightner, Theodore M. (1983). *Introduction to English Derivational Morphology*. Amsterdam and Philadelphia: Benjamins.

Lyons, John (1968). *Introduction to Theoretical Linguistics*. Cambridge: Cambridge University Press.

Lyons, John (1991). *Chomsky*. 3rd edn. London: Fontana.

McCawley, James D. (1971). Where do noun phrases come from? In Danny D. Steinberg & Leon A. Jakobovits (eds), *Semantics*. Cambridge: Cambridge University Press, 217–31.

McGilvray, James (ed.) (2005). *The Cambridge Companion to Chomsky*. Cambridge: Cambridge University Press.

Smith, Neil (1999). *Chomsky: Ideas and Ideals*. Cambridge: Cambridge University Press.

Smith, Neil (2005). *Language, Frogs and Savants*. Malden MA: Blackwell.

9

Form and function

The distinction between form and function is one of the fundamental distinctions in linguistics, yet it causes problems surprisingly often. The basic insight is very simple, yet failure to understand it leads to many complications in linguistic descriptions.

The basics

We need to begin with some definitions of some linguistic terms. Parts of speech were introduced in section 5. Words belonging to many of these classes can be the most important word in a phrase which contains them. In *red onions*, for example, the most important word (or HEAD) is *onions* because it is obligatory within the construction and because the phrase as a whole denotes a subset of onions. *Onions* is a noun, and *red onions* is a NOUN PHRASE. By a similar logic, *extremely unusual* is an adjective phrase, *in the park* is a prepositional phrase, and so on.

In a sentence like *Kim runs the video shop*, the noun phrase *Kim* is not compatible with a verb form *run* (as we might find if the initial noun phrase were *Kim's family*). This noun phrase is called the SUBJECT of the sentence, and is traditionally often equated with the person or thing that carries out the action of the verb. There are instances, though, where there is not much action for the subject to carry out: in *The video costs $30*, for example, the subject is *the video*. In *Kim runs the video shop*, *the video shop* acts as the (direct) object of the verb *run*. The object is closely related to the verb (compare *ate the cake* with **ate the water*, **ate the sky*, etc.). Just as the subject is commonly thought of as the performer of the action of the verb, the object is commonly thought of as the receiver or patient of the action of the verb. In the sentence *Kim wrote Pat a* *letter, a letter* is the direct object, while *Pat* is the INDIRECT OBJECT. (In some older treatments, *Pat* would still be considered an indirect object in *Kim wrote a letter to Pat*, but it is more often treated differently, reflecting the grammatical structure rather than the meaning.) Finally, in *Kim is the owner, the owner* is called the SUBJECT COMPLEMENT. *The owner* refers to the same person as the subject does (namely, Kim), and while objects can become the subjects of passive verbs (*The video shop is run by Kim*), subject complements cannot (**The owner is been by Kim*).

With those preliminaries out of the way, we can turn to form and function.

A potato can be used for a number of things. It can be cooked in various ways and eaten, whether in boiled, mashed, baked, fried or chipped form. It can be turned into potato flour; it can be used to hold cocktail sticks carrying lumps of cheese or other delicacies; it can be used to make stamps for printing with; it can be used to make pellets to fire from a potato gun. The same basic item, the potato, has various functions.

In the same way, the phrase *the mouse*, while remaining a noun phrase, may have any one of a number of jobs in a sentence. Consider the ways it used in (1)–(5).

(1) The mouse ran away.
(2) I've caught the mouse.
(3) I gave the mouse a piece of cheese.
(4) They showed me a picture of the mouse.
(5) I trod on the mouse's tail.

In (1) *the mouse* is the subject of the sentence, in (2) it is the direct object of the verb, in (3) it is the indirect object, in (4) it is the object of a preposition, part of the post-modifier for *picture*, and in (5) it is part of the determiner. The form remains the same, but the functions in the sentence have changed. In this particular case the difference between form and function is captured by the terminology used. Phrase types are form labels, while *subject, object*, etc. are function labels. So although our terminology does not specifically draw attention to what is a form and what is a function, in this instance it provides us with distinct terms for talking about the two aspects of the thing we are describing.

Similarly, we can find a prepositional phrase such as *in the garden* used with different functions, and again we have, or can find, terminologies which allow us to make the distinctions.

(6) The chair in the garden is more comfortable than this one.
(7) After lunch we walked in the garden.
(8) The cat is in the garden.

In (6) *in the garden* is a post-modifier to the head noun *chair*, in (7) it is an adverbial of place (which may be given some other label). In (8) there is dispute in the literature as to whether *in the garden* should be seen as an adverbial or as a subject complement, but in either case its function is given a label distinct from its form. Its form remains a prepositional phrase.

So why does this create problems?

The problems with form and function arise in different places, depending on the sophistication of the analyst. Beginning students may confuse nouns with subjects until they have the difference specifically drawn to their attention. Since it is not always clear that the ancient Greek grammarians kept the distinction in mind, we cannot be too surprised by this error, though today we do want to recognise it as an error.

Problems arise more easily where the terminology does not make any distinction between form and function. Two examples will make this point.

Consider words which can occur between an article and a noun, for example in *the _ bracelet*. One obvious set of words which can occur in this position is made up of words for colour, description and size and so on: words like *blue, cheap, long, shiny, thick, yellow*. These words are usually called adjectives. Another set of words which can occur here, though, is words for materials: words like *amber, copper, silver*, and the like. These are words which usually occur in noun phrases and in functions like those shown in (1)–(4). They are usually nouns. And they do not behave like adjectives in that we cannot say **the rather/very/so amber bracelet*, **the copperest/most copper bracelet*. So these are not adjectives. The problem is that many grammatical models do not give us a function label for what it is that both an adjective and a noun can do – what their function can be – when they appear before a noun in such a phrase. We can easily invent one. We can call these *pre-modifiers*, and determine that this is the functional label we will use. But in the absence of such a label, we occasionally find *amber, copper* and *silver* treated as adjectives in constructions like *the amber bracelet*. Thus *The Chambers Dictionary* (9th edition, 2003) says under *amber*, after defining it as a fossilised resin, '*adj* made of amber; the colour of amber'. The same dictionary does not call *crocodile* an adjective, even though the word occurs in expressions such as *crocodile handbag, crocodile shoes, crocodile tears*. There is a case to be made for accepting *amber* as an adjective in *an amber light*, but it is unnecessary to extend this to *an amber necklace*. Not only adjectives and nouns may be pre-modifers, as is illustrated by *the then leader* (adverb), *the down train* (preposition), *an I don't-want-to-know reaction* (sentence).

As a second example, consider the typology of languages according to the order of the subject, verb and object. Languages are typically classified as SVO,

SOV, VSO, etc., where *S* stands for 'subject', *O* stands for 'object' and *V* stands for 'verb'. As we have seen, subject and object are functions. We would assume, therefore, that verb is also a function, and, indeed, it must be understood as one in such a classification. However, a verb is also a form. A verb, we might say in English, is a word which can take a third person singular *-s*, which has a past tense form and a past participle form (which will be homophonous if the verb is regular), and which has a form ending in *-ing*. These are all statements about forms. Just as *noun* and *adjective* are labels referring to form, so too is *verb*. But now we have a paradox: verb is a label relating to form sometimes, and it is sometimes a functional label. Some scholars have used the term PREDICATOR for the functional label, and retained *verb* for the form. Unfortunately, the use of the label *verb* in the two distinct ways is very widespread, and care is required not to confuse the two.

Reference

The Chambers Dictionary. (2003). 9th edn. Edinburgh: Chambers Harrap.

10

Contrast and substitution

Imagine the situation where you want to play Ludo with four players. You have four green counters for the first player, four blue counters for the second and four yellow counters for the third. However, you have only three red counters. Rather than give up the game, you might look for something which can be used as a fourth counter for red. Even if you have a fifth green counter, that will not be suitable, because it is indistinguishable from the counters being used by the first player. But if you have a white counter, this can be used. It might not be red, but it can be distinguished from the green, blue and yellow counters.

In this situation, a linguist would say that green, blue, yellow and red CON-TRAST with each other. For this to be the case, it is important that all members of each of these sets can be distinguished from all members of the other sets which can occur on the same game-board. In the situation outlined above white 'acts as' a red, and does not contrast with red, even though perceptually there is as big a difference between white and red as there is between yellow and red. The contrast is defined by the game. In Ludo we have to be able to tell what happens if two counters end on the same square. Does one take the other, or do they accumulate to create a block to the progress of others? Red and white will accumulate; red and yellow will take.

Note that we need to distinguish here between things we can tell apart physically and things which act as different in the system we are working with. Red and white can be told apart, but they function as 'the same colour' in the system we are working with. The same principles apply in the linguistic analysis of language.

Consider, as an example, past tense marking in regular English verbs. Given a set of bases such as /djuːp, lɑːf, lʊk, wɔːk, bæn, briːð, dræg, fɪl/ , and a set of past tense forms such as /djuːpt, lɑːft, lʊkt, wɔːkt; bænd, briːðd, drægd, fɪld/, we can see that we have two markers of the past tense which we are able to distinguish, namely /t/ and /d/. But we also need to know whether the two contrast. To discover this we can do a COMMUTATION TEST, sometimes called a SUBSTITUTION TEST.

In a commutation test we ask whether replacing one element in the analysis with another leads to a change on another level of analysis, specifically on the semantic level (this is the equivalent to asking whether this is important for the rules of the game in the Ludo analogy). So if we take the analysed final /t/s from the sets provided above and replace them with /d/s, do we get to a regularly different meaning? The answer is 'no: we get impossible combinations: /*djuːpd, *laːfd, *lʊkd, *wɔːkd/'.

We can compare this with what happens when we put an /ɪŋ/ in place of the /t/. Then we get /djuːpɪŋ, laːfɪŋ, lʊkɪŋ, wɔːkɪŋ/, each of which is an occurring word, but one which does not mean the same as the original word. By this method we discover that /ɪŋ/ and /t/ CONTRAST in this position. We can also discover that each is associated with its own meaning, and that the contrast is not restricted to the particular examples we have chosen here, but is very general when we add these different endings to a verb stem.

A pair of words like /djuːpt/ and /djuːpɪŋ/ differ in just one element and mean different things, and we talk of a MINIMAL PAIR. A minimal pair is proof of contrast. It is the result of a commutation test having shown that contrasting elements are involved. Note that the 'elements' being discussed here are elements at the relevant level of analysis. The fact that /ɪŋ/ is made up of two speech sounds is irrelevant, because neither of those two sounds carries a meaning on its own.

So contrast is more than just being able to tell that two things are different; contrast implies functioning within the system to provide different messages.

The same notion of contrast can be used within phonology and syntax. In phonology, minimal pairs such as [tɪk] and [tʊk] show that [ɪ] and [ʊ] contrast in English, because *tick* and *took* do not mean the same. On the other hand, although we can hear the difference between [ɫ] and [l], when they occur in words like *plead* [pɫiːd] and *bleed* [bliːd] in English we cannot use them to distinguish meanings, and so they do not contrast. They may contrast in other languages, but they do not contrast in English.

In syntax, pairs of sentences such as *I love my wife* and *I love your wife* equally provide minimal pairs which prove the contrast between *my* and *your*, but which equally prove the parallel function of the two. Minimal pairs are more often used in syntax for this second reason. For example, the fact that you can substitute *it* for the underlined section in <u>*The weather we have been having all this month*</u> *has been awful* shows that the two have parallel function. We could have said the same for [ɪ] and [ʊ] in *tick* and *took*, where both have the same function in the syllables in which they occur.

Items which contrast are, by definition, in a PARADIGMATIC relationship with each other (see section 7), although we tend to call (1) a PARADIGM, where we see the relationship between morphological elements, but not (2), where we see the relationship between phonological elements.

(1) dominus
     domine
     dominum
     dominī
     dominō
     dominō
(2) pliːt
     bliːt
     fliːt
     sliːt
     kliːt

Contrast, based on substitution, is one of the fundamental notions of linguistics. We can see it as being based on the notion from information structure that there can be no meaning unless there is contrast: if you have no choice as to what to say, what you say doesn't mean anything. (Though if we want to be picky we can point out that there is always the option of saying nothing, and that saying something predictable may nevertheless have affective social value.) This is what underlies Saussure's (1969 [1916]: 166) famous dictum 'dans la langue il n'y a que des différences', usually translated into English as 'in language, only the differences count'. Those important differences are the contrasts. There are also differences which do not count: the different kinds of [l] sound or the different ways of marking past tense in English which are distinguishable but not contrastive. We could perhaps rephrase Saussure: we cannot have language without differences, but some of the observable differences are not important for the system, while others are crucial. Languages depend on contrast.

Reference

Saussure, Ferdinand de (1969 [1916]). *Cours de linguistique générale*. Paris: Payot.

11

Binarity

Binarity is, in effect, a hypothesis about the way in which language is structured. The hypothesis states that contrasts are all built on two-way oppositions.
The hypothesis used to be applied in particular to distinctive features, and is
these days more often applied to tree structure.

There is a sense in which any distinction can be reduced to a number of
binary oppositions. Suppose, for example, that we have a series of three
things, *A*, *B* and *C*, all of which are equivalent. We can describe that as being
a three-way choice, or we can describe that as being a choice first between
A and something else and then, if it is not-*A*, as a choice between *B* and *C*.
In the latter case we have imposed a binary structure on something which
was stated not to be inherently binary. The difficulty with such a description
is that we might equally well have described it another way: first, we might
have said, we choose between *C* and not-*C*, and then if it is not-*C*, we
choose between *A* and *B*. If *A*, *B* and *C* are not strictly ordered in some
way, there is also another choice – see (1). The binary hypothesis, therefore, implies that, in dealing with language, there will always be a motiva-
tion for choosing one of the options over the others for providing a binary
structure.

(1) A B C; (A B) C; A (B C); (A C) B.

The academic origins of the binary hypothesis are not easy to track down,
but I believe that it goes back originally to communication theory in the mid-
twentieth century, and ultimately to the belief (now disproved) that neurons
in the brain either fire or do not fire, that is, that they have just two possible
states.

Distinctive features

Within the Prague School of linguistics in the 1930s, binarity in phonological distinctive features such as [± voiced] or [± back] is related to markedness. There is a marked value for every feature (the + value) and an unmarked value. In early markedness theory, the marked value is given to something which is physically present in some environment (e.g. nasalisation in [m] or [ã]), but absent elsewhere. However, as markedness theories became more sophisticated, it has become harder to maintain the principle that for any feature the same value is marked or unmarked in all environments. For example, 'voiced' seems to be the normal state for vowels (that is, we would want to say that [+ voice] is the unmarked value for vowels), but the opposite is true for obstruents (the norm is for them to be voiceless).

In a deservedly widely ignored paper, Halle (1957) appears to argue that because binarity works in many places it should be used everywhere. This seems to disregard the received wisdom of the period, inherited from the Prague School, that there are several types of distinctive feature only some of which are binary in nature. Thus we find scholars like Ladefoged (1971) reverting to features with many values (multinary features) for things like vowel height, since binary features (a) do not allow easily for five distinctive vowel heights and (b) do not allow for simple statements of rules which raise or lower vowels by a single step. We also find alternative approaches, such as the use of unary features (features with just one value; that is, the feature is either present or not) within Dependency Phonology. Even within Generative Phonology, once feature values are filled in by general rules, problems can start to arise with ostensibly binary features actually having three contrastive values (Stanley 1967). For instance, if we suppose that a feature whose value has not yet been assigned is marked as u, we could imagine the three rules in (2) which would in effect be using u as a third contrastive value of the feature.

(2) [u voice]   →   [+ sonorant]
     [− voice]   →   [− sonorant]
     [+ voice]   →   [− sonorant]

The question of binarity has never been definitively settled within phonology, although modern versions of feature geometry seem to ignore it. It seems safe to conclude that it is at least not universally accepted.

Binarity has not been questioned to the same extent in semantic features, perhaps because semantic features themselves have rather fallen out of fashion. Morphosyntactic features, such as those used to mark tense and case in abstract structures, lost an absolute requirement for binarity at least as early as Gazdar et al. (1985), where it is argued (p. 22) that 'a feature value is either an atomic symbol or a category', that is, that a feature such as Case can have a value such as [accusative]. Similar extensions of feature theory are found in A-Morphous Morphology, for example. Binarity, to judge by the way that it is currently used by linguists in features, is all very well, but it is certainly not universal.

Tree structure

In the meantime, tree structure has been moving in precisely the opposite direction, away from multiply branching trees towards binary-branching. Scalise (1984) introduces what he terms the Binary Branching Hypothesis with respect to morphological trees, and argues that such a restriction can be justified in that domain.

In syntax, a restriction to binary branching can be seen as being implicit in X-bar theory (though Chomsky 1970, probably the location of the introduction of X-bar into Chomskyan linguistics, does not use binary-branching trees). It was generally adopted following Kayne (1984). Although Kayne introduces the notion of binary branching for technical reasons, it seems to have been welcomed as a principled constraint on the format of trees. Binary branching appears to fail in the case of coordination but only there (see also Wells 1957 [1947]). We might wonder, however, how principled the limitation is if it fails at all.

Interestingly, a restriction to binarily branching trees has been resisted in phonology. Not only have widely supported suggestions that the syllable might have a binarily branching structure like that in (3) been fiercely debated, but arguments for structuring consonant sequences (such as those that arise in both the onset and the coda of *strengths*) seem remarkably weak in models which look for constituent structure, with the result that a 'flat' tree like that in (4) might be preferred. (Dependency Phonology uses sonority as a guide to headedness, and is able to assign heads to these clusters; but the arguments for some of them

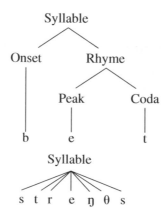

being more closely related as constituents than others are elusive.) Thus the acceptance of binary branching in syntax and morphology has not been matched by a corresponding acceptance of the same principle in phonology.

Conclusion

A hypothesis that linguistic structure or some part of linguistic structure is binary is one way of constraining and simplifying theories about language. But like all hypotheses, it is subject to counter-examples which might show the hypothesis to be in error. At the moment, the hypothesis does not seem to have been disproved in morphological structures, the situation in syntax is not clear, and the hypothesis seems to be ignored by many phonologists both for trees and for distinctive features. We need to recognise that the hypothesis of binarity in syntax is very new, and that it may not have been fully tested. We also need to recognise that binarity in other areas of grammar does not have a good record. Binarity is simple, and elegant where it works well, but not necessarily observationally adequate.

References

Chomsky, Noam (1970). Remarks on nominalization. In Roderick A. Jacobs & Peter S. Rosenbaum (eds), *Readings in English Transformational Grammar*. Waltham MA: Ginn, 184–221.

Gazdar, Gerald, Ewan Klein, Geoffrey Pullum & Ivan Sag (1985). *Generalized Phrase Structure Grammar*. Oxford: Blackwell.

Halle, Morris (1957). In defence of the number two. In Ernst Pulgrum (cd.), *Studies Presented to Joshua Whatmough on his Sixtieth Birthday*. The Hague: Mouton, 65–72.

Kayne, Richard S. (1984). *Connectedness and Binary Branching*. Dordrecht: Foris.

Ladefoged, Peter (1971). *Preliminaries to Linguistic Phonetics*. Chicago and London: Chicago University Press.

Scalise, Sergio (1984). *Generative Morphology*. Dordrecht: Foris.

Stanley, Richard (1967). Redundancy rules in phonology. *Language* 43: 393–436.

Wells, Rulon S. (1957 [1947]). Immediate constituents. Reprinted in Martin Joos (ed.), *Readings in Linguistics I*. Chicago and London: Chicago University Press, 186–207

12

Trees

It is a fundamental of linguistic structure that some parts of the string of linguistic elements belong together more closely than others. The nature of the 'belonging together' might be in doubt, but the basic observation is at the root of theorising about linguistic structure. So given a string of phonemes such as /drʌŋkəndraɪvəz/ we would want to say that the /ən/ go together more closely than the /nd/, for instance, or given a string of words like *Drunken drivers cause suffering* we would want to say that *drunken* and *drivers* go together more closely than *drivers* and *cause*. An obvious way of capturing this intuition graphically is to bracket the bits that go together, the CONSTITUENTS of the larger construction: *[drunken drivers][cause suffering]*, for instance. This allows us to capture the difference between a *[French history] teacher* 'a teacher of French history' and a *French [history teacher]* 'a history teacher who is French', and so on. If we want to say what status each of the bits has, we can use a labelled bracketing to do it: *[drunken drivers]$_{NP}$ [cause suffering]$_{VP}$* (where NP means 'noun phrase' and VP means 'verb phrase', assuming that these are the categories you wish to mark). There are two problems with this: it becomes typographically complex, and, with less simple examples, becomes extremely difficult to work out. Consider (1), for example. Although it would be possible to label opening brackets as well as closing ones, to make it easier to see which pairs belonged together, (1) would never be easy to read.

(1) $[[[\text{drunken}]_{ADJ} [\text{drivers}]_N]_{NP} [[\text{cause}]_V [[\text{immense}]_{ADJ} [\text{suffering}]_N]_{NP}]_{VP}]_S$

A labelled tree provides an exact equivalent of the labelled bracketing in (1) which, although it takes up more room on the page, is considerably easier to read. See (2).

(2)

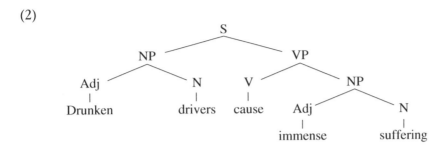

However difficult it may be to produce a tree like (2) in your own documents, its great virtue is that it is easier to absorb than the labelled bracketing like (1).

Terminology

In mathematical terms, a tree of the kind we are discussing here is a rooted acyclic directed graph. The properties of such structures are well understood in mathematical and computational terms, where each of the features of such structures can be important. In linguistics it is not clear that we are concerned with precisely those qualities that make a tree a tree for mathematicians. More relevantly for linguistics students, there is a large terminology associated with trees which it will be useful to know. We will begin with the very simplest possible tree, as in (3).

(3)

Each of the labelled points in (3) is a NODE, so A, b and c are all nodes. But b and c are TERMINAL NODES: they are those parts of the tree which have no tree structures below them. In syntactic trees, the terminal nodes will usually represent words (sometimes morphs) or, in trees which show the structure without any lexical content, the terminal nodes will be those nodes on which lexical material is to be grafted by some process of lexical insertion. Node A, being the origin of the tree, is termed the ROOT of the tree.

Relationships between nodes are discussed using female relationship terms. So in (3) A is the MOTHER of b and c, b and c are the DAUGHTERS of A, and b and c are SISTER nodes. There is rarely any need to refer to more distant nodes, though the same conventions would presumably be used.

Any node which lies in a direct line between a node being discussed and the root of the tree is said to DOMINATE the node being discussed. If there are no intervening nodes, then we talk of IMMEDIATE DOMINANCE. So A in (3) IMMEDIATELY DOMINATES both b and c. This becomes more relevant in a tree like (4) which has more than one branching structure in it. In (4), A dominates D, but immediately dominates C. Mothers immediately dominate their daughters. As well as showing dominance relationships, trees like those in (3) and (4) also

(4)

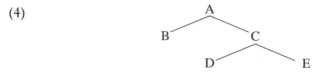

indicate LINEAR PRECEDENCE. In (4), for example, B comes before (to the left of) D. Although we might be able to envisage a tree in which the BRANCH linking C to D was lengthened, and B occurred between D and E, it is generally taken that this would not be a legal tree structure: it would involve crossed branches, and crossed branches are not permitted.

Although trees show both dominance and precedence relationships, the two are usually treated together as a single set of relationships. Occasionally, rules for dominance are distinguished from rules for precedence in an ID/LP (Immediate Dominance / Linear Precedence) format (Gazdar et al. 1985). Standard phrase-structure rules (rules of the general form A → b + c) cannot distinguish between these two aspects of the tree structure, with the result that it would be impossible to write a standard phrase-structure rule to generate trees with crossing branches.

Some conventions

Conventionally, syntactic trees are drawn as being binary branching (i.e. no mother can have more than two daughters) except in instances of coordination. This is a recent convention, and not necessarily adhered to by all syntacticians. (For more discussion see section 11.) Binary-branching trees are generally accepted in morphology, but are not always accepted in phonology, where the arguments for assigning a binary structure to a sequence of three (or more) adjacent consonants in a word like *sixths* may not always be clear. However, even here, some scholars enforce binary-branching trees, and nearly all scholars prefer them.

Another convention, again generally accepted in syntax, but not always in phonology, is sometimes referred to as the Single Mother Convention. The Single Mother Convention states that every node except the root must have one and only one mother. This is important for establishing the mathematical structure of the tree, and seems relatively uncontroversial in syntax and morphology. In phonology, however, there has been a great deal of discussion of ambisyllabicity, whereby the medial consonant in a word like *silly* may be seen as being simultaneously the coda of the first syllable and the onset of the second syllable. This accounts for two things: /ɪ/ cannot occur in a stressed syllable in

English without a following consonant, and so the /l/ must belong to the first syllable; the /l/ in *silly* is clear not dark, and thus in varieties of English which make this distinction belongs to the second syllable. Ambisyllabicity breaks the Single Mother Convention, and strictly speaking means that a structure which shows this is no longer a tree, although this terminological nicety is largely ignored.

Finally, we need to note that there is a notational convention for dealing with trees where one does not wish to give all the detail. A triangle over a particular piece of language data indicates that the author is not concerned with the internal structure of that particular section. This is illustrated in (5).

(5)

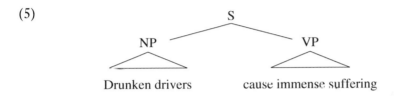

Extending trees

Although trees like those outlined above are typically used to display information about constituency, it is also possible to use trees to show other things.

Dependency trees directly encode information about headedness which has to be inferred in constituent structure trees or guaranteed by some complex mechanism. Dependency trees also give information on constituency. Dependency trees were developed by Anderson (1971), although slightly different versions are used by other scholars. A dependency tree is presented in (6).

(6)

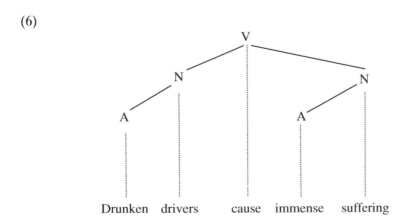

In (6), the solid lines show dependency relations, with elements higher up the tree being the heads of their constructions and GOVERNING their DEPEN- DENTS lower down the tree. The dotted lines show lexical filling of nodes – note that all nodes are terminal nodes in this tree. Linear precedence is shown by the order of the elements in the tree.

Trees are also used to represent one model of historical relationships between languages. These trees are not binary, and distance between languages left-to-right is supposed to indicate closeness of relationship (see (7)). There are various objections to the family-tree model of language development, but this is nevertheless a widespread use of tree notation.

(7)

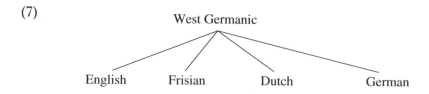

References

Anderson, John M. (1971). *The Grammar of Case*. Cambridge: Cambridge University Press.

Gazdar, Gerald, Ewan Klein, Geoffrey Pullum & Ivan Sag (1985). *Generalized Phrase Structure Grammar*. Oxford: Blackwell.

Sampson, Geoffrey (1975). The single mother condition. *Journal of Linguistics* 11: 1–11.

13

State versus process

Consider the following two statements.

(1) In English nasalised vowels immediately precede nasal consonants
(2) In English vowels become nasalised before nasal consonants.

Either of these is a perfectly reasonable statement of the situation in English. It is just that the first of these views the situation as a state, while the second views that state as the outcome of a process.

Linguists vary between these two ways of talking about language structure. To generalise, we can say that the structuralists in the first part of the twentieth century saw language as a state, while the transformationalists in the second half of the twentieth century saw any state as resulting from a process.

The dynamic or processual metaphor has become ingrained in linguistic terminology and practice. We write rules with a dynamic-looking arrow, which seems to imply change; we talk of phonemes BECOMING nasalised; we talk of MOVEMENT to head position; and so on. All of this implies that there is some kind of underlying or original structure from which actual linguistic production diverges. In many instances this may seem harmless. We know, for instance, that speakers perceive languages like English in terms of phoneme-size chunks, and fail to hear differences between, for example, clear and dark [l], until these things are specifically pointed out to them. We have no problem with the notion that a sentence like *Pity I don't need* is somehow a variant of a more neutral *I don't need pity*.

The suitability of such a view seems to be supported by the fact that we regularly make such statements in historical linguistics: word-initial /k/ WAS DROPPED before /n/ in the history of English so that *knight* (cognate with

German *Knecht* with initial /kn/) is now pronounced with initial /n/; Old English was an SOV language but it has TURNED INTO SVO in modern English.

At the same time, any notion that a non-standard variety of English (or any other language) is derived from the standard version is likely to be historically, socially and even structurally unsound. It is not far removed from the prescriptivism against which all linguistics students are warned early in their careers. Similarly, any implication that spoken language is in some way derived from a written norm is likely to be at best misleading and at worst dangerous.

What this means is that you have to recognise the process terminology as being a metaphor, and you have to consider whether it is helping you or misleading you. In many cases it provides an easy way of viewing a complex situation.

At one point there was something of a fashion among psycholinguists for considering the rules (process terminology) proposed by linguists and seeing whether there was any evidence that equivalent processes were taking place in the brain. Here we have a simple illustration of a particular group of scientists presupposing that the process metaphor should be taken literally. A failure to get a positive correlation between mental processes and linguists' rules could arise because the wrong rules had been postulated, but could also arise because the rules are merely one way of stating a relationship and human brains deal with the relationship in a non-processual way.

The history of the study of morphophonemic variation provides an interesting case study. For Trubetzkoy, the /aɪ/ in *divine* and the corresponding /ɪ/ in *divinity* are a set of distinct phonemes perceived as a unit, called a morphophoneme. Bloomfield recognised that a good description could be given using a single original form, an underlier, and a set of rules to derive the attested form (for example, by saying that vowels in stressed syllables three from the end of a word become short). Bloomfield (1935: 213) said overtly that any such presentation 'is a fiction and results simply from our method of describing the forms'. By the time of Chomsky & Halle's *Sound Pattern of English* (1968), it was assumed that such a set of morphophonemic rules corresponded to processes taking place in the brain, and that the underlier did not necessarily have a form which appears on the surface. The processes were said to be PSYCHOLOGICALLY REAL. Some of the reactions against Chomsky & Halle (1968) were caused by precisely this problem. Various scholars, e.g. those like Hooper (e.g. Hooper 1976) who were part of the school of Natural Generative Phonology, and Jackendoff (1975), presented series of statements about links (called VIA-RULES in the first case and REDUNDANCY RULES in the second) whose job was to show a link between forms such as *divine* and *divin(ity)* without deriving one from the other. Some more recent approaches have tried to distinguish between those morphophonemic alternations which speakers do manipulate and where we must assume some psychological mechanism for generating forms and those which they simply learn. An initial analysis in terms of states led first to an analysis in terms of processes viewed as a fiction, then to an analysis in terms of processes viewed as a fact about language users, and finally to the view that some of the alternations are best described as states, others as processes.

The moral is that too strict an adherence to either a static or a processual view may end up being counter-productive, and that it is worthwhile considering whether the view that has been taken is a helpful one or not in the particular context in which you are working. You should also realise that data presented in either view can be reformulated so as to appear with the other, and that each formulation may make assumptions that the other does not.

References

Bloomfield, Leonard (1935). *Language*. London: George Allen and Unwin.

Chomsky, Noam & Morris Halle (1968). *The Sound Pattern of English*. New York: Harper and Row.

Hooper, Joan B. (1976). *An Introduction to Natural Generative Phonology*. New York : Academic Press.

Jackendoff, Ray (1975). Morphological and semantic regularities in the lexicon. *Language* 51: 639–71.

14

Native speaker

The native speaker of a language has been given great status by both structuralist and generative linguists, in both theoretical and applied linguistics. The notion of 'native speaker' is highly problematic, though this has largely gone unnoticed.

For many of us, there is no apparent problem at all. I grew up in an environment which was (to all intents and purposes) monolingual. I was literate in English before I learnt any other language. In the course of my formal education, I acquired, to various degrees, a number of extra languages. Some of these I can speak reasonably fluently, well enough to be taken on superficial acquaintance as a member of the relevant language community. Despite this facility, it is still less tiring for me to spend an evening talking to friends in English than in any other language, I can use English in a wider range of circumstances (including writing) than I can use any other language, I can read English more quickly and efficiently than I can read any other language, and I feel confident about what is or is not English over a wider range of constructions than I feel confident about in any other language. There are tasks which I can carry out in English that I can carry out only with great difficulty in any other language (performing arithmetical calculations, for instance). Even if I had chosen to spend the larger part of my life in a country where English was not the major language of interaction, and had learnt to function well in that environment, I feel that this imbalance would have remained. I am a native speaker of English.

Even within these parameters, we can question what exactly I am a native speaker of. My parents grew up in different parts of the United Kingdom, and I was brought up in a third. Thus I was exposed to three varieties of English from early in my life. My grandmothers spoke different varieties again. I have lived for extended periods in three different English-speaking countries, being exposed to people whose English is like mine to very different extents. In some measure my English changes its characteristics depending on whether the person I am speaking to comes from one of those areas. It is probable that I am a speaker of a unique variety, spoken by nobody else in the world. Am I still a native speaker of English? (See also section 1.)

When we start looking at the concept more widely, and at the uses to which it is put, the notion of native speaker becomes more difficult to tie down.

Who is a native speaker?

A native speaker of a language must have acquired that language naturally by growing up in the community in which it is spoken before the age of puberty.

There is some evidence that children whose parents did not also grow up in the same community show slightly different speech patterns from those whose parents were already part of the community. So perhaps I am not a native speaker of anything because I did not grow up in the community in which both of my parents grew up.

What should we then say about people who grow up in bilingual or multi-lingual communities? Such people are more common than monoglots (people who speak just one language) in the world. Are they native speakers only if both parents grew up in the same community and speak the same language to the child within that community? Is it possible for children to grow up as native speakers of two languages, or can they only be native speakers of one, and if so, can it be determined by simple principles which language they are native speakers of? Is it possible for children who arrive in a community near the cut-off point for language acquisition to forget their chronologically first language and operate fully in their chronologically second language, and if so do they then become people who are not native speakers of any language?

Can people lose native-speaker status if they move away from their own community? Just as interestingly, can people acquire native-speaker status by staying long enough in a community which is not their original one? After all, even if I am more confident about what is English than I am about what is French, I still have intuitions about what sounds like good French (just not such extensive ones as I have for English). Are those intuitions inevitably second-class citizens of the intuition world?

We also know that not all people who use a particular language do so with the same effectiveness. A few people have the ability to produce great works of literature or to make speeches which move others and stir them to action. Most of us do not. Some people are more aware of the speech of outsiders than others. Some find it harder to understand people with a foreign accent than others do. Are all these people equal in the status as native speakers? Or are there, perhaps, good native speakers and bad native speakers? And if there are, is this status in any way correlated with literacy in cultures where literacy is a relevant consideration?

Are all people who speak only one language *ipso facto* native speakers of that language? This becomes relevant in countries where, for example, English was once a colonial language and has been adopted for local use. Some people feel uncomfortable with the idea that a person who speaks only Indian, Nigerian or Singaporean English can be a 'native speaker of English'. This is probably tied up with rather extravagant ideals about what 'English' is, but it becomes a real political problem in some places, especially when native-speaker status may be used as a tool of discrimination.

Is there a test which will prove that a person is a native speaker of a particular language?

The simple answer to the question in the title of this section is 'No'. A more complex answer might mention that if any such test is in theory possible, it has not yet been devised or shown to be accurate in any sense at all. This, of course, raises the further question of whether 'native speaker' is a term which has a precise definition at all. And this in turn raises the question of whether native speakers of a particular language are a definite category of people or whether the notion of native speaker is a PROTOTYPE, a presupposed perfect model, which real speakers may resemble more or less closely.

What does a native speaker do?

Native speakers are generally assumed to have reliable intuitions about what is or is not part of their own language, and to be able to make judgements about the structures of their language: for example, they can state reliably whether something is ambiguous, and which parts of the utterance belong together. As a result of this, they are able to guide linguists in determining the grammar of their language, even though they themselves do not have conscious access to their grammar of their own language.

The whole notion of intuition is taken up in a separate section (see section 15). But there is plenty of evidence that intuition is variable, both within the same speaker and between speakers, at least in the subtler cases. At the level at which intuitions are probably the most constant, the level at which we judge that *Syntax not my functioning is* is not a legitimate sentence of English (even though it is an occurrent one: I have heard someone say this), we probably do not need native speakers to bring us the news.

We also need to recall that one of the things we have learnt from late twentieth-century linguistics is that production is variable. While some of this may be accessible to introspection, it seems unlikely that all of it is. That is, while a speaker may be able to tell you that more than one of *I haven't a car, I don't have a car* and *I haven't got a car* sound reasonable, they probably cannot tell you precisely how to distinguish them. When it comes to phonetic/phonological facts such as when or how often to say /ʌŋkaɪnd/ rather than /ʌnkaɪnd/, any overt information provided by a native speaker is likely to be misleading.

We must remember, too, that even where native speakers are able to make judgements appropriately, they may not do so for external reasons: the desire not to contradict the linguist, the desire to provide an answer even when they are guessing, the desire to seem confident where they are not.

Are there different definitions of 'native speaker'?

Unfortunately, there are occasions when the term 'native speaker' is, in any case, used in a rather different sense from the one most often intended by linguists. For example, in Singapore people are assigned a native language or, rather, a 'mother tongue', of which they may then be considered native speakers, independent of their actual speech habits (Lim & Foley 2004: 5). A speaker of Hokkien may be designated a mother-tongue speaker of Mandarin, for example, since only standardised variants are recognised as languages which may function as a 'mother tongue'. Here we may just need a richer terminology: there can be mother tongues, first languages, community languages and heritage languages, any of which may or may not coincide with a native language (if we can define that term). A MOTHER TONGUE is quite literally the tongue learned from one's mother (though in most cases, that language will be modified by the language of the speaker's peers); a FIRST LANGUAGE is the language the speaker feels most comfortable using — usually, but not necessarily the mother tongue; a COMMUNITY LANGUAGE is the language used by a particular community, perhaps a small community functioning within a larger one, as is the case with groups of immigrants in a foreign country; a HERITAGE LANGUAGE is a language which may not be spoken at all, but in which some important facets of the local culture are encoded and which has some historical and emotional tie for people, even if they do not speak it. Italian might be a heritage language for monolingual English speakers descended from Italians in some parts of the USA or Australia, for example.

Conclusion

The notion of native speaker, and also the notion of native language, are not as simple as they might seem. In this section, more questions have been asked than have been answered. The intention is to draw attention to possible problems with a term which is often used glibly. This does not necessarily mean that the term should simply be abandoned or that the notion behind the term should be discarded. There are plenty of instances where the term 'native speaker' can act as a perfectly informative and useful label, communicating an appropriate idea economically. But it is a term which needs to be used with appropriate care because a precise definition is, if not impossible, at least difficult, and precisely who is covered by the label may not be clear in individual cases. For much fuller discussion, see Coulmas (1981), Paikeday (1985) and Davies (2003).

References

Coulmas, Florian (ed.) (1981). *A Festschrift for Native Speaker*. The Hague: Mouton.

Davies, Alan (2003). *The Native Speaker: Myth and Reality*. Clevedon: Multilingual Matters.

Lim, Lisa & Joseph A. Foley (2004). English in Singapore and Singapore English. In Lisa Lim (ed.), *Singapore English*. Amsterdam and Philadelphia: Benjamins, 1–18.

Paikeday, Thomas M. (1985). *The Native Speaker is Dead!* Toronto and New York: PPI.

15

The data of linguistics

It may seem obvious that linguistics is about language and that language provides the primary data for linguistic theorising. However, different kinds of language data have been fashionable at different times and in different sub-branches of linguistics. Each of these different kinds of data has advantages and disadvantages associated with it, so that it is often beneficial to consider a range of possible data-sources when trying to answer a particular linguistic question. The various data-sources listed below are not all mutually exclusive, and it may be desirable to get data from a number of sources to provide a solid empirical foundation for a particular argument.

Literary texts

Literary texts are generally seen as being texts of great inherent value, illustrating the very best use of language – highly polished, well expressed, effective and reflecting high points of cultural achievement. It is for this reason that literary texts have been preserved, while less highly regarded texts have often been treated as ephemeral, discarded as soon as they have served their purpose. As a result, literary texts of great antiquity are still available (not necessarily, it is true, in their original linguistic form) for most European languages and some Asian ones.

It has to be recognised, though, that the very features of literary language which contribute to its literary value mean that it does not correspond in any easily measurable way to the ordinary language of the streets at the same period. Literary texts are usually formal and conservative, typically more ornate and complex than texts written in other styles.

Possible benefits of this type of data for linguists include:

- The texts are interesting.
- The texts provide good coverage of a range of historical periods.

Possible disadvantages of this type of data include:

- The patterns illustrated in the data are not necessarily representative.
- There is a certain artificiality associated with literary styles.
- The topics discussed are often restricted.

Non-literary texts

There is a huge range of non-literary texts ranging from personal letters through newspaper editorials to science textbooks. Each individual type has its own advantages and disadvantages. Personal letters, for example, are more likely to be a relatively accurate reflection of the language of the period than are literary texts, but are rarely kept. Examination scripts are likely to contain a large number of errors of performance (see section 8) because they are written hurriedly and under pressure. Newspaper editorials and columns look as though they provide relatively reliable diachronic data, but the style of newspaper reporting has probably changed over the last century, and is possibly continuing to evolve. Science textbooks use very unusual vocabulary, and are likely to overuse the passive construction (which used, at least, to be seen as part of a good scientific writing style). In the current period, many business and government communications seem to be written in a form of officialese, often involving particularly convoluted syntax and a strange use of many lexical items. Nevertheless, there is so much non-literary textual material easily available that it is often possible to find data-sources which will match the linguist's requirements in terms of vocabulary, grammar or text type.

Possible benefits of this type of data include:

- Large amounts of material are available for standard languages in developed countries.
- It is relatively easy to match sources or to get a range of sources.
- Data collection costs are relatively low.

Possible disadvantages of this type of data include:

- Very little material is available for the huge number of languages which serve what are still fundamentally oral cultures.

- There is variability between sources as to style, etc., although this can be exploited.
- The texts display an unknown amount of editorial interference and standardisation.
- Newspaper sources are typically anonymous, which makes it hard to use them for sociolinguistic enquiry.

Dictionaries and word-lists

Dictionaries look like a linguist's heaven: they are full of words, each word is provided with one or more meanings, some of them provide illustrations of the use of the words (and thus of the syntactic patterns in which they occur), and more and more they are available in electronic format, which makes them easier to search.

However, care is required with dictionary data. First, all words are treated the same, so that *fiacre* and *fiancé* have similar entries, despite the fact that one is much more common that the other. Second, dictionaries given no direct information on word frequency, and very little on the ways in which words are used – their collocations and typical grammatical patterning. Sometimes dictionaries aimed at non-native speakers are more useful than dictionaries for native speakers in this regard. Third, dictionaries do not necessarily make it simple to take a random sample of words, although they appear to do that. The problem is that a word like *combust* may have an entry consisting of just a few lines, while a word like *come* may have an entry which spills over several columns or pages. While there are more words like *combust*, more room is given to words like *come*, and any simple counting or sampling procedure (such as consider the first new word on every fifth page) is likely to end up with a biased sample. Fourth, dictionaries inevitably involve compromises between academic integrity and commercial feasibility, and there is a certain random element in what happens to be included in them. Having said that, *The Oxford English Dictionary*, particularly in its on-line incarnation, is an invaluable tool for anyone dealing with the history of English or the vocabulary of English.

It should be recalled that as well as ordinary monolingual and translating dictionaries, there are dictionaries of special vocabularies, dialect dictionaries, dictionaries of pronunciations, dictionaries of synonyms and antonyms, dictionaries of etymology, dictionaries of Indo-European roots, and a host of other works which provide fascinating reading and a wealth of valuable information.

Possible benefits of this type of data include:

- It provides easy access to large amounts of data.
- The existence of competing dictionaries provides simple checks on the accuracy of the available data.

- It provides analyses and decisions about pronunciation, polysemy, fixed collocations, etc. which are independent of the linguist's ideas.
- Dictionaries can be excellent sources of historical data.

Possible disadvantages of this type of data include:

- Search engines for electronic dictionaries do not always make it easy to carry out the search you need for your query.
- Examples of 'usage' are often invented, and may not give a true picture of the language.
- Dictionaries provide limited syntagmatic information.
- The arrangement of the entries can mask information which is important for the linguist.
- There is a relatively high concentration of rare, obscure or technical words in some dictionaries.
- Criteria for decisions about inclusion of items, layout, spelling conventions, entry-division, etc. may not be clear or consistent.

Sound recordings

The advent of sound recording had a profound effect on the data available for linguistic study. This is most obvious in the fields of phonetics, conversation analysis, the study of child language and the study of pathological language. However, the importance of recorded data for the study of syntax should not be ignored.

We can distinguish here between two kinds of recorded data: recordings of conversations, lectures, meetings, etc. which would have taken place whether or not the sound recording had been made, and recordings which are deliberately made to capture particular linguistic events. The latter includes the reading of texts (sometimes larded with examples relevant to the linguist), the utterance of individual words (whether these are read or prompted for by the interviewer in some way), and the establishment of experimental situations designed to elicit particular types of linguistic behaviour (perhaps the asking of questions, for example).

Recordings of naturally occurring events

Possible benefits of this type of data include:

- This is presumably the most natural kind of data available, illustrating language use with the least possible conscious control.
- Recording provides the only way to get accurate data on a number of the phenomena in spoken language, including hesitation, pausing,

back–channelling, interruption and the precise phonetic nature of what is produced by infants.

Possible disadvantages of this type of data include:

- It takes an extremely long time to transcribe tapes, and accuracy of transcription is often difficult to achieve.
- The observer's paradox states that an observed interaction is not exactly like an unobserved one precisely because it is observed.
- Structures of interest may occur very rarely, and thus require very large amounts of data.
- It can be difficult to search the data (though this is becoming easier with various electronic analysis tools).
- There are ethical and legal concerns in collecting data of this kind, and careful planning is required.

Recordings of word-lists, read texts, etc.

Possible benefits of this type of data include:

- It allows the linguist to focus of points of interest.
- It allows relatively rapid collection of relevant data.
- It allows collection of data which occurs naturally only rarely.

Possible disadvantages of this type of data include:

- Some speakers have difficulty in reading fluently.
- Read text is not pronounced just like naturally produced text, partly because it is done with rather more conscious control.
- Words are not pronounced precisely the same way in word-lists as they are in ordinary conversation.
- Word-lists are typically spoken with listing intonation, which may have effects on the pronunciation of the individual words, as well as making words early in a list different from the final items in a list.
- The concentration of particular phenomena in a short text or word-list may make the focus of the enquiry obvious.
- People willing to undertake the required tasks are often not randomly spread across the required gender/socio-economic/ethnic/age groups, which means that careful planning may be required in collecting suitable data.

Although a binary division has been made here between naturally occurring events and elicited material, there are various attempts made to create events which can be recorded but which involve rather less unnatural production of speech than is provided in reading tasks: role playing, doing a 'map task' (where two participants are given partial maps showing some of the same features and are asked to reconstruct some route across the map, without seeing each other's maps), and similar exercises. The difficulty here is often to create a meaningful task which will produce the requisite language behaviour, but the data produced can be very valuable.

Electronic corpora

While it is possible to create one's own electronic corpus and to annotate it in any way desired, it will be assumed in what follows that the use of electronic corpora involves the analysis of one of the standard corpora now more and more readily available. The great benefit of corpora is that somebody has already collected a number of texts, probably with some attempt at representativeness, and has already done the transcription in the case of spoken texts. Electronic corpora thus provide some of the best features of literary and non-literary texts and sound recordings, with the added advantage that they are relatively easy to search (or, in most cases, are easy to search as long as the search can be carried out in terms of specific lexical material). Some corpora have also been tagged, i.e. marked with information about the word classes of the items in the texts. The best corpora of spoken language can now link the transcriptions direct to the sound files and to the files containing speaker information, so that it is possible to search for an occurrence of /e/ before /l/ spoken by a woman. Where part-of-speech tagging has been manually checked it is more useful than when it has been done entirely automatically, in which case the analyst has to be aware that there may be errors in the labels assigned. A very few corpora have also had the syntactic constructions in them analysed and marked. As well as those collections of texts put together specifically for the use of linguists, there is a growing number of electronically searchable bodies of text, which may also be of value. Many newspapers are now republished retrospectively on CD, and there are collections of literary and non-literary texts from various periods. The largest body of electronically searchable text is provided by the world-wide web. Ironically, given that one of the problems with newspapers as sources of data is that there may be editorial interference, one of the major problems with the web is that there is no editorial control, and that spelling mistakes and syntactic errors abound. For example, a query on *few person* will not only turn up reference to *a few person-hours* and the like, but will also provide examples such as *Is it possible that a few person participate using the same computer?* Also, a search of the web may turn up several occurrences of the same document, and thus apparently inflate the occurrence of a particular structure. Despite such problems, the web is an invaluable source of data on some topics. When interpreting corpus data, it must always be recalled that any result holds for the corpus rather than for the language as a whole.

Possible benefits of this type of data include:

- There is good software available for searching corpora quickly and efficiently.
- Experiments based on freely available corpora are replicable.
- It is possible to search large amounts of data for relatively rare constructions.
- The text collection and transcription of spoken material are done in advance.
- Experiments based on corpus data allow for the meaningful statistical analysis of results.

Possible disadvantages of this type of data include:

- There are some constructions which it is very difficult to search for in most corpora, for example, relative clauses with a zero relativiser.
- For some queries huge amounts of data are required if any meaningful results are to be obtained.
- The analyst can be faced with too much data.
- In most cases a search has to be done on lexical data.

Descriptive grammars

Even when dealing with our own language, we all turn to descriptive grammars to discover what is going on in various constructions or what the difference between two similar constructions might be. When it comes to learning another language, we turn either to specific pedagogical grammars, which compare the target language with our own first language, or to more general descriptive grammars in order to aid our learning of that language. When it comes to knowing how a more exotic language works, we are often dependent on what we are told in a descriptive grammar of that language, written by an expert. These three types of descriptive grammar are not entirely parallel, but we will consider them all together here.

Descriptive grammars may or may not be overt about the linguistic theory or grammatical model which informs their description. In principle, the best grammars are readable independent of the model they base themselves on, but the questions that are answered may depend on the assumptions made by the author(s). Every descriptive grammar must be selective in the material it presents, none can ever hope to be exhaustive, and room for illustrative material is always at a premium. The result is that some constructions will not be covered, and that it can often be difficult to find multiple examples of the same phenomenon, even when it would be useful to the reader. Even with the best descriptive grammars, therefore, the reader often has to work quite hard to find an answer to any specific question, and with brief descriptions it is frequently impossible. That is why multiple descriptions and journal articles focusing on particular structures or functions in a given language are often a useful support for a grammar of that language.

Possible benefits of this type of data include:

- They provide the most efficient way to gain data on a range of languages which the investigator does not speak; the alternative of eliciting information from native speakers is frequently not available.
- They allow access to a wide range of languages.

Possible disadvantages of this type of data include:

- A descriptive grammar may presuppose familiarity with the writing system of the language concerned.
- A descriptive grammar may presuppose some familiarity with the language concerned, or may require access to a dictionary.
- The data may be patchy or insufficient for the investigator's purposes.
- Different models of description and terminologies may make individual grammars difficult to interpret or to compare with descriptions of other languages. In the phonetics/phonology sections of such grammars, different theoretical presuppositions may provide incompatible analyses of even fundamental material.

Introspection

Introspection is probably one of the most useful and one of the most condemned ways of collecting data in linguistics. In phonetics, introspection about what one's articulators are doing in a particular utterance is usually encouraged. In syntax, introspection about marginal syntactic constructions is often vilified. Introspection about matters of discourse is probably even more difficult. In either case, it should be pointed out, experience makes for better introspection. But it is probably always safer to verify the results of introspection in some independent way if at all possible.

Possible benefits of this type of data include:

- It makes it possible to consider very rare constructions.
- It is an efficient mode of data collection.
- It provides an efficient way of examining alternatives.
- It provides a good way to start an investigation.

Possible disadvantages of this type of data include:

- Speakers who are asked to make judgements about a set of very similar constructions can easily become confused about what is and is not possible.
- Different varieties of the same language sometimes differ on how they treat constructions that are taken as crucial for some theoretical point. Unverified data from introspection can lead to ultimately fruitless arguments about whether the theoretical point is justified on the basis of one variety, when it may not be justified on the basis of another.
- Introspection is often not reliable (see also elicitation, below).

Random (or systematic) observation

Random observations can lead to good scientific outcomes: we only have to remember Newton's apple to see that. Many a piece of good linguistic description has likewise started from an observation of a particular utterance and a question as to what the systematic pattern underlying the utterance might be. Following a random observation, there may be a period of more systematic observation: listening for similar utterances from newsreaders, passengers on the bus, colleagues in meetings, interlocutors, and so on. One colleague I know went from a random observation about the lines from the song 'Diamonds are a girl's best friend'

> And that's when those louses
> Go back to their spouses

to enquire into the figurative use of irregular plural forms in English. This kind of serendipity is a crucial source of questions about linguistic structure, and linguists in general seem to be very aware of the benefits of such observations.

Possible benefits of this type of data include:

- It provides an extremely valuable source of insights into linguistic structures.
- It draws attention to rare or innovative structures.

Possible disadvantages of this type of data include:

- An observation of the existence of a particular structure says nothing about how frequently it occurs or who uses it.
- The initial observation may be misleading – for instance, if the speaker made a speech error.
- Such a means of data collection is insufficient by itself.

Elicitation

Elicitation is asking speakers about their language. Despite the fact that this method of collecting data is virtually inescapable, and despite the fact that some linguists believe that speakers will have good intuitions about their own language, direct elicitation has to be treated with great caution. Problems may include things such as speakers not liking to contradict the linguist in any way because that would not be considered polite, speakers saying that something is impossible in their language when what they mean is that they cannot immediately think of a situation in which they might say it (linguists are far more used to thinking about sentences out of context than most speakers are), speakers becoming confused because they are asked about too many similar structures at once, speakers being sidetracked by matters which are irrelevant for the linguist (e.g. Kim wouldn't do that, but I'd believe it of Lee; I couldn't say that, but it would be in order for a prince/woman/rude person to say it; we all know that happened last year, so you can't use the present tense to describe it), and speakers not being able to put their intuitions about some usage into words. In some cases, speakers seem to be just plain wrong. Quirk & Svartvik (1966: 49) point out that in an experiment they carried out *A keeps changed very when* and *Not if I have anything to do with it* got very similar results for acceptability. For all these reasons, elicitation is best if carefully planned so that the informant or consultant is not inadvertently led to give a particular set of responses or exhausted in any particular session, and so that the elicitation uses behaviour which is as natural as possible. The other side of this particular coin is that some speakers, even if they cannot express what is going on in linguistic terms, may have very good intuitions about what is important in their language.

For all these reasons, a number of techniques have been designed in an attempt to make data elicitation as accurate as possible, and indirect methods of elicitation are often to be preferred over direct ones. There are, of course, traps. If you ask a speaker of English 'Do you say *diaper* or *nappy*', they may give you the answer they think you are looking for (for example, you may be more likely to get *diaper* if you speak with an American accent), but if you show them a picture of a baby wearing the relevant garment and ask what the baby is wearing, they may give you an answer depending on whether they perceive the garment as being made of cloth or some artificial fabric. In principle, there is a distinction to be made between the situation of the linguist trying to elicit details of a language from a single speaker of that language, and the linguist trying to elicit details of a language from large numbers of speakers (where statistical techniques may be used to determine degrees of acceptability, for instance). In practice, both require similar care. For some discussion of these matters see Quirk & Svartvik (1966), Greenbaum & Quirk (1970), and Newman & Ratliff (2001).

Possible benefits of this type of data include:

- It allows for efficient data collection.
- It allows the linguist to focus on important details.
- It allows multiple approaches to similar data.
- It allows access to speakers' intuitions.

Possible disadvantages of this type of data include:

- Speakers' introspection and therefore responses may not always be reliable or consistent.
- Reasons for speaker's reactions may be irrelevant. In one recently reported case (Hay et al. 2006) the accent of the person who greeted the speakers when they arrived influenced their reactions.

Experimentation

Precisely what counts as experimentation in linguistics is not clearly delimited: it may very well include elicitation, and may even include introspection. On the other hand, it certainly includes the very elaborate experiments set up by many psycholinguists and people working within the field of experimental or laboratory phonology (Ohala & Jaeger 1986; Pierrehumbert et al. 2000). Prototypical experimental approaches to linguistic questions (a) are aimed at answering very specific questions, (b) involve the collection of controlled and balanced data, and (c) involve statistical treatments to draw conclusions. This notably says nothing about the origins of data, which may be elicited, the result of recording natural interactions, derived from dictionaries or word-lists, or from corpora, etc.

Possible benefits of this type of data include:

- Experiments seem to get to the heart of how real people use language; this is a God's-Truth approach to linguistics.
- Even limited experiments can make a genuine contribution to theory.
- Formulating a good experiment demands considerable thought about the issues to be tackled.

Possible disadvantages of this type of data include:

- Experiments can, and frequently do, contradict each other.
- Linguistic data which will allow the author to distinguish between two competing hypotheses may not exist.
- Progress is slow, since each experiment is closely controlled to answer a specific question.

- Negative results can be frustrating, even if, theoretically, they tell you a lot.
- Really sound experiments can be difficult to devise, and some demand sophisticated technical equipment.

References

Greenbaum, Sidney & Randolph Quirk (1970). *Elicitation Experiments in English*. London: Longman.

Hay, Jen, Katie Drager & Paul Warren (2006). Cross-dialectal exemplar priming. Poster presented at the 10th conference on laboratory phonology, Paris.

Newman, Paul & Martha Ratliff (eds) (2001). *Linguistic Fieldwork*. Cambridge: Cambridge University Press.

Ohala, John & Jeri J. Jaeger (eds) (1986). *Experimental Phonology*. Orlando FL: Academic.

Pierrehumbert, Janet, Mary E. Beckman & D. R. Ladd (2000). Conceptual foundation of phonology as a laboratory science. In Noel Burton-Roberts, Philip Carr & Gerard Docherty (eds), *Phonological Knowledge*. Oxford: Oxford University Press, 273–303.

Quirk, Randolph & Jan Svartvik (1966). *Investigating Linguistic Acceptability*. The Hague: Mouton.

Part II: Notation and terminology

16

Notational conventions

Linguistics is full of notation, with notational conventions varying from theory to theory and from topic to topic. This section describes some of the more obvious notational conventions and what they mean.

Asterisks and the like

Grammaticality judgements

The asterisk (*) is conventionally prefixed to some construction which is considered to be ungrammatical. So a central use of the asterisk would be as in (1).

(1) *A this not sentence is.

However, the asterisk is also used to indicate that a construction is deemed unacceptable (see e.g. Lyons 1968: 142), which is far less clear cut. Should Chomsky's (1957: 15) example in (2) be given an asterisk or not? The answer may depend on the extent to which you believe that the oddity of (2) is caused by the grammar and how far it is caused by the pragmatics which makes (2) an unlikely utterance in real language use.

(2) Colourless green ideas sleep furiously.

Even were it not for problems of pragmatics versus grammaticality, there are problems in deciding about grammaticality. Many people find the notion to be a matter of degree rather than a straight distinction between grammatical and ungrammatical. This leads to a proliferation of intermediate steps,

usually marked (rather informally) with question marks. Any such intermediate steps are not well defined, and the relative grammaticality or acceptability of the constructions under consideration is the important feature.
Radford (1981) is fairly conservative, apparently working with three degrees
of ungrammaticality, illustrated by the sentences in (3) (from Radford 1981:
72).

(3) a.   John certainly washed the dishes.
     b.   ?John washed certainly the dishes.
     c.   *John washed the certainly dishes.

Other authors propose rather more degrees of ungrammaticality, with Ross
(1973: 190) explicitly ranking six: OK, ?, ??, ?*, *, **.

Ungrammaticality is distinguished in principle from semantic oddity, sometimes called semantic ill-formedness, which is shown by an exclamation mark.
Radford (1981: 10) illustrates this with examples such as those in (4), but he
points out that the borderline between ungrammaticality and unsemanticity
may not be clear cut.

(4) a.   !I killed John, but he didn't die.
     b.   !All my friends are linguists, but I don't have any friends.

Unfortunately, the use of the exclamation mark is not completely general.
For example, Huddleston & Pullum (2002) use the hash mark '#' for
'semantically or pragmatically anomalous' and the exclamation mark for
'non-standard'. Other idiosyncratic markers include '@ ' (ambiguous or
attested depending on the source), '&' (ambiguous) and '%' (dialectally variable).

Reconstruction

An asterisk is also used to mark a reconstructed form in historical linguistics.
A reconstructed form is one for which there is no direct evidence, but which
seems to be presupposed given the later developments in related languages.
The starred word is a hypothesis about the form a word is likely to have had at
an earlier stage of the language. Consider, for example, modern Romance
words for 'uncle', as in (5).

(5) French   oncle
     Italian   zio
     Spanish   tío
     Portuguese tiu

Given these forms, and no others, we would probably be tempted to reconstruct an earlier Romance form of the word for 'uncle' as *tiu*, with the assumption that French *oncle* had been borrowed from somewhere else. It is only
because we know more about the history of the Romance languages (and have
other languages to draw upon besides those mentioned in (5)) that we know that
the Latin word was *avunculus*, and that the Italian, Spanish and Portuguese
forms derive from a Greek loan-word in Vulgar Latin (Elcock 1960: 162). A
reconstructed *tiu* would be a hypothesis about the form of the word for 'uncle'
which would be only partly correct, a best guess on the basis of the available
evidence. The asterisk marks that status.

Optimality Theory

In Optimality Theory tableaux, an asterisk is used to show a breach of a particular constraint. If the constraint is broken more than once, more than one asterisk is used. If the breach of the constraint is FATAL (that is, if that particular breach
leads to the candidate under discussion being rejected), the asterisk is followed
by an exclamation mark. A simple example comes from Pater (2000). The two
contradictory constraints concerned are NON-FIN (i.e. Non-final: the head of the
prosodic word, the stressed syllable, must not be final) and ALIGN-HEAD (Align
the right edge of the prosodic word with the right edge of the head of the prosodic
word, i.e. the stressed syllable). Applied to the word *horizon*, this gives the tableau
in (6). Output (a) breaks the ALIGN-Head constraint because the stressed syllable is not at the right-hand edge of the word; output (b) breaks the same constraint twice because there are two syllables after the stressed syllable; output (c)
breaks NON-FIN because the stress is final. Since breaking NON-FIN is more
serious than breaking ALIGN-HEAD, and since (a) breaks ALIGN-HEAD less than
(b) does, (a) is the optimal candidate here, as indicated by the pointing finger.

(6) NON-FIN >> ALIGN-HEAD

horizon	NON-FIN	ALIGN-HEAD
☞ a. ho[rí]zon		*
b. [hóri]zon		**!
c. [hòri][zón]	*!	

Autosegmental and Metrical Phonology

In Autosegmental Phonology, an asterisk is used to mark a syllable which has
pitch prominence. Thus in Japanese *kokoro* 'heart' the second syllable is

marked with an asterisk to show that it is the one which stands out from the low tones which are the default. In intonational uses of this notation, H* stands for a high-tone pitch accent.

In Metrical Phonology, grids are often drawn with asterisks, though other characters (e.g. *x*'s) are also used)

Notation involving font style

Small capitals

Small capitals are generally used to mark lexemes, using a notation introduced by Matthews (1965) and Lyons (1968), although Lyons himself uses at least three different notations in different works. Thus if we say that 'BE has the forms *am, is, are, was, were, be, being* and *been*', we can read this as 'the lexeme BE . . .'.

Constraint names in Optimality Theory are also usually written in small capitals, as illustrated in (6).

In interlinear glosses, grammatical categories are glossed in small capitals (see section 30).

Wells's lexical sets (introduced in Wells 1982) are also marked with small capitals. For example, the FLEECE lexical set is the set of words which share the same stressed vowel as the word *fleece*: words such as *caesar, heap, keep, oestrus*, and so on. By generally accepted shorthand, that vowel is then referred to as 'the FLEECE vowel'. Wells's lexical sets are used as cue words for the introduction of the transcription system used in this book on p. ix.

Italics

Italics (represented in manuscript by underlining) are used to show language mention as opposed to language use (see section 31). Since what is mentioned is usually a form, italics can be used to show word forms (as opposed to lexemes) and morphs (as opposed to morphemes) where such distinctions are being made or are relevant.

Brackets

Brackets are used in rule notation and also to isolate various theoretical structures. Although it would in many ways be easier to consider the various types of use independently, from the user's point of view it is probably of more value to know how the different kinds of brackets are used. This part is thus organised in terms of the brackets involved, with the result that some themes (such as rule notation) recur.

(. . .)

The most frequent use of parentheses is to indicate something which is optional. Thus *kiwi(s)* should be read as '*kiwi* or *kiwis*' and *judg(e)ment* should be read as '*judgment* or *judgement*'. The same meaning attaches to parentheses in rule notation, so that (7) – which could be phrased more generally – applies whether or not there is [l] before the [m], so that we get both [hẽm] and [hẽlm].

$$(7) \quad e \;\rightarrow\; \tilde{e} \,/ \underline{\quad} (l)\, m$$

In interpreting rules such as (7) you should always try the longest possible expansion first (here the one which includes the [lm] cluster) before trying the shorter one (here the one which has only [m] in the environment).

In sociolinguistics, parentheses are used to enclose the name of a variable, so that '(ng)' could refer to the variability between [ŋ] and [n] in words like *hunting, shooting fishing*, etc.

<. . .>

Angle brackets are usually employed to enclose an orthographic representation, so that we might want to say that '<ough> is pronounced [ʌf] in *enough* but [əʊ] in *though*.'

In phonological rule notation angle brackets used to be used to enclose parts of the string which must either be all present or all absent for the rule to apply. Sommerstein (1977: 140) gives the example of rule (8), which is to be read as 'any vowel becomes short before two consonants, except that if the vowel is of height 1, it requires that there either should be three consonants or that the two consonant cluster should be word-final for this rule to apply'. (Vowels of height 1 are open vowels in Sommerstein's notation.)

$$(8) \begin{bmatrix} V \\ \text{<1 height>} \end{bmatrix} \;\rightarrow\; [-\,\text{long}] \,/ \underline{\quad} CC < \begin{Bmatrix} C \\ \# \end{Bmatrix} >$$

In early variable rule notation, angle brackets are used to enclose a set of realisations of some variable in a given context (see, e.g., Trudgill 1974: 156–9), or to show variable constraints (see Mesthrie 1994: 4906).

In Optimality Theory, angle brackets are sometimes used to indicate extrametrical constituents shown on tableaux.

[. . .]

The most obvious use of square brackets is to enclose phonetic transcriptions. The use of square brackets here contrasts with the use of slashes (see below) in ways which may not be obvious. The default notation is to use square brackets; the use of slashes makes particular claims about the transcription being used.

The term 'phonetic transcription' is unfortunately ambiguous. It may mean no more than a transcription using phonetic symbols. It may also be used to contrast with a 'phonemic transcription', in which case 'phonetic transcription' may be more or less synonymous with 'narrow transcription'. Narrowness, of course, is a matter of degree: one transcription may be narrower than another. When 'phonetic' is used in this sense, it covers all degrees of narrowness.

Note that in rule notation (and, increasingly, elsewhere) phonetic transcriptions (of whichever kind) are not enclosed in brackets at all. See (7) for an example. This is partly for clarity, and partly because the status of an element in a rule may be unclear, or variable from one application to the next.

Square brackets are also used to enclose distinctive features (like the [– long] in (8)) or arrays of distinctive features defining a single unit: in phonology, that unit is generally the segment, in syntax and semantics it may be the word. Thus we find examples like those in (9).

(9)

$$
\text{a.} \quad C \begin{bmatrix} +\text{vocalic} \\ +\text{long} \\ -\text{back} \end{bmatrix} \# \quad \text{b.} \begin{bmatrix} +\text{verb} \\ +\text{3rd person} \\ -\text{plural} \\ -\text{past} \end{bmatrix} \quad \text{c.} \begin{bmatrix} +\text{bovine} \\ +\text{female} \\ -\text{adult} \end{bmatrix}
$$

More generally, square brackets are used to mark parenthetical material inside a parenthesis. This includes uses such as the notation 'Smith (1999 [1905])', meaning that the reference is to a 1999 edition of a work first published in 1905. Square brackets are also used for interpolations and corrections within quotations, including such annotations as *sic*.

/. . ./

The technical printers' name for the characters involved here is VIRGULES, but the notation is also referred to as obliques, slash-brackets or just slashes. Slashes enclose a phonetic transcription which meets certain criteria. Where a single segment appears between slashes, it must refer to the phoneme, so that '/p/' can be read as 'the phoneme /p/'. Where a longer stretch of speech is transcribed between slashes, the claim is that each of the elements in the transcription represents a phoneme and no extra information is provided. The reason that this is not necessarily clear is that the term 'phoneme' tends to be used differently within different schools of phonology. You therefore have to use it according to the norms you have been taught. It is clear that any transcription which details the minutiae of actual pronunciation cannot be enclosed within slashes. The items enclosed between slashes always represent some abstract analysis of the raw data.

|. . .|, ||. . .||

These notations are used synonymously to enclose morphophonemic transcriptions where these are distinguished from phonemic transcriptions. Thus the word *right*, phonemically /raɪt/, has been argued to be morphophonemically |rixt|. The vertical line is also known as a pipe.

{. . .}

In rule notation, braces or curly brackets enclose options; that is, the rule will work with any one of the things listed in braces. So in (8) we find C and # listed as options, and that can be read as 'followed by either C or #'. The vertical layout of the options in (6) is usual, and is easy to read, but an alternative layout, which would mean precisely the same thing, would be '{C, #}'. This has the advantage of being space-saving, and the disadvantage of being harder to read. The ease-of-reading advantage becomes clearer when there are several options to be considered and not just two, or when one or more of the options is itself complex.

Braces are also used to enclose morphemes where these are distinguished from morphs. The morpheme is usually given in its default form, for example '{-able}' for the morpheme that appears in both *defendable* and *defensible*. However, when the morpheme represents some inflectional morphological property, a description of the morpheme may be given instead, e.g. '{present tense}'.

Since braces may be used to enclose morphemes, they are occasionally also used to enclose morphophonemic transcriptions.

Single character notation

A number of alphanumeric characters have particular meaning in linguistic notation, and some of the main ones are presented in table 16.1. Specific phonetic symbols are not given here, and neither are initialisms and abbreviations such as *VOT* ('voice onset time') or *Infl* ('inflection').

Table 16.1 Single character notation

A	adjective (sometimes also including adverb); adverbial; agent, subject of a transitive verb; argument
C	consonant; complement; complementiser
D	determiner
F	formant; F_0 means 'fundamental frequency'
G	glide
H	high tone; heavy syllable; high form in diglossic situation
I	inflection
K	case
L	liquid; low tone; light syllable; low form in diglossic situation; language (esp. when followed by a number, e.g. *L1* 'first language')
N	noun; nasal
O	object (if not further specified, direct object)
P	phrase; preposition (perhaps more generally, adposition); predicator; predicate; patient of a transitive verb
Q	question marker; quantifier
R, r	root
S	sentence; subject; subject of an intransitive verb
T	tense; familiar second person; transformation
V	vowel; verb; polite second person
X, Y, Z	variables; in X-bar grammar X is a variable over A, N, P and V; in Autosegmental phonology, X is a slot in the skeleton; elsewhere these represent any sequence of relevant units including none at all
a	adjective
e	empty node
f	feminine
i, j	used to mark co-reference between NPs
m	masculine
n	neuter; noun
t	trace of a node whose contents have been moved
v	verb
#	a phonological and morphological boundary; usually loosely glossed as 'word boundary' but having more specific meaning in some theories
$	syllable boundary
+	a phonological and morphological boundary; usually loosely glossed as 'morpheme boundary' but having more specific meaning in some theories
=	a phonological and morphological boundary, less strong than '+'; indicating word divisions in a gloss
. (full stop)	syllable boundary; indicating word divisions in a gloss
-	morpheme boundary; intermediate intonational boundary
· (decimal point)	morph boundary
'	glottal stop; equivalent to a single bar in X-bar theory
"	equivalent to a double bar in X-bar theory
†	obsolete
|	foot boundary; minor tone unit boundary
||	(major) tone unit boundary
%	dialectally variable; intonational phrase boundary

Table 16.1 continued

~	alternates with
1, . . . 9	indication of vowel height, tone height, stress level as specified within a particular theory; indicator of person
φ	foot; phonological phrase
μ	mora; morpheme
σ	syllable
θ	thematic
ω	phonological word
Σ	sentence; super-foot; foot

References

Chomsky, Noam (1957). *Syntactic Structures*. The Hague: Mouton.

Elcock, W. D. (1960). *The Romance Languages*. London: Faber and Faber.

Huddleston, Rodney & Geoffrey Pullum (2002). *The Cambridge Grammar of the English Language*. Cambridge: Cambridge University Press.

Lyons, John (1968). *Introduction to Theoretical Linguistics*. Cambridge: Cambridge University Press.

Matthews, P. H. (1965). The inflectional component of a word-and-paradigm grammar. *Journal of Linguistics* 1: 139–71.

Mesthrie, R. (1994). Variation, linguistic. In R. E. Asher (ed.), *The Encyclopedia of Language and Linguistics*. Oxford: Pergamon, Vol. 9, 4900–9.

Pater, Joe (2000). Non-uniformity in English secondary stress. *Phonology* 17: 237–74.

Radford, Andrew (1981). *Transformational Syntax*. Cambridge: Cambridge University Press.

Ross, John Robert (1973). Nouniness. In Osamu Fujimura (ed.), *Three Dimensions of Linguistic Theory*. Tokyo: TEC, 137–257.

Sommerstein, Alan (1977). *Modern Phonology*. London: Edward Arnold.

Trudgill, Peter (1974). *The Social Differentiation of English in Norwich*. Cambridge: Cambridge University Press.

Wells, J. C. (1982). *Accents of English*. Cambridge: Cambridge University Press.

17

Frequent abbreviations and initialisms

Giving a complete list of abbreviations which might be used in a linguistics paper is completely impossible: new ones are being added all the time, sometimes not surviving the paper in which they are presented. Thus the list given in table 17.1 is selective. It is selective in two ways. First, the abbreviations given here are considered common enough that writers might justifiably feel that they can use the abbreviation without a gloss. Second, abbreviations which are clipped forms of the original are not given here. It is assumed that the reader stands a better chance of reconstructing *ModEng* 'modern English' than *ME* 'Middle English'.

Table 17.1 Abbreviations and initialisms

AAVE	African American Vernacular English
AP	adjective phrase
ASL	American Sign Language
ATR	advanced tongue root
BEV	Black English Vernacular
BNC	British National Corpus
BSL	British Sign Language
CA	conversation analysis
CALL	computer-assisted language learning
CDS	child-directed speech
CF	context-free
CP	complementiser phrase
cps	cycles per second
CS	context-sensitive
CV	consonant vowel
dB	decibel

Table 17.1 continued

DF	distinctive feature
DG	dependency grammar
DO	direct object
DP	determiner phrase
ECP	Empty Category Principle
EFL	English as a foreign language
ELT	English language teaching
EME	Early Modern English
ESL	English as a second language
FLOB	Freiburg–Lancaster–Oslo–Bergen (a corpus parallel to the LOB corpus collected in Freiburg)
GA	General American
GB	Government and Binding
GPSG	Generalised Phrase-Structure Grammar
GVS	great vowel shift
HPSG	Head-driven Phrase-Structure Grammar
Hz	Hertz
IA	item and arrangement
IC	immediate constituent
ICE	International Corpus of English
IDLP	immediate dominance, linear precedence
IE	Indo-European
IO	indirect object
IP	item and process; inflection phrase; intonational phrase
IPA	International Phonetic Association; International Phonetic Alphabet
LAD	language acquisition device
LAGB	Linguistics Association of Great Britain
LAS	language acquisition system
LF	logical form
LFG	Lexical Functional Grammar
LOB	Lancaster-Oslo-Bergen (a corpus collected in those centres)
LSA	Linguistic Society of America
LSP	Language for Special (or Specific) Purposes
ME	Middle English
MF	Middle French
MHG	Middle High German
MIT	Massachusetts Institute of Technology, hence the linguistics associated with the institution, especially through Chomsky
MLU	mean length of utterance
MP	morphophoneme, morphophonemic
NLP	natural language processing
NP	noun phrase
OCP	Obligatory Contour Principle
OCS	Old Church Slavonic
OE	Old English
OED	*The Oxford English Dictionary*
OF	Old French
OHG	Old High German

Table 17.1 continued

ON	Old Norse or Old Icelandic
OS	Old Saxon
OT	Optimality Theory
OV	object–verb
P-D	present-day (e.g. in *P-DE* 'present-day English')
PF	phonetic form; perfect
PIE	Proto-Indo-European
PP	prepositional phrase; past participle
PS	phrase structure
PSG	phrase-structure grammar
RG	Relational Grammar
RP	Received Pronunciation (sometimes remotivated as 'reference pronunciation')
RRG	Role and Reference Grammar
SC	structural change
SD	structural description
SIL	Summer Institute of Linguistics
SPE	*The Sound Pattern of English* (influential book by Noam Chomsky and Morris Halle, published in 1968).
SSBE	Standard Southern British English
SSE	Standard Scottish English
SVO	(or any other ordering of the same letters) Subject–Verb–Object
T(G)G	transformational (generative) grammar
TAM	tense, aspect, mood
TEFL	teaching English as a foreign language
TESL	teaching English as a second language
TESOL	teaching English as a second or other language
UG	Universal Grammar
Vi	intransitive verb
VO	verb-object
VOT	voice onset time
VP	verb phrase
Vt	transitive verb
WFR	word-formation rule
WP	word and paradigm
XP	a phrase of any type

18

Terminology: ambiguity

There are, unfortunately, many terms in linguistics which mean one thing in one place and another in another. These are not terms like *phoneme* and *morpheme* which mean (subtly or considerably) different things to different scholars, but words which are used as technical terms in different sub-areas of linguistics. In principle, these terms are rendered unambiguous by the sub-area of linguistics in which they are used, but in practice the use of the same term can cause transient or even long-term problems of understanding. Detailed definitions are not attempted in table 18.1: as is the case with phoneme and morpheme the precise definition may depend upon the individual writer. However, a rough guide is given to the meanings, as well as the sub-area of linguistics where the term is used. It should be noted that, especially with adjectives, the particular use may be made clear by the linguistic environment: *natural* means one thing in *natural language* and another in *natural phonology*, and these meanings may be largely predictable from the collocations in which the word occurs.

Table 18.1 Ambiguous terminology

Term	Area 1	Area 2
abstract	syntax: of a noun, denoting a quality	phonology: making reference to elements which are not found in the phonetic record
accent	phonetics: frequently equivalent to *stress*, sometimes another form of prominence	sociolinguistics: the phonetic qualities of the speech of a particular group of people

Table 18.1 continued

Term	Area 1	Area 2
active	syntax: a verb which has an agent as its subject, opposed to *passive*	lexicology: of words which you actually use as opposed to those which are merely recognised
analytic	morphology: used of a language in which (ideally) every word comprises a single morpheme	semantics: used of a statement which is necessarily true
argument	general: a reasoned attempt to convince	syntax: an element which obligatorily accompanies a verb
blocking	morphology: the lack of a particular word because its meaning has already been pre-empted by another word clinical linguistics: in stuttering, an impediment to uttering a required sound	psycholinguistics: the inability to produce a particular word because you can only think of a closely related word
bound	morphology: of a morpheme which cannot form a word form on its own	syntax: of elements which are coindexed
checked	phonology: the name of a distinctive feature used for glottalisation	phonology: of a vowel, followed by a consonant in the same syllable
class	phonology, morphology, syntax, semantics: a set of items which share some property	sociolinguistics: socio–economic status seen as a correlate of linguistic variation
closed	phonology: of a syllable, ending in a consonant	syntax: of a class of words whose members can in principle be listed
coda	phonology: consonants occurring after the peak of a syllable	discourse analysis: that part of an interaction which summarises and completes the interaction or narrative
command	speech-act: an order or to order	syntax: a relationship defined over nodes in a phrase-structure tree; to stand in such a relationship to another node
common	morphology: a gender comprising both masculines and feminines	syntax: of a noun which is not a proper noun
comparative	morphology, syntax: a form used to compare two things, as *bigger, more intelligent*	historical linguistics: involving comparing different languages or dialects

Table 18.1 continued

Term	Area 1	Area 2
complex	phonetics: of a vowel or a tone made up of two (or more) targets syntax: of a sentence made up of a main clause and at least one subordinate clause phonetics: of a tone, comprised of sounds of different frequencies	morphology: of a word made up of more than one morpheme syntax: a set of features which define a word class
compound	morphology: a word made up of two (or more) stems morphology: of a tense expressed periphrastically	syntax: of a sentence made up of two (or more) coordinated clauses sociolinguistics: of bilingualism of a particular type
concrete	syntax: of a noun, denoting a real-world object	phonology: anchored in actual phonetic production
conjunct	syntax: any of the items linked by coordination	syntax: a type of adverbial
contrastive	phonology, morphology, syntax: distinctive	applied linguistics: involving comparison between two languages
coordinate	sociolinguistics: of bilingualism of a particular type	syntax: of elements of equivalent status linked together
cycle	phonetics: a complete vibration of the vocal folds	phonology, syntax: the application of a set of rules of a certain type, especially ones which can be applied more than once in a derivation
daughter	historical linguistics: a language directly derived from another one	syntax: a node immediately dominated by another one
declarative	speech-act: a sentence which makes a statement	meta-theory: any theory which works by providing constraints on possible structures rather than by deriving one level of structure from another
derivation	morphology: that part of morphology concerned with the creation of new lexemes by processes of affixation, conversion	phonology, morphology, syntax: any process of successive changes between an underlying form and its surface representation
diffuse	phonology: a now little-used distinctive feature, the	sociolinguistics: used to describe a community in which

Table 18.1 continued

Term	Area 1	Area 2
	opposite of *compact*	there is little standardisation; the opposite of *focused*
domain	phonology, morphology, syntax: the places in the system where a particular rule or process applies	sociolinguistics: a social situation that calls forth particular linguistic behaviour
double articulation	duality of structure	phonetics: the circumstance where a particular sound is made with two equal strictures at different places of articulation
dynamic	phonetics: of a tone, changing in pitch	morphology, syntax: of a verb, denoting an action
emphatic	phonetics: pharyngealised	pragmatics: giving emphasis
empty	morphology: having no meaning	syntax: having no form; unexpressed
expletive	pragmatics: a swear-word	syntax: an element seen as carrying no meaning, a dummy word
falling	phonetics: of pitch or tone, becoming lower	phonetics: of a diphthong, having the first element the more prominent
formal	meta-theory: based on form rather than on meaning pragmatics: a relatively explicit style used on occasions of high prestige	meta-theory: based on a mathematical system
formant	morphology: sometimes used as equivalent of *formative*	phonetics: a band of energy in the spectrum of a sonorant sound
free	morphology: of a morph, with the potential to stand alone as a word form	syntax: of word order, in which the order of elements is determined by pragmatic and stylistic factors rather than by strictly grammatical ones
	phonology: of stress, not constrained so as to fall on a particular syllable in the word syntax: of a pronoun, not bound in its construction	translation: determined by the requirements of the target language rather than sticking literally to the source language
gender	morphology, syntax: a subdivision of nouns on the basis of prototypical reference to entities having a particular sex	sociolinguistics: the social construction of an identity usually thought to correlate with biological sex

Table 18.1 continued

Term	Area 1	Area 2
gesture	semiotics: a meaningful movement of the body	phonology: a planned articulatory movement seen as the basis of phonological performance
hard	phonetics, historical linguistics: velar and/or plosive	phonetics: velarised
head	phonology, morphology, syntax: obligatory or most important element in a construction	phonetics: that part of an intonation contour before the main pitch movement
high	phonetics: spoken with high pitch phonetics: pronounced with the tongue close to the roof of the mouth	sociolinguistics: having social prestige
hypercorrection	sociolinguistics: the overuse of a particular feature belonging to a standard variety in an effort to sound more standard	sociolinguistics: the use of a particular variant more often by a class which aspires to prestige than it is used by the prestige group
idiomatic	semantics: having a meaning which cannot be deduced from the meanings of its elements	language teaching: fluent and native-like
inclusive	morphology, syntax: a form of first person plural which involves the speaker and the person spoken to semantics: a disjunction is termed inclusive if it is possible for both disjuncts to be true – *these people are blonde or blue-eyed* is inclusively disjunctive if some may be both	sociolinguistics: of language which avoids bias or stereotyping
inflection	morphology: one of the major branches of morphology phonetics: an intonation pattern	morphology: an inflectional affix
instrumental	phonetics: which uses instruments to carry out an investigation rather than the human senses	morphology, syntax: a case which is used to mark the thing with which some action is performed

Table 18.1 continued

Term	Area 1	Area 2
	pragmatics: achieving some practical goal	
jargon	sociolinguistics: a set of words known only to insiders, such as the words associated with a particular profession psycholinguistics: unintelligible words used by speakers with some language pathologies	sociolinguistics: a pre-pidgin phase in the development of a new language
level	general linguistics: distinguishing between e.g. phonetics, morphology, syntax as areas requiring description phonology, morphology: an ordered set of rules and representations	phonetics: of a tone or intonational nucleus, not kinetic syntax: a quasi-independent domain of description
lexical	historical linguistics, morphology: to do with words, e.g. *lexical diffusion* morphology, syntax, semantics, lexicography: to do with the dictionary or lexicon, e.g. *lexical rule*	morphology, syntax, semantics: having content as opposed to expressing function, e.g. *lexical word*
lexicalisation	morphology: the historical process of becoming listed and opaque	semantics: the provision of a lexeme for a particular meaning
local	morphology, syntax: of cases which are used to mark location rather than grammatical function	morphology, syntax: which is restricted to or by the immediate environment (sometimes more narrowly specified)
localisation	psycholinguistics: the attempt to say which parts of the brain deal with (which parts of) language	phonetics, psycholinguistics: pinpointing the source of a sound
low	phonetics: spoken with low pitch phonetics: pronounced with the tongue relatively low in the mouth	sociolinguistics: not having social prestige

Table 18.1 continued

Term	Area 1	Area 2
marker	morphology: an affix or other way of showing that a particular category applies	sociolinguistics: a variable which shows social stratification
modal	phonetics: of voice, normal, not falsetto, creaky, etc.	syntax: an element or describing an element indicating possibility, obligation, necessity, etc.
natural	meta-theory: of a language, arising due to normal evolution, not deliberately created phonology, morphology, syntax: using explanations based on human perception and cognition	phonology: of a class of sounds, acting in parallel ways in some process morphology: of gender classes, based on real-world sex
neologism	morphology: a new word entering a language	psycholinguistics: a nonsense word created for experimental purposes or by a speaker with some language deficit
network	semantics: a series of meaning relationships between words psycholinguistics: a model of language production or perception in which inputs are related to outputs without overt rules or defaults	sociolinguistics: a series of relationships between speakers in a community
noise	phonetics: random fluctuations in the spectrum of a sound wave	communications: anything which makes a message more difficult to perceive
open	phonetics: pronounced with the tongue low in the mouth syntax, psycholinguistics: of a class allowing new members	phonology: of a syllable not having any coda
passive	syntax: a marked form of a verb in which a patient is typically the subject, opposed to *active*	lexicology: of words which are recognised but not actually used
register	phonetics: voice produced with a particular laryngeal setting	sociolinguistics: a variety associated with a particular topic or subject
relational	sociolinguistics: dealing with interaction between individuals	syntax: dealing with functions rather than forms

Table 18.1 continued

Term	Area 1	Area 2
relevance	morphology: the importance of a semantic link between an affix and the root to which it is attached	pragmatics: a mechanism for constraining interpretations of utterances by considering the environment in which the utterance occurs
rising	phonetics: of pitch or tone, becoming higher	phonetics: of a diphthong, having the second element more prominent
root	phonetics: that part of the tongue which lies opposite the pharynx wall syntax: the initial node in a tree	morphology: the part of a word which remains when all affixes have been removed
simple	morphology: expressed without periphrasis	syntax: having a single clause
soft	phonetics, historical linguistics: coronal and/or fricative	phonetics: palatalised
strong	phonology, historical linguistics: not likely to change phonology: relatively prominent	morphology: a label for certain inflection classes
subject	pragmatics, rhetoric: the matter being discussed	syntax: the sentence element which is normally taken to denote the undertaker of the action of the verb
tag	syntax: a brief addition to a sentence, e.g. *That's her, isn't it?*	corpus linguistics: a label given to each word in a text which provides information about that word, e.g. word class
tense	phonetics: an ill–defined quality of the muscles of the vocal tract in the production of some vowels, now usually replaced by a feature [±ATR]	morphology/syntax: a morphosyntactic category referring to time
topic	pragmatics, rhetoric: the matter under discussion discourse, syntax: the element in a sentence about which something is said	syntax: an element emphasised prosodically or by syntactic movement to indicate importance in the utterance
variable	phonology, syntax: any symbol in a rule whose content is not specified by the rule	sociolinguistics: a position in the linguistic system where variation between two or more possible forms is

Table 18.1 continued

Term	Area 1	Area 2
		exploited to mark social differences
voice	phonetics: the sound caused by vibration of the vocal folds	morphology, syntax: the category, usually marked on the verb, which allows different arguments of the verb to be treated as new information (active, passive, etc.)
weak	phonology, historical linguistics: likely to change phonology: relatively less prominent	morphology: label for certain inflection classes phonetics: made with relaxed muscles

19

Terminology: synonymy

Like any technical area, linguistics is full of jargon. What is more, the jargon has been developing for thousands of years. The result is that some has been rejected, some has been redefined, some is used as much to mark the theory in which comments are being made as to mark a difference in content, and some is misused. In this section a glossary is provided in table 19.1 with terms that may be synonymous (and if they are not, it will sometimes be because they are defined by a particular person or within a particular theory as not being synonymous). In some cases, terms have multiple usages, and only one set of equivalents may be given here: *formant* may be used in morphology or in phonetics (see section 18), but only in morphology does it have *formative* as an equivalent term. Words marked with a dagger '†' are believed to be now superseded by newer terminology, and are never put on the right-hand side of the glossary as an explanation. Otherwise, any term on the right-hand side of an equivalence is also listed on the left-hand side.

Table 19.1 Synonymous terminology

abbreviation	alphabetism, initialism
Ablaut	apophony
accidence (†)	inflectional morphology
adjective	epithet
adjective clause	relative clause
African American Vernacular English (AAVE)	Black English (Vernacular), Ebonics
agglutinating	agglutinative
agglutinative	agglutinating
agraphia	dysgraphia
agreement	concord

Table 19.1 continued

alexia	dyslexia
allomorph	(a) morpheme alternant
	(b) morpheme variant
allophone	phoneme alternant
alphabetism	abbreviation, initialism
alveolar ridge	alveolum, teeth ridge
alveolum	alveolar ridge, teeth ridge
a-morphous morphology	word-and-paradigm morphology
analytic	isolating
anomia	dysnomia
anticipatory assimilation	regressive assimilation
antonym	opposite
aorist	simple past
apex	(of the tongue) tip
aphasia	dysphasia
aphonia	dysphonia
apophony	Ablaut
approximant	frictionless continuant, glide, semi-vowel
apraxia	dyspraxia
artificial language	auxiliary language
Aryan (†)	Indo-European
ATR (advanced tongue root)	tense/lax
auxiliary language	artificial language
baby-talk	caregiver language, child-directed speech, motherese
back-derivation	back-formation
back-formation	back-derivation
bahuvrihi	exocentric compound, possessive compound
bivalent	divalent, transitive
Black English (Vernacular) (BEV)	African American Vernacular English, Ebonics
blend	(a) portmanteau word
	(b) cluster
breath group	intonational phrase, tone group
breathy voice	murmur
cacuminal (†)	retroflex
calque	loan translation
caregiver language	baby-talk, child-directed speech, motherese
centre	(a) determinant, head
	(b) nucleus, peak
centre-embedding	self-embedding
cerebral (†)	retroflex
checked syllable	closed syllable
checked vowel	lax vowel, short vowel (in English)
child-directed speech (CDS)	baby-talk, caregiver language, motherese
clear	palatalised
close vowel	high vowel
closed syllable	checked syllable
close-mid	half-close

Table 19.1 continued

cluster	blend
code	lect, variety
coinage	neologism
commutation	substitution
concord	agreement
constructional homonymy	structural ambiguity
consultant	informant
content word	full word, lexical word
continuous	progressive
contour tone	kinetic tone
contrastive	distinctive
conversion	functional shift, zero–derivation
coordinating conjunction	coordinator
coordinator	coordinating conjunction
cranberry morph(eme)	unique morph(eme)
creaky voice	laryngealisation
CV-tier	skeletal tier
cycles per second (cps)	Hertz
dangling participle	misrelated participle
dark	velarised
dative movement	dative shift
dative shift	dative movement
defining relative clause	restrictive relative clause
degree	grade (of comparison)
desinence (†)	inflectional affix/ending
determinans	modifier
determinant	centre, head
determinative compound	tatpurusa
diachronic linguistics	historical linguistics
diaerisis	umlaut (the written accent)
diathesis (†)	voice
dictionary	lexicon
distinctive	contrastive
ditransitive	trivalent
divalent	bivalent, transitive
domal (†)	retroflex
double articulation	duality of patterning
duality of patterning	double articulation
dysgraphia	agraphia
dyslexia	alexia
dysnomia	anomia
dysphasia	aphasia
dysphonia	aphonia
dyspraxia	apraxia
Ebonics	African American Vernacular English, Black English (Vernacular)
embedded	nested, subordinate
emphatic	pharyngealised

Table 19.1 continued

ending	(inflectional) suffix
epithet	adjective
exocentric compound	bahuvrihi, possessive compound
exponence	manifestation, realisation
felicity conditions	happiness conditions
First Germanic Consonant Shift	Grimm's Law
first language	mother tongue, native language
flap, flapping	frequently used for tap, tapping, although strictly distinct
flectional	flexional, fusional, inflecting, inflectional, inflexional
flexional	flectional, fusional, inflecting, inflectional, inflexional
folk etymology	popular etymology
formal word	function word, functor, grammatical word
formant (†)	formative
formative	morpheme
fortis	tense
fortition	strengthening
fossilisation	idiomatisation, lexicalisation
fossilised	lexicalised
free vowel	long vowel, tense vowel, unchecked vowel (in English)
frictionless continuant	approximant, glide, semi-vowel
full verb	lexical verb
full word	content word, lexical word
function word	formal word, functor, grammatical word
functional shift	conversion, zero-derivation
functor	formal word, function word, grammatical word
fusional	flectional, flexional, inflecting, inflectional, inflexional
genitive	possessive
glide	approximant, frictionless continuant, semi-vowel
glottal	laryngal, laryngeal
grade (of comparison)	degree
grammatical word	(a) formal word, function word, functor (b) morphosyntactic word
grammaticalisation	grammaticisation
grammaticisation	grammaticalisation
Grimm's Law	First Germanic Consonant Shift
half-close	close-mid
half-open	open-mid
happiness conditions	felicity conditions
head	centre, determinant
headword	lemma
Hertz (Hz)	cycles per second
high vowel	close vowel

Table 19.1 continued

historical linguistics	diachronic linguistics
hypernym	hyperonym, superordinate
hyperonym	hypernym, superordinate
iambic reversal	rhythm rule, stress shift
idiomatisation	fossilisation, lexicalisation
inceptive	inchoative
inchoative	inceptive
inflecting	flectional, flexional, fusional, inflectional, inflexional
inflectional	flectional, flexional, fusional, inflecting, inflexional
inflexional	flectional, flexional, fusional, inflecting, inflectional
informant	consultant
Ingvaeonic (†)	Anglo–Frisian
initialism	abbreviation, alphabetism
intonational phrase	breath group, tone group
intransitive	monovalent
introflection	transfixation
isolating	analytic
kinetic tone	contour tone
labio–palatal (†)	labial–palatal
labio–velar (†)	labial–velar
LAD (language acquisition device)	LAS
laryngal	glottal, laryngeal
laryngeal	glottal, laryngal
laryngealisation	creaky voice
LAS (language acquisition system)	LAD
lax	(a) with retracted tongue root (b) lenis
lax vowel	checked vowel, short vowel (in English)
lect	code, variety
lemma	headword
length	quantity
lenis	lax
lenition	weakening
lexical	word (as a modifier in e.g. *lexical stress = word stress*)
lexical category	part of speech, word class
lexical item	listeme
lexical verb	full verb
lexical word	content word, full word
lexicalisation	fossilisation, idiomatisation
lexicalised	fossilised
lexicon	dictionary
lexis	vocabulary
linguistic area	Sprachbund
linguistic relativity	Sapir-Whorf hypothesis

Table 19.1 continued

listeme	lexical item
loan translation	calque
long vowel	free vowel, tense vowel, unchecked vowel (in English)
low vowel	open vowel
manifestation	exponence, realisation
mass	non-count, non-countable
mass comparison	multilateral comparison
mediae (†)	voiced plosives
misrelated participle	dangling participle
modifier	determinans
monophthong	pure vowel
monovalent	intransitive
morpheme	formative
morpheme alternant	allomorph
morpheme variant	allomorph
morphonology	morphophonology, morphophonemics
morphophonemics	morphonology, morphophonology
morphophonology	morphonology, morphophonemics
morphosyntactic word	grammatical word
mother tongue	first language, native language
motherese	baby-talk, caregiver language, child-directed speech
multilateral comparison	mass comparison
murmur	breathy voice
native language	first language, mother tongue
neologism	coinage
nested	embedded, subordinate
non-count(able)	mass
non-restrictive relative clause	parenthetical relative clause
normative	prescriptive
noun	substantive
nuclear syllable	sentence stress, tonic
nucleus	centre, peak
occlusive (†)	plosive
open vowel	low vowel
open-mid	half-open
opposite	antonym
palatalised	(a) clear (e.g. 'clear [l]') (b) soft (e.g. of a Russian consonant)
palato-alveolar	post-alveolar
parenthetical relative clause	non-restrictive relative clause
part of speech	lexical category, word class
peak	centre, nucleus
persevatory assimilation	progressive assimilation
pharyngealised	emphatic
phonation	voicing
phone	speech sound

Table 19.1 continued

phoneme alternant	allophone
popular etymology	folk etymology
portmanteau word	blend
possessive	genitive
possessive compound	bahuvrihi, exocentric compound
post-alveolar	palato-alveolar
prescriptive	normative
progressive	continuous
progressive assimilation	persevatory assimilation
pure vowel	monophthong
quantity	length
r-colouring	rhotacisation
realisation	exponence, manifestation
rection (†)	government
regressive assimilation	anticipatory assimilation
relative clause	adjective clause
resonant (*n*)	sonorant (*n*)
restrictive relative clause	defining relative clause
rhotacisation	r-colouring
rhotacism	rhoticity
rhoticity	rhotacism
rhythm rule	iambic reversal, stress shift
roll	trill
Sapir-Whorf hypothesis	linguistic relativity
self-embedding	centre-embedding
semi-vowel	approximant, frictionless continuant, glide
sentence stress	nuclear syllable, tonic
short vowel	checked vowel, lax vowel (in English)
simple past	aorist
skeletal tier	CV-tier
soft	palatalised
soft palate	velum
sonorant (*n*)	resonant (*n*)
speech sound	phone
spirant (†)	fricative
Sprachbund	linguistic area
strengthening	fortition
stress shift	iambic reversal, rhythm rule
structural ambiguity	constructional homonymy
subordinate	embedded, nested
substantive	noun
substitution	commutation
suffix	ending (used esp. for inflectional suffix)
superfix	suprafix
superordinate	hypernym, hyperonym
suprafix	superfix
surd (†)	voiceless consonant
tatpurusa	determinative compound

Table 19.1 continued

teeth ridge	alveolum, alveolar ridge
tense	(a) fortis
	(b) with advanced tongue root
tense vowel	free vowel, long vowel, unchecked vowel (in English)
tenues (†)	voiceless plosives
termination (†)	(inflectional) ending, (inflectional) suffix
Teutonic (†)	Germanic
theme (†)	stem
tip (of the tongue)	apex
tone group	breath group, intonational phrase
tonic	nuclear syllable, sentence stress
transfixation	introflection
transitive	bivalent, divalent
trill	roll
trivalent	ditransitive
umlaut	diaerisis (the written accent)
unchecked vowel	free vowel, long vowel, tense vowel(in English)
unique morph(eme)	cranberry morph(eme)
unvoiced	voiceless
variety	code, lect
velarised	dark
velum	soft palate
vocabulary	lexis
vocal bands (†)	vocal folds, vocal cords
vocal cords	vocal folds
vocal folds	vocal cords
vocal lips (†)	vocal folds, vocal cords
voiceless	unvoiced
voicing	phonation
weakening	lenition
wh-question	X-question
word class	lexical category, part of speech
word (used as a modifier)	lexical (e.g. *word stress* = *lexical stress*)
word-and-paradigm morphology	a-morphous morphology
X-question	wh-question
zero-derivation	conversion, functional shift

Part III: Reading linguistics

20

The International Phonetic Association

The International Phonetic Association grew out of Dhi Fonètik Ticerz' Asóciécon, founded in 1886 in Paris. Because of its close links with practical language learning, there was considerable focus in the early years on the development of a phonetic alphabet whose function was to give a practical teaching alphabet which marked distinctive sounds. The phonetic alphabet propagated by the Association has developed considerably since those early days, both in terms of its domains of use and in terms of its sophistication.

In terms of its use, the IPA's alphabet has become the world's standard phonetic notational system. It is used not only in foreign language teaching, but also in such diverse areas as speech recognition systems and representations of pronunciation for mother-tongue speakers. If we just look at its use in English dictionaries, for example, the International Phonetic Alphabet was adopted for use in *The Collins English Dictionary* (1979), *The Macquarie Dictionary* (1981), the eighth edition of *The Concise Oxford Dictionary* (1990) and *Chambers 21st Century Dictionary* (1996). Of course, these various dictionaries do not use precisely the same transcription system for English, but they are all based on the IPA system. Not all dictionaries have adopted IPA systems whole-heartedly, though a majority now have: the tenth edition of *Merriam-Webster's Collegiate Dictionary* (1996) and *The New Penguin Dictionary* (2000) both hold out – though even they have both adopted the use of [ə] and IPA stress marks, and the Penguin dictionary uses the IPA alphabet for the transcription of foreign words.

For linguists, the IPA's alphabet has become the default way of presenting foreign-language data. That is why it is so important that linguistics students should be familiar with the IPA chart and have some ability to read its symbols. While grammars aimed at native speakers of any language will typically be based on the orthographic system used in the language, even these grammars will often explain the orthographic system in terms of IPA categories and symbols, and linguists presenting material for other linguists will frequently translate the orthography into some IPA-based transcription.

Although the original idea of the alphabet was to provide symbols for phonemes but not for allophones (hence, for example, the lack of a symbol for a labio–dental plosive in the alphabet), and to avoid diacritics for phonemic symbols as much as possible, continuing discoveries about languages which were unknown to the founders of Dhi Fonètik Ticerz' Asóciécon have now blurred that distinction, and we find that we need diacritics to show the phonemes of some languages and also that we can mark some allophones without using diacritics (for example, the labio–dental nasal in English or Italian). This is just a side-effect of the alphabet having become far more inclusive over the years. The last major overhaul of the alphabet was in 1989, with minor modifications last having been made in 1996 and 2005. Discussions about possible changes to the alphabet continue in the pages of the Association's journal, the *Journal of the International Phonetic Association*.

Some scholars find the phonetic theory on which the alphabet is based to be flawed or at least overly simplistic. For example, the Association defines [p] as a voiceless bilabial plosive, with no attention being paid to what the tongue might be doing during the articulation of that plosive, to the precise detail of what the vocal folds are doing (or when they do it), to the lip position during that plosive, to the fact that the plosive may be lacking a shutting phase or an opening phase, and so on. The vowel charts that are used by the Association do not appear to correlate closely with either an articulatory description of what happens in the production of a vowel or the description of the acoustic structure of the sound wave produced during the articulation of the vowel. Phonological theory has also advanced so much that talk of 'phonemes' and 'allophones' is in itself suspect. Despite these shortcomings, the alphabet has had, and continues to have, a huge practical value; provided that it is recalled that the alphabet was first created as a way of producing writing systems (rather than, say, a way of producing full phonetic descriptions of articulation), gaps in the description can be filled in on the basis of an initial analysis in terms of the IPA categories.

The theory underlying the IPA chart, examples of the various sounds and the ways in which the IPA system may be used for the transcription of individual languages are not dealt with here (see IPA 1999). But the IPA chart is provided as figure 20.1 as a reference tool.

CONSONANTS (PULMONIC)   © 2005 IPA

	Bilabial	Labiodental	Dental	Alveolar	Postalveolar	Retroflex	Palatal	Velar	Uvular	Pharyngeal	Glottal
Plosive	p b			t d		ʈ ɖ	c ɟ	k ɡ	q ɢ		ʔ
Nasal	m	ɱ		n		ɳ	ɲ	ŋ	N		
Trill	ʙ			r					R		
Tap or Flap		ⱱ		ɾ		ɽ					
Fricative	ɸ β	f v	θ ð	s z	ʃ ʒ	ʂ ʐ	ç ʝ	x ɣ	χ ʁ	ħ ʕ	h ɦ
Lateral fricative				ɬ ɮ							
Approximant		ʋ		ɹ		ɻ	j	ɰ			
Lateral approximant				l		ɭ	ʎ	L			

Where symbols appear in pairs, the one to the right represents a voiced consonant. Shaded areas denote articulations judged impossible.

CONSONANTS (NON-PULMONIC)

Clicks		Voiced implosives		Ejectives	
ʘ	Bilabial	ɓ	Bilabial	ʼ	Examples:
ǀ	Dental	ɗ	Dental/alveolar	pʼ	Bilabial
ǃ	(Post)alveolar	ʄ	Palatal	tʼ	Dental/alveolar
ǂ	Palatoalveolar	ɠ	Velar	kʼ	Velar
ǁ	Alveolar lateral	ʛ	Uvular	sʼ	Alveolar fricative

OTHER SYMBOLS

ʍ	Voiceless labial-velar fricative	ɕ ʑ	Alveolo-palatal fricatives
w	Voiced labial-velar approximant	ɺ	Voiced alveolar lateral flap
ɥ	Voiced labial-palatal approximant	ɧ	Simultaneous ʃ and x
ʜ	Voiceless epiglottal fricative		
ʢ	Voiced epiglottal fricative		Affricates and double articulations can be represented by two symbols joined by a tie bar if necessary. k͡p t͡s
ʡ	Epiglottal plosive		

VOWELS

Where symbols appear in pairs, the one to the right represents a rounded vowel.

SUPRASEGMENTALS

ˈ	Primary stress	ˌfoʊnəˈtɪʃən
ˌ	Secondary stress	
ː	Long	eː
ˑ	Half-long	eˑ
˘	Extra-short	ĕ
ǀ	Minor (foot) group	
‖	Major (intonation) group	
.	Syllable break	ɹi.ækt
‿	Linking (absence of a break)	

DIACRITICS   Diacritics may be placed above a symbol with a descender, e.g. ŋ̊

̥	Voiceless	n̥ d̥		̤	Breathy voiced	b̤ a̤		̪	Dental	t̪ d̪
̬	Voiced	s̬ t̬		̰	Creaky voiced	b̰ a̰		̺	Apical	t̺ d̺
ʰ	Aspirated	tʰ dʰ		̼	Linguolabial	t̼ d̼		̻	Laminal	t̻ d̻
̹	More rounded	ɔ̹		ʷ	Labialized	tʷ dʷ		̃	Nasalized	ẽ
̜	Less rounded	ɔ̜		ʲ	Palatalized	tʲ dʲ		ⁿ	Nasal release	dⁿ
̟	Advanced	u̟		ˠ	Velarized	tˠ dˠ		ˡ	Lateral release	dˡ
̠	Retracted	e̠		ˤ	Pharyngealized	tˤ dˤ		̚	No audible release	d̚
̈	Centralized	ë		̴	Velarized or pharyngealized	ɫ				
̽	Mid-centralized	e̽		̝	Raised	e̝	(ɹ̝ = voiced alveolar fricative)			
̩	Syllabic	n̩		̞	Lowered	e̞	(β̞ = voiced bilabial approximant)			
̯	Non-syllabic	e̯		̘	Advanced Tongue Root	e̘				
˞	Rhoticity	ɚ a˞		̙	Retracted Tongue Root	e̙				

TONES AND WORD ACCENTS

LEVEL			CONTOUR		
e̋ or ˥	Extra high		ě or ˩˥	Rising	
é or ˦	High		ê or ˥˩	Falling	
ē or ˧	Mid		e᷄ or ˦˥	High rising	
è or ˨	Low		e᷅ or ˩˨	Low rising	
ȅ or ˩	Extra low		e᷈ or ˧˦˧	Rising-falling	
↓	Downstep		↗	Global rise	
↑	Upstep		↘	Global fall	

Figure 20.1 The International Phonetic Alphabet (revised to 2005)

Reference

International Phonetic Association (1999). *Handbook of the International Phonetic Association*. Cambridge: Cambridge University Press.

21

Reading phonetics and phonology

Despite the word 'international' in its title, the International Phonetic Association was for many years a European association, with very little influence outside Europe. Even within Europe, because the Association's alphabet was not finally established until 1899, it had competition from local phonetic alphabets used in Europe by dialectologists and in the Americas by anthropologists and linguists writing down the languages of the New World. Some of these alternative phonetic alphabets have persisted until the present day, others have gradually been replaced by the International Phonetic Association's alphabet. As late as 1991, Brink et al. were using the Dania transcription symbols (though they also give IPA 'translations' for their symbols in an introductory section).

In any case, until very recently, using a phonetic alphabet involved almost insuperable problems. Although printers were in principle capable of setting IPA symbols, they frequently did not have the symbols in all type sizes, they were unused to setting them and many were not very good at it, symbols had to be entered by hand in typescripts and were frequently difficult for printers to read (with the inevitable result that there were many typographic errors in transcriptions). While in principle these problems were lessened by the advent of micro-computer-based word-processing in the 1970s (or, for most of us, the 1980s), in practice it took a lot longer for suitable fonts to be available to all potential users. It is only since the mid-1990s that the pressure has been removed for writers to restrict themselves to the symbols of the Roman (possibly Roman and Greek) alphabet, for technical reasons.

There were also less technical reasons for avoiding IPA symbols. Many publishers felt that readers had enough difficulty coping with a single alphabet, let alone two, and so chose to mark pronunciations with a system of respelling, using easily available characters from the keyboard (but giving them specific meanings within their respelling systems). Merriam-Webster's Collegiate dictionaries still use such a system, the Oxford dictionaries changed to using IPA symbols fairly recently, as did *Chambers 21st Century Dictionary*. Similar problems faced those who were creating writing systems for languages which had previously not been written. The symbols used by the IPA were seen as technical and difficult, and it was nearly always preferred to develop an orthography based entirely on the Roman alphabet: this can be seen in the writing systems for most Australian languages, for example.

So not only has there been a range of possible phonetic alphabets since phonetic alphabets were first used, there has been pressure not to use phonetic alphabets for many purposes – and these purposes include the writing of grammars. The result is that in order to understand a particular phonetic/phonological description, the reader has to know whether it is written using a phonetic alphabet or not (and if so, which one) in order to translate the system used into something with which they are familiar. Where respelling systems are used, we need to know what language the respelling is treating as fundamental: is <ch> to be understood as in Spanish, as in French or as in German, for example? Is <j> to be understood as in Spanish or as in German? Is <u> to be understood as in German, as in French or as in English? It is important that we do not make assumptions about the phonetic or phonological system used by the writer of the description we are reading.

The function of this section is to give you some clues for things to look for.

Changes in the IPA

The IPA itself has made modifications to its alphabet over time. Sometimes, this has just been the addition of symbols; sometimes symbols have been removed from the approved set of symbols; occasionally, symbols have been reassigned (which may also be the effect of adding or deleting symbols).

One change, however, is a difference of terminology. The place of articulation which is now called 'post-alveolar' used to be termed 'palato-alveolar'. The label remains (surprisingly) in the current IPA chart for a place of articulation for clicks. This label also explains the label alveolo-palatal. Something which is palato-alveolar is basically alveolar, but heading in the direction of the palate; something with is alveolo-palatal is basically palatal, but heading in the direction of the alveolar ridge. Thus palato-alveolar sounds are produced slightly further forward in the mouth than alveolo-palatal ones. (For the fricatives [ʃ] and [ç] there is also a difference in tongue profile, [ʃ] being a grooved fricative, unlike [ç]. This is similar to the distinction between [s] and [θ], and is not directly shown on the IPA chart.)

A series of symbols for voiceless implosives had brief currency, but are no longer part of the official IPA chart.

There are some differences to diacritics, too, most of which will be ignored here. Importantly, what is now [lʲ] (etc.) used to be [ļ] (etc.), and what is now [lˠ] (etc.) used to be [ł] (etc.).

Other important changes to IPA practice are set out in table 21.1.

Implications of IPA practice

There are a number of facets of IPA practice which lead to what I will here call SYMBOL SPREADING: the situation where a given IPA symbol may have a wider potential range of application than is obvious from its definition on the IPA chart.

First, there is a certain amount of vagueness built into the IPA chart. Where the IPA chart provides no contrasting symbol, any symbol for a trill may be used as the symbol for the corresponding tap or flap; any symbol for a voiced fricative may be used as the symbol for the corresponding approximant. Where vowels are concerned, any vowel symbol covers quite a large area of the chart. But even taking this into consideration, the requirement that any vowel be represented by the nearest symbol on the vowel chart is open to a fair amount of flexibility, especially where the variety being described has more than one contrasting vowel in a particular area of the vowel chart (for example, in New Zealand English the vowels in STRUT and START differ mainly in terms of length, not quality, but may be given different symbols which look as though they are quality-based).

The most important point to note here, however, is the preference for romanic symbols. This means that, other things being equal, a symbol will be chosen which is a letter of the Roman alphabet, or, where that is not possible, a symbol will be chosen which is like a letter of the Roman alphabet rather than something which is more exotic in shape. This has particularly important consequences in the transcriptions of vowels, where [a] may 'really' mean [æ], [ɑ] or [ɐ], where [e] may 'really' mean [ɛ], [o] may 'really' mean [ɔ], and, in transcriptions of English, where [ʌ] usually does mean [ɐ]. The consequences in consonant transcription may also be important. The IPA itself (IPA 1949: 13) recommends using [ʃ] rather than [ʂ] where the two do not contrast; [r] may stand for [ɾ], [ɹ], [ɻ] or even [ʁ] or [ʀ]; and [c] and [ɟ] are normal replacements for [tʃ] and [dʒ] respectively.

Finally note that transcriptions like [ee] and [rr] may be ambiguous. Either they may represent two repetitions of the same segment (so, in the case of [ee] a disyllabic sequence), or they may represent a long segment (in the case of [ee] something which could also be transcribed as [eː], in the case of [rr] probably something which would be transcribed [r] or [rː] as opposed to [ɾ]).

Table 21.1 Some important changes to IPA practice

Symbol	Previous use	Current use
ʙ	new symbol	voiced bilabial trill
ʟ	new symbol	voiced velar lateral
ɰ	new symbol	voiced velar approximant (for which [ɣ] had to be used earlier)
ʇ	voiceless dental click	replaced by [ǀ]
ʗ	voiceless alveolar click	replaced by [!]
ʖ	voiceless alveolar lateral click	replaced by [ǁ]
ɼ	voiced alveolar fricative trill	no longer used
ɪ	near-close front unrounded vowel	no longer used, only [ɪ] recognised for this vowel
ɷ	near-close back rounded vowel	no longer used, only [ʊ] recognised for this vowel
ə	any central vowel between [ɨ] and [ɐ]	specifically a mid-central unrounded vowel
ɘ	new symbol	close-mid central unrounded vowel
ɵ	any central rounded vowel	close-mid central rounded vowel
ɜ	any central vowel	open-mid central unrounded vowel
ɞ	new symbol	open-mid central rounded vowel

Non-IPA practice

Because the IPA alphabet tends to use symbols with values that they have in many national Roman-alphabet spelling systems (for example, the use of the symbol [s]), many non-IPA transcription systems are partly compatible with the IPA. This is both a blessing and a problem: it is a blessing because you do not have to reinterpret everything you read; it is a problem because it may not be clear at first whether or not an IPA system is being used for transcription.

It is not my purpose here to reproduce the Dania system for Danish dialectological work, Sapir's system for the transcription of native American languages or Ellis's forerunner of the IPA. People who wish to read these in detail will need to work out the details or find expositions of the details of the individual systems being used. Nevertheless, certain generalisations can be made.

Where consonants are concerned, there are so many alternatives that they are set out in table 21.2. While there are many correspondences here, note in particular the use of the symbol <y> for IPA [j], something which is so widespread that the IPA has on a number of occasions considered permitting it within its own system.

Table 21.2 Non–IPA symbols in common use

	Bilabial	Labio-dental	Dental	Alveolar	Post-alveolar	Retroflex	Palatal	Velar	Uvular	Pharyngeal	Glottal
Plosive						ṭ ḍ	ky gy kʲ gʲ		g̣		q ʔ
Affricate				c ¢	č ǰ ch j	č̣					
Nasal						ṇ	ñ ny	ng			
Trill				ř r̃							
Tap or flap				D ř̃		ŗ					
Fricative	ƀ ʋ		ƀ ɖ δ		š ž sh zh x	ṣ ẓ		kh g̶ j	x̣ ɣ̣	ḥ	
Lateral fricative											
Approximant						r i̯	y ly				
Lateral approximant											

Notes: Symbols under each other in the same slot have the same meaning.

Other symbols

IPA symbol				ɥ	dⁿ		dˡ				
Non-IPA variants				ẅ	dᴺ		dᴸ				

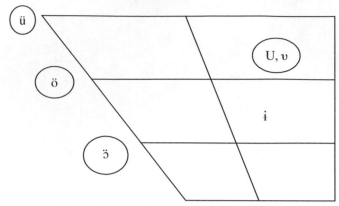

Symbols with circles round them indicate rounded vowels.

Figure 21.1 Non–IPA symbol for vowels

There are far fewer vowel symbols to worry about. They are presented in Figure 21.1. Note the generalisation that where an umlaut in IPA notation means 'centralised' (i.e. moved closer to the centre line on the IPA vowel chart), in non–IPA transcriptions it is used to mark a front vowel (following the use made of it in the national spelling systems used for German, Swedish and Finnish, for example). Note that here, as with the consonants in table 21.2, the value of a given symbol may not be clear without some description of the segment involved.

Stress is frequently marked with an acute accent for primary stress and a grave accent for secondary stress: [sékəndèri].

References

Brink, Lars, Jørn Lund, Steffen Heger & J. Normann Jørgensen (1991). *Den Store Danske Udtaleordbog*. København: Munksgaard.

IPA (1949). *The Principles of the International Phonetic Association*. London: IPA.

22

Foreign expressions

Although fewer people learn Latin in schools than used to be the case, there is still a tradition of using Latin words and phrases (and occasionally some from other languages as well) in academic prose, as if these were part of English. Some of these which are used in bibliographical references are mentioned in section 34, but are repeated in table 22.1 for ease of reference. All these expressions may or may not be italicised.

Table 22.1 Foreign expressions

Foreign expression	Abbreviation (if used)	Language (if not Latin)	Meaning
a fortiori			with stronger reason
a posteriori			from the latter; by experiment
a priori			from the preceding (often used to indicate argument from basic principles)
ad hominem			against the man (as opposed to arguing against the principle)
caveat			warning of conditions or stipulations (literally: 'let him beware')
ceteris paribus			other things being equal
(conditio) sine qua non			indispensable condition
confer	cf.		compare
et alii, et aliae	et al.		and others
ex hypothesi			from the hypothesis, hypothetically

Table 22.1 continued

Foreign expression	Abbreviation (if used)	Language (if not Latin)	Meaning
exempli gratia	e.g.		for the sake of an example, for example
Festschrift		German	a publication in honour of a person
grosso modo			more or less, approximately
hapax legomenon		Greek	word or expression found once only in a given body of text (literally 'said once')
ibidem	ibid.		in the same place or passage
id est	i.e.		that is
idem	id.		the same
inter alia			among other things
ipso facto			by this very fact
lapsus linguae			slip of the tongue
loco citato	loc. cit., l.c.		in the place or passage just cited
mutatis mutandis			making the necessary changes
non sequitur			something which does not follow logically
nota bene	NB		note well, pay attention
opere citato	op. cit.		in the work cited
pace			by leave of (usually used to indicate that the author is aware of a contradicting opinion)
passim			everywhere, in many places
post hoc			after the event
post hoc ergo propter hoc			after this and so because of this (a fallacious mode of argumentation)
quod vide	q.v.		which see (i.e. a cross-reference to some other heading or section in a work)
sic			thus (i.e. this is an accurate copy)
status quo			the situation as it was
sub verbo	s.v.		under the word
tabula rasa			blank page
traduttore, traditore		Italian	the translator is necessarily unfaithful to the original
ut infra			as (mentioned or explained) below
ut supra			as (mentioned or explained) above
vide	v		see
videlicet	viz.		that is to say, namely

23

Letters, accents and diacritics

There are a number of extra markings which are often found on the letters of the Roman alphabet which it is difficult to talk about if you don't have names for them. In tables 23.1 and 23.2 some common ones are considered, their names are provided, and some of their common uses are discussed. For details of how these symbols are used in transcriptions see Pullum & Ladusaw (1986). For details about what marks are used in individual languages, see Ritter (2002), and for usage and meaning in the Slavic languages in particular, see Comrie & Corbett (1993).

It is also the case that some languages add to the number of letters used in the standard Roman alphabet in several ways, and some of these are also mentioned in these tables, and given names for easy reference.

Table 23.1 Accents or diacritics

Accent	E.g.	Name	Discussion
´	é	acute	Used to mark vowel quality in French and Icelandic, but for stress in e.g. Spanish and for length in Hungarian. In many African languages used to mark high tone. Used over a consonant, usually indicates some degree of palatality or palatalisation, e.g. in Polish and in some transliterations of Sanskrit.
ˇ	š	caron, háček, hachek	Used in a number of Slavic languages to mark a post-alveolar consonant, and in Czech to mark a fricative trilled <r>. Sometimes informally termed 'wedge'. *Hachek* is the Slavicists' name for this character, while *caron* is the typographers' name.

Table 23.1 continued

Accent	E.g.	Name	Discussion
,	ç	cedilla	In French used to mark an /s/ rather than a /k/ pronunciation for the letter <c>. In Turkish used to show a post-alveolar quality.
ˆ	î	circumflex	In French usually used to show a following etymological <s> is missing. Sometimes used to mark length. In African languages sometimes used to mark falling tone. Also used to mark tone in Vietnamese.
¨	ü	di(a)eresis	Used to indicate that vowel letters belong to separate syllables in a word like *naïf*. In German and Finnish, etc. used to mark a front vowel, and often then called an UMLAUT, reflecting the name of the vowel modification process.
″	ő	double acute	Used in Hungarian for the combination of diaerisis and length.
`	à	grave	Used to mark vowel quality in French on an <e>, and used for stress in Italian. In English occasionally used to show that a vowel is not silent, as in *murderèd*. In many African languages used to mark low tone.
¯	ō	macron	Used to mark a long vowel, and in Vietnamese to mark tone.
˘	ă	micron, breve	Used to mark a short vowel, and in Vietnamese to mark tone.
˛	ę	ogonek or Polish hook	Used in Polish to mark a nasalised vowel.
˚	ů	ring	A rarely used accent with varying value.
.	ṣ	subdot, under-dot	Used in transliterations to indicate retroflection in Indian languages.
˙	ċ	superdot	Used in Maltese to show post-alveolar articulation.
˜	ñ	tilde	In Spanish used on an <n> to mark a palatal nasal. In Portuguese used to mark a nasal vowel.

Table 23.2 Letters

Letter	Name	Value or use
ŋ	agma, angma, engma, eng	Usually used for a voiced velar nasal.
ß	*Eszett*, beta–ess	Used in some varieties of German as a symbol for a double <s>.
Æ æ	ash, æsc	A vowel intermediate between <a> and <e>. Used thus in Old English, Danish, Norwegian, Icelandic.
Ð ð	eth, edh	Used for a voiced dental fricative, e.g. in Icelandic.
ə	schwa, shwa	Used as a phonetic symbol for an unrounded central vowel; the name derives from Hebrew.
Þ, þ	thorn	Used for a voiceless dental fricative, e.g. in Old English.
j	yod	The name is used for the phonetic symbol for a voiced palatal approximant.
ʒ ʒ	yogh	Used in Old English for a voiceless palatal fricative.
Ł ł	crossed 'l', Polish 'l'	In modern Polish pronounced [w], but derived historically from a dark [l].
Ø ø	slashed o	Used for a front rounded vowel, e.g. in Danish.
ƿ ƿ	wyn	Used in Old English for a [w].

References

Comrie, Bernard & Greville G. Corbett (eds) (1993). *The Slavonic Languages*. London and New York: Routledge.

Pullum, Geoffrey K. & William A. Ladusaw (1986). *Phonetic Symbol Guide*. Chicago and London: University of Chicago Press.

Ritter, R. M. (2002). *The Oxford Guide to Style*. Oxford: Oxford University Press.

24

Journals

If you want to know what is going on in linguistics, you have to read the journals. Very often important developments do not appear in books until several years after they first make their appearance in the pages of periodicals or learned journals.

Table 24.1 simply provides a list of some of the more important linguistics journals. Brief comments are added as necessary. The list provided here is clearly a biased one: it does not list journals written in Asian languages, for example. Nevertheless, the list is extensive, and shows just how much is published on linguistics and language-related areas.

What I have called 'national' journals in this list are often journals produced by a national linguistics society. They often carry articles in the language of the nation they serve and articles about the languages of the area they serve. At the same time, these journals may carry articles in 'international languages' (whose definition varies depending on the particular country involved, but usually including English and French), including articles by linguists from outside their national boundaries, and they often carry articles of general interest.

The coverage of many of the journals is made clear by their titles. The journal *English language and linguistics* deals with just that and requires little other comment. Journals which do not specialise in terms of their topic are said to deal with 'general' linguistics.

Some journals have had several publishers in their lifetimes; only the most current one known about is listed. In some cases, the imprint under which a journal is published may actually be owned by a different publishing house. Finally, since new journals are being introduced all the time, this list is bound to be slightly out of date.

Table 24.1 Linguistics journals

Acta linguistica hafniensia. Copenhagen: Reitzel, 1939–. Two series with a break between them.
  A general linguistics journal.
Acta linguistica Hungarica. Budapest: Akadémiai Kiadó, 1988—. A major national journal.
Anthropological linguistics. Bloomington IN: Dept of Anthropology, Indiana University, 1959-.
Archivum linguisticum. London: Mansell, 1949–80. A journal dealing with general linguistics.
Australian journal of linguistics. Abingdon: Routledge, 1981–. A major national journal.
  Particularly strong on Australian languages.
Brain and language. San Diego: Academic Press, 1974–.
Cahiers de lexicologie. Paris: Campion, 1959–.
Canadian journal of linguistics / La revue canadienne de linguistique. Ottawa: Canadian
  Linguistic Association, 1961–. A major national journal.
Clinical linguistics & phonetics. London and New York: Taylor & Francis, 1987–.
Cognitive linguistics. Berlin and New York: Mouton de Gruyter, 1990–.
Cognitive science. Norwood N.J.: Ablex, 1977–.
Discourse processes. Mahwah NJ: Erlbaum, 1978–.
Discourse studies. London: Sage, 1998–.
English language and linguistics. Cambridge and New York: Cambridge University Press, 1997–.
Folia linguistica. Berlin: Mouton de Gruyter, 1967–. A pan-European general linguistics
  journal.
Folia linguistica historica. Berlin: Mouton de Gruyter, 1980–. A companion to *Folia linguistica*.
  One of the major journals for the history of linguistics.
Foundations of language. Dordrecht and Boston: Reidel, 1965–76. A leading journal of
  generative linguistics during its lifetime.
Functions of language. Amsterdam and Philadelphia: Benjamins, 1994–. Deals with functional
  approaches to language.
General linguistics. Binghamton NY: State University of New York at Binghamton, 1955–. Has
  a focus on Indo-European and language change.
Georgetown University papers on languages and linguistics. Washington DC: Georgetown
  University Press, 1976–. Thematic volumes.
Glossa. Burnaby, British Columbia: Dept of Modern Languages, Simon Fraser University,
  1967–97. A general linguistics journal.
Historiographia linguistica. Amsterdam: Benjamins, 1974–. One of the major journals for the
  history of linguistics.
International journal of American linguistics. Chicago: University of Chicago Press, 1982–.
  Deals almost exclusively with native American languages.
International journal of corpus linguistics. Amsterdam and Philadelphia: Benjamins,
  1996–.
International journal of lexicography. Oxford: Oxford University Press, 1988–.
International journal of psycholinguistics. The Hague and New York: Mouton de Gruyter,
  1972–81.
International review of Chinese linguistics / Guo ji Zhongguo yu yan xue ping lun. Amsterdam:
  Benjamins, 1996–.
International review of sign linguistics. Mahwah NJ: Erlbaum, 1996–.
IRAL, International review of applied linguistics in language teaching. Heidelberg: Groos,
  1963–.
Journal of Celtic linguistics. Cardiff: University of Wales Press, 1992–.
Journal of comparative Germanic linguistics. Dordrecht: Springer, 1997–.
Journal of East Asian linguistics. Dordrecht: Springer, 1992–.

Table 24.1 continued

Journal of English linguistics. Thousand Oaks CA: Sage, 1967–. Particularly strong on corpus-based work and variationist studies.

Journal of language and social psychology. Clevedon: Multilingual Matters, 1982–.

Journal of linguistics. Cambridge: Cambridge University Press, 1965–. Highly prestigious; the main British journal for general linguistics.

Journal of memory and language. New York: Academic Press, c.1985–. Formerly called *Journal of verbal learning and verbal behavior.*

Journal of neurolinguistics. Tokyo: Language Sciences, 1985–.

Journal of phonetics. London: Academic Press, 1973–. One of the leading phonetics journals.

Journal of pragmatics. Amsterdam: North-Holland, 1977–. The leading journal on pragmatics.

Journal of psycholinguistic research. New York: Springer/Plenum, 1971–.

Journal of sociolinguistics. Oxford and Malden MA: Blackwell, 1997–. A leading sociolinguistics journal.

Journal of the International Phonetic Association. Cambridge: Cambridge University Press. Formerly called *Le maître phonétique.* Particularly strong on matters of transcription and descriptive phonetics.

La Linguistique. Paris: Presses universitaires de France, 1965–.

Langages. Paris: Didier-Larousse, 1966–. Each volume is thematic.

Language. Washington, DC: Linguistic Society of America, 1925–. The leading journal for general linguistics, with excellent review sections.

Language and cognitive processes. Hove: Psychology Press, 1985–.

Language & communication. Amsterdam: Elsevier, 1981–.

Language and education. Clevedon: Multilingual Matters, 1987–.

Language and speech. Twickenham: Kingston Press Services, 1958–. Strong on interdisciplinary and experimental research.

Language in society. Cambridge and New York: Cambridge University Press, 1972–. The leading sociolinguistics journal.

Language learning. Malden MA: Blackwell, 1948–.

Language learning journal. Rugby: The Association, 1990–.

Language sciences. Oxford and New York: Pergamon, 1979–.

Language testing. London: Edward Arnold, 1984–.

Language variation and change. Cambridge and New York: Cambridge University Press, 1989–. The major journal for variationist linguistics.

Levende talen tijdschrift. Amsterdam: Vereniging van Leraren in Levenden Talen, 1914–. Formerly called *Levende talen.*

Lingua. Amsterdam: North-Holland, 1947–. A major European journal for general linguistics, with generative preferences.

Lingua e stile. Bologna: il Mulino, 1966–.

Linguistic bibliography for the year. Utrecht: Spectrum, 1948–.

Linguistic inquiry. Cambridge MA: MIT Press, 1970–. A very influential journal for MIT linguistics.

Linguistic reporter. Arlington VA: Center for Applied Linguistics, 1959–1983.

Linguistic review. Dordrecht: Foris, 1981–.

Linguistic typology. Berlin and New York: Mouton de Gruyter, 1997–.

Linguistics. Berlin: Mouton de Gruyter, 1963–. A major journal for general linguistics.

Linguistics abstracts. Oxford: Blackwell, 1985–. A good bibliographical journal.

Table 24.1 continued

Linguistics and language behavior abstracts: LLBA. La Jolla CA: Sociological Abstracts, 1967–. Probably the major bibliographical source for linguistics; now available on-line in major libraries.

Linguistics and philosophy. Dordrecht and Boston: Reidel 1977–.

Linguistische Berichte. Wiesbaden: Steiner, 1969–. A major journal with a very wide range of articles.

Mind & language. Oxford: Blackwell, 1986–.

Natural language & linguistic theory. Dordrecht and Boston MA: Reidel, 1983–. A major generative linguistic journal.

Natural language semantics: an international journal of semantics and its interfaces in grammar. Dordrecht: Springer, 1992–.

Nordic journal of linguistics. Cambridge: Cambridge University Press, 1978–. A focus on formal syntax, but with many articles covering Scandinavian languages.

Oceanic linguistics. Honolulu: University of Hawaii Press, 1962–. Deals mainly with the languages of Oceania.

Orbis. Leuven: Peeters, 1952–. A journal on dialectology.

Phonetica. Basel and New York: Karger, 1957–. One of the major phonetics journals.

Phonology. Cambridge and New York: Cambridge University Press, 1984–. Formerly called *Phonology yearbook.* The leading journal specialising in phonology.

Revista española de lingüística. Madrid: Gredos, 1971–.

Revue roumaine de linguistique. Bucarest: Editions de l'Académie de la République populaire roumaine, 1964–. A major national journal.

Rivista di linguistica. Torino: Rosenberg & Sellier, 1989–.

Russian linguistics. Dordrecht and Boston: Reidel, 1974–.

Second language research. London: Edward Arnold, 1985–.

Sign language & linguistics. Amsterdam: Benjamins & HAG Publications, 1998–.

Sociolinguistics: newsletter of the Research Committee on Sociolinguistics, International Sociological Association. Missoula MT: The Committee, 1983–. Formerly called *Sociolinguistics newsletter.*

Speech and language. New York: Academic Press, 1979–84.

Sprache im technischen Zeitalter. Berlin: Kohlhammer, 1961–.

Sprachtypologie und Universalienforschung. Berlin: Akademie Verlag, 1993–.

Sprachwissenschaft. Heidelberg: Carl Winter, 1976–.

Studia linguistica. Oxford: Blackwell, 1947–. Once a major national journal, this is now expanding as a general linguistics journal.

Studies in language. Amsterdam: Benjamins, 1977–. A leading journal on language typology.

Studies in the linguistic sciences. Urbana IL: Dept of Linguistics, University of Illinois, 1971–.

Syntax. Oxford: Blackwell, 1998–. A specialist journal for syntax.

Te Reo. Christchurch: Linguistic Society of New Zealand, 1958–. Particularly good on Oceanic and Pacific languages.

Text. The Hague: Mouton, 1981–.

Theoretical linguistics. Berlin and New York: Mouton de Gruyter, 1974–. Deals mainly with formal semantics.

Travaux de linguistique. Gand: Service de linguistique française, 1969–.

Travaux linguistiques de Prague. Prague: Ceskoslovensk·α akademie, 1966–71.

Voprosy iazykoznaniia. Moskva: Izd-vo Akademii nauk SSSR, 1952–.

Table 24.1 continued

Word: journal of the Linguistic Circle of New York. New York: Vanni, 1945–. A major non-MIT American journal.

Word structure. Edinburgh: Edinburgh University Press, 2008–. A new journal dealing with morphology.

Yearbook of morphology. Dordrecht: Springer, 1988–. To be renamed *Morphology*. The first journal devoted to the study of morphology.

Zeitschrift für Phonetik, Sprachwissenschaft und Kommunikationsforschung. Berlin: Akademie-Verlag, 1961–92. A major national journal from the former East Germany.

Zeitschrift für Sprachwissenschaft. Göttingen: Germany, 1982–. A major national journal.

25

Linguists' names

It can sometimes be difficult to know how to pronounce the names of individual linguists, and this can be awkward, especially if you are presenting a seminar or conference paper. However, giving pronunciations raises a number of questions: for non-English names, should a pronunciation in English be given, or a pronunciation in the source language? Should we use the version the linguists themselves use, or should we use a standard version frequently heard? How many foreign names should be included on any such list, particularly if they are pronounced as expected in the language concerned? Do we need to worry about first names as well as surnames?

There is a related problem with the sex of some linguists. This is particularly true for those who publish using only their initials or those who have names which are not widely recognised by English speakers: names of Chinese, Finnish, Japanese, Korean origins and many more, for example, but also sometimes names from closer to home of Celtic or Scandinavian origin.

This last problem is too large to be dealt with comprehensively here, but the matter of pronunciation can be broached. In table 25.1 are the surnames of a number of linguists, along with a pronunciation of that name where it may not be obvious to the English-speaking reader. The pronunciation is given as it can be used by a monoglot Anglophone. Indications of gender are given as well. It is assumed that readers of these names speak English and are familiar with English names, so that Philip Carr, for example, does not require an entry.

Any list of this kind is problematic: some quite standard names can be mispronounced on occasions, and with many foreign names all one really needs to know is whether it is pronounced with an anglicised pronunciation or not, which may depend on what country the person lives in. Accordingly, the list given here is very much a matter of personal judgement, with names chosen because they are met often in writings in English or because of the importance of the scholar.

Table 25.1 Linguists' names

Name	Pronunciation	Sex
Aronoff, M.	'ærənɒf	M
Baldi, P.	'bɔːldi	M
Baudoin de Courtenay, J.	'bəʊdwæn dɪ 'kɔːtneɪ	M
Bauer, L.	'baʊə	M
Bavin, E.	'bævɪn	F
Besnier, N.	'bezniei	M
Blevins, J.	'blevɪnz	M/F[1]
Bloch, B.	blɒk	M
Bolinger, D.	'bəʊlɪndʒə	M
Booij, G.	bɔɪ	M
Botha, R. P.	'bəʊtə	M
Bybee, J. L.	'baɪbiː	F
Chierchia, G.	'kɪəkɪə	M
Chung, S.	tʃʌŋ	F
Crowley, T.	'kraʊli, 'krəʊli[2]	M
Culicover, P.	'kʌlikəʊvə	M
Di Sciullo, A-M.	diː 'ʃʊləʊ	F
Fairclough, N.	'feəklʌf	M
Fischer-Jørgensen, E.	fɪʃə'jɜːgənsən	F
Fisiak, J.	'fɪʃjæk	M
Gimson, A. C.	'gɪmsən	M
Hagège, C.	æ'ʒeʒ	M
Halle, M.	'hæli	M
Haugen, E.	'haʊgən	M
Hjelmslev, L.	'jelmslef	M
Hoeksema, J.	'huːksmə	M
Jakobson, R.	'jækəbsən	M
Jespersen, O.	'jespəsən	M
Kaisse, E.	keɪs	F
Kiefer, F.	'kiːfə	M
Koerner, E. F. K.	'kɜːnə	M
Koptjevskaja Tamm, M.	kɒp'tʃefskəjə 'tæm	F
Labov, W.	lə'bəʊv, lə'bɒf[3]	M
Ladefoged, P.	'lædɪfəʊgəd	M
LaPolla, R.	laː'pəʊlaː	M
Laver, J.	'leɪvə	M
Malkiel, Y.	'mælkiːel	M
Marchand, H.	maː'ʃɒn	M
Martinet, A.	'maːtɪneɪ	M

Table 25.1 continued

Name	Pronunciation	Sex
McMahon, A.	mək'mɑːn	F
Mey, J.	meɪ, maɪ[4]	M
Mithun, M.	mɪ'θuːn	F
Paul, H.	paʊl	M
Pierce, C. S.	pɜːs	M
Pullum, G. K.	'pʊləm	M
Ramsaran, S.	ræm'sɑːræn	F
Robins, R. H.	'rəʊbɪnz	M
Roeper, T.	'rəʊpə	M
Sadock, J. M.	'seɪdɒk	M
Sapir, E.	sə'pɪə	M
Seuren, P. A. M.	'sjuːrən	M
Siewierska, A.	ʃe'vɪəskə	F
Trask, R. L.	træsk	M
Trudgill, P.	'trʌdgɪl	M
Wasow, T.	'wuːsəʊ	M
Wierzbicka, A.	vɪəʒ'bɪtskə	F

[1] Juliette is female, Jim (J. P.) is male.
[2] I once asked Terry which he preferred, and he answered (unhelpfully) that he was happy with either.
[3] The first pronunciation given here is the American one (and thus the one used by Labov himself) and follows the American tradition of taking foreign vowels to be equivalent to English tense vowels, while the second is the British pronunciation, which follows the British tradition of taking foreign vowels to be short vowels (contrast the American and British pronunciations of *adios*, which vary in precisely the same way).
[4] The Dutch diphthong falls between the two English diphthongs, and may be heard as either.

26

Laws and principles

A number of general laws and principles are freely referred to in linguistics texts, and it is often assumed that the reader will be familiar with these. Unfortunately, the list of laws and principles which are thought of as being well enough known not to require a gloss keeps changing, so that a definitive list is not possible. Here some of the most important are listed. Note that the words *condition*, *constraint* and *principle* often seem to be used synonymously and promiscuously in these titles.

Behaghel's Law

Behaghel's Law, as expressed in Behaghel (1932: 4), is that items which belong together mentally will be grouped together syntactically.[1]

Binding theory

In principle, a theory is not the same as a hypothesis or a set of constraints or conditions. However, binding theory is made up of a set of three statements which are various termed 'conditions' or 'principles'. As set out in Chomsky (1981: 188) they are:

  (A) An anaphor is bound in its governing category
  (B) A pronominal is free in its governing category
  (C) An R-expression is free.

[1] 'Das oberste Gesetz ist dieses, daß das geistig eng Zusammengehörige auch eng zusammengestellt wird.'

An *anaphor* refers to a reflexive or reciprocal pronoun, a *pronominal* to any other pronoun, and an *R-expression* to a nominal which is not a pronoun. Each of these three types of category has an empty category counterpart.

Complex Noun Phrase Constraint

See Island constraints.

Coordinate Structure Constraint

See Island constraints.

Elsewhere Condition

Kiparsky (1973: 94) formulates the Elsewhere Condition as follows:

> Two adjacent rules of the form
> A → B / P __ Q
> C → D / R __ S
> are disjunctively ordered if and only if:
> (a) the set of strings that fit PAQ is a subset of the set of strings that fit RCS, and
> (b) the structural changes of the two rules are either identical or incompatible.

Kiparsky notes that this principle is also used explicitly in the grammar of Panini, which is why it gets the alternative name of the Panini Principle. The rule is provided in a rather different formulation, which may be easier to understand, by Anderson (1992: 12): 'Application of a more specific rule blocks that of a more general one.'

Empty Category Principle (ECP)

Chomsky (1986: 18) expresses this as follows: 'Every trace must be properly governed.'

Full-Entry Theory

The full–entry theory (Jackendoff 1975) is the theory that all existing words (possibly including all inflectional forms; see Halle 1973) have their own independent entries in the mental lexicon.

Functional Load

Madonia (1969: 84) summarises the notion of functional load as 'the worth of an opposition in a given language'[2] (My translation). Madonia considers only the functional load of phonemic distinctions, which she measures either by the frequency of the opposition in words which can appear in the same context or by the frequency of the phonemes in discourse. This is viewed as part of the economy of linguistic structure. Phonemes with a higher functional load are more stable, i.e. more resistant to change.

Grassmann's Law

Grassmann's Law was set out in Grassmann (1863). It concerns the deaspiration of the first of a sequence of two aspirated consonants in Sanskrit.

Grimm's Law

Grimm's Law is essentially a statement of regular correspondences between certain consonants in Indo-European (inherited in Sanskrit, Greek, Latin and other Indo-European languages) and those in the Germanic languages. The implication is that there was a change which set Germanic off from its Indo-European parent language, and that change is usually called the first Germanic Consonant Shift. The correspondences are set out in (1).

> (1) Indo-European voiced plosives correspond to voiceless plosives in Germanic.
> (e.g. Latin *dens, dentis* corresponds to Danish *tand*, English *tooth.*)
> Indo-European voiceless plosives correspond to voiceless fricatives in Germanic.
> (e.g. Latin *tres* corresponds to English *three.*)
> Indo-European voiced aspirated plosives correspond to voiced fricatives (often to voiced plosives in the modern languages) in Germanic.
> (e.g. Indo-European **bhrāter-* corresponds to English *brother.*)

This correspondence was stated in Grimm (1822). There has been some discussion of the extent to which Grimm's Law was really discovered by Grimm and the extent to which it was really discovered by Rasmus Rask, but it seems clear that the statement of the shift as a unitary process is properly Grimm's. For an extension to Grimm's Law, *see* Verner's Law.

---

[2] 'Par rendement fonctionnel, on entend l'importance d'une opposition dans une langue donnée.'

Head Movement Constraint

This constraint is formulated by Chomsky (1986: 71) as: 'Movement of a zero-level category β is restricted to the position of a head α that governs the maximal projection γ of β, where α θ-governs or L-marks γ if α ≠ C.'

Is-a Condition

The Is-a condition is the name given by Allen (1978) to the fact that an endocentric compound is a hyponym of its head, so that, for example, a *tennis-ball* IS A *ball* of some kind.

Island constraints

Island constraints were introduced by Ross (1986 [1967]) as an improvement upon the earlier A-over-A Constraint, which turned out to be an inadequate solution to an observed problem. The problem was to restrict the things that could be moved by transformations, a problem which has remained important although various solutions have been proposed since 1967. Ross proposed four constraints:

> *The Complex NP Constraint* (Ross 1986 [1967]: 76)
> No element contained in a sentence dominated by a noun phrase with a lexical head noun may be moved out of that noun phrase by a transformation.

> *The Coordinate Structure Constraint* (Ross 1986 [1967]: 98–9)
> In a coordinate structure, no conjunct may be moved, nor may any element contained in a conjunct be moved out of that conjunct.

> *The Left Branch Condition* (Ross 1986 [1967]: 127)
> No NP which is the leftmost constituent of a larger NP can be reordered out of this NP by a transformational rule.

> *The Sentential Subject Constraint* (Ross 1986 [1967]: 149)
> No element dominated by an S may be moved out of that S if that node S is dominated by an NP which is itself immediately dominated by S.

Island constraints were superseded by the Subjacency Condition, which attempted to do the same task but in a simpler statement.

Left-Branch Condition

See Island constraints.

Level-Order Hypothesis

Although the term is not introduced in her work, level ordering is introduced by Siegel (1979 [1974]), who suggests that the behaviour of various kinds of affix in English can be accounted for if 'the lexicon is so ordered that Class I affixation precedes Class II affixation' (Siegel 1979: 103). Class II affixation involves the so-called 'stress-neutral' affixes, while Class I affixation involves those affixes whose addition has the potential to influence stress patterns. Crucially for the level-order hypothesis, the rules dealing with stress are introduced between the rules introducing the two classes of affix.

Lexicalist Hypothesis

Chomsky (1970: 190) introduces the lexicalist hypothesis as the proposition that 'a great many items appear in the lexicon with fixed selectional and strict subcategorization features, but with a choice as to the features associated with the lexical categories noun, verb, adjective.' Elsewhere on the same page he refers to such a lexical entry as a 'neutral' lexical entry, one which does not determine in the lexicon whether we are dealing with, for example, *destroy*, *destruction* or *destructive*.

More recently, the term 'lexicalist hypothesis' has been used of something also called the 'strong lexicalist hypothesis' or the Lexical Integrity Principle, namely that syntactic operations have no access to the internal structure of words, so that the operation of syntactic processes cannot depend on the presence of particular word-internal elements, and elements within a word cannot be referred to by anaphoric processes.

Linguistic Relativity principle

See Sapir–Whorf hypothesis.

Multiple Application Constraint

See Repeated Morph Constraint.

Natural Serialisation Principle

This principle is associated with Theo Vennemann (see Bartsch & Vennemann 1972), who suggested that the order of operand and operator is consistent in any language. This is a generalisation of work on word-order typologies. The principle is too strong in its bald form.

Neogrammarian Hypothesis

The neogrammarian hypothesis is usually quoted in English in Lehmann's translation: '[E]very sound change, inasmuch as it takes place mechanically, takes place according to laws that admit of no exception' (Osthoff & Brugman 1967 [1878]: 204). This is not the earliest formulation of the idea, but it is perhaps the most influential one. This stands in conflict with the idea, summarised in the slogan associated with the work of the Swiss dialectologist Jules Gilliéron, 'chaque mot a son histoire' ('every word has its own history'), where the regularity of sound change is implicitly challenged. It is sometimes also seen as being in conflict with the notion of LEXICAL DIFFUSION, that is, that sound change does not affect all words at the same rate.

No-Phrase Constraint

The No-Phrase Constraint is a corollary of the Word-Based Hypothesis. As stated by Botha (1984: 137) it is 'Lexical rules do not apply to syntactic phrases to form morphologically complex words.' As stated, this constraint is too strong to account for data from at least some languages.

Obligatory Contour Principle (OCP)

The OCP is formulated by Goldsmith (1979 [1976]: 36), with reference to the work of Leben, as: 'at the melodic level of the grammar, any two adjacent tonemes must be distinct. Thus H[igh] H[igh] L[ow] is not a possible melodic pattern; it automatically simplifies to H[igh] L[ow].' This formulation has subsequently been found to be too general, in that not all languages adhere to the principle. But the statement has also been generalised so that it can apply to things other than tonemes.

Ockham's Razor

Ockham's razor is named after William (of) Ockham (also spelt <Occam>, <Okham> and in various other ways) (1285–1347) who came from the village of Ockham near East Horsley in Surrey. It is usually cited in Latin as *entitia non sunt multiplicanda praeter necessitatem* 'entities should not be multiplied beyond what is necessary', even though this form does not arise in Ockham's own writings, but was familiar long before Ockham. This is a simplicity metric for theory-building.

One form one meaning

'One form one meaning' refers to a supposed typological preference for languages to avoid homonymy and synonymy. It is thus argued that an ideal language would have a single meaning for every form, and a single form for every meaning.

Panini's Principle

Panini's Principle or the Panini Principle are other names given to the Elsewhere Condition.

Principle of least effort

The principle of least effort is based on work by Zipf, who states the principle in its most general form as: '[A] person will strive to minimize the *probable average rate of his work-expenditure* (over time)' (Zipf 1949: 1; italics in original). This has been interpreted in a number of ways in the study of language (see for example, discussion of Zipf's Law, below). It is often held to imply that speakers will simplify their pronunciation as much as possible, for example through assimilation and the loss of consonants and vowels. However, speakers are also listeners, and need to minimise the effort that it will take to understand the spoken language as well as the effort it will take to produce it; these two opposing forces need to be considered in understanding the principle.

Projection Principle

Chomsky (1981: 29) formulates this principle as follows: 'Representations at each syntactic level (i.e. LF, DS and SS) are projected from the lexicon, in that they observe the subcategorization properties of lexical items.'

Repeated Morph Constraint

The Repeated Morph Constraint is also known as the Multiple Application Constraint. Lieber (1981: 173) phrases this as: 'No word formation process . . . can apply iteratively to its own output.' In other words, no word can contain a sequence of identical affixes. There are known exceptions, but they tend to be marginal.

Right-hand Head Rule

Williams (1981: 248) states the Right hand Head Rule as 'In morphology, we define the head of a morphologically complex word to be the righthand member of that word.' There are languages for which this does not seem to be true across the board, and the statement has given rise to a large amount of discussion, but has been extremely influential.

Sapir-Whorf Hypothesis

The Sapir–Whorf hypothesis, also known as the linguistic relativity principle, was developed in the eighteenth and nineteenth centuries but is associated with Edward Sapir and Benjamin Lee Whorf, who made it a part of modern linguistics. It states that '[E]ach language . . . is itself the shaper of ideas . . . . We dissect nature along lines laid down by our native languages' (Whorf 1940a: 212–13), and that speakers of different languages have, by virtue of the grammatical systems of the languages they speak, different views of the world (Whorf 1940b: 221). The hypothesis is extremely controversial.

Sentential Subject Constraint

See Island constraints.

Separation Hypothesis

The separation hypothesis is the notion, expounded particularly by Beard (e.g. 1977, 1995), that processes of derivation (e.g. the creation of a nominalisation of a particular verb) and processes of affixation (e.g. the addition of the suffix *-ation*) should be kept distinct and not conflated into a single set of processes.

Specified Subject Condition and Tensed S Condition

These are two constraints on movement within a transformational syntax. They are summarised by Ouhalla (1999: 86) in the following terms:

> Move NP to an empty subject position provided NP is
> (i) not contained in a tensed S
> (ii) not separated from the target position by a specified subject.

Structure Preserving Hypothesis

This hypothesis is stated by Lasnik & Uriagereka (2005: 113) as: 'No transformational rule can involve positions X and Y if X and Y do not share property P.'

Subjacency Condition

For discussion of what the Subjacency Condition does, *see* Island constraints. Freidin (1992: 109) gives the simplest form of this condition as:

$$* [_\alpha \cdots [_\beta \cdots e_i \cdots] \,]$$

where α, β are bounding categories (NP, IP) and e_i is free in α.

Tensed S Condition

See Specified Subject Condition.

Θ-Criterion/Theta-Criterion

In the formulation from Chomsky (1981: 36), this constraint states that: 'Each argument bears one and only one θ-role. Each θ-role is assigned to one and only one argument.'

Uniformitarian Principle

The Uniformitarian Principle is borrowed from geology, and was apparently first formulated as early as 1785 by James Hutton. Briefly, it states that the forces which have always operated are precisely the forces which can be seen to be applying now, or, as phrased by Labov (1972: 275), 'We posit that the forces operating to produce linguistic change today are of the same kind and order of magnitude as those which operated in the past five or ten thousand years.'

Uniformity of Theta Assignment Hypothesis (UTAH)

This is formulated by Baker (1988: 46) as: 'Identical thematic relationships between items are represented by identical structural relationships between those items at the level of D-structure.'

Unitary Base Hypothesis

According to Aronoff (1976: 48), '[T]he syntacticosemantic specification of the base [in a process of derivational morphology], though it may be more or less complex, is always unique. A W[ord] F[ormation] R[ule] will never operate on either this or that.'

Unitary Output Hypothesis

Following from the Unitary Base Hypothesis, Scalise (1984: 137) proposes a Unitary Output Hypothesis which 'does not allow a particular phonological form to be considered a single affix if it produces outputs with different category labels or different semantics.'

Verner's Law

Verner's Law explains some of the apparent exceptions to Grimm's Law. Historically, this was important because it strengthened the position of the neogrammarians (*Junggrammatiker*) that sound changes operated as exceptionless 'laws', not just as tendencies. Verner's Law (first published in Verner 1877) states that Germanic word-internal voiceless fricatives (many of which had arisen through the application of Grimm's Law) were voiced when the stress did not fall on the immediately preceding syllable. Old English *brōþar* 'brother' and *fadar* 'father' have different medial consonants, even though there was a **t* in the corresponding position for both in Indo-European (compare Greek *phrātēr* and *pater*, respectively), because the Indo-European word for 'brother' is stressed on the first syllable, the word for 'father' on the second.

Wackernagel's Law

Wackernagel (1953 [1892]) draws attention to the fact that clitics in the Indo-European languages occur preferentially in second position in the sentence. This is now sometimes called the Wackernagel position.

Word-Based Hypothesis

According to Aronoff (1976: 21): 'All regular word-formation processes are word-based. A new word is formed by applying a regular rule to an already existing word. Both the new word and the existing one are members of major lexical categories [defined elsewhere as noun, adjective, verb and adverb, LB.]'

    Word formation, in this text, must be understood as derivational morphology, and *word* must be understood as 'lexeme'.

Zipf's Law

Zipf formulated several laws about linguistic behaviour. The one that is usually referred to as 'Zipf's Law' can be formulated as

$$r \times f = C$$

where r is the rank of a word in a particular text (that is, its position in terms of frequency in the text: a word which occurs 72 times has a higher rank than one which occurs 63 times), f is its frequency of occurrence in the same text, and C is a constant (Zipf 1949: 23–7).

    Zipf (1965 [1935]: 38) states what he terms his 'law of abbreviation' as follows: '[T]he length of a word tends to bear an inverse relationship to its relative frequency.' In other words, short words tend to be common, long words tend to be rare. This law is perhaps better known than the first law.

Zipf also pointed out that the more frequent a word is, the more meanings it is likely to have. He calls this the 'law of meaning'.

Zipf (1949) relates all these laws to the principle of least effort.

References

Allen, Margaret R. (1978). Morphological Investigations. Unpublished PhD dissertation, University of Connecticut.

Anderson, Stephen R. (1992). *A-Morphous Morphology*. Cambridge: Cambridge University Press.

Aronoff, Mark (1976). *Word Formation in Generative Grammar*. Cambridge MA: MIT Press.

Baker, Mark C. (1988). *Incorporation*. Chicago and London: University of Chicago Press.

Bartsch, Renate & Theo Vennemann genannt Nierfeld (1972). *Semantic Structures: A study in the relation between semantics and syntax*. Frankfurt-am-Main: Athenäum.

Beard, Robert (1977). On the extent and nature of irregularity in the lexicon. *Lingua* 42: 305–41.

Beard, Robert (1995). *Lexeme-Morpheme Base Morphology*. Albany: State University of New York Press.

Behaghel, Otto (1932). *Deutsche Syntax. Vol. IV*. Heidelberg: Winter.

Botha, Rudolf P. (1984). *Morphological Mechanisms*. Oxford: Pergamon.

Chomsky, Noam (1970). Remarks on nominalization. In Roderick Jacobs and Peter Rosenbaum (eds), *Readings in English Transformational Grammar*. Waltham MA: Ginn, 184–221.

Chomsky Noam (1981). *Lectures on Government and Binding*. Dordrecht: Foris.

Chomsky Noam (1986). *Knowledge of language*. New York: Praeger.

Freidin, Robert (1992). *Foundations of Generative Syntax*. Cambridge MA and London: MIT Press.

Goldsmith, John (1979 [1976]). *Autosegmental Phonology*. New York and London: Garland.

Grassmann, Hermann (1863). Über die Aspiranten und ihr gleichzeitiges Vorhandsein im An- und Auslaute der Wurzeln. *Zeitschrift für Vergleichende Sprachforschung* 12: 81–138.

Grimm, Jacob (1822). *Deutsche Grammatik*. Vol. I. 2nd edition. Göttingen: Dieterich.

Halle, Morris (1973). Prolegomena to a theory of word formation. *Linguistic Inquiry* 4: 3–16.

Jackendoff, Ray (1975). Morphological and semantic regularities in the lexicon. *Language* 51: 639–71.

Kiparsky, Paul (1973). 'Elsewhere' in phonology. In Stephen R. Anderson & Paul Kiparsky (eds), *A Festschrift for Morris Halle*. New York: Holt, Rinehart and Winston, 93–106.

Labov, William (1972). The social setting of language change. In William Labov, *Sociolinguistic Patterns*. Philadelphia PA: University of Pennsylvania Press, 260–325.

Lasnik, Howard & Juan Uriagereka (2005). *A Course in Minimalist Syntax*. Malden MA: Blackwell.

Lieber, Rochelle (1981). *On the Organization of the Lexicon*. Bloomington IN: Indiana University Linguistics Club.

Madonia, Giovanna (1969). Économie. In André Martinet (ed.), *La Linguistique: Guide alphabétique*. Paris: Denoël, 81–6.

Osthoff, Hermann & Karl Brugman (1967 [1878]). Preface to *Morphologische Untersuchungen auf dem Giebiet der indogermanischen Sprachen I* (Leipzig: Hirzel). Reprinted and translated in Winfred P. Lehmann (ed.), *A Reader in Nineteenth-Century Historical Indo-European Linguistics*. Bloomington IN and London: Indiana University Press, 197–209.

Ouhalla, Jamal (1999). *Introducing Transformational Grammar*. 2nd edition. London: Arnold.

Ross, John Robert (1986 [1967]). *Infinite Syntax!* Norwood NJ: Ablex.

Scalise, Sergio (1984). *Generative Morphology*. Dordrecht: Foris.

Siegel, Dorothy (1979 [1974]). *Topics in English Morphology*. New York and London: Garland.

Verner, Karl (1877). Eine Ausnahme der ersten Lautverschiebung. *Zeitschrift für Vergleichende Sprachforschung* 23: 97–130.

Wackernagel, Jacob (1953 [1892] Über ein Gesetz der indogermanischen Wortstellung. In *Kleine Schriften von Jacob Wackernagel*. Göttingen: Vandenhoeck und Ruprecht, 1–103.

Whorf, Benjamin Lee (1940a). Science and linguistics. *Technological Review* 42: 229–31, 247–8. Reprinted in John B. Carroll (ed.), *Language Thought and Reality*. New York: Wiley, and London: Chapman and Hall, 1956: 207–19.

Whorf, Benjamin Lee (1940b). Linguistics as an exact science. *Technological Review* 43: 61–3, 80–3. Reprinted in John B. Carroll (ed.), *Language Thought and Reality*. New York: Wiley, and London: Chapman and Hall, 1956: 220–32.

Williams, Edwin (1981). On the notions 'lexically related' and 'head of a word'. *Linguistic Inquiry* 12: 245–74.

Zipf, George K. (1949). *Human Behavior and the Principle of least Effort*. New York: Addison-Wesley. Reprinted in facsimile by Hafner of New York, 1965.

Zipf, George K. (1965 [1935]). *The Psycho-biology of Language*. Cambridge MA: MIT Press.

27

Statistics

For many linguists, the ability to understand a statistical presentation is an unnecessary skill. But for a growing number, particularly those that work with sociolinguistics, psycholinguistics, corpus linguistics or some relatively recent models of phonology and morphology, at least a reading knowledge of statistics is a requirement.

This is not the place to teach statistics. If you are in one of the areas of study that requires a sound understanding of statistics, you should take a statistics course or find some other way to gain the knowledge you need. If, however, you are an irregular consumer of statistics, you can work out the crucial bits of information you need without too much difficulty as long as you do not try to get too involved. If you are such a person and you find you really need to understand the statistics that others produce in greater depth, or if you need to produce your own statistics to prove some point, consult a professional. The simplified presentation here is for those who are not trying to be expert in the field.

Populations

The questions that linguists typically want to answer are large ones: what is happening to such and such a vowel in the English spoken in Birmingham? Do Americans use *that* and *which* differently from Britons? Are long words rarer than short words? Do languages with a particular stress pattern also show particular patterns of grammatical behaviour? And so on. These questions are enquiring about the nature of a particular vowel in every utterance spoken by any speaker from Birmingham within a particular time frame, between all instances of *that* ever used in American English and those instances of it used in British English, about every long word in the language under consideration (or perhaps every long word in every language ever spoken), about all languages with the relevant stress pattern. These are called the POPULATIONS about which we are asking questions and making inferences.

(The reason that statisticians talk in terms of 'populations' is of some marginal interest. The science of statistics was developed to help deal with what was happening in countries or states – hence the name *statistics*. In states, the rulers and administrators are concerned with the number of people who are likely to need particular services, or likely to be able to offer particular services, such as paying tax, in times of need. In other words, they are dealing with the people in the state or, in other terms, with the population of the state. This terminology has carried across to instances where we are not dealing with actual people.)

The types of questions we ask about populations are usually about particular properties, or PARAMETERS, of those populations. We might want to know the proportion of occasions where speakers use *that* rather than *which* or *who* in a restrictive relative clause, or we want to determine the average quality of a particular vowel sound from all utterances of that sound in Birmingham. We might then want to ask if the values of those parameters differ between distinct populations: how different are the parameters of speakers from Birmingham from those in Coventry?

In order to make valid inferences about a population we should be able to select and survey every member of that TARGET POPULATION. This is the ideal situation, and we might like to consider how often it applies in linguistic research. While some projects allow for every member of the city they are discussing to be chosen, very few are as open as that. Instead we often compromise by selecting from a different population, usually a subset of the target population. This is the SURVEY POPULATION: the population it is practicable to survey. Our survey population might be the utterances made by colleagues, or linguistics students, or by people who shop at a particular shopping centre in Birmingham. Since our survey data comes exclusively from the survey population, then strictly speaking all of our conclusions should only be about the survey population.

However, we usually want to generalise from the survey population to the target population. It is for the linguist (rather than the statistician) to make the case that the properties of the target and survey populations are the same, at least in so far as those properties that are being measured are concerned. If the survey and target populations differ significantly then we have the possibility of BIAS. If students speak differently from everyone else, then a study which uses students as the survey population will yield perfectly good estimates of the speech of students, but biased estimates of the speech of the whole population. People who do opinion polls or political polls often survey by selecting phone numbers, either from the phone book or randomly and calling those numbers; this means that they have to argue that people who do not have access to a phone do not differ in important ways from those who do have a phone and are at home to answer it.

Quantifying the bias caused by a mismatch between target and survey populations is not easy. Since we never have any data from those parts of the target population that are missing from the survey population, we cannot use the collected survey data *post hoc* to justify an assumption that the two populations truly are similar. Instead we have to appeal to results from other studies, to our knowledge of the demographics and history of the population, or perhaps even to common sense.

Samples

There are huge numbers of utterances spoken by people from Birmingham in a given time frame which we could in principle record (i.e. those utterances are part of a practicable survey population). However, we quite clearly cannot possibly survey them all, and we have to look at just some of those utterances. The utterances that we actually consider (or the instances of *that* and *which* that we look at, or the long words we make calculations about, and so on) are our SAMPLE from the population.

If we want to make some informed estimate about the population from which our sample comes, it is important that we should take a sample in an appropriate way. If we were to sample a single person saying our Birmingham vowel on one day, any number of things might go wrong. We might find that our speaker has a cold, that she's only just settled in Birmingham and speaks with an Italian accent, that the speaker makes a mistake in saying the relevant word, that the social or ethnic group of the speaker is more important to the way she sounds than the fact that she is from Birmingham, etc. To overcome such accidents, we want a large enough sample of vowels to be sure that we are getting a reasonable idea of what this vowel sounds like in Birmingham. At the same time, we do not want to have to track down every last inhabitant of Birmingham to find out how they say the vowel on a particular occasion. Part of what statistics tells us is how large a sample we need in order to feel reasonably certain that we are finding an accurate value of this vowel. The fewer people we survey, and the fewer tokens each of them produces for our sample of the population of vowel sounds, the less certain we are likely to be (see below).

If the inferences we draw from a sample about the population are to be valid, then we need to select the sample in an appropriate and well-defined way. Ideally this means taking a RANDOM SAMPLE of the tokens of our vowel in Birmingham (or whatever it might be that we are trying to measure). This means giving a known, though not necessarily equal, chance of selection to every token in the population. In the simplest case (called simple random sampling) it means that the chance of selection of any token of our vowel in the sample is not in any way connected to the selection of any other token in the sample. In linguistics, what it means to have a random sample is frequently fudged. Does it mean that no two tokens are produced by the same speaker? In the simplest case it does, but this requirement is rarely met in linguistic sampling. A thousand tokens from a single speaker clearly tell us less about the population than 10 tokens from each of 100 speakers. And if we have 10 tokens from 100 speakers who live in the same street then we'll learn less than if those 100 speakers come from all over the city. There are statistical methods, some quite complex, for taking such associations between sample members into account when making inferences. However, all the linguist needs to keep in mind is that although in general we learn more from larger samples, if the individual responses are linked to each other in any way at all precision is lost.

So far, the assumption has been made that you just want to know something about your sample as a homogeneous set: what the quality of a vowel is in Birmingham, for example. But you may believe that speakers in one suburb speak differently from speakers in another suburb, or that people over 190 cm in height speak differently from speakers under 160 cm in height. In such cases you are in effect dividing your survey population into a number of subpopulations, and then comparing the subpopulations. If the subpopulations are large you may be confident of finding enough people in a random sample (e.g. a random sample of students in most subjects ought to net a large number of both males and females, even if the proportions are not 50:50). However, sampling for minority groups, such as people above 190 cm tall, requires a purpose-built sampling scheme to make sure you get enough sample members from that subpopulation. You might need, for example, to visit basketball clubs to find people over 190 cm tall. Such an approach may complicate the analysis somewhat, and statistical advice should be sought at the planning stage if you need to design a complex sampling scheme. How you create a random sample of the relevant population is an important matter, as is how you ensure a response from your random sample.

Presenting the sample

Having taken a sample and derived such information as you require from that sample, you are ready to describe the behaviour of that sample. Where your sample is one of actual people, you will need to get those people to produce a certain piece of information for you in a recordable way. Where your sample is a number of words or sentences, you will need to analyse them in the way relevant to your experiment (e.g. count how long the words are in letters and/or phonemes; count how many subordinate clauses there are in each sentence; and so on). At this point you know everything that you need to know about the sample, and can describe it in detail. So it is at this point that you draw graphs, if graphs are required, or set up tables showing how many occurrences of particular categories were found.

Again, it is not the function of this text to teach you how to do this, though you should recognise that drawing appropriate graphs is a skill in itself and that even interpreting graphs and tables may not always be as straightforward as it seems. Readings for your various courses should give you plenty of practice at the interpretative task involved in dealing with such presentations. If you really want to know about when to draw a line graph and when to draw a bar graph, what the difference is between a bar graph whose bars touch and one whose bars are separated out from each other, and why pie charts are no longer seen as a preferred way of presenting data, you need to do a course in statistics or read a good statistics book.

At this stage you can also present some summary statistics about your sample. For example, if you want to know what the average vowel used by speakers in Birmingham is in some given word, you might simply find some way of turning the quality you have heard or recorded into numbers (for example, by carrying out an acoustic analysis, or by assigning a number to each of several perceptually different versions) and then producing a MEAN from those figures (the word 'average' is used in so many different ways that most statisticians prefer to be specific and use words like *mean*, *median* and *mode*; if your secondary school mathematics is not sufficient to let you know the difference, you might want to check these three words in some suitable reference work[1]). As well as the mean, you probably need to record the STANDARD DEVIATION, which tells you how much variation there was away from that mean in your figures. The mean and standard deviations are precisely known for your sample, because you know values for every member of the sample, but they are also estimates of what the mean and standard deviation are for the population as a whole, ON THE ASSUMPTION THAT YOUR SAMPLE IS REPRESENTATIVE OF THE POPULATION AS A WHOLE. Remember that if this assumption is not correct your figures will tell us only about the sample: this situation very often applies in small–scale undergraduate projects, and you must be careful not to claim too much for these.

For example, we might find that 17 per cent of restrictive relative clauses in written British English use *that* and that 77 per cent contain *which* or *who* (the

---

[1]   If you really don't know enough mathematics to distinguish between these terms, Huff (1954) is a very good and entertaining place to start. The book is now over fifty years old, and rather quaint in some ways, but it is still readable for those who have always tried to avoid such matters in the past.

numbers do not add up to 100 per cent because there are other possibilities). Thus 17 per cent is our best guess at this proportion among the whole population of written restrictive relative clauses. However, since we have only taken a sample of the population our result must be expressed tentatively, acknowledging the uncertainty introduced by examining only a subset of the population rather than taking a census (in this particular case, a census would not even be possible). So rather than reporting a simple value, statisticians often prefer to quote a CONFIDENCE INTERVAL (i.e. a range of values within which we are reasonably confident the true population value lies).

Statistical inference

When you have collected your data, and made some estimates of various quantities of interest, you may simply wish to report those estimates, with their uncertainties. Most commonly, however, you want to go a step further and answer a specific research question: e.g. do the speakers in two different suburbs really behave in a different way? In particular do the mean values of a particular vowel differ? You will have collected samples from both suburbs and calculated means in the two samples. Those sample means will undoubtedly differ, at least slightly. But does that mean that the population means are different? You will probably have individuals in each sample whose behaviour is atypical of the population they came from, for reasons such as those suggested above, but you want to know whether the differences between the two samples are due entirely to chance (because of the individuals you recorded when trying to find out the answer to your question) or whether the two populations they came from are really behaving differently. Statisticians prefer us to ask this question in a very particular way. Let us assume, they say, that there is no difference between our two populations (i.e. the people from the different suburbs, the very tall and not-so-tall people, are in principle behaving identically). This is the NULL HYPOTHESIS. It is, in a sense, the hypothesis of the person who is sceptical about your expectations and believes that the two groups do not differ in terms of the feature we are trying to measure. Statistical tests are then framed so as to answer the question: what evidence do we have that the null hypothesis is wrong? In a statistical test we start from the null hypothesis, and look to see if we have evidence to persuade us out of that position.

p-values

At this stage we have stopped asking about the nature of the sample, and we are trying to use the sample to draw inferences about the population as a whole. The null hypothesis is that the two samples we are dealing with really belong to the same population, that each sample you have collected is a different random sample from the same population. So the null hypothesis or the sceptic's position is that your two samples, though not identical, are not different enough to be samples of different populations.

Statisticians have various tests available to them for deciding whether the null hypothesis is or is not correct, and which test is appropriate depends upon factors such as the kind of data you are using (e.g. whether it is measurements on a physical scale or simple categorical answers to individual questions – yes versus no, occupational types, and so on), and if you have a physical scale whether the scale is extendable in both directions or just one. As you read you will start to become familiar with the names of some of these tests, such as Student's t (one- or two-tailed t-tests), chi-squared (χ^2), Wilcoxon, etc. If you want to be well informed, you will check out when each should be used. But if you assume that each has been appropriately used, you will eventually come to a p-value, which is a statement of the probability that your samples could have come from a population for which the null hypothesis is true. A value of p will be given which will be between zero and one. Large values close to $p = 1$ support the null hypothesis, low values close to $p = 0$ indicate that the data set is inconsistent with the null hypothesis. This is probably what you were hoping for when you asked the question. In practice we never see p-values of exactly zero or one, but an answer near to zero is good enough to conclude that there is a real difference between the two sets of samples you have taken. But how close does it have to be to zero before you can claim success?

If the probability is greater than 0.05, statisticians agree that it is not SIG-NIFICANT. This is a technical usage of the word *significant* (though one based on the ordinary language term). For any value greater than that, you cannot assume that the null hypothesis is incompatible with the data from your samples. Because *significant* is used in this very precise way in statistics, if you do not mean it in its statistical sense you should avoid it in favour of some synonym (*important, indicative, suggestive, telling*) when discussing results to which you might in principle have applied a statistical test.

What does it mean if we say that $p = 0.05$, or, more likely $p < 0.05$ ('p is less than 0.05')? What it means is that you have seen quite a large or quite a consistent difference in the properties of the samples (e.g. the sample means), and that there is only one chance in twenty that the two samples you took could be samples from the same population and still look that different. If you think of this in terms of betting money, those odds seem pretty good. If you put up £1, and nineteen times out of twenty you win £1, and the other time you lose your £1, you will be able to afford your own beer all evening. But if you think of it in terms of something more serious, you would not like those odds. You would not drive on a motorway if the odds of having a serious accident there were one in twenty. So $p < 0.05$, while statistically significant, might seem a relatively low level of significance for some things.

Accordingly, there are two other levels of significance which are regularly taken to be meaningful: $p < 0.01$ (there is only one chance in one hundred that things turned out the way they did purely by accident) and $p < 0.001$ (there is only one chance in a thousand that things turned out the way they did purely by accident).

So imagine our research project: we've collected two samples of people from two subpopulations, measured the values of a particular vowel, found a large difference between the samples and concluded that we have evidence against the null hypothesis (by calculating a small p-value from some appropriate statistical test). This small p-value can arise in two ways: either there is a real difference and our experiment has detected it, or alternatively we were unlucky, and chose a sample with too many atypical people. The p-value gives us a measure of how unlucky we would have to be if the null hypothesis was actually true, but we found samples that differed as strongly as the ones we just collected.

Alternatively we might have found samples that looked very similar, and found a large p-value from a statistical test. This lack of evidence against the null hypothesis can also come from two sources: there might really be no difference and our experiment correctly found none, or alternatively our sample was too small to detect the difference (e.g. we selected only two people from each suburb). So we should be careful. Finding no evidence for a difference can sometimes mean we just have not looked hard enough yet.

In summary, the lower the p-value the greater your confidence in dismissing the null hypothesis, and thus the greater your confidence in the hypothesis that you are dealing with two distinct populations. In other words, low values for p support the notion that the speakers from different suburbs or people of different heights do not speak the same way.

Some final warnings

Apart from the importance of using the term *significant* only in its proper meaning if you are discussing sets of figures like these, there are two things to note about figures of this kind.

The first is that, if you have a significance level of $p < 0.05$, and it took you twenty tests to come to this conclusion, the answer to one of them is wrong, but you don't know which it is. After all, if there is a one in twenty chance of getting the answer wrong and you try twenty times, then one of those answers should be wrong by your own statistics. Twenty tests is not very many, which is another reason for being a bit careful with low levels of significance. It also means that you should not carry out too many tests in the hope that something will turn out to be significant; the more tests you do, the higher the number that give misleading information.

The second is that these statistical tests are probably predicated on the assumption that each sample is independent of every other sample. Recall what was said above on this topic. Again, it should make you wary of accepting low significance levels when dealing with linguistic data collected in the way that most linguists go about collecting data.

Reference

Huff, Darrell (1954). *How to Lie with Statistics*. London: Gollancz.

28

Some on-line resources for linguists

It is always dangerous to give on-line sources because even if they persist, they have a habit of changing their names. Nevertheless, a list of some valuable resources is presented here with some brief commentary. Most of these sources will also have links to further resources, some of them listed here. These lists are only a starting point, and there is a lot more out there. You just need to take care that you get sites which are likely to be authoritative. Most of the sites listed directly here are run and maintained by professional linguists, but much that appears on the web is not subject to peer review and is prone to error — occasionally grossly.

http://www.arts.gla.ac.uk/IPA/ipa.html

The International Phonetic Association's site provides information about the association and its publications, and also the association's chart of symbols and information on where to get phonetic fonts.

http://www.ciplnet.com/

The Permanent International Committee of Linguists (CIPL) has a page on endangered languages with links to related sites.

http://www.essex.ac.uk/linguistics/clmt/other_sites/

This site at the University of Essex provides a well-structured list of sites connected with linguistics.

http://www.ethnologue.com/

The *Ethnologue* contains a list of the world's languages with information on where each is spoken, how many speakers it has and what language family it belongs to. You may also find this work published as a book, but the on-line version is often easier to search and more up to date.

http://www.eva.mpg.de/lingua/

This site, from the Max Planck Institute of Evolutionary Anthropology in Leipzig, has rules for glossing languages as well as material on endangered languages and some other links.

http://www.lagb.org.uk/

The Linguistic Association of Great Britain's site also has some discussion of linguistic questions, as well as links to British departments of linguistics.

http://www.ling.rochester.edu/links.html

This Rochester site provides links to many university departments of linguistics around the world.

http://www.linguistlist.org/

The Linguist List provides a vast amount of information, including discussion of topics of general interest, information about new publications, information about forthcoming conferences, and a list of linguists. It also has many links to other sites dealing with languages, language families, writing systems, and the like.

http://www.lsadc.org/

This is the Linguistic Society of America's site, and as well as having some material which is available only to members, it has some interesting discussion papers on general topics about linguistics.

http://www.sil.org/linguistics/

The Summer Institute of Linguistics site is perhaps best known for providing computer fonts for linguists, but it contains other resources as well, including a glossary and, at http://www.sil.org/linguistics/topical.html, useful links to other sites.

http://www.zompist.com/langfaq.html

This site provides some interesting answers to frequently asked questions, but has not been updated recently.

Part IV: Writing and presenting linguistics

29

Essay writing

Many of the assignments you will write as a student of linguistics will be data-analysis questions. In order to get the right answers for these questions, you may not need to write very much, and what you have to write is likely to be constrained by the questions you are asked. In answering such problems, it is often a direct disadvantage to launch yourself into connected prose: if you say more than you are asked for, you may start divulging your ignorance. It may even be the case that you are not asked for further comment because your teachers know that you have not yet reached the stage where you can be expected to give suitably informed further comment.

At some stage, though, you will have to write a real essay, a task which seems all the more scary because you have rarely been asked for sustained argument in this subject area before. What is more, your notion of an 'essay' may derive from high school or from notions that have been inculcated in different subject areas: anthropology, history, literary studies, philosophy. You may feel that you do not quite know what is expected in linguistics, and you may suspect that it is not quite what is expected in some of these other areas.

There are innumerable books and self-help packages, as well as tertiary-level courses, whose aim is to teach you 'to write'. That is not my aim here. Those programmes may or may not have something to offer you – the best of them will definitely have something to offer whether you are a beginning beginner or a famous and published author. Here my focus is on matters which might be specifically required in linguistics.

You were probably taught in school to plan an essay. If you were any good at writing essays, you probably found such advice tedious and tendentious: you did not need to draw a plan, you had it all in your head; the best way to discover your plan was to read the finished essay and see what plan you had in fact used. So a plan may not be on paper, it may be in your head. However, as you go further from 1,500-word essay to 3,000-word essay to 6,000-word project to research paper to Masters thesis to PhD to book, the time will come when you really do need a plan, one written down on paper. You may still not write it all down carefully before you begin writing, but you will need to know what is happening where in your work, if only so that you do not presuppose at point p^1 something which is not introduced until a later point p^2. If you ever get to the stage of writing books, your publishers will not accept a book project from you without a fairly detailed plan. So at some stage you will need to get used to writing a plan, even if it is no more than a few scribbled points on the back of a cinema ticket. Even fairly basic essays can be improved by having the right plan. The right plan is

- one that means you do not have to repeat yourself;
- one where you introduce theoretical notions before you need them;
- one that puts the most similar points close to each other;
- one that gives you a small number of headings under which all the things you need to say will fit;
- one that allows parallel treatment of parallel aspects of your data or argument;
- one that guarantees you will answer the question you have been asked to answer;
- one that does not let you wander off into irrelevancies.

With the right plan, your essay is half written before you begin.

Style sheet

Your teachers will almost certainly have a style sheet for use in the programme of which you are a member. Read it through, and use it. Some of the points it mentions will be discussed here as well. Where there is a conflict between your local style sheet and what is said here, you will gain more kudos by following your local advice.

The style sheet will tell you to provide a reference list and to provide bibliographical entries in a standard format. Detailed help on such matters is provided in the sections 34 and 35, and nothing further will be added here. If your local style sheet is more narrowly prescriptive than the advice here, follow the local advice for maximum advantage.

Sections and numbered paragraphs

One of the differences between an essay in linguistics and one in a more literary subject is that in linguistics you are often encouraged to provide headings for your sections. These headings in effect provide the plan for the essay. They have a dual function:

- They show the fundamental structure of your work.
- They remind you, as writer, what material needs to go in to each section (and, by implication, what is not relevant in that section).

Some of these section titles are sanctioned by usage: 'Introduction' and 'Conclusion' may be boring titles, but they are safe. (For more on their content, see below.) 'Discussion' will typically follow a section entitled 'Results', and will elaborate on the possible reasons for particular results of a survey, experiment, etc.

Furthermore, in linguistics essays, just as in linguistics articles and books, you may be encouraged to number your paragraphs. There are several ways of doing this, so you may find varying practice in your reading, but here a standard method will be described, which is usually called 'decimal numbering' (however misleading that may be).

Let us assume that you have been asked to write an essay on the classification of consonants in the system used by the International Phonetic Association. In this system, you are aware, there are three labels for any consonant, a voicing label, a place label and a manner label. Accordingly you might say there are three main areas you have to cover in your essay, and you may set out your fundamental plan as in (1)

(1) *   Voicing
     *   Place
     *   Manner

To this fundamental structure, we can add the ubiquitous Introduction and Conclusion, to make five major points for the essay, and they will be numbered, as in (2).

(2) 1. Introduction
     2. Voicing
     3. Place
     4. Manner
     5. Conclusion

(You may find that some people use a number '0' for an introduction, but this is not usually a favoured approach these days, and it is not recommended: start at '1'.) Under 'Voicing' you are going to have to deal with at least two options: consonants are usually classified as either voiced or voiceless, though extra

THE LINGUISTICS STUDENT'S HANDBOOK

variants may be worthy of discussion. Let us assume that you just want to explain these two. We will now expand heading 2 in (2), to say we need subsections dealing with these two categories. We will get the new version in (3).

(3) 1. Introduction
     2. Voicing
          2.1 Voiced
          2.2 Voiceless
     3. Place
     4. Manner
     5. Conclusion

Section 3 will similarly be expanded to discuss the various places of articulation from Bilabial through to Glottal, and section 4 will have manners such as Plosive (or Stop) through to Approximant (or whatever label is preferred in your institution). But you might decide that Approximants are better split into two sub-subsections, one dealing with median approximants (such as [j] and [w]), the other dealing with lateral approximants (such as [l] and [ʎ]). Having made that decision, you might decide to subdivide the Fricative section in the same way. You might end up with the pattern in (4).

(4) 1. Introduction
     2. Voicing
          2.1 Voiced
          2.2 Voiceless
     3. Place
          3.1 Bilabial
          3.2 Labio-dental
          3.3 Dental
          3.4 Alveolar
          3.5 Post-alveolar
          3.6 Retroflex
          3.7 Palatal
          3.8 Velar
          3.9 Uvular
          3.10 Pharyngeal
          3.11 Glottal
     4. Manner
          4.1 Plosive (or Stop)
          4.2 Fricative
               4.2.1 Median
               4.2.2 Lateral

Notice the structure evident here. Subheadings have been indicated in (4) by being indented, but that is unnecessary: the number shows the level of subordination. The longer the number, the greater the notional indentation is, and this implies the less important the section heading is. The use of three levels of heading (as illustrated here) is fairly normal. If you can manage with just two, that is good. In very complex documents (such as theses) you might need four. You should never exceed four if you can possibly help it (though you may have bullet points or numbered lists within a fourth-level discussion). Never use any level of subheading if there are not at least two equivalently numbered paragraphs (if you have 2.1 it implies there will be at least a 2.2; if you have a 4.5.1, it implies there will be at least a 4.5.2).

Use and mention

For discussion of use and mention, see section 31. What this amounts to for present purposes is that when you are referring to morphs, words (specifically word forms) or phrases in the middle of your own text, these should be marked as being mentioned by the use of italics (underlining in typescript or manuscript). Alternatively, where it is relevant, the forms may be transcribed (and thus in [...] or /.../ brackets as appropriate; see section 16).

Occasionally you will see elements which are being mentioned enclosed in single quotation marks rather than being italicised – and in newspapers it may be a struggle to gain even this small amount of marking. Since single quotation marks are used in linguistics to show meanings or glosses (as in (5)), this alternative is definitely a less favoured choice.

(5) The -s plural occurs rarely with the lexeme LOUSE, giving *louses* /lausɪz/ (it does not rhyme with *houses*), but it always means 'unpleasant person' rather than 'type of insect' under such circumstances.

Data

Where you are producing an analysis of data as part of your essay, there are certain conventions you should observe.

The first is that where you are giving examples which consist of whole sentences, or pieces of text or dialogue which are longer than one sentence, or sets of words, you should set them off, number them consecutively throughout the essay, and refer to them by number. This is what has been done in this section for examples like (5).

Where you present foreign language data, you may need to gloss that data. Information on glossing is given in section 30.

You need to ensure that

- your data is relevant;
- your data is comprehensible;
- your data is representative;
- your data is consistent with your analysis;
- your data is sufficient in extent to indicate why alternative analyses are not appropriate.

(Incidentally, if you object to the singular use of *data*, you are in good company: many journal editors would agree with you, especially in psychology journals. I insist upon my right to treat *data* as a mass singular noun, as it is used in normal language by large numbers of English speakers. I would sometimes try to say *data set* to avoid the problem, but that would not make sense here. *Evidence* would have been an alternative.)

Introduction and conclusion

In these days of word-processors, you are no longer restricted to writing your essay in the order in which it will appear in the final version. This is liberating. It means two things: (a) you can write a section when you have enough information to do so and fit it in to the whole later; (b) you do not need to write the introduction first and the conclusion last.

One good procedure is to write the body of the essay first. Once you have done that, you can write the conclusion, because you know what you have done in the essay. Your conclusion should provide a basic summary of the essay. It should remind the reader of the points you have made, the line your argumentation has taken, the kind of data you have adduced to support your argument. If your essay is data-based, it should say where your data takes you, what you wish to conclude on the basis of the evidence which the data has provided. Once you have written your conclusion, you are in a position to write the introduction. The introduction will be a mirror of the conclusion. If the conclusion says 'I have shown that x, and then that y, with the result that z', your introduction will say 'I will conclude that z on the basis of x and y.' For most essays, this is probably sufficient. For longer documents such as research papers and theses, it is probably not: there you might need to define some basic terms, to set out the background to the problem to be treated, to justify a discussion of the topic, or to indicate that there is a genuine problem to be solved. While any of these may be useful in an essay, undergraduate essays are usually so constrained in topic and in length that there is little room for this kind of material. What you should certainly NOT do, either in the introduction or in the conclusion, is try to relate your discussion to 'life, the universe and everything'. Your essay topic should be specific, and your introduction and conclusion should relate to that specific topic.

Writing and rewriting

How good an essay do you want to write? If you really do not care, then the first thing you put down on paper is presumably good enough. If you do care, then the first thing you put down on paper is rarely good enough.

Different people work in different ways to do their writing, and there is no simple correct way for you to work. Some spend a long time in initial preparation, getting a quite detailed plan of what they will say (and even how) before they start writing. Others start writing, and then go back as they realise that gaps have arisen. Some combination of the two approaches is probably a norm. But whichever way is your dominant approach (and it may vary from one essay to the next), you still need to work over your essay.

At a minimum you should proof-read your essay carefully. Have you inserted the relevant phonetic symbols if you do not have phonetic fonts?[1] Have you missed the word *not* out of one of your vital quotations? Have you used correct notation for the linguistic concepts? Have you spelt words central to your theme correctly? Does each sentence make sense and is it grammatical? Do all language names (including *English*) begin with a capital letter?

Some writers expect to spend at least twice as long in rewriting as they did in writing. They will be checking things such as:

- Is there any unnecessary repetition?
- Is everything that is said relevant to the argument?
- Is what is said said in the most useful place in the argument?
- Are the main stages in the argument or presentation clearly signposted?
- Where something has been quoted, is it advantageous to quote it rather than to refer to it?

[1] Fonts with phonetic symbols for Macintosh and Windows computers can be obtained from http://www.chass.utoronto.ca/~rogers/fonts.html and from http://www.sil.org/linguistics/computing.html#fonts. The latter site also gives details about obtaining commercial fonts for the IPA and for things like drawing trees.

- Where there is reference to someone else's work, has it been accurately paraphrased and without plagiarism?
- Are the sentences as clear as they can be? Are there any ambiguous sentences which can be removed or reworded?
- Do the sentences go together to make a text? Are the connectors such as *so, thus, therefore, nevertheless* placed meaningfully?
- Are parallel points made in a parallel way for extra clarity?
- Is the style too repetitive because it uses the same structures too often?
- Is the text as easy to read as it is possible to make it?

All of these and other things are the kinds of things you can check to help improve your essay. For other suggestions, see books on essay writing.

30

Glosses

GLOSSES are the interlinear translations of foreign-language data that allow you to see the structure of the language being dealt with. In providing a gloss, the writer has to present enough information for the reader to be able to understand the structure sufficiently to be able to follow the general argument. This means that sometimes you need to be specific about the internal structure of a foreign word, and sometimes you do not. For example, suppose you were glossing the French sentence *Il va à l'église le dimanche* 'He goes to church on Sundays.' If you are only worried about the use of the definite article in French for church and for Sunday, you will probably gloss *va* as 'goes'. If you are concerned with the details of the present tense in French, you will probably gloss it to show that it is the third person singular of the present tense of the verb meaning 'go'. Because there is variation of this kind depending on the aims of the writers, it is not possible to give absolute guidelines about glossing. Some generalities, though, hold true. It should also be noted that there is more than one way of writing glosses: be prepared to meet alternatives!

A three-line gloss

If you have to gloss foreign-language data, you should expect to give a three-line example. The first line presents the foreign-language data. Where appropriate (see above) the data will have marks showing the boundaries between morphs/morphemes. The second line provides the gloss, a translation of each of the elements marked out in the first line. The beginning of each word is aligned with the word from line one which it translates. The third line (which may be omitted if it would not be significantly different from the second) is an idiomatic translation of the first line, enclosed in single quotation marks. If we use the same French sentence as above, we get the layout shown in (1).

(1) Il   va   à   l'·église   le   dimanche
    He   go.PRES.3SG to   the·church   the   Sunday
    'He goes to church on Sundays'

Features of the gloss line

In glosses, the translations of lexical items are presented in lower case roman type, while glosses of grammatical information are presented in small capitals. Each morph or morpheme separated out in the first line must receive its own gloss. This will sometimes involve the insertion of zeros in the first line in order to have an element to gloss, as, for example, in the Russian example in (2). Similarly, empty morphs may be glossed as 'Ø'. I use the decimal point to separate morphs from each other since it is clearly not a part of the orthography and because it is less obtrusive, but the hyphen is more frequently used. Some authors distinguish various types of boundary.

(2) komnat·Ø
    room·GEN.PL
    'of the rooms'

Elements in the glosses are divided in the same way as elements in the words in the first line. That has been illustrated in (1) and (2). However, there are many occasions when the gloss will contain more elements than the first line, either because of the nature of translation (e.g. 'go up' for French *monter*) or because of morphological cumulation (as in (2)). Where this happens, the elements in the gloss have to be separated, but a space cannot be used, since this would look as though it was the beginning of a new word in the first line. The usual notation is to use a full stop / period, as has been done above, though an equals sign (=) or an underscore (_) is sometimes used instead.

Note that the situation where there are more elements in the original than in the language used for the glossing is covered by the translation line. If we imagine glossing English for French speakers, we would get something like what we see in (3), where the English word *hedgehog* is analysable, but the French word *hérisson* is not.

(3) The   hedge·hog   is   dead
    DÉF   haie·cochon   est   mort
    'Le hérisson est mort'

There are standard lists of abbreviations for the grammatical categories used in glossing. Lehmann (1982) is the major work in this area, and he provides an extensive list. Another list is provided by the Department of Linguistics at the Max Planck Institute for Evolutionary Anthropology at Leipzig, http:// www.eva. mpg.de/lingua/files/morpheme.html. But most people use their own abbreviations, and, in any case, you MUST PROVIDE A LIST OF THE ABBREVIATIONS USED. The major point is to avoid providing the same abbreviation for, say subject and subjunctive or absolute and ablative, particle and participle, imperative and impersonal, and so on. The use of the figures 1, 2, 3 is standard for first, second and third persons, while big roman numerals are used for declension or conjugation classes.

Discontinuous elements provide problems for glossing – problems which are solved in a number of different ways. Fortunately, these are rare enough not to cause too many problems, and can sometimes be treated as instances of morphological cumulation.

Dealing with the morphophonologically complex

Where languages are particularly morphophonologically complex, it may be necessary to add a fourth line to the gloss. In this situation, the first line will be the surface form, the second line the underlying morphemic form, the third line the gloss and the fourth line the translation. A very simple example from Yimas (see Foley 1991: 51) in (4) makes the point.

(4) taɲa
     taj–nak
     see–IMP
     'look at it'

Note in this case that the second line shows morphemes and not morphs (and hence my use of the hyphen rather than the decimal point which is used to separate morphs). However, for many purposes this degree of sophistication will not be necessary. Lehmann (1982: 211) suggests that where morphemes whose boundaries are not marked in the foreign language text are nevertheless translated in the gloss, they should be separated by colons. Using this convention, (4) could be represented as (5).

(5) taɲak
     see:IMP
     'look at it'

Most authorities, however, seem to see this situation as equivalent to that illustrated with the gloss of *va* in (1), and simply use the period notation.

Some questions about glosses

The present tense is not marked in the language I am glossing: what do I do?

It is frequently the case that there is no morpheme for an unmarked category and yet you want to show this in your gloss. In some cases you can use zeros here, but this may seem artificial if there is no particular reason to suppose that the tense marker would otherwise hold a particular position: zeros are much easier when they are in complementary distribution with overt morphs. There are at least two possible answers here: the first is to leave it to the translation to show that present tense is implied by the lack of marking; the second is to put the category name in parentheses: '(PRES)'.

How do I deal with proper names?

Where proper names are not inflected, you can leave them unglossed, simply gloss them with an initial, or gloss them as '[name]'. Where they are inflected, you will probably need to put a name in the gloss as well, so that there is something to which to add the inflectional categories. Some writers translate names where there is a ready equivalent, e.g. French *Jean*, English *John*, or Italian *Napoli*, English *Naples*.

How do I punctuate glosses?

You do not punctuate glosses. You punctuate the first line of your set according to the conventions of the foreign language being dealt with, and the last line according to the conventions of the glossing language. In addition you mark divisions into morphs or morphemes. The middle line is complicated enough without extra punctuation marks.

Do I have to gloss every language?

Conventions are changing on what languages are glossed. While it used to be thought reasonable to expect a reader to be able to cope with at least French, German and Latin (and in the nineteenth century, Greek was virtually never translated, let alone glossed), this is no longer so obviously the case (after all, people who grew up in India or China or Japan would not necessarily have learnt any of these languages, even if they speak several languages). Certainly, if you are making a point about the structures of the languages, you should gloss everything. You cannot, of course, gloss the language you are writing in.

References

Foley, William A. (1991). *The Yimas Language*. Stanford: Stanford University Press.
Lehmann, Christian (1982). Directions for interlinear morphemic translations. *Folia Linguistica* 16: 199–224.

31

Use versus mention

I recall the first time I had a cryptic crossword clue explained to me. The clue was 'Cheese that is made backwards (4)' and the answer was, of course, 'Edam'. I thought this was terribly witty – which probably says more about my age at the time than anything else! Later in life, I came back to this clue, now dissatisfied with it. The clue is deliberately misleading. The process of making the cheese is not reversed in the production of Edam, which is what, on the face of it, the clue says. Rather, the name of the cheese is the word *made* written backwards. Cryptic crossword clues are designed to exploit such potential ambiguities in language. But as linguists we want to be clearer than that, and to avoid such ambiguities.

The difference can be explained as a distinction between USE and MENTION. The reason my crossword clue is misleading is that we assume that the word *made* is being used in the clue as a normal word of English. But to get the answer, we have to see that *made* is really being mentioned: we have to reinterpret *made* and see it not as part of the verb but as the name of a particular orthographic word. As linguists, we would want to write 'Cheese that is *made* backwards (4)', thus destroying the ambiguity (and making the clue at lot easier to solve). Mentioned words are set in italics (underlined in manuscript). The convention has already been used in this section, and is used generally in this book.

As linguists we regularly mention bits of language. Some examples are given in (1)–(5), where italics are used to show that mention is involved.

(1) *Red* in *red chair* is an epithet, while in *red wine* it is a classifier.
(2) Chomsky's (1957: 15) famous example of *Colourless green ideas sleep furiously* can be interpreted in several ways.

(3) The suffixes *-s*, *-ed* and *-ing* are all inflectional.
(4) The words *skinny* and *slim* show the power of connotations.
(5) *To* and the infinitive or the *-ing* form after *start* appear to be synony-
     mous.

When words or sentences are being cited in arrays (e.g. in tables or in numbered examples) it is usual to avoid the use of italics, because it is clear from the
context that these are linguistic examples being cited. Where there might be
ambiguity, you should use the notational convention of using italics to make
your meaning absolutely clear.

A colleague once told me of a student who had written something along the
lines of 'The fox, like many common animals, has three letters.' We might wish
to query the accuracy of the observation (after all, are foxes or rabbits more
common?), but let us ignore that point here. The point for current purposes is
that while the fox may be a common animal, it is *fox* (i.e. the word *fox*) which
has three letters. The student was mixing use and mention. Foxes do not have
letters; it is the words for foxes which have letters (or phonemes or belong to
declension classes, etc.).

So foxes are mammals, but *foxes* is a five-letter word. Note that the difference
can be crucial. (6) is a valid syllogism; (7) is not.

(6) He hates foxes.
     That animal is a fox.
     Therefore he hates that animal.
(7) He hates *foxes*.
     That animal is a fox.
     Therefore he hates that animal.

The first premise of (7), but not of (6), is true if he hates the sound of the
word *foxes*, or if he, on principle, hates all five-letter words. But even if the
difference is not always as clear cut as these examples suggest, it is worth
making an effort to distinguish between use and mention in order to be a little
clearer (possibly even in your own mind) about what you are saying.

Reference

Chomsky, Noam (1957). *Syntactic Structures*. The Hague and Paris: Mouton.

32

Reification

The Macquarie Dictionary (3rd edition) defines *reify* as 'to convert into or regard as a concrete thing'. Where linguistics is concerned, the problem is regarding the constructs of linguists as concrete objects which have a reality independent of the linguists who thought them up. Nowhere is that tendency stronger than with the notion of languages.

One of the differences between a lay approach to the notion of a language like German and that of the linguist is that lay people tend to imagine languages having a definition 'out there'. Linguists, on the other hand, see a language like German being made up of such agreement as there is between those people who believe that they are speaking and listening to German. In this latter view, it is very difficult to point to something and say 'that is the German language', though easy to point to something and say 'that is a use of German'. Part of the distinction between prescriptive and descriptive approaches to language lies in whether we believe that there is some external reality to which we can refer for how 'the language' ought to be. Most linguists would say there is no such external authority except an artificial one imposed by a certain class of speakers. To find out what the language is like, we have to observe the behaviour of its speakers. If speakers of English say *It is me*, then *It is me* is part of the English language, even if some self-appointed guardians tell us that we ought to prefer *It is I*. (See further, section 1.)

But even linguists reify languages. We find statements like 'English has no future tense' (Palmer 1971: 193), 'German is a V2 language', or 'Our primary concern . . . is to describe the grammar of English' (Quirk et al. 1985: 14). Most of the time, this is probably a harmless enough metaphor. But it does set up languages as realities. Formulations such as 'English does not allow us to . . . ' are worse. Here the language is not only reified but in some sense made animate.

Turns of phrase like Schibsbye's (1970: 37) 'The subjunctive in principal clauses cannot be said to be living in modern English' are in principle better, since they allow us to understand them as 'in modern English usage', but even they reify 'English' as opposed to the forms produced by English speakers or the speakers themselves. A formulation such as Gimson's (1962: 158) 'Some RP speakers will also use [?] to replace /t/ . . . ' clearly shows where the variation (in this case) arises: with the speakers. (Gimson also uses other formulations, of course.)

How important is all this? As long as one is aware of the reification, it is probably not very important. But it is easy to lose track of the fact that one is dealing with a reification, and then it can be important. For example, if we say 'New Zealand English is in the process of merging the NEAR and the SQUARE vowels' we get a rather different picture from if we say 'Speakers of New Zealand English are less and less likely to distinguish the NEAR and SQUARE vowels.' Only in the latter case do we see a reason to ask, 'Why should people behave in this way?' Asking why language changes in a particular way might be seen as a very different question, with a different set of possible answers. So there are times when it is valuable to remind ourselves that a language such as English or German or Japanese is a reification of an abstract idea.

It is probably less of a problem to remind ourselves that theoretical constructs such as the Right-hand Head Rule or Move-Alpha or a particular morphophonemic transcription are equally abstract constructs. While we remain aware of them as hypotheses, or structures and concepts generated within a particular theory, there is little danger of misusing them. If we start to think of them as realities which inhabit the world of linguistics, there is the potential for problems to arise.

The result is that a statement such as 'English has /p/' is a theory-laden statement. It presents a reification of English, it assumes a notion of a phoneme, which it assumes has some kind of reality, and it assumes the correctness of a classification in which 'p' is meaningful. Every one of these assumptions has been challenged at some point. If we don't make assumptions about our theoretical bases, on the other hand, it becomes extremely difficult to talk about things at all. 'Speakers of English have been observed to used a [p]-sound contrastively' is not only far more long-winded than 'English has /p/', it fails to cancel all of the assumptions in that shorter statement. Reification is unavoidable; at times, making a deliberate effort to overcome the reification can be a useful thing to do.

References

Gimson, A. C. (1962). *An Introduction to the Pronunciation of English*. London: Arnold.

Palmer, Frank (1971). *Grammar*. Harmondsworth: Penguin.

Quirk, Randolph, Sidney Greenbaum, Geoffrey Leech & Jan Svartvik (1985). *A Comprehensive Grammar of the English Language*. London and New York: Longman.

Schibsbye, Knud (1970). *A Modern English Grammar*. 2nd edn. London: Oxford University Press.

33

Spelling

As linguists we know that spelling is a by-product of linguistic behaviour, and that our ability to spell is on the whole independent of our ability to manipulate language in other ways. Nevertheless, your spelling is part of the face you present to the world, and people judge you by your spelling as well as by the other more meaningful things you do. That being the case, it is worthwhile getting the spellings of the fundamental terms of the trade right, just to avoid looking stupid. Remember that the best spelling-checker in the world will not

Table 33.1 Spelling

assimilation	double S, one M - I
auxiliary	one L
complementary distribution	L – E – M
dependency	D – E – N
diphthong	P – H – T – H
genitive	N – I – T
grammar	A – R
Jakobson	O – N
Jespersen	E – N
monophthong	P – H – T – H
occurred	double R
occurrence	double R
possessive	double S, double S
pronunciation	N – U – N
psycholinguistics	P – S – Y – C – H
rhotacism	T – A – C (contrast *rhoticity*)
rhythm	R – H, only one Y
vocal cords	C – O – R (say 'vocal folds' if in doubt)

help your spelling if you have told it that something is right or if there are homophones spelt differently. Fortunately, there are not many words that cause problems. A short list of words that linguists need to be able to spell is presented in table 33.1.

Part V: Bibliographies

34

Citation etiquette

Until relatively recently in the history of ideas, it was assumed that anyone who was writing anything of value would already have read everything there was to read on the subject. Moreover, anyone who was going to read a new work would also have read everything there was to read. So if a particular author quoted a bit of Plato without acknowledgement, it scarcely mattered – all the readers would recognise the quotation from Plato anyway.

With the arrival of the industrial revolution, the expansion of the world's population and the corresponding increase in highly educated people, the arrival of computer typesetting, the sudden expansion of the world-wide web, and the modern trend towards specialisation, this is no longer true. It is quite literally impossible to read everything that might be relevant on almost any subject, and you certainly cannot assume that your reader has read and will remember the particular passage you wish to cite. Accordingly you have to do two things: you have to help your reader and you have to declare your intellectual antecedents. The first of these is a matter of politeness; the second is a matter of honesty. Just as it is clearly cheating if you get someone else to write your essay for you (since the essay is being submitted, and possibly assessed, in your name), so it is a matter of cheating for you to put forward ideas on bits of text as though they are your own when they are not. This kind of cheating is called PLAGIARISM. Most universities take plagiarism very seriously: a vice-chancellor was forced to resign from an Australian university in 2002 because of accusations of plagiarism. It is not only students for whom this is important.

In this section it is not my purpose to get into definitions of plagiarism (for which see any reputable dictionary), or to discuss methods of marking references, but to provide some help on what you should be providing references for, and how to do it in awkward instances.

When should I give a reference?

The short answer is every time you are taking an idea or some words from another author (whether the other author is Chomsky or your friend at the next desk). Some instances should be obvious.

(1) Chomsky believes that this is because …
(2) Chomsky says that this only happens if …
(3) Chomsky calls this '…'
(4) As Chomsky says, '…'

In any of the cases above, we want to know where this appears in Chomsky's work, so that we know that you can justify your claim. In each of these cases, give a reference.

(5) Many scholars believe …
(6) It is a paradox often cited that …
(7) Earliest mentions of this idea seem to come from the Greeks, …

Again, in each of (5)–(7) we need to be told how you know: which scholars believe it (or alternatively, who has made the same claim before you), who cites the paradox, where have you discovered these early mentions? Provide references.

More subtly, you need references when you could have given the kind of introduction that is provided in (5)–(7) but did not. If instead of putting in a phrase such as that given in (5) or 'It is commonly believed' or 'Some suggest' or an equivalent, you simply said 'Syllables are divided into an Onset constituent and a Rhyme constituent', you still need to give references in the same way. (I have here chosen a controversial matter, to make it clear that a reference is needed. There comes a point where something is so generally accepted that no reference is needed. For example, 'Adjectives in English pre-modify nouns' would not require a reference. In general, if you can tell something by looking at the data or if you know it from your own experience it does not need a reference; if you have to check it, it needs a reference.)

How specific a reference should I give?

If you are giving an actual quotation or referring to a very specific point, you should always give a page reference. If you are not referring to any specific passage in the work in question, it is sufficient to cite the work. So we would expect things like

(8) Chomsky (1965: 3) calls these 'formatives'.

(9) Chomsky (1965) provides a statement of what later became known as the 'standard' theory of syntax.

In some instances, particularly in referring to reference works or works which have appeared in several editions (e.g. translated into several languages), it may make more sense to refer to a section or paragraph number rather than a page number. The symbol '§' can be used to mean 'section'. It is not always absolutely clear when you should give a page or section number and when you should not: individual authors or editors may prefer more or fewer page numbers. For beginners, it is recommended that a page number should be given whenever there is a reference to a specific passage, and omitted only in the general cases illustrated by (9), where the reference is to the whole book.

How do I refer?

In general, the name–date–page method of reference illustrated in (8) and (9) is used in linguistics, and will be assumed here. However, if you are using some other system of referencing, you should make sure that you give information equivalent to that which is available in the name–date–page system. You will certainly need to be able to read other referencing systems if you read works from before the middle of the last century.

Where do I put the reference?

Most commonly, it will be obvious that the date and page should come immediately after the name of the author, so that in (1) we will say 'Chomsky (1957: 32) believes that this is because …' and so on. The problem becomes more acute when the name of the author is not part of your sentence. For example, references for a sentence like (5) might be inserted immediately after the word *scholars* or at the end of the sentence. Thus we might get 'Many scholars (e.g. Smith 1935; Brown 1950; Jones 1986) believe that …' or we might get 'Many scholars believe that the morpheme is a physical reality (see e.g. Smith 1935; Brown 1950; Jones 1986)'. In such lists, authors may be listed in chronological order (as here) or in alphabetical order – be consistent! Even harder is the case where we mention the name of the author, and then provide a direct citation. For example, 'Lyons in his book published in 1968 makes on page 425 the comment that '"reference" necessarily carries with it the presupposition of "existence".' The rule is to formulate this so as to give the reference just once and all in the same place. An obvious way of doing this is to say 'Lyons (1968: 425) comments that " 'reference' necessarily carries with it the presupposition of 'existence'".' An alternative might be to say that 'It must be recalled that "'reference' necessarily carries with it the presupposition of 'existence'" (Lyons 1968: 425).' Do not split the page reference from the name and date reference if you can possibly avoid it.

How do I refer to a work I have not seen?

Presumably, if you have not seen the work, but wish to refer to it, it is because you have seen a reference to it in another source. Let us therefore distinguish between your SOURCE, and the WORK REFERRED TO. Let us further assume that the source is a work published by Robinson in 2000, and that the work referred to is an article published by Smithers in 1991.

In your text, you should say

> Smithers (1991; cited in Robinson 2000: 25)

or, more generally

> *Work referred to* (year(: page); cited in *Source* year: page)

with the usual use of page references. If you have a page reference for the source (which you will, of course, get from Robinson (2000)), you should give that as necessary. There is a certain amount of variation in wording here: *cited in* may be *cited from*, for example, or just *in*.

In your reference list you should give full details of BOTH your source AND the work referred to.

This 'cited in' format should be used ONLY if you have not seen the work to which you are referring. If you have seen it, you should use the normal citation conventions. Since you should try to check out the original if it is important for your work, the cited-in format should be used sparingly.

What if I have two people with the same name?

You may often have references to two people with the same family name. Where this is the case, the two people will normally be distinguishable by their initials. If you never refer to works by these two people published in the same year, in principle the name–and–date in-text reference is sufficient, but you may feel that it is unhelpful. In that case, you may use the initial as well as the family name in the in-text reference. There are two ways to work this: the first is to use the initial only for the person who is cited least often, and where family name alone may thus be misleading (perhaps only for C. Chomsky and not for N. Chomsky); the second is to use initials for both (e.g. both J. Milroy and L. Milroy). You will then get an in-text reference such as: 'see L. Milroy (1987); J. Milroy (1992: 85)'.

How do I refer to something which is in another person's book?

The general rule for citations is that you are citing the AUTHOR of the work. If you are referring to a work written by Joseph Greenberg but which appears in a volume which has the names of Elizabeth Closs Traugott and Bernd Heine on the cover, you refer to it as 'Greenberg (1991)' (the date comes from the instance of this I know of). Your reference list will make it clear that the paper by Greenberg appeared in a volume edited by Traugott and Heine. But they did not write the material themselves, and so you do not refer to that paper under their names. This principle also applies to things like entries in encyclopedias if it is possible to discover the author of the individual entry: you should refer by the name of the person who wrote the entry, not the name of the person in charge of the encyclopedia.

How do I refer to unpublished work?

There are a number of types of unpublished work which you might want to refer to. These include assignments (either your own, or those of fellow students), theses, conference papers, works due for publication, websites, lectures, discussions with other people from whom you are taking major ideas. Let us deal with each of these in turn.

You can refer to your own and others' assignments as you would refer to any published piece of work. But instead of a place of publication, you should say 'Assignment for [Course identifier] at [Institution name]'. So we might get a reference such as the following:

> Jones, Susan (2002). 'How American is New Zealand English?' Assignment for LING 322 'New Zealand English' at Victoria University of Wellington.

Theses and dissertations are referred to in precisely the same way. They are usually treated as articles rather than as books (which is unexpected, but not crucial), and specifically cited as being 'unpublished'. (If they are subsequently published, it is better to refer to the published version if possible, on the grounds that it will be more easily available for an international audience.) The nomenclature ('thesis' versus 'dissertation' etc.) should ideally follow that used in the relevant institution, but if you have to guess, use 'thesis' for British, Australian and New Zealand and 'dissertation' for American works. We thus get references such as the following:

> Matthewson, Lisa (1991). 'An application of Autosegmental Morphology to some nonconcatenative phenomena in Germanic languages.' Unpublished MA thesis, Victoria University of Wellington.

Conference papers require the title of the paper and the name, date and place of the conference involved. You should refer to a conference presentation only if you do not have a subsequently published version of the paper to refer to. We find references such as:

> Bauer, Laurie (2000). 'What you can do with derivational morphology.' Paper presented at the IXth International Morphology Meeting, Vienna, 24–8 February.

Work which is not yet published goes through a number of stages on the way to publication. First, the work goes through a number of drafts and revisions, some of which may encompass only a part of the final work. At this stage the work may be said to be 'in preparation' (or 'in prep.' for short). Then a full draft form is produced for submission to a publisher. While you will occasionally see bibliographical references to work which is in draft form or which has been submitted, it is better to call this still 'in preparation'. Typically, a publisher will accept something for publication, subject to certain amendments being made. At this stage there is a commitment to publish the material, and it can be termed 'to appear', or 'forthcoming'. Finally, the final version is submitted to the publishers, who begin the (often lengthy) process of editing and setting the material, prior to publication. At this stage it can be said to be 'in press' (sometimes abbreviated to 'i.p.'), or 'forthcoming' may be retained. With 'forthcoming', 'to appear' and 'in press' it should be possible to give some bibliographic references, since the publisher is known, though it will often not be possible to be specific. Some writers prefer not to use 'in preparation' and instead simply say 'unpublished paper' or 'prepublication draft'. Some authors prefer not to have their work cited at this provisional stage, and may mark their drafts 'do not cite without permission'. You should, of course, adhere to any such requests.

You should cite websites you use as sources just as you would cite books or papers. The difficulty with websites is that they may change without warning. Thus you should always give not only the URL, but also the date on which you accessed the material. Thus we get references like the following:

> Quinion, Michael (1997). People versus persons. When should we use which? http://www.worldwidewords.org/articles/people.htm (created 19 July 1997; accessed 14 November 2002).

Lectures can be referred to in the same way as course papers, making sure that the date and the relevant course are provided. Thus we might have a reference such as

> Bauer, Laurie (2002). 'Consonantal phenomena'. Lecture to LING
> 322 'New Zealand English', Victoria University of Wellington, 9
> September.

Material derived from private discussions with individuals (whether these take place in face-to-face interaction, by email or by letter) are generally termed 'personal communications'. 'Personal communication' is often abbreviated to 'pers. comm.' or 'p.c.'. Typically, there will be nothing to put in a reference list, and '(personal communication)' in the text is sufficient; occasionally you may want to refer to a letter of a particular date, in which case you can put that information in the list of references.

How do I refer to work by more than one person?

Assuming that you are using a name, year and page system of referencing, then you will be familiar with the format of 'Bauer (1988: 16)', where *Bauer* is the family name of the author. This is the format used for referring to a work which has a single author.

When a work has TWO authors, you must mention both of them. Thus we find 'Chomsky & Halle (1968)', 'Fromkin & Rodman (1974)' and so on. Some publishers replace the ampersand (&) by the word 'and', others prefer the ampersand since it is space-saving, and can allow disambiguation in cases like 'Work by Chomsky & Halle and Fromkin & Rodman suggests ...'.

When a work has more than two authors, they should all be listed in the references. Some publishers insist that they should all be named on the first mention in any given work, as well, though nowadays this is not the norm. Certainly after the first mention, the work should be referred to by the name of the first author with 'et al.' added afterwards. Thus a reference to the textbook written by Andrew Radford, Martin Atkinson, David Britain, Harald Clahsen and Andrew Spencer would normally be in the form 'Radford et al. (1999)'. Note there is no full stop/period after the *et*, since this is a complete Latin word.

How do I refer to something which occurs in a footnote?

If you are citing material which appears in a footnote in the original, you say so in your reference. Thus you might write:

> the term 'lexicalised' appears to be widely accepted in this sense (see
> Bauer 1983: 48 note 4).

If there is only one footnote on the relevant page, you might not need to cite the number of the note, and it may be possible to write *fn* (for 'footnote') rather than *note*. If the material is in an endnote which appears on a page where there are only endnotes, it may be sufficient to cite the page number, though it is more helpful to cite the note number. In such a case, of course, the term 'footnote' is inappropriate.

What do all these abbreviations mean?

Particularly in works which do not use the name, year, page system of giving references, you will often find a number of abbreviations used in references which may be unfamiliar (table 34.1). Although you will not need to use most of these, you need to understand them if you meet them in the works of others. There are not very many of them. Like the other foreign expressions listed in section 22, these may or may not be italicised.

Something which is not strictly a bibliographical convention is the use of *sic* in quotations (*sic* is usually pronounced [sɪk], although [siːk] is an alternative rather closer to the Latin). *Sic* is Latin for 'thus', and means that even though it may look wrong, this is really what was said in the original. Although it is possible to use '*sic*' to draw attention to minor matters such as spelling mistakes, this is rather rude, and should be restricted to instances where the original has been complaining about people who make spelling mistakes. A preferable convention is to correct the spelling mistake, putting the corrected word in square brackets: 'Jones (1999: 25) says that his "[accommodation] was better than expected in such a poor area".' The square brackets can also be used to change the person in a quotation, to change capitalisation to fit in with your own conventions, and so on: 'Jones (1999: 25) complains about this. "[I]n some cities [he] was unable to get a decent cup of coffee anywhere."' The general rule is that where it is blindingly obvious what the author meant, you can correct it using square brackets. Where it is important for your point that the author wrote something which is probably not correct, then you can use *sic*. So you might say, for example: 'Smith (2000: 25) talks about "morphemes [sic] which are in complementary distribution", although by his own definitions these should presumably be morphs.'

Is all the fuss worthwhile?

This question can be answered in respect to short-term advantages or to long-term ones. Short-term, yes it is all worthwhile, because if you don't do it you will end up losing marks or failing courses.

But is that just to allow your teachers to feel superior to you and keep you under control or is there some more fundamental principle involved? As I said above, the two main principles are politeness and honesty: politeness to your reader, but also to those from whom you have derived ideas; honesty to your

Table 34.1 Abbreviations in references

Abbreviation	Full form	Meaning	Comment
et al.	*et alii* (masculine or mixed gender)/*et aliae* (feminine)	'and others'	Used to indicate multiple authorship
ib., ibid.	*ibidem*	'in the same place'	May either mean 'in the same work' – in which case a page number may be given – or 'at the same place in the work mentioned'; frequently used to mean 'in the last work you were referred to'; used only if a single work is given in the last reference
id.	*idem*	'the same'	Means the same person; used to replace the author's name in successive references
loc. cit.	*loco citato*	'in the place cited'	Means on the same page as the last reference
op. cit.	*opere citato*	'in the work cited'	Requires an author's name and a page number; refers to the most recently cited work by this author
s.v.	*sub verbo*	'under the word'	Really useful for citing dictionaries and glossaries where the information is best located by the headword rather than by the page number; for example, you can find references to a nun's hen in *The Oxford English Dictionary* s.v. *nice*

marker (in the short term) or your peers (in the longer term) who want to be able to trace the development of ideas. For an entertaining but sobering perspective on what happens when it all goes wrong, read Pullum (1991), which makes the point that even fully fledged linguists are often not careful enough with their referencing, and that this can lead to gross misinformation. Proper referencing should allow gross misinformation to be avoided.

Reference

Pullum, Geoffrey K. (1991). The great Eskimo vocabulary hoax. In Geoffrey K. Pullum, *The Great Eskimo Vocabulary Hoax and Other Irreverent Essays on the Study of Language*. Chicago and London: Chicago University Press, 159–71.

35

Reference lists

Reference lists versus bibliographies

The general practice in linguistics is to list at the end of any work the books and articles that have been referred to in it. This means that something is listed at the end if and only if there is a reference in the text to that work (i.e. the work is specifically mentioned in the text). To make it clear that the list is restricted in this way, it is usually entitled 'References', although alternatives such as 'Works cited' would be possible. The label 'Bibliography' is also used in the same way by some, but it is potentially misleading, since it can also mean 'Bibliography of works consulted'. Such a list would include everything the author had read in order to write what has been written, whether those items have been cited or not. In most cases, you will probably find that you are encouraged to provide a reference list; if you are not, it is helpful to distinguish between 'References' and 'Bibliography of works consulted' just to be absolutely unambiguous. This means you should avoid a heading 'Bibliography' without any further elaboration.

Subdividing the reference list

It is sometimes useful to subdivide your reference list into two or more subsections. You should do this only if there will be a reasonable number of works in each subsection.

One type of division that is likely to be useful in writing about historical linguistics or about points of grammar is that between texts and general works. Texts are those works which are used as sources of data; general works are those which you used to help with the theoretical background or the analysis. Texts may include published editions of texts, manuscripts, novels and other literary works, articles from newspapers, or large-scale computer corpora. Where there are a lot of references to texts, some authors use different referencing systems for texts and for general works, using the author and date system only for general works. Texts are sometimes called primary sources or primary literature, with general works then being referred to as secondary.

Another division which can be useful on occasions is a distinction between dictionaries (or lexica) and general works. Most dictionaries are referred to by their titles rather than by the names of their authors or editors, so this allows two distinct ways of entering references in a reference list by the most useful piece of information. Thus it would be more usual to refer to *The Canadian Oxford Dictionary* (or even to *CanOD*) than to Barber (1998); even though either is possible. The name and date system works in favour of the latter method; separating dictionaries from other works lets you list the dictionary by its title (or handy abbreviation).

The core of a reference

There are certain vital pieces of information that you must give when giving a reference: the name of the author, the year of publication, the title of the book, the place of publication, the title of the item in the book if the whole book is not relevant, and so on. In this section we will consider each of these pieces of information in turn, pointing out traps and potential difficulties.

Name

Reference lists are presented in alphabetical order of the family name of authors. Editors are included under 'authors' in this. The family name of authors may take a little thought, especially with authors from other language backgrounds. Not all people habitually present their names in the order given name + family name, and it is not always clear whether English-language publications retain the preferred order of the author or impose their own default order on the name. You may need to check if you are in doubt.

European names with *de, van, von* etc. also cause problems. While these may be alphabetised according to one set of principles in French, German or Dutch, that same set of principles is not always carried forward to English. So while Van Valin would be alphabetised as *Valin, Robert van* in Dutch, in English he is more likely to be called *Van Valin, Robert*. For all these particles, the native use is to put them at the end of the name. In Dutch, *van* is capitalised if it is the first part of the name to occur, and has a lower case *v* if it is immediately preceded by the given name (thus *Jaap van Marle*, but *Van Marle*). Probably the best solution here is to alphabetise such names as the authors themselves do.

Alphabetical order may not be obvious. For example, the relative order of the names *Smith-Fenwick* and *Smithers* may be in doubt. However, this problem is not restricted to alphabetising proper names, and need not delay us here. More serious is that jointly authored works should be listed after works written by the first author alone. So Chomsky & Halle (1968) will be listed after Chomsky (1972). This may seem fairly obvious, but word-processors will impose just the opposite ordering if left to themselves, and so care has to be taken.

Because authors are listed in order of their family names, the first author's name is usually given in the format '[Family name], [Given name]'. If there are second or subsequent authors, there is variation in the way in which their names are dealt with: either they can be ordered in the same way as the first author's name, or they can be ordered in the 'natural' order (the order you would use them if you were introducing yourself, for example). The latter requires less punctuation, which makes it the simpler version to use. Whichever you choose (or whichever is chosen for you by your publisher), be consistent!

Where papers from edited works are cited, there is the problem of citing the name or the names of the editor(s) as well as the names of the author(s). If the paper is cited as 'Bloggs, Joe (2000) 'Words'. In . . . ' there is nothing to prevent you using the natural order for the editor's (or editors') name(s). Nevertheless, some publishers prefer the same ordering as for authors' names, so take care to be consistent.

In a case like that just cited, if you are referring to several works from the same edited volume it may be more economical to give the edited volume its own entry in the reference list to which you can cross-refer. The alternative is to give full details of edited works every time they are mentioned. Thus the options are as in (1) or as in (2) (note the use of 'et al.' in the first reference in (2)).

(1) Bauer, Laurie (2002). 'What you can do with derivational morphology'. In S. Bendjaballah, W. U. Dressler, O. E. Pfeiffer & M. D. Voiekova (eds), *Morphology 2000*. Amsterdam and Philadelphia: Benjamins, 37–48.

(2) Bauer, Laurie (2002). 'What you can do with derivational morphology'. In Bendjaballah et al., 37–48.
Bendjaballah, S., W. U. Dressler, O. E. Pfeiffer & M. D. Voiekova (eds) (2002). *Morphology 2000*. Amsterdam and Philadelphia: Benjamins.

The listing in (2) brings up the question of whether to spell out given names or whether to give initials. Some publishers demand one or the other. The obvious answer is to use what the author (or editor) uses, since this is clearly what they prefer. Occasionally this may involve problems where a particular author usually uses one form of the name but is forced to use another for editorial (or other) reasons. For example, if we go by what is on the cover, we would give the references in (3):

(3) Matthews, P. H. (1993). *Grammatical theory in the United States from Bloomfield to Chomsky*. Cambridge: Cambridge University Press. Matthews, Peter (2001). *A Short History of Structural Linguistics*. Cambridge: Cambridge University Press.

The two are written by the same person. Such discrepancies are not unusual; the problem is how to deal with them. The simplest answer is to leave them alone. But it is possible to spell things out a little, using the notation in (4):

(4) Matthews, P[eter] H. (1993). *Grammatical theory in the United States from Bloomfield to Chomsky*. Cambridge: Cambridge University Press.

The main difficulty with (4) is that it may not be possible to carry it through consistently, since you may not know or be able to discover the given names of all the relevant people (in the case of the edited volume listed in (2), for instance, I know the given names of only two of the four editors). This leads to even less consistency in presentation.

An alternative is to use initials for everyone, and many publishers prefer this. It is certainly simpler to apply consistently. Some feminists argue that it gives less visibility to women writers because people tend to assume that authors are male, but it could also be argued to be treating women and men equally by masking everyone's gender. Less controversially, full given names may allow someone trying to locate the work to distinguish between various J. Smiths in a library catalogue or bibliographic database, and this can be helpful.

Occasionally, especially with reference works, there may be no author or editor mentioned. One possible solution here is to use 'anon.' (meaning 'anonymous'), but that is usually restricted to cases where a single, unknown author is involved. The alternative is to list such works by their titles, rather than by their authors, even though it goes against the general pattern of the references used.

Publication date

In principle, the date that you want to give for a work is the date of publication of the edition you have consulted. In the case of periodical articles, this is seldom a problem, since the journal will be clearly marked with a year. However, in some cases the year of publication may not match the ostensible year to which the periodical belongs, and it is then the year of publication which should be given. Thus the *Yearbook of Morphology 1995* was actually published in 1996, and should be cited as 1996.

Books are not quite as straightforward. The date of publication will normally be found on the reverse of the title page, at least in books published recently in English. Where a book has been published in several editions, there are two competing conventions. One is that the dates of each of the editions will be listed, in which case you should cite the last new edition. The other is that dates will be given such as '1978; 1974'. This means that the current edition was published in 1978, based on an earlier 1974 edition.

If it is important — for example, to illustrate the order in which ideas were put forward — you can indicate the date of the first edition of a work as well as the date of the edition being cited. This is done as follows:

(5) Fromkin, Victoria A. & Robert Rodman (1978 [1974]). *An Introduction to Language*. Second edition. New York, etc.: Holt, Rinehart and Winston.

The first date represents the date of the edition whose page numbers you will cite in in-text references; the date in square brackets is the original date of publication. Sometimes scholars put both dates in the in-text references, using the same notation as in (5). Note the addition of the comment 'Second edition', which may be abbreviated, e.g. as '2nd edn.'. This type of reference may be especially important in citing works which have a very long publication history, such as Saussure's *Cours de Linguistique Générale* or Paul's *Prinzipien der Sprachgeschichte*. It may also be used when you are citing a paper by a particular author which has been collected in a series of papers. While you need the edition you are citing for page references, you may also want to note the original date of publication. So Twaddell's paper on defining the phoneme from 1935, reprinted in Joos's 1957 collection *Readings in Linguistics*, might be listed as Twaddell (1957 [1935]).

It is important to note that it is the date of the publication which is required, not the date of the printing. This may be of particular importance in two situations. The first is where a distinction is made between, for example, the second edition and the third impression. It is the date for the edition which is needed; 'impression' just means it has been reprinted. The second arises more often with books published in non-English-speaking countries, where you may find, sometimes on the last page of the book, something saying 'Printing completed on' and then a date. While that date of printing may match the year of publication, it cannot be assumed that it does. If you are in doubt about the year of publication, but have hints such as these, you may prefer to mark the year of publication as 'c. 1936', though your in-text reference would probably still be '1936'.

If you are using a name-and-date system of referencing and you find two or more works by the same author(s) published in the same year, you should distinguish them by lower case 'a', 'b', etc. following the year. You will then refer to these works in text as, for example, 'Smith (2000a)' or 'Jones (1999b)'. You can still use this system if the works have not been published but are 'forthcoming' or 'in press' or any other similar annotation: 'Smith (forthcoming c)'. If the two works you are citing in this way are clearly ordered, it might be preferable to order the 'a' and 'b' to reflect the order in which they were written; the norm, however, is simply to use the order in which you want to refer to them or to use alphabetical ordering of the titles to determine the order of presentation.

If all else fails and you really cannot find a date, you can mark it as 'n.d.', short for 'no date'.

Title

Deciding what the title of a particular piece is should provide no great problem. Two things might, though: how to punctuate the title, and how much of the title to report.

The punctuation of titles is largely a matter of where capital letters should be used in them. Where titles in English are concerned there are two competing conventions. The first is to capitalise all content words and the longer prepositions; the second is to capitalise only those words which require a capital letter for independent reasons. The two references in (3) illustrate these two conventions (each copied faithfully from the cover of the relevant book). Despite the accuracy of doing what is done in the original, most publishers will insist on your following one convention or the other. Where other languages are concerned, you should follow the principles of capitalisation used for the relevant language, e.g. capitalising all nouns in German.

How much of the title you should report is a matter of subtitles. Many books have subtitles, some of them relatively brief, some of them very unwieldy. Some examples are given in (6).

(6) *Phonology: theory and analysis*
Phonology: an introduction to basic concepts
Phonology: theory and description
Morphology: a study of the relation between meaning and form
Morphology: an introduction to the theory of word-structure
Morphological Mechanisms: lexicalist analysis of synthetic compounding
Theoretical Morphology: approaches in modern linguistics
Inflectional Morphology: a theory of paradigm structure

There are three things you can do with subtitles like these.

1. ignore them completely;
2. include them, but use the minimum number of capital letters in them;
3. include them all, capitalising just as you did in the main title.

Subtitles may be useful in some instances (for example, in distinguishing between the various books called *Phonology* or *Morphology*). Mainly they are intended as some kind of clarification of the approach or content for the reader, and the main title alone will be sufficient for identification.

If you are listing titles in alphabetical order, e.g. when giving lists of dictionaries, you should omit the words *a, an, the* from the bit you alphabetise: '*Oxford English Dictionary, The* . . .'.

Very occasionally, you may find some item which has been given no title. Such an item may be listed as 'Untitled'.

Place of publication

The place of publication should always be a city, never a country or a state or a province or a county. Publishers, who once inhabited the larger cities, have in recent times been fleeing to the country for cheaper accommodation, with the result that some quite small places may be the seat of some major publishers. Nevertheless, that is the place that should be cited.

You must take care to cite the place of publication and not the place of printing. The publishers are the people who take the financial risk of issuing the book, arrange for its distribution and lend it their imprint as a quality mark; the printers contract to put the text on paper. In these days of globalisation, a work published in London may be printed in Hong Kong, so it is important to get the right place. Printers very often put their address on works they print as well as the publisher's name, so confusion can arise.

Where a publisher has branches in two cities (usually, but not always, in different countries) you should cite both cities: Chicago and London, Berlin and New York, Amsterdam and Philadelphia. Where the publisher has branches in more than two cities, you have a choice:

1. cite all of them; this is rare;
2. cite the first and then put 'etc.' as in (5); this is becoming less frequent;
3. cite only the first city; this is becoming the most usual solution.

As with so many of these things, publishers may take a decision for you, but left to yourself, you should be consistent with whichever solution you adopt.

'Cambridge' will be understood as being 'Cambridge, England', so that you will need to specify 'Cambridge, Mass.' or 'Cambridge, MA' for MIT Press or Harvard University Press. The system of specifying states for American cities is sometimes generalised, even when there is no ambiguity, though it is rarely applied to the largest cities such as Chicago, Los Angeles or New York.

If your city of publication is one which has different names in different languages (e.g. *Munich* and *München*; *Venice, Venise, Venedig* and *Venezia*), use consistently either the version of the name that corresponds to the language in which the book is published or the version which is used in the book itself.

Very occasionally you will not be able to find a place of publication, especially in old books. On these occasions you can use the notion 'n.p.', standing for 'no place (given)'.

Publisher

We can roughly divide publishers into three groups: the big international conglomerates, the university presses, and the small firms, sometimes still run by an individual. Of course, the division is sometimes more apparent than real: the Edward Arnold imprint is now owned by one of the big conglomerates. The distinction may nevertheless be helpful.

For the big firms, you need to give the name of the firm, but without any 'Inc.', 'Ltd.', '& Co.' or similar notation. So you write 'Harcourt Brace Jovanovich' not 'Harcourt Brace Jovanovich, Inc.', even if the 'Inc.' is there in the book. Note that the spelling and punctuation used by the firm is followed: this particular publisher uses no commas, and so you should not do so either.

For university presses, you should always give the full title of the press as mentioned in the book: very often the university press is a different commercial body from the university to which it is nominally attached, and so should not be confused with the university itself (although it takes part of its prestige from the university it serves).

The smaller firms often have or had the name of the (original) owner of the firm: Basil Blackwell, Edward Arnold, Gunter Narr, John Benjamins. Again you should omit any mention of commercial status. You may use both the names as the name of the publisher or you may use the family name alone, the latter being more common.

Where you are faced with a publisher's name in a foreign language which you do not understand, you may simply have to copy out the whole thing, though in principle the same rules apply.

Where things are less formally published it may be difficult to ascertain the publisher. For instance, it may be the university department which issued the volume or the society (for example, the International Phonetic Association or the Philological Society) for whom the book was printed.

Title of the journal article or chapter in a book

In most cases this should give no problems. For newspaper articles use the headline as the title. If something does not have a title at all, it may be listed as 'Untitled'.

Periodical title

On the whole this is a simple matter of copying from the volume in front of you. There are a few potential snares, though.

The first is if there are two journals with very similar titles which you need to distinguish. The main example of this in linguistics is *Acta Linguistica*, which may be *Acta Linguistica Hafniensia* or *Acta Linguistica Hungarica*. If there is doubt, put the city of publication in parentheses after the title: '*Acta Linguistica* (Copenhagen)'.

The second point is that some writers abbreviate journal titles. There are standard sets of abbreviations of journal titles which you should use if you are going to do this (see e.g. Alkire 2001). It is good practice to spell out all journal titles for ease of recognition by your reader, but some abbreviations such as *JL, Lang., EWW* are common and easily interpretable. In a thesis, give a list of any abbreviations you do use at the head of the reference list.

Finally, there are so many newspapers called things like *Daily News* or *Chronicle* that you will almost certainly have to specify the town or city that such a paper comes from (and, if it is American, which state that city is in), even if that information is not strictly part of the newspaper's title. '*Omak (Washington) Chronicle*' has simply *The Chronicle* as its title.

Periodical volume number

The point here is to identify unambiguously the bit of the periodical a reader should take down from the shelf to find the article you are referring to. Different periodicals label themselves in different ways. We will look at three possibilities.

The most common pattern is for a periodical to have a numbered volume every year, frequently with several parts (or numbers) going together to make up that volume. If this is the case you may cite the part for extra clarity, but it is not necessary as long as the whole volume is paginated right through (so that part 2 of volume 45 starts on page 156 rather than on page 1). If the numbering restarts for every part, you MUST give the part number as well. There are various notations for this: '24/3', '24, 3' or '24(3)' meaning 'part 3 of volume 24'. Some people cite the part number in every reference in order to be more explicit and in case a particular library has not bound the parts together.

The next most likely pattern is that each bound fascicule is given its own number (sometimes called things like 'Number 134'). These numbers may be assigned to a date (e.g. October, 2001; Spring, 2002; 26 October–1 November 2002). You should always give the number, and usually give the date as well if there is one. Put the date in parentheses.

Lastly, you may find something which has no volume number or part number, but just a date. This is typically true of newspapers, for example. Here you should give the date.

If you meet any other exceptional circumstances, give enough information for your reader to be able to identify the correct bound item.

Page numbers

Page numbers are usually self-explanatory. If you are citing a newspaper you may have to give the section as well as the page (e.g. 'C45') and, particularly in older newspapers, you may have to give the column number (e.g. 'col. 4'). If there are no page numbers, then you can write 'Unpaginated'.

When you are citing an extended discussion from someone's work, the usual thing is to give the beginning page and the final page of the discussion: 'Smith (2000: 94–105)', for example. You will sometimes see the notation 'Smith (2000: 94f)' or 'Smith (2000: 94ff)', where 'f' stands for 'following (page)' and 'ff' means 'following (pages)'. The first of these is equivalent to 'Smith (2000: 94–5)'. The second is inexplicit, since it does not say how many following pages the discussion is spread over (just that it is more than one), and should be avoided unless the discussion has an unclear ending point. While you will need to recognise this notation, you should use it extremely sparingly.

In brief

The idea with a reference is to make it easy for a reader who wants to look at a work you cite to find that work in a good library. The information you provide should be sufficient for anyone to do this (or to ask to interloan the item if it is not in their library). So you should always try to give enough information for it to be totally unambiguous where the work is to be found. You should also do this in a consistent manner, giving similar information for similar types of work, so that your reader knows what to expect. For more detail on any of the topics covered here, see *The Chicago Manual of Style*.

References

Alkire, Leland G. (ed.) (2001). *Periodical Title Abbreviations*. 13th edn. Detroit, etc.: Gale.

Chicago Manual of Style, The (1993 [1906]). 14th edn. Chicago and London: University of Chicago Press.

Part VI: Language file

Language file

In this last part of the book, details are given of some 280 languages. Given that there are somewhere between 5,000 and 7,000 languages in the world, this is clearly a very small sample, and the chances of finding a language which is not on the list are considerably higher than those of finding a language which is treated. However, the sample here is not a random one (and this may have implications for the uses to which the list can put) but a sample of opportunity, which means that well-described languages and major languages stand a far better chance of figuring here than poorly-described languages and minor languages. Nevertheless, some extinct or near-extinct languages are listed, especially where these are isolates or otherwise of linguistic interest.

Warnings

Although every effort has been made to ensure that the information provided here is as accurate as possible, there are inevitably a large number of gaps and inaccuracies. Not only is it incredibly easy to misunderstand a description (for instance, to read an unusual construction as being a typical one), but much of the material here is provided at second or third hand, which magnifies the possibility of error. In some cases, sources may even disagree quite radically. Where number of speakers is concerned, this is normal, figures fluctuating according to the latest census figures or the latest estimates in the *Ethnologue* (Grimes 1988). Often these figures show a disheartening drop in the numbers of speakers still using minority languages, as more and more languages head for language death. It is perhaps less expected when it is a matter of structural factors, yet sources can still disagree, and the outcome here is simply a matter of guesswork. For example, Maddieson (1984) states that Haida has three vowels, while Mithun (1999) states that it has six. This does not appear to be a matter of how to analyse long vowels, though it might well be a matter of dialect. The outsider cannot judge.

Consequently, although the information provided here can be used to give readers some idea of the languages mentioned, where any particular piece of information becomes crucial in the testing of some hypothesis it is suggested that it should be thoroughly rechecked.

Interpreting the data provided

Data was collected by checking descriptions of the various languages against a short questionnaire. Since it was not always possible to find descriptions which answered all the questions on the questionnaire, there are inevitably gaps in the data. Accordingly a blank may mean that no information was found on this topic. In such a case, it may simply be because the source did not say anything (or the reader failed to find or interpret it), or it may mean that there is nothing to say. For example, in some, but not all, tone languages, the category of word stress is simply irrelevant, so it may be appropriate that no information is provided.

Language name

The language name provided in **bold** type is usually the one which was used in the description from which the data is taken. Occasionally alternative spellings are given where these are current, but this has not been done systematically. This row also gives current alternative names for the language, and a guide to pronunciation of the first name given.

Alternative language name

Where a language has several apparently very different names used in English, alternatives are provided and cross-references have been added. Again, this has not been done systematically (as a glance at Grimes 1988 will show), but major alternatives have been listed. Sometimes this involves taking political decisions. Croatian and Serbian, for example, have been given different listings, as have Hindi and Urdu. In other cases, the political decisions may not even have been ones of which we were aware: no offence is intended by any such decisions.

Pronunciation of the language name

The pronunciation of the language name is the way the name is likely to be pronounced by English speakers rather than a reflection of the native pronunciation of the name. Thus, for example, no attempt has been made to transcribe the initial aspirated lateral click in the name of the language Xhosa. Where this field has been left blank, no information was discovered, and while the pronunciation may or may not be perfectly transparent from the orthography it seemed safer to err on the side of caution. Occasionally alternative pronunciations have been offered, though there are rather more alternatives differing only in stress than have been listed.

Autonym

In many cases the language is known by the name the speakers of the language themselves use, but in other instances the English name may derive from a name originally given by a third party. It is often very difficult to find reliable information about autonyms, and this space is accordingly left blank far more often than would be desirable. In many cases where it is filled in, a phonetic rendition is provided rather than an orthographic one (sometimes for obvious reasons, sometimes because that was what was available in sources).

Language family

Language families are remarkably controversial. Not only is it often in doubt what is related to what, the precise membership of several sub-branches of the major families is also often in doubt. In principle, an attempt was made to provide a two-term guide to language families, corresponding to names such as Indo-European and Germanic for English. In practice this is difficult because sources written at different periods will reflect the scholarship of their time and may use different labels for the same families, and because it is often difficult to judge what the most useful family label is likely to be. Although some attempt has been made to standardise some of the nomenclature, there may still be inconsistencies (or even errors seen from the position of recent scholarship).

Place spoken

The place or places where the language is spoken is or are usually given in terms of country names, but sometimes with the names of states or provinces (in which case the country is given in parenthesis after the name of the state or province). Pockets of migrants who carry their language to a new country have usually been ignored.

Number of speakers

As was noted above, the number of speakers of any language is changing rapidly, and the numbers given in different sources often diverge by 100 per cent or more. Thus these figures should be taken as no more than a guide to whether a language is likely to be extremely stable or very threatened.

Writing system

Very often the writing system used for a particular language is more a matter of the colonial power than anything linguistic, and in many cases writing systems change either from country to country or as the colonial powers change or for religious reasons. A blank here often means that the language is not written a great deal at all, but may well be a matter of the information not having been readily available.

Stress

In many languages, particularly in tone languages, stress is not a relevant concept, and often this section is correspondingly left blank for that reason. Where stress falls in a relatively regular position in the word, this is noted. Where the position of stress is known to be dependent on vowel length or syllable weight this is also noted. In such cases it is not usually stated whether stress falls on a heavy/long syllable near the beginning or near the end of the word.

Rare consonants

Consonants which were included as rare types were retroflex, uvular and pharyngeal consonants and clicks, ejectives and implosives. Any consonant type not having an IPA symbol was noted. No distinction is made between a language which has a single retroflex consonant (for example) and one which has a whole series of retroflex consonants.

Number of vowels

The number of vowels a language has is, of course, a matter of analysis rather than something which is an automatic given. Where there were five vowel qualities but ten contrastive vowel elements because the second five were distinguished by length or nasalisation, this is noted as '5 + length' or '5 + nasalisation' rather than as '10'. Where the long or nasalised vowels are not as numerous as the basic vowel qualities, the number is provided in parentheses. Diphthongs are noted separately. It should be noted that it is frequently difficult to tell from descriptions whether a diphthong or a vowel sequence is intended, and usually the terminology of the source has been respected.

Marked vowel types

Marked vowel types were front rounded vowels and back non-low unrounded vowels. Central vowels were not listed where it was stated that they were central.

Tone

Different sources give different amounts of information about tone, using different terminologies. The distinction used here is basically that between register tone languages and contour tone languages, with tonal accent languages noted as a third option. 'None' is a default marking here.

Rhythm

Very few sources give information on rhythm type, partly because the whole area is extremely controversial. However, some sources do distinguish between stress-timed, syllable-timed and mora-timed languages, and the information has been added where available. The default here is 'No information'.

Vowel harmony

It is not always clear from descriptions exactly what is involved in vowel harmonic patterns, some of which are in any case much more pervasive than others. Any relevant information has been included, though occasionally this is no more than that there is some vowel harmony operating.

Morphology

Four possible morphological types are marked: isolating, agglutinative, fusional and polysynthetic (or, of course, some combination of these). Since a polysynthetic language may be agglutinative or fusional, the label 'polysynthetic' may not be maximally clear. In addition, an attempt has been made to note whether the morphology is word-based or stem-based (Bloomfield 1935); that is, whether there is a form of the word which has no affixes attached to it, or whether every noun or verb must have at least one affix (e.g. the case/number suffix on Latin nouns). This was often one of the hardest questions to answer, not only because the answer is sometimes different for nouns and verbs, but also because it is often not clear that an affixless form of some word exists at some point in the paradigm where it is not the citation form.

Formation types

This gives information on which languages use prefixes, suffixes, etc. Following Bauer (1988), a SYNAFFIX is any affix made up of two or more formal elements which must all co-occur to give a particular meaning. A circumfix is thus a type of synaffix. Apophony (ablaut) was added late as a category, and may not be reported in every relevant language. Categories in parentheses are rare.

Word order

Word order is divided into three parts: the order of major sentence elements, the ordering within a noun phrase, and whether prepositions or postpositions are used. The first is given in terms of the ordering of S[ubject] V[erb] and O[bject], with alternatives being V2 (verb second, common in Germanic languages), Free or Focus-based where the word order is not determined by these grammatical categories. Where the word order is completely free, even the word order with a noun phrase may not be fixed, but the unmarked order of noun and adjective (NA or AN) (sometimes other modifiers, especially in languages which do not have adjectives) and the unmarked order of possessor and possessed noun are also given where possible. The possessor–noun ordering (poss N or N poss) is based on what happens when the possessor is a full noun or a proper noun, not when it is a pronoun. Often these orders had to be deduced from example sentences or texts. In many cases it is ambiguous whether a language has postpositions or case suffixes, and although we have largely followed the sources, there may be some inconsistencies here. Parenthesised values are rare.

Syntactic phenomena

It was difficult to know what phenomena to look for in this category, but a list was provided for research assistants which included absolutive/ergative marking (not necessarily inflectional), classifiers, genders, inclusive/exclusive 1st person plural marking, inflecting adpositions, inflectional aspect, nominative/accusative marking, noun classes, peculiarities in the number system, peculiarities in the person system, verb conjugations and a vague 'other points of interest'. Of these, the distinction (if it is a real one) between gender and noun classes was hard to uphold, peculiarities in the persons system were rarely commented on, and verb conjugations were sometimes confused with verb classes. Alienable/inalienable possession was added late, and is probably not consistently noted, as were serial verbs, often hard to find since the label itself is relatively recent.

Points of interest

This final heading was a general one under which many points could be noted, including matters of sociolinguistic interest. The points raised here are largely ones raised directly in the sources consulted as being matters of particular interest in the language concerned, but not even all such matters have been reported.

Sources

A bibliography of sources is provided at the end of the list. Grimes (1988) is not mentioned specifically as a source, but of course was consulted regularly.

References

Bloomfield, Leonard (1935). *Language*. London: George Allen & Unwin.

Grimes, Barbara F. (1988). *Ethnologue. Languages of the World*. Dallas TX: Summer Institute of Linguistics.

Maddieson, Ian (1984). *Patterns of Sound*. Cambridge: Cambridge University Press.

Mithun, Marianne (1999). *The Languages of Native North America*. Cambridge: Cambridge University Press.

Language name	Acooli		ɔˈtʃɔli
Autonym (if known and different)		Acholi	
Language family	Nilotic		
Spoken in	Uganda, Sudan		
Approximate number of speakers	674k		
Writing system	Roman		
Phonetics/phonology			
Stress			
Contains following rare consonant (types)	retroflex		
Said to have how many vowels?	11 + 2 degrees of length		
Marked vowel types			
Tone	register		
Rhythm	no information		
Vowel harmony	limited height harmony		
Morphology	agglutinative	word-based	
Particular formation types	prefix; partial prefixed and full reduplication; suffix; tone used morphologically		
Syntax			
Word order	SVO	NA NPoss	prepositions
Particular syntactic phenomena	conjugation classes		
Points of interest			
Sources	Asher (1994), Crazzolara (1955)		

Language name	Abkhaz		əpˈhɑːz
Autonym (if known and different)			
Language family	Caucasian	NW Caucasian	
Spoken in	Georgia		
Approximate number of speakers	90k		
Writing system	Cyrillic + extra letters		
Phonetics/phonology			
Stress			
Contains following rare consonant (types)	retroflex, uvular, pharyngeal; ejective		
Said to have how many vowels?	2		
Marked vowel types			
Tone	none		
Rhythm	no information		
Vowel harmony	none		
Morphology	agglutinative	stem-based	
Particular formation types	dvandva; prefix; full reduplication		
Syntax			
Word order	SOV	NA PossN	postpositions
Particular syntactic phenomena	absolutive/ergative; evidentials; gender; morphological aspect; inclusive/exclusive 1st plural		
Points of interest			
Sources	Campbell (1991), Haspelmath et al. (2005), Hewitt & Khiba (1979), Lyovin (1997)		

Acholi see **Acooli**

Language name	Ainu	'amu:
Autonym (if known and different)	(the name derives from the word ['ajnu] meaning 'person')	
Language family	Isolate	
Spoken in	Hokkaido Island (Japan)	
Approximate number of speakers	10	
Writing system	Roman, Japanese kana	
Phonetics/phonology		
Stress		
Contains following rare consonant (types)		
Said to have how many vowels?	5	
Marked vowel types		
Tone	tonal accent	
Rhythm	no information	
Vowel harmony	traces of front–back harmony	
Morphology	polysynthetic in process of moving to isolating	
Particular formation types	prefix; full reduplication; suffix	
Syntax		
Word order	SOV	AN PossN	postpositions
Particular syntactic phenomena	inclusive/exclusive 1st plural; morphological aspect; evidentials	
Points of interest		
Sources	Campbell (1991), Haspelmath et al. (2005), Katzner (1977), Maddieson (1984), Ruhlen (1976), Shibatani (1990)	

Language name	Afrikaans	æfrɪˈkɑːns
Autonym (if known and different)		
Language family	Indo-European	Germanic
Spoken in	South Africa	
Approximate number of speakers	6m	
Writing system	Roman	
Phonetics/phonology		
Stress	root-initial	
Contains following rare consonant (types)		
Said to have how many vowels?	8 + length; 6 diphthongs	
Marked vowel types	front rounded	
Tone	none	
Rhythm	no information	
Vowel harmony	none	
Morphology	agglutinative	word-based
Particular formation types	prefix; suffix; apophony	
Syntax		
Word order	SVO, SOV in subordinate clauses	AN PossN	prepositions
Particular syntactic phenomena		
Points of interest		
Sources	Campbell (1991), Donaldson (1993), Gordon (2002), Lyovin (1997), Ruhlen (1976)	

Language name	Akan	Twi	əˈkæn
Autonym (if known and different)			
Language family	Niger-Congo	Kwa	
Spoken in	Ghana		
Approximate number of speakers	8m		
Writing system	Roman		
Phonetics/phonology			
Stress			
Contains following rare consonant (types)	retroflex		
Said to have how many vowels?	8 + nasality (5) + long nasal (2)		
Marked vowel types	front rounded		
Tone	register, terrace tone		
Rhythm	no information		
Vowel harmony	ATR		
Morphology	agglutinative and fusional	stem-based	
Particular formation types	prefix; prefixed partial reduplication; suffix		
Syntax			
Word order	SVO	NA PossN	postpositions
Particular syntactic phenomena	conjugation classes		
Points of interest			
Sources	Campbell (1991), Clements (2000), Maddieson (1984)		

Language name	Albanian		ælˈbeɪniən
Autonym (if known and different)	Giuha Shqipe		
Language family	Indo-European		
Spoken in	Albania, Yugoslavia, Italy, Greece		
Approximate number of speakers	5m		
Writing system	Roman		
Phonetics/phonology			
Stress	word-penultimate		
Contains following rare consonant (types)			
Said to have how many vowels?	7		
Marked vowel types	front rounded		
Tone	none		
Rhythm	no information		
Vowel harmony	none		
Morphology	fusional	stem-based	
Particular formation types	prefix; suffix		
Syntax			
Word order	SVO	NA NPoss	prepositions
Particular syntactic phenomena	gender; nominative/accusative marking; evidentials		
Points of interest			
Sources	Buchholz & Fiedler (1987), Campbell (1991), Gordon (2002), Haspelmath et al. (2005), Maddieson (1984)		

Language name	Amharic		æm'hærik
Autonym (if known and different)	amhariñña		
Language family	Afro-Asiatic	Semitic	
Spoken in	Ethiopia, Sudan		
Approximate number of speakers	20m		
Writing system	its own alphabet		
Phonetics/phonology			
Stress	not relevant		
Contains following rare consonant (types)	ejective		
Said to have how many vowels?	7		
Marked vowel types			
Tone	none		
Rhythm	syllable timed		
Vowel harmony	none		
Morphology	agglutinative and fusional	stem-based	
Particular formation types	prefix; root-and-pattern; suffix		
Syntax			
Word order	SOV	AN PossN	prepositions and postpositions
Particular syntactic phenomena	gender; morphological aspect; nominative/accusative marking		
Points of interest			
Sources	Bender (2003), Ullendorf (1965)		

Language name	Amele		
Autonym (if known and different)			
Language family	Trans-New-Guinea	Gum	
Spoken in	Papua New Guinea (S of Madang)		
Approximate number of speakers	6k		
Writing system	Roman (introduced by missionaries)		
Phonetics/phonology			
Stress	weight-based		
Contains following rare consonant (types)			
Said to have how many vowels?	5		
Marked vowel types			
Tone	none		
Rhythm	stress-timed		
Vowel harmony	limited height and front–back harmony		
Morphology	agglutinative and some fusion	word-based	
Particular formation types	dvandva; incorporation; partial prefixed and full reduplication; suffix		
Syntax			
Word order	SOV	NA PossN	postpositions
Particular syntactic phenomena	morphological aspect; dual; serial verbs		
Points of interest			
Sources	Roberts (1987)		

Language name	Apalai	Aparai
Autonym (if known and different)		
Language family	Cariban	
Spoken in	Brazil	
Approximate number of speakers	350	
Writing system	Roman	
Phonetics/phonology		
Stress	word–penultimate	
Contains following rare consonant (types)		
Said to have how many vowels?	6 + nasality (6)	
Marked vowel types		
Tone		
Rhythm	no information	
Vowel harmony	none	
Morphology	agglutinative	word-based for nouns, stem-based for verbs
Particular formation types	incorporation; prefix; partial prefixed reduplication; suffix; synaffix	
Syntax		
Word order	OVS	NA PossN postpositions
Particular syntactic phenomena	morphological aspect	
Points of interest	particularly complex pronoun system; no overt coordination markers; shape of object determines relative postposition	
Sources	Asher (1994), Koehn & Koehn (1986)	

Aparai see Apalai

Language name	Anejom	
Autonym (if known and different)	aneɟomᵂ	
Language family	Austronesian	Southern Oceanic
Spoken in	Aneityum (Vanuatu)	
Approximate number of speakers	800	
Writing system		
Phonetics/phonology		
Stress	word–penultimate mora	
Contains following rare consonant (types)		
Said to have how many vowels?	5 + length	
Marked vowel types		
Tone	none	
Rhythm	no information	
Vowel harmony	optional vowel-height harmony	
Morphology	isolating and agglutinative	word-based
Particular formation types	prefix; partial prefixed and full reduplication; suffix	
Syntax		
Word order	VOS	NA NPoss prepositions
Particular syntactic phenomena	inclusive/exclusive 1st plural; noun classes; serial verbs; trial	
Points of interest		
Sources	Lynch (2000, 2002a)	

Annamite see Vietnamese

Language name	Arabic		'ærəbɪk
Autonym (if known and different)	Al Arabiya		
Language family	Afro-Asiatic	Semitic	
Spoken in	widely used from Morocco to the Persian Gulf, and also as a minority language in countries as far apart as Nigeria, Turkey and Iran also a language of religion		
Approximate number of speakers	150m		
Writing system	Arabic		
Phonetics/phonology			
Stress	quantity-based		
Contains following rare consonant (types)	uvular, pharyngeal		
Said to have how many vowels?	3 + length (3) + 2 diphthongs (but some modern dialects have more vowels)		
Marked vowel types			
Tone	none		
Rhythm	stress-timed		
Vowel harmony	none		
Morphology	fusional	stem-based	
Particular formation types	prefix; root-and-pattern; infix; suffix		
Syntax			
Word order	VSO	NA NPoss	
Particular syntactic phenomena	gender; nominative/accusative; dual		
Points of interest			
Sources	Campbell (1991), Katzner (1977), Nasr (1967)		

Language name	Arabana-Wanggannguru		ˌarabʌnʌ 'wʌŋgəŋ'uːru;
Autonym (if known and different)			
Language family	Pama-Nyungan	Karnic	
Spoken in	South Australia		
Approximate number of speakers	8		
Writing system			
Phonetics/phonology			
Stress	word-initial		
Contains following rare consonant (types)	retroflexes		
Said to have how many vowels?	3		
Marked vowel types			
Tone	none		
Rhythm	no information		
Vowel harmony	some restrictions on vowel co-occurrence, such that *iCu	word-based	
Morphology	agglutinative		
Particular formation types	partial prefixed, partial suffixed, full reduplication; suffix		
Syntax			
Word order	SOV	NA NPoss	neither
Particular syntactic phenomena	mixed absolutive/ergative; inclusive/exclusive 1st plural; morphological aspect; noun classes; trial		
Points of interest			
Sources	Gordon (2002), Hercus (1994), Maddieson (1984)		

Language name	Archi		ɑːˈtʃʼi
Autonym (if known and different)			
Language family	Caucasian	N–NE Lezghian	
Spoken in	Daghestan		
Approximate number of speakers	850		
Writing system	unwritten		
Phonetics/phonology			
Stress	word-initial		
Contains following rare consonant (types)	uvular, pharyngeal		
Said to have how many vowels?	8		
Marked vowel types	front rounded		
Tone	none		
Rhythm	no information		
Vowel harmony	none		
Morphology	fusional and polysynthetic	word-based	
Particular formation types	prefix; partial suffixed reduplication; suffix		
Syntax			
Word order	SOV		postpositions / case affixes
Particular syntactic phenomena	gender		
Points of interest	over 1.5m word forms in a verbal paradigm		
Sources	Kibrik (1998), Ruhlen (1976)		

Language name	Aramaic		ærəˈmeɪk
Autonym (if known and different)			
Language family	Afro-Asiatic	North Semitic	
Spoken in	Iran		
Approximate number of speakers	23k		
Writing system	Aramaic (its own form of Semitic script)		
Phonetics/phonology			
Stress	word-final		
Contains following rare consonant (types)	uvular, pharyngeal, pharyngealised consonants		
Said to have how many vowels?	3		
Marked vowel types			
Tone	none		
Rhythm	no information		
Vowel harmony	none		
Morphology	fusional	stem-based	
Particular formation types	root-and-pattern; suffix		
Syntax			
Word order	SVO	NA NPoss	prepositions
Particular syntactic phenomena	morphological aspect; conjugation classes		
Points of interest	two types of plural formation		
Sources	Campbell (1991), Gordon (2002), Ruhlen (1976)		

Aranda see Arrernte

Language name	Arrernte	Aranda	ˈaranda
Autonym (if known and different)			ˈaranda
Language family	Pama-Nyungan	Arandic	
Spoken in	Northern Territory (Australia)		
Approximate number of speakers	1,500		
Writing system			
Phonetics/phonology			
Stress			
Contains following rare consonant (types)	retroflex		
Said to have how many vowels?	2		
Marked vowel types			
Tone	none		
Rhythm	no information		
Vowel harmony	none		
Morphology	agglutinative	stem-based	
Particular formation types	infix; full reduplication; suffix		
Syntax			
Word order		NA / NPoss	postpositions
Particular syntactic phenomena	ergative / absolutive; dual		
Points of interest	pronouns depend upon kinship relations		
Sources	Katzner (1977), Strehlow (1944)		

Language name	Armenian		ɑːˈmɛnɛn
Autonym (if known and different)	Ashkharhabar		
Language family	Indo-European		
Spoken in	Armenia, Georgia, Iran		
Approximate number of speakers	5m		
Writing system	Armenian		
Phonetics/phonology			
Stress	word-final (in general)		
Contains following rare consonant (types)	uvular, pharyngeal, ejective		
Said to have how many vowels?	7		
Marked vowel types			
Tone	none		
Rhythm	no information		
Vowel harmony	none		
Morphology	agglutinative and fusional	word-based	
Particular formation types	partial reduplication; suffix		
Syntax			
Word order	S-Predicate	AN / PossN	prepositions and postpositions (the latter predominate now)
Particular syntactic phenomena	nominative / accusative marking; conjugation classes		
Points of interest			
Sources	Asher (1994), Campbell (1991), Gordon (2002), Maddieson (1984), Ruhlen (1976)		

Language name	Basque		bɑːsk, bæsk
Autonym (if known and different)	Euskara		
Language family	Isolate		
Spoken in	NW Spain, SW France		
Approximate number of speakers	500k		
Writing system	Roman		
Phonetics/phonology			
Stress	penultimate (in E'ern dialects; variable elsewhere)		
Contains following rare consonant (types)	apical / laminal alveolar fricative contrast		
Said to have how many vowels?	5 + diphthongs (6)		
Marked vowel types			
Tone	tonal accent in some dialects		
Rhythm	no information		
Vowel harmony	some traces in some dialects		
Morphology	agglutinative	word-based	
Particular formation types	dvandva; suffix		
Syntax			
Word order	SOV	NA PossN	postpositions
Particular syntactic phenomena	ergative/absolutive		
Points of interest	a pre-Indo-European language of Europe		
Sources	Asher (1994), Gordon (2002), Katzner (1977), Maddieson (1984), de Rijk (2003), Ruhlen (1976), Saltarelli (1988), Tovar (1957), Wälchli (2005)		

Batak see Toba Batak

Language name	Babungo		
Autonym (if known and different)	ghaŋ vəˈŋɔ́o		
Language family	Niger-Congo	W Grassfields Bantu	
Spoken in	Congo, Cameroon		
Approximate number of speakers	14k		
Writing system	Roman		
Phonetics/phonology			
Stress	irrelevant		
Contains following rare consonant (types)			
Said to have how many vowels?	9 + length (8)		
Marked vowel types			
Tone	register, 8 tones		
Rhythm	no information		
Vowel harmony	none		
Morphology	isolating and fusional	stem-based	
Particular formation types	prefix; full reduplication; suffix; suprasegmentals used morphologically		
Syntax			
Word order	SVO	NA NPoss	prepositions
Particular syntactic phenomena	inclusive / exclusive 1st plural; noun classes; morphological aspect		
Points of interest			
Sources	Bendor-Samuel (1989), Schaub (1985)		

Bahasa Indonesia see Indonesian

Language name	Bella Coola		'belaˈkuːla
Autonym (if known and different)	Nuxalk		
Language family	Salishan		
Spoken in	British Columbia (Canada)		
Approximate number of speakers	50		
Writing system			
Phonetics/phonology			
Stress	not distinctive		
Contains following rare consonant (types)	uvular, ejective		
Said to have how many vowels?	3		
Marked vowel types			
Tone	none		
Rhythm	no information		
Vowel harmony	none		
Morphology	polysynthetic	stem-based	
Particular formation types	prefix; full and partial reduplication; suffix		
Syntax			
Word order	VSO	NPoss	prepositions
Particular syntactic phenomena	morphological aspect; conjugation classes; evidentials		
Points of interest	extremely complex consonant clusters		
Sources	Bright (1992), Campbell (1991), Haspelmath et al. (2005), Ruhlen (1976)		

Language name	Bengali		beŋˈgɔːli
Autonym (if known and different)			
Language family	Indo-European	Indic	
Spoken in	Bangladesh, West Bengal (India)		
Approximate number of speakers	165m		
Writing system	Bengali script, a version of Devanagari		
Phonetics/phonology			
Stress	word-initial		
Contains following rare consonant (types)	retroflex; voiced aspirated plosives		
Said to have how many vowels?	7 + nasalisation		
Marked vowel types			
Tone	none		
Rhythm	no information		
Vowel harmony	none		
Morphology	fusional	word-based	
Particular formation types	dvandva; suffix		
Syntax			
Word order	SOV	AN NPoss	neither
Particular syntactic phenomena	classifier; conjugation classes		
Points of interest	honorific inflections		
Sources	Bright (1992), Campbell (1991), Katzner (1977), Ruhlen (1976), Wälchli (2005)		

Language name	Bislama		ˈbislama:
Autonym (if known and different)			
Language family	Creole	Pacific	English-based
Spoken in	Vanuatu		
Approximate number of speakers	1,200		
Writing system	Roman		
Phonetics/phonology			
Stress	initial and final		
Contains following rare consonant (types)			
Said to have how many vowels?	5 + diphthongs		
Marked vowel types			
Tone	none		
Rhythm	probably syllable-timed		
Vowel harmony	none		
Morphology	isolating	word-based	
Particular formation types	suffix		
Syntax			
Word order	SVO	AN NPoss	prepositions
Particular syntactic phenomena	dual; inclusive / exclusive 1st plural		
Points of interest			
Sources	Guy (1974)		

Language name	Berber		ˈbɜːbə
Autonym (if known and different)	Tamaziɣt		
Language family	Afro-Asiatic	Berber	
Spoken in	Northern Africa		
Approximate number of speakers	12m		
Writing system	Arabic, Roman, Tifinag		
Phonetics/phonology			
Stress			
Contains following rare consonant (types)	retroflex, uvular		
Said to have how many vowels?	9		
Marked vowel types			
Tone	none		
Rhythm	no information		
Vowel harmony	none		
Morphology	fusional	stem-based	
Particular formation types	prefix; suffix; synaffix; root-and-pattern		
Syntax			
Word order	VSO	NA NPoss	prepositions
Particular syntactic phenomena	gender; morphological aspect; conjugation classes		
Points of interest	a language family rather than a single language		
Sources	Campbell (1991), Katzner (1977), Kossmann (2003)		

Bini see Edo

Language name	Blackfoot	'blækfʊt	
Autonym (if known and different)	Siksika ('black foot')		
Language family	Algonkian		
Spoken in	Montana, Alberta (Canada)		
Approximate number of speakers	6k		
Writing system			
Phonetics/phonology			
Stress			
Contains following rare consonant (types)	uvular		
Said to have how many vowels?	3 + length		
Marked vowel types			
Tone	none		
Rhythm	no information		
Vowel harmony	none		
Morphology	polysynthetic	stem-based	
Particular formation types	incorporation; prefix; suffix; synaffix		
Syntax			
Word order	SVO	AN PossN	prepositions
Particular syntactic phenomena	inclusive / exclusive 1st plural; conjugation classes: gender		
Points of interest			
Sources	Campbell (1991), Katzner (1977), Ruhlen (1976)		

Language name	Bontok, Bontoc	bɒn'tɒk	
Autonym (if known and different)	Kali ('the language')		
Language family	Austronesian	Malayo-Polynesian	
Spoken in	Philippines		
Approximate number of speakers	40k		
Writing system			
Phonetics/phonology			
Stress			
Contains following rare consonant (types)			
Said to have how many vowels?	4		
Marked vowel types			
Tone	none		
Rhythm	no information		
Vowel harmony	none		
Morphology	agglutinative	word-based	
Particular formation types	prefix; infix; partial prefixed reduplication and full reduplication; suffix; synaffix		
Syntax			
Word order	VSO	AN and NA PossN	neither
Particular syntactic phenomena			
Points of interest			
Sources	Reid (1976)		

Language name	Bulgarian		bʌlˈgeərɪən, bʊlˈgeərɪən
Autonym (if known and different)			
Language family	Indo-European	Slavic	
Spoken in	Bulgaria		
Approximate number of speakers	8m		
Writing system	Cyrillic		
Phonetics/phonology			
Stress	variable		
Contains following rare consonant (types)			
Said to have how many vowels?	6 + nasalisation + diphthongs (2)		
Marked vowel types			
Tone	none		
Rhythm	no information		
Vowel harmony	none		
Morphology			
Particular formation types	fusional	stem-based	
	prefix; suffix		
Syntax			
Word order	SVO	AN PossN	prepositions
Particular syntactic phenomena	morphological aspect; conjugation classes		
Points of interest			
Sources	Campbell (1991), Katzner (1977), Ruhlen (1976), Scatton (1993)		

Language name	Breton		ˈbretən
Autonym (if known and different)	brəzõnɛk		
Language family	Indo-European	Celtic	
Spoken in	Brittany (France)		
Approximate number of speakers	500k		
Writing system	Roman		
Phonetics/phonology			
Stress	word-penultimate		
Contains following rare consonant (types)	uvular; pharyngeal		
Said to have how many vowels?	9 + nasal (5)		
Marked vowel types	front rounded		
Tone	none		
Rhythm	no information		
Vowel harmony	none		
Morphology			
Particular formation types	fusional	word-based	
	prefix; suffix		
Syntax			
Word order	VSO (with much variation)	NA NPoss	prepositions
Particular syntactic phenomena	gender; morphological aspect; dual; inflecting prepositions		
Points of interest	initial mutations		
Sources	Press (1986), Wmffre (1998a)		

Language name	Bungandity	Buwandik	
Autonym (if known and different)	Drualat-ngolonung ('speech of the man')		
Language family			
Spoken in	South Australia, Victoria (Australia)		
Approximate number of speakers	0		
Writing system			
Phonetics/phonology			
Stress			
Contains following rare consonant (types)	retroflex		
Said to have how many vowels?	3		
Marked vowel types			
Tone	none		
Rhythm	no information		
Vowel harmony	none		
Morphology	agglutinative	stem-based	
Particular formation types	reduplication; suffix		
Syntax			
Word order	free	NA and AN PossN	neither
Particular syntactic phenomena	dual; ergative /absolutive; inclusive / exclusive 1st plural		
Points of interest			
Sources	Blake (2003)		

Language name	Burmese		bɜ̀ˈmiːz
Autonym (if known and different)			
Language family	Sino-Tibetan	Lolo-Burmese	
Spoken in	Myanmar		
Approximate number of speakers	30m		
Writing system	Burmese		
Phonetics/phonology			
Stress			
Contains following rare consonant (types)	voiceless nasal		
Said to have how many vowels?	7+ diphthongs (4)		
Marked vowel types			
Tone	tonal accent		
Rhythm	no information		
Vowel harmony	none		
Morphology	agglutinative	stem-based	
Particular formation types	dvandva; prefix; full reduplication; suffix; suprasegmentals used morphologically		
Syntax			
Word order	Argument-V	NA PossN	postpositions
Particular syntactic phenomena	nominative / accusative marking; classifier; morphological aspect		
Points of interest	pronouns of deference		
Sources	Campbell (1991), Katzner (1977), Ruhlen (1976), Wälchli (2005), Wheatley (2003), Yip (2002)		

Language name	Buryat		
Autonym (if known and different)	'burɪæt		
Language family	Altaic	Mongolian	
Spoken in	Russian Federation round Lake Baikal		
Approximate number of speakers	360k		
Writing system	Cyrillic		
Phonetics/phonology			
Stress			
Contains following rare consonant (types)			
Said to have how many vowels?	7 long + 6 short + 4 diphthongs		
Marked vowel types	front rounded		
Tone	none		
Rhythm	no information		
Vowel harmony	front–back and rounding		
Morphology	agglutinative	word-based	
Particular formation types	suffix		
Syntax			
Word order	SOV	AN PossN	postpositions
Particular syntactic phenomena	nominative / accusative marking		
Points of interest			
Sources	Haspelmath et al. (2005), Skribnik (2003)		

Buwandik see **Bungandit̪j**

Language name	Burushaski		
Autonym (if known and different)	burʊ'ʃæski		
Language family	isolate		
Spoken in	Kashmir		
Approximate number of speakers	60k		
Writing system	unwritten		
Phonetics/phonology			
Stress	quantity-based		
Contains following rare consonant (types)	retroflex, uvular		
Said to have how many vowels?	5		
Marked vowel types			
Tone	tonal accent		
Rhythm	no information		
Vowel harmony	none		
Morphology	agglutinative and fusional	stem-based for verbs; word-based for nouns	
Particular formation types	dvandva; prefix; suffix		
Syntax			
Word order	SOV	AN PossN	postpositions
Particular syntactic phenomena	ergative / absolutive; nominative / accusative; gender		
Points of interest			
Sources	Bashir (2005), Katzner (1977), Maddieson (1984), Ruhlen (1976), Wälchli (2005), Yip (2002)		

Language name	Cahuilla		kə'weə
Autonym (if known and different)			
Language family	Aztec-Tanoan	Uto-Aztecan	
Spoken in	California (USA)		
Approximate number of speakers	10		
Writing system			
Phonetics/phonology			
Stress			
Contains following rare consonant (types)	uvular		
Said to have how many vowels?	5 + length (4)		
Marked vowel types			
Tone	none		
Rhythm	no information		
Vowel harmony	none		
Morphology	agglutinative	stem-based	
Particular formation types			
Syntax			
Word order	SOV	AN PossN	neither
Particular syntactic phenomena	evidentials		
Points of interest			
Sources	Haspelmath et al. (2005), Ruhlen (1976), Seiler (1977)		

Cambodian see Khmer

Language name	Canela-Krahô		kæ'nɛlə 'krɑːhau
Autonym (if known and different)			
Language family	Jê		
Spoken in	Brazil		
Approximate number of speakers	2k		
Writing system	Roman		
Phonetics/phonology			
Stress	word-final		
Contains following rare consonant (types)			
Said to have how many vowels?	10 + nasalisation (7)		
Marked vowel types	back unrounded		
Tone	none		
Rhythm	no information		
Vowel harmony	none		
Morphology	isolating and agglutinative	word-based	
Particular formation types	prefix; suffix		
Syntax			
Word order	SOV	NA PossN	postpositions
Particular syntactic phenomena	inclusive / exclusive 1st plural; alienable / inalienable possession		
Points of interest			
Sources	Haspelmath et al. (2005), Popjes & Popjes (1986)		

Cant see Shelta

Language name	Carrier		ˈkærɪə
Autonym (if known and different)			
Language family	Na-Dene	Athabaskan	
Spoken in	British Columbia (Canada)		
Approximate number of speakers	2,200		
Writing system			
Phonetics/phonology			
Stress			
Contains following rare consonant (types)			
Said to have how many vowels?	23		
Marked vowel types			
Tone	tonal accent		
Rhythm	no information		
Vowel harmony	none		
Morphology	polysynthetic		
Particular formation types	prefix	stem-based and word-based	
Syntax			
Word order	SOV	NA PossN	postpositions
Particular syntactic phenomena			
Points of interest	five sets of numerals, usage depending on what is being counted		
Sources	Katzner (1977), Mithun (1999), Morice (1932), Yip (2002)		

Language name	Cantonese		kæntəˈniːz
Autonym (if known and different)			
Language family	Sino-Tibetan	South-Sinitic	
Spoken in	Southern China, Singapore, Malaysia, etc.		
Approximate number of speakers	55m		
Writing system	Chinese characters		
Phonetics/phonology			
Stress			
Contains following rare consonant (types)			
Said to have how many vowels?	11 + 11 diphthongs		
Marked vowel types	front rounded		
Tone	contour		
Rhythm	no information		
Vowel harmony	none		
Morphology	isolating	word-based	
Particular formation types	dvandva; prefix; suffix; infix; partial prefixed reduplication, full reduplication; tone used morphologically		
Syntax			
Word order	SVO VSX	AN PossN	prepositions and postpositions
Particular syntactic phenomena	classifiers		
Points of interest	no tense, but many aspectual markers		
Sources	Bauer & Matthews (2003), Campbell (1991), Matthews & Yip (1994), Ruhlen (1976), Yip (2002)		

Language name	Cashinahua	
Autonym (if known and different)		
Language family	Ge-Pano-Carib	Macro-Panoan
Spoken in	Peru, Brazil	
Approximate number of speakers	2k	
Writing system	Roman	
Phonetics/phonology		
Stress		
Contains following rare consonant (types)		
Said to have how many vowels?	4 + length	
Marked vowel types	back unrounded	
Tone	tone present	
Rhythm	no information	
Vowel harmony		
Morphology		
Particular formation types		
Syntax		
Word order	SOV	NA Poss N
		postpositions
Particular syntactic phenomena		
Points of interest		
Sources	Maddieson (1984), Ruhlen (1976)	

Language name	Catalan		ˈkætələn
Autonym (if known and different)			
Language family	Indo-European	Romance	
Spoken in	Spain, Andorra, Balearic Islands		
Approximate number of speakers	6m		
Writing system	Roman		
Phonetics/phonology			
Stress	word–penultimate or word-final		
Contains following rare consonant (types)			
Said to have how many vowels?	7		
Marked vowel types			
Tone	none		
Rhythm	no information		
Vowel harmony	none		
Morphology	fusional	stem-based	
Particular formation types	prefix; suffix		
Syntax			
Word order	SVO	NA NPoss	prepositions
Particular syntactic phenomena	gender classes; verb conjugations		
Points of interest			
Sources	Campbell (1991), Haspelmath et al. (2005), Hualdo (1992), Katzner (1977), Ruhlen (1976)		

Language name	Cherokee		'feraoki; fere'ki:
Autonym (if known and different)	Tsaligi		
Language family	Macro-Siouan	Iroquoian	
Spoken in	Oklahoma, North Carolina (USA)		
Approximate number of speakers	30k		
Writing system	its own syllabary		
Phonetics/phonology			
Stress			
Contains following rare consonant (types)	lateral fricative		
Said to have how many vowels?	6 + length		
Marked vowel types			
Tone	register		
Rhythm	no information		
Vowel harmony	none		
Morphology	polysynthetic	stem-based for verbs, word-based for nouns	
Particular formation types	incorporation; prefix; suffix; synaffix		
Syntax			
Word order	SVO or VSO	AN PossN	prepositions
Particular syntactic phenomena	inclusive / exclusive 1st plural; classifiers; morphological aspect; gender; verb classes; dual; evidentials		
Points of interest			
Sources	Campbell (1991), Cook (1979), Haspelmath et al. (2005), Holmes & Smith (1977), Katzner (1977), Mithun (1999), Yip (2002)		

Language name		Cayubaba	Cayuvava
Autonym (if known and different)			
Language family		Andean-Equatorial	Equatorial
Spoken in		Bolivia	
Approximate number of speakers		0	
Writing system			
Phonetics/phonology			
Stress		word antepenultimate	
Contains following rare consonant (types)			
Said to have how many vowels?		6	
Marked vowel types			
Tone		none	
Rhythm		stress-timed	
Vowel harmony		none	
Morphology		agglutinative	word-based
Particular formation types		prefix; suffix; partially prefixed, partially suffixed and full reduplication; synaffix	
Syntax			
Word order		VOS (SVO)	AN NPoss — prepositions
Particular syntactic phenomena		nominative / accusative marking; morphological aspect	
Points of interest			
Sources		Aikhenvald & Dixon (1999), Gordon (2002), Haspelmath et al. (2005), Key (1967), Ruhlen (1976)	

Cayuvava see Cayubaba
Cheremis see Mari

Language name	Chinook		tʃɪˈnʊk, tʃɪˈnuːk
Autonym (if known and different)			
Language family	Penutian	Chinookan	
Spoken in	Oregon, Washington (USA)		
Approximate number of speakers	12		
Writing system			
Phonetics/phonology			
Stress			
Contains following rare consonant (types)	uvular; ejective		
Said to have how many vowels?			
Marked vowel types			
Tone	none		
Rhythm	no information		
Vowel harmony	none		
Morphology	agglutinative	stem-based	
Particular formation types	prefix; suffix		
Syntax			
Word order	VOS	AN NPoss	prepositions and postpositions
Particular syntactic phenomena	inclusive / exclusive 1st plural; evidentials; ergative / absolutive marking; gender; dual; inflected postpositions		
Points of interest			
Sources	Amith & Smith-Stark (1994), Haspelmath et al. (2005), Mithun (1999), Silverstein (1972a)		

Language name	Chinanteco		
Autonym (if known and different)			
Language family	Oto-Manguean	Chinantecan	
Spoken in	Mexico		
Approximate number of speakers	30k		
Writing system			
Phonetics/phonology			
Stress	on last tone-bearing vowel in the word		
Contains following rare consonant (types)			
Said to have how many vowels?	7 + length + nasalisation		
Marked vowel types	front rounded; back unrounded		
Tone	register		
Rhythm	no information		
Vowel harmony	none		
Morphology	isolating and agglutinative	word-based	
Particular formation types	dvandva; prefix; incorporation		
Syntax			
Word order	VSO	NA NPoss	
Particular syntactic phenomena	noun classes; evidentials		
Points of interest	tonal harmony		
Sources	Haspelmath et al. (2005), Merrifield (1968), Ruhlen (1976), Wälchli (2005), Yip (2002)		

Language name	Chinook Jargon			tʃ'ɪnʊk'dʒɑːɡən
Autonym (if known and different)				
Language family	pidgin based on Chinook, Nootka, English and French			
Spoken in	California, Oregon, Washington, Alaska (USA), British Columbia (Canada)			
Approximate number of speakers				
Writing system				
Phonetics/phonology				
Stress	word-initial			
Contains following rare consonant (types)	ejective, uvular			
Said to have how many vowels?	6			
Marked vowel types				
Tone	none			
Rhythm	no information			
Vowel harmony	none			
Morphology	isolating	word-based		
Particular formation types	prefix			
Syntax				
Word order	SVO	AN PossN	prepositions	
Particular syntactic phenomena	serial verb; inclusive / exclusive 1st plural			
Points of interest				
Sources	Silverstein (1972b), Thomason (1983), Zenk (1988)			

Language name	Chipewyan			tʃɪpəˈwaːən
Autonym (if known and different)				
Language family	Na-Dene	Athabaskan		
Spoken in	Canada			
Approximate number of speakers	4k			
Writing system				
Phonetics/phonology				
Stress				
Contains following rare consonant (types)	ejectives; implosives			
Said to have how many vowels?	5 + length (3) + nasalisation			
Marked vowel types				
Tone	register			
Rhythm	no information			
Vowel harmony	none			
Morphology	fusional	stem-based		
Particular formation types	suffix			
Syntax				
Word order	SOV	NA PossN	postpositions	
Particular syntactic phenomena	classifiers; morphological aspect; conjugation classes; evidentials			
Points of interest				
Sources	Campbell (1991), Haspelmath et al. (2005), Maddieson (1984), Ruhlen (1976)			

Chippewa see Ojibwa

Language name	Chrau		ʧrau
Autonym (if known and different)			
Language family	Austro-Asiatic	Mon-Khmer	
Spoken in	Vietnam		
Approximate number of speakers	15k		
Writing system			
Phonetics/phonology			
Stress			
Contains following rare consonant (types)	retroflex, implosive		
Said to have how many vowels?	8 long, 6 short, 2 diphthongs		
Marked vowel types			
Tone	none		
Rhythm	no information		
Vowel harmony	none		
Morphology	isolating	word-based	
Particular formation types	infix; prefix; full reduplication		
Syntax			
Word order	SVO	NA NPoss	prepositions
Particular syntactic phenomena	classifiers; noun classes		
Points of interest	most affixation is no longer productive		
Sources	Ruhlen (1976), Thomas (1971)		

Language name	Chukchee	Chukchi	ˈʧʊktʃiː
Autonym (if known and different)	Luoravetlat		
Language family	Paleo-Asiatic	Chukchi	
Spoken in	Chukchi Peninsula (USSR)		
Approximate number of speakers	10k		
Writing system	Cyrillic		
Phonetics/phonology			
Stress	word-initial		
Contains following rare consonant (types)	retroflex, uvular		
Said to have how many vowels?	7		
Marked vowel types			
Tone	none		
Rhythm	no information		
Vowel harmony	yes, strong–weak or dominant–subordinate		
Morphology	polysynthetic	stem-based	
Particular formation types	incorporation; prefix; partial suffixed reduplication; suffix; synaffix		
Syntax			
Word order	SOV	AN PossN	postpositions
Particular syntactic phenomena	absolutive/ergative and nominative/accusative systems; morphological aspect; gender; conjugation classes		
Points of interest			
Sources	Haspelmath et al. (2005), Maddieson (1984), Ruhlen (1976)		

Chukchi see Chukchee
Circassian see **Kabardian**

Language name	Cornish		
Autonym (if known and different)	'kɔːnʃ		
Language family	Indo-European	Celtic	
Spoken in	Cornwall (UK)		
Approximate number of speakers	died out in about 1800, but is being revived		
Writing system	Roman		
Phonetics/phonology			
Stress	word-penultimate		
Contains following rare consonant (types)	nasalised bilabial fricative		
Said to have how many vowels?	6 + length (5) + 7 diphthongs		
Marked vowel types			
Tone	none		
Rhythm	stress-timed		
Vowel harmony	none		
Morphology	fusional	stem-based verbs; word-based nouns	
Particular formation types	infix (dialectally variable); suffix; apophony		
Syntax			
Word order	SVO	NA NPoss	prepositions
Particular syntactic phenomena	gender; dual; inflected prepositions		
Points of interest	initial mutation		
Sources	George (1993), Haspelmath et al. (2005), Wmffre (1998b)		

Language name	Coeur d'Alene		
Autonym (if known and different)	k3ːdəˈlem		
Language family	Salishan		
Spoken in	Idaho (USA)		
Approximate number of speakers	<5		
Writing system			
Phonetics/phonology			
Stress	weight-based system		
Contains following rare consonant (types)	uvular, pharyngeal, ejective, labialised uvulars and pharyngeals		
Said to have how many vowels?	5		
Marked vowel types			
Tone	none		
Rhythm	no information		
Vowel harmony	vowels restricted in terms of following consonants		
Morphology	polysynthetic		
Particular formation types	prefix; suffix; infix; partial prefixed reduplication; incorporation		
Syntax			
Word order	SVO	AN NPoss	prepositions
Particular syntactic phenomena	ergative / absolutive marking; morphological aspect		
Points of interest			
Sources	Doak (1997)		

Language name	Croatian	Serbo-Croat	krɔuˈɛtʃən
Autonym (if known and different)			
Language family	Indo-European	Slavic	
Spoken in	Croatia, Montenegro		
Approximate number of speakers	10m		
Writing system	Roman		
Phonetics/phonology			
Stress			
Contains following rare consonant (types)			
Said to have how many vowels?	5 + length		
Marked vowel types			
Tone	tonal accent		
Rhythm	no information		
Vowel harmony	none		
Morphology	fusional	stem-based	
Particular formation types	prefix; suffix		
Syntax			
Word order	SVO	AN PossN and NPoss	prepositions
Particular syntactic phenomena	gender; morphological aspect; nominative / accusative marking; conjugation classes		
Points of interest	see also Serbian		
Sources	De Bray (1980), Browne (1993)		

Language name	Cree		krⁱⁱ:
Autonym (if known and different)	hahiyawāwak		
Language family	Algonkian	Cree	
Spoken in	Ontario, Manitoba, Saskatchewan (Canada)		
Approximate number of speakers	60k		
Writing system	its own syllabary		
Phonetics/phonology			
Stress	word-antepenultimate		
Contains following rare consonant (types)			
Said to have how many vowels?	7		
Marked vowel types			
Tone	none		
Rhythm	no information		
Vowel harmony	none		
Morphology	polysynthetic		
Particular formation types	suffix; synaffix		
Syntax			
Word order	SVO	AN PossN	postpositions
Particular syntactic phenomena	inclusive / exclusive 1st plural; noun classes; obviative		
Points of interest			
Sources	Haspelmath et al. (2005), Mithun (1999), Ruhlen (1976)		

Language name	Crow		krɔu
Autonym (if known and different)			
Language family	Macro–Siouan	Siouan	
Spoken in	Montana (USA)		
Approximate number of speakers	5k		
Writing system			
Phonetics/phonology			
Stress			
Contains following rare consonant (types)	ejective		
Said to have how many vowels?	5 + length		
Marked vowel types			
Tone	register		
Rhythm	no information		
Vowel harmony	none		
Morphology	polysynthetic	word-based	
Particular formation types	incorporation; prefix; suffix		
Syntax			
Word order	SOV	NA PossN	postpositions
Particular syntactic phenomena	switch reference; alienable / inalienable possession; conjugation classes		
Points of interest			
Sources	Campbell (1991), Mithun (1999), Rood (1979), Ruhlen (1976)		

Language name	Czech		tʃɛk, tʃɛx
Autonym (if known and different)	Čeština		
Language family	Indo-European	Slavic	
Spoken in	Czech Republic		
Approximate number of speakers	10m		
Writing system	Roman (with diacritics)		
Phonetics/phonology			
Stress	word-initial		
Contains following rare consonant (types)	alveolar fricative trill		
Said to have how many vowels?	5 + length + 1 diphthong		
Marked vowel types			
Tone	none		
Rhythm	no information		
Vowel harmony	none		
Morphology	fusional	stem-based	
Particular formation types	prefix; suffix		
Syntax			
Word order	SVO (with much variation)	AN NPoss	prepositions
Particular syntactic phenomena	gender; nominative / accusative marking; morphological aspect; conjugation classes		
Points of interest			
Sources	Campbell (1991), Gordon (2002), Ruhlen (1976), Short (1993a, 2003)		

Dagur see Daur

Language name	Dan	Gio, Yakuba
Autonym (if known and different)		dæn
Language family	Niger-Congo	Eastern Mande
Spoken in	Ivory Coast	
Approximate number of speakers	300k	
Writing system		
Phonetics/phonology		
Stress		
Contains following rare consonant (types)	implosive	
Said to have how many vowels?	9 + nasalisation (8)	
Marked vowel types	back unrounded	
Tone	register	
Rhythm	no information	
Vowel harmony	none	
Morphology	agglutinative	
Particular formation types	suffix	
Syntax		
Word order	SOV	NA PossN postpositions
Particular syntactic phenomena		
Points of interest		
Sources	Maddieson (1984), Ruhlen (1976)	

Language name	Dakota		dəˈkəutə
Autonym (if known and different)			
Language family	Macro-Siouan	Siouan	
Spoken in	North Dakota, South Dakota, Montana, Nebraska (USA)		
Approximate number of speakers	10k		
Writing system	Roman		
Phonetics/phonology			
Stress	second-syllable		
Contains following rare consonant (types)	ejective (including fricative)		
Said to have how many vowels?	5 + nasalisation (3)		
Marked vowel types			
Tone	none		
Rhythm	no information		
Vowel harmony	none		
Morphology	agglutinative and fusional	word-based	
Particular formation types	incorporation; infix; prefix; suffix		
Syntax			
Word order	SOV	NA PossN	postpositions
Particular syntactic phenomena	noun classes		
Points of interest			
Sources	Campbell (1991), Haspelmath et al. (2005), Maddieson (1984), Ruhlen (1976)		

Language name	Danish		ˈdɛmʃ
Autonym (if known and different)	dansk		
Language family	Indo-European	Germanic	
Spoken in	Denmark, Faroe Islands, Greenland		
Approximate number of speakers	5m		
Writing system	Roman + extra letters		
Phonetics/phonology			
Stress	root-initial		
Contains following rare consonant (types)	uvular		
Said to have how many vowels?	12 + length		
Marked vowel types	front rounded		
Tone	none: *stød* or glottal catch replaces the Scandinavian tonal accent in Eastern Standard Danish		
Rhythm	stress timed		
Vowel harmony	none		
Morphology	agglutinative	word-based	
Particular formation types	prefix; suffix; apophony		
Syntax			
Word order	V2	AN PossN	prepositions
Particular syntactic phenomena	gender		
Points of interest			
Sources	Bredsdorff (1956), Campbell (1991), Diderichsen (1972), Gordon (2002), Ruhlen (1976)		

Language name	Dani		
Autonym (if known and different)			
Language family	Trans-New-Guinea	Dani-Kwerba	
Spoken in	Iriyan Jaya		
Approximate number of speakers	270k		
Writing system			
Phonetics/phonology			
Stress	word-final		
Contains following rare consonant (types)			
Said to have how many vowels?	7 + 5 diphthongs		
Marked vowel types			
Tone	none		
Rhythm	no information		
Vowel harmony	none		
Morphology	agglutinative	stem-based	
Particular formation types	prefix; suffix		
Syntax			
Word order	SOV	NA PossN	postpositions
Particular syntactic phenomena	conjugation classes		
Points of interest	reported as having only two basic colour terms		
Sources	Bromley (1981), Gordon (2002), Maddieson (1984), Ruhlen (1976)		

Language name	Daur	Dagur	dauə
Autonym (if known and different)			
Language family	Altaic	Mongolian	
Spoken in	Inner Mongolia (China)		
Approximate number of speakers	120k		
Writing system	Manchu, Roman, Cyrillic		
Phonetics/phonology			
Stress			
Contains following rare consonant (types)			
Said to have how many vowels?	5 + length + 6 diphthongs		
Marked vowel types			
Tone	none		
Rhythm	no information		
Vowel harmony	low–non-low and rounding		
Morphology	agglutinative	word-based	
Particular formation types	partial prefixed and full reduplication; suffix		
Syntax			
Word order	SOV	AN NPoss	postpositions
Particular syntactic phenomena	inclusive / exclusive 1st plural; morphological aspect; nominative / accusative marking		
Points of interest			
Sources	Tsumagari (2003), Wu (1996)		

Dieri see Diyari

Language name	Dinka	Jieng	'dɪŋkə
Autonym (if known and different)			
Language family	Nilo-Saharan	Eastern Sudanic	
Spoken in	Sudan, Ethiopia		
Approximate number of speakers	2m		
Writing system	Roman		
Phonetics/phonology			
Stress			
Contains following rare consonant (types)			
Said to have how many vowels?	8 + length (4) + 1 diphthong		
Marked vowel types			
Tone	register		
Rhythm	no information		
Vowel harmony	none		
Morphology	isolating	word-based	
Particular formation types	prefix; suffix; tone used morphologically		
Syntax			
Word order	SOV SVO	NA PossN	prepositions and postpositions
Particular syntactic phenomena	nominative / accusative marking		
Points of interest			
Sources	Campbell (1991), Haspelmath et al. (2005)		

Language name	Dumi		
Autonym (if known and different)	Dumī Raī		
Language family	Sino–Tibetan	Tibeto–Burman	
Spoken in	Nepal		
Approximate number of speakers	1k		
Writing system	Devanagari		
Phonetics/phonology			
Stress	initial in nouns, root-final in verbs		
Contains following rare consonant (types)			
Said to have how many vowels?	8 + length (5) + 5 diphthongs		
Marked vowel types	front rounded		
Tone	tonal accent		
Rhythm	no information		
Vowel harmony	none		
Morphology	agglutinative and fusional	stem-based	
Particular formation types	prefix; suffix		
Syntax			
Word order	SOV	AN PossN	postpositions
Particular syntactic phenomena	absolutive / ergative marking; gender; inclusive / exclusive 1st plural; morphological aspect; dual; conjugation classes		
Points of interest			
Sources	Van Driem (1993)		

Language name	Diyari	Dieri	'diaɻi
Autonym (if known and different)	dijiaɻi		
Language family	Pama–Nyungan		
Spoken in	South Australia		
Approximate number of speakers	<10		
Writing system			
Phonetics/phonology			
Stress	root-initial		
Contains following rare consonant (types)	retroflex, pre-stopped sonorants		
Said to have how many vowels?	3		
Marked vowel types			
Tone	none		
Rhythm	no information		
Vowel harmony	none		
Morphology	agglutinative	stem-based	
Particular formation types	partial prefixed reduplication; suffix		
Syntax			
Word order	SOV	NA PossN	prepositions
Particular syntactic phenomena	dual number; ergative / absolutive marking and nominative / accusative marking; gender		
Points of interest			
Sources	Austin (1981)		

Language name	Dyirbal	ˈdjɜːbəl
Autonym (if known and different)		
Language family	Pama-Nyungan	
Spoken in	Queensland (Australia)	
Approximate number of speakers	40	
Writing system		
Phonetics/phonology		
Stress	word-initial	
Contains following rare consonant (types)	retroflex	
Said to have how many vowels?	3	
Marked vowel types		
Tone	none	
Rhythm	no information	
Vowel harmony	none	
Morphology	agglutinative	word-based
Particular formation types	partially prefixed and full reduplication; suffix	
Syntax		
Word order	determined by focus	NA / NPoss / neither
Particular syntactic phenomena	absolutive / ergative and nominative / accusative marking; gender; morphological aspect; conjugation classes; dual; alienable / inalienable possession	
Points of interest	'mother-in-law language' is an avoidance variety used reciprocally to and in the hearing of certain taboo relatives, including mothers-in-law	
Sources	Dixon (1972), Ruhlen (1976)	

Language name	Dutch	dʌʃ
Autonym (if known and different)	Nederlands	
Language family	Indo-European	Germanic
Spoken in	Netherlands, Belgium, Surinam, Dutch Antilles	
Approximate number of speakers	19m	
Writing system	Roman	
Phonetics/phonology		
Stress	word-initial	
Contains following rare consonant (types)		
Said to have how many vowels?	13 + 8 diphthongs	
Marked vowel types	front rounded	
Tone	none	
Rhythm	no information	
Vowel harmony	none	
Morphology	fusional	word-based
Particular formation types	prefix; suffix; synaffix; apophony	
Syntax		
Word order	V2	AN / PossN / prepositions
Particular syntactic phenomena	gender; conjugation classes	
Points of interest	Flemish (Vlaams), spoken in Belgium, sometimes considered a separate language, can be viewed as a variety of Dutch	
Sources	Campbell (1991), Koolhoven (1949), Ruhlen (1976)	

Language name	Edo	Bini	'edɔu
Autonym (if known and different)			
Language family	Niger-Congo	Benue-Congo	
Spoken in	Nigeria		
Approximate number of speakers	1m		
Writing system			
Phonetics/phonology			
Stress			
Contains following rare consonant (types)	implosive		
Said to have how many vowels?	7		
Marked vowel types			
Tone	register		
Rhythm	no information		
Vowel harmony	none		
Morphology	fusional	stem-based	
Particular formation types	prefix; tone used morphologically		
Syntax			
Word order	SVO	NA NPoss	prepositions
Particular syntactic phenomena	serial verbs		
Points of interest			
Sources	Bendor-Samuel (1989), Haspelmath et al. (2005)		

Language name	Efik		'efik
Autonym (if known and different)			
Language family	Niger-Congo	Benue-Congo	
Spoken in	Nigeria		
Approximate number of speakers	750k		
Writing system	Roman, Nsibidhi script		
Phonetics/phonology			
Stress			
Contains following rare consonant (types)			
Said to have how many vowels?	7		
Marked vowel types			
Tone	register, terrace-level		
Rhythm	no information		
Vowel harmony	front-back		
Morphology	agglutinative	stem-based	
Particular formation types	prefix; suffix		
Syntax			
Word order	SVO	AN and NA NPoss	prepositions
Particular syntactic phenomena	morphological aspect; conjugation classes; serial verbs; noun classes		
Points of interest			
Sources	Campbell (1991), Cook (1969), Givon (1975), Maddieson (1984), Williamson & Blench (2000)		

Language name	English	'ɪŋglɪʃ	
Autonym (if known and different)			
Language family	Indo-European	Germanic	
Spoken in	USA, Canada, United Kingdom, Australia, New Zealand, West Indies, South Africa, Ghana, Zimbabwe, Nigeria, Liberia, India, Singapore, etc.		
Approximate number of speakers	350m		
Writing system	Roman		
Phonetics/phonology			
Stress	variable		
Contains following rare consonant (types)			
Said to have how many vowels?	approx. 20 including diphthongs, depending on variety		
Marked vowel types			
Tone	none		
Rhythm	stress-timed		
Vowel harmony	none		
Morphology	isolating and agglutinative and fusional	word-based	
Particular formation types	prefix; suffix		
Syntax			
Word order	SVO	AN PossN	prepositions
Particular syntactic phenomena			
Points of interest			
Sources	Campbell (1991), Ruhlen (1976)		

Language name	Erromangan	Sye	
Autonym (if known and different)	Nam Eromaga		
Language family	Austronesian	Malayo-Polynesian	
Spoken in	Vanuatu		
Approximate number of speakers	1.4k		
Writing system	Roman		
Phonetics/phonology			
Stress	word-penultimate		
Contains following rare consonant (types)			
Said to have how many vowels?	6		
Marked vowel types			
Tone	none		
Rhythm	no information		
Vowel harmony	none		
Morphology	agglutinative and fusional	stem-based	
Particular formation types	prefix; full reduplication; suffix; synaffix		
Syntax			
Word order	SVO	NA NPoss	prepositions
Particular syntactic phenomena	inclusive / exclusive 1st plural; morphological aspect; noun classes; conjugation classes		
Points of interest			
Sources	Crowley (1998)		

Erse see Irish

Language name	Etruscan		ʼtraskən
Autonym (if known and different)			
Language family	isolate		
Spoken in	Italy		
Approximate number of speakers	spoken from c. 700 BCE to 50 CE		
Writing system	own alphabet derived from Greek		
Phonetics/phonology			
Stress	word-initial		
Contains following rare consonant (types)			
Said to have how many vowels?	4 + 4 diphthongs		
Marked vowel types			
Tone	none		
Rhythm	no information		
Vowel harmony	none		
Morphology	agglutinative (fusional)	word-based	
Particular formation types	prefix; suffix; apophony		
Syntax			
Word order	SOV	NA (in late Etruscan) PossN (changes to NPoss)	postpositions
Particular syntactic phenomena	nominative / accusative marking; gender		
Points of interest			
Sources	Bonfante & Bonfante (2002), Rix (2004)		

Language name	Estonian		eˈstəʊnɪən
Autonym (if known and different)	Eeste		
Language family	Uralic	Finno-Ugric	
Spoken in	Estonia		
Approximate number of speakers	1m		
Writing system	Roman		
Phonetics/phonology			
Stress	word-initial		
Contains following rare consonant (types)			
Said to have how many vowels?	9 + length		
Marked vowel types	front rounded		
Tone	none		
Rhythm	no information		
Vowel harmony	none in standard dialect		
Morphology	agglutinative and fusional	stem-based	
Particular formation types	dvandva; suffix		
Syntax			
Word order	SVO	AN PossN	postpositions
Particular syntactic phenomena	nominative / accusative marking; 4th person as an impersonal; evidentials		
Points of interest	has long and extra-long vowels		
Sources	Collinder (1957), Harms (1962), Haspelmath et al. (2005), Wälchli (2005)		

Language name	Evenki	Ewenki, Tungus	e'veŋkı
Autonym (if known and different)			
Language family	Altaic	Northern Tungusic	
Spoken in	Siberia, Northern China		
Approximate number of speakers	29k		
Writing system	Cyrillic (previously Roman)		
Phonetics/phonology			
Stress	free stress		
Contains following rare consonant (types)			
Said to have how many vowels?	7 + length (6)		
Marked vowel types	back unrounded		
Tone	none		
Rhythm	no information		
Vowel harmony	short–long or soft–hard–neutral		
Morphology	fusional	stem-based	
Particular formation types	suffix		
Syntax			
Word order	SOV	AN PossN	postpositions
Particular syntactic phenomena	inclusive / exclusive 1st plural; morphological aspect; nominative / accusative marking		
Points of interest	no compounds		
Sources	Campbell (1991), Maddieson, (1984), Nedjalkov (1997), Ruhlen (1976)		

Language name	Ewe		'ewei, 'ewei
Autonym (if known and different)			
Language family	Niger-Congo	Kwa	
Spoken in	Ghana, Togo, Benin		
Approximate number of speakers	3m		
Writing system	Roman		
Phonetics/phonology			
Stress			
Contains following rare consonant (types)			
Said to have how many vowels?	7 + nasalisation		
Marked vowel types			
Tone	register		
Rhythm	no information		
Vowel harmony	none		
Morphology	isolating and agglutinative	word-based	
Particular formation types	partial prefixed and full reduplication; suffix		
Syntax			
Word order	SVO	NA PossN	prepositions
Particular syntactic phenomena	serial verbs		
Points of interest			
Sources	Campbell (1991), Maddieson (1984), Westermann (1967)		

Ewenki see Evenki

Language name	Farsi	Persian	
Autonym (if known and different)		'fɑːsiː; fɑːˈsiː	
Language family	Indo-European	Indo-Iranian	
Spoken in	Iran, Afghanistan, Tadzhikistan		
Approximate number of speakers	40m		
Writing system	Arabic		
Phonetics/phonology			
Stress	word-final		
Contains following rare consonant (types)	uvular		
Said to have how many vowels?	3 + length		
Marked vowel types	back unrounded		
Tone	none		
Rhythm	no information		
Vowel harmony	none		
Morphology	fusional	stem-based	
Particular formation types	prefix; suffix		
Syntax			
Word order	SOV	NA NPoss	prepositions
Particular syntactic phenomena	classifier; morphological aspect; nominative / accusative marking; conjugation classes		
Points of interest			
Sources	Campbell (1991), Maddieson (1984), Mahootran (1997), Windfuhr (2003)		

Language name	Faroese		feɔrɔʊˈiːz
Autonym (if known and different)	Føroysk		
Language family	Indo-European	Germanic	
Spoken in	Faroe Islands		
Approximate number of speakers	45k		
Writing system	Roman + extra letters		
Phonetics/phonology			
Stress	word-initial or root-initial		
Contains following rare consonant (types)	pre-aspirated plosives; retroflex		
Said to have how many vowels?	10 + length + 3 diphthongs		
Marked vowel types	front rounded		
Tone	none		
Rhythm	no information		
Vowel harmony	none		
Morphology	fusional	stem-based	
Particular formation types	prefix; suffix; apophony		
Syntax			
Word order	V2	AN PossN	prepositions
Particular syntactic phenomena	gender; nominative / accusative marking; conjugation classes		
Points of interest			
Sources	Campbell (1991), Lockwood (1964)		

Language name	Fijian	fiː'dʒiːən, fɪ'dʒiːən
Autonym (if known and different)		
Language family	Austronesian	Malayo-Polynesian
Spoken in	Fiji	
Approximate number of speakers	300k	
Writing system	Roman	
Phonetics/phonology		
Stress	on long syllables or word-penultimate	
Contains following rare consonant (types)		
Said to have how many vowels?	5 + length	
Marked vowel types		
Tone	none	
Rhythm	no information	
Vowel harmony	none	
Morphology	isolating agglutinative	word-based
Particular formation types	prefix; suffix	
Syntax		
Word order	VSO (and SVO)	NA PossN	prepositions
Particular syntactic phenomena	classifiers; inclusive / exclusive 1st plural; dual and trial	
Points of interest		
Sources	Campbell (1991), Milner (1972)	

Language name	Finnish	'fɪnʃ
Autonym (if known and different)	Suomi	
Language family	Uralic	Finno-Ugric
Spoken in	Finland, Sweden, Karelia	
Approximate number of speakers	5m	
Writing system	Roman	
Phonetics/phonology		
Stress	word-initial	
Contains following rare consonant (types)		
Said to have how many vowels?	8 + length	
Marked vowel types	front rounded	
Tone	none	
Rhythm	no information	
Vowel harmony	front-back	
Morphology	agglutinative	word-based
Particular formation types	dvandva; suffix	
Syntax		
Word order	SVO	AN PossN	prepositions and postpositions
Particular syntactic phenomena	nominative / accusative marking	
Points of interest	complex morphophonology; large number of cases	
Sources	Campbell (1991), Maddieson (1984), Ruhlen (1973), Sulkala & Karjalainen (1992), Wälchli (2005)	

Flemish see Dutch

Language name	French		fren(t)ʃ
Autonym (if known and different)	français		
Language family	Indo-European	Romance	
Spoken in	France, Belgium, Switzerland, Canada and colonial territories		
Approximate number of speakers	109m		
Writing system	Roman		
Phonetics/phonology			
Stress	phrase-final		
Contains following rare consonant (types)	uvular		
Said to have how many vowels?	12 + nasalisation (4)		
Marked vowel types	front rounded		
Tone	none		
Rhythm	syllable-timing		
Vowel harmony	none (or only marginally in a few words)		
Morphology	fusional	word-based	
Particular formation types	prefix; suffix		
Syntax			
Word order	SVO (though contemporary spoken forms show deviation from this)	NA NPoss	prepositions
Particular syntactic phenomena	gender; conjugation classes		
Points of interest			
Sources	Byrne & Churchill (1993), Campbell (1991), Gordon (2002), Maddieson (1984)		

Language name	Fore		ˈfɔːreɪ
Autonym (if known and different)			
Language family	Indo-Pacific	Central New Guinea	
Spoken in	Eastern Highlands of New Guinea		
Approximate number of speakers	13k		
Writing system	Roman		
Phonetics/phonology			
Stress	variable		
Contains following rare consonant (types)			
Said to have how many vowels?	6 + 4 diphthongs		
Marked vowel types			
Tone	tonal accent		
Rhythm	mora timing		
Vowel harmony	rounded–unrounded		
Morphology	agglutinative	verbs stem-based; nouns word-based	
Particular formation types	dvandva; prefix; full reduplication; suffix		
Syntax			
Word order	SOV	AN NPoss	none
Particular syntactic phenomena	morphological aspect; nominative/accusative marking; conjugation classes		
Points of interest	conjunctions are affixed; 5 levels of distance in the determiner system		
Sources	Foley (1986), Ruhlen (1976), Scott (1978), Wälchli (2005)		

Language name	Friesian	Frisian		ˈfriːʒən, ˈfrɪʒən
Autonym (if known and different)	Frysk			
Language family	Indo-European	Germanic		
Spoken in	Netherlands, Germany			
Approximate number of speakers	730k			
Writing system	Roman			
Phonetics/phonology				
Stress	word-initial or root-initial			
Contains following rare consonant (types)				
Said to have how many vowels?	9 + length + 13 diphthongs			
Marked vowel types	front rounded			
Tone	none			
Rhythm	stress-timed			
Vowel harmony	none			
Morphology	agglutinative	word-based		
Particular formation types	prefix; suffix; apophony			
Syntax				
Word order	V2	AN PossN		prepositions
Particular syntactic phenomena				
Points of interest	the closest language to English			
Sources	Tiersma (1985)			

Frisian see Friesian
Ful see Fula

Language name	Fula	Ful, Fulani, Fulfulde Pulaar and other variants		ˈfuːla, fuˈlaːni
Autonym (if known and different)				
Language family	Niger-Congo	Atlantic		
Spoken in	Nigeria, Benin, Senegal, Gambia, Mali, Niger, Chad, Cameroon			
Approximate number of speakers	10m			
Writing system	Arabic, Roman			
Phonetics/phonology				
Stress	mainly word-initial			
Contains following rare consonant (types)	implosive			
Said to have how many vowels?	5 + length			
Marked vowel types				
Tone	none			
Rhythm	no information			
Vowel harmony	none			
Morphology	agglutinative	stem-based		
Particular formation types	suffix			
Syntax				
Word order	SVO	NA NPoss		prepositions
Particular syntactic phenomena	morphological aspect; noun classes; inclusive / exclusive 1st plural; nominative / accusative marking			
Points of interest				
Sources	Arnott (1970), Campbell (1991), Dunstan (1969)			

Fulani, Fulfulde see Fula

THE LINGUISTICS STUDENT'S HANDBOOK

	Gaelic	Scottish Gaelic	
Language name	Gaelic	Scottish Gaelic	
Autonym (if known and different)			ˈgeɪlɪk, ˈgælɪk
Language family	Indo-European	Celtic	
Spoken in	Scotland		
Approximate number of speakers	100k		
Writing system	Roman		
Phonetics/phonology			
Stress	word-initial		
Contains following rare consonant (types)			
Said to have how many vowels?	9 + length + 10 diphthongs		
Marked vowel types	back unrounded		
Tone	none		
Rhythm	no information		
Vowel harmony	none		
Morphology	fusional	stem-based	
Particular formation types	apophony; prefix; suffix	suffix	
Syntax			
Word order	VSO	NA NPoss	prepositions
Particular syntactic phenomena	gender; nominative / accusative marking		
Points of interest	considerable phonological mutation of initial consonants		
Sources	Campbell (1991), Gillies (1993), Katzner (1977)		

	Ganda	Luganda	
Language name	Ganda	Luganda	
Autonym (if known and different)			ˈgændə
Language family	Niger-Congo	Bantu	
Spoken in	Uganda, Tanzania		
Approximate number of speakers	4m		
Writing system			
Phonetics/phonology			
Stress			
Contains following rare consonant (types)			
Said to have how many vowels?	5 + length		
Marked vowel types			
Tone	register		
Rhythm	no information		
Vowel harmony	none		
Morphology	agglutinative	word-based	
Particular formation types	prefix; suffix		
Syntax			
Word order	SVO	NA NPoss	prepositions
Particular syntactic phenomena	noun classes		
Points of interest			
Sources	Katzner (1977), Snoxall (1967)		

Galla, Gallinya see Oromo

Language name	Geez	Ge'ez, Gŭʿz, Old Ethiopic	'giːez
Autonym (if known and different)	Gaʿəz [ˤ represents a voiced pharyngeal fricative]		
Language family	Afro-Asiatic	Semitic	
Spoken in	Ethiopia		
Approximate number of speakers	extinct		
Writing system	Ethiopic syllabary		
Phonetics/phonology			
Stress			
Contains following rare consonant (types)	pharyngeal, ejective		
Said to have how many vowels?	7		
Marked vowel types			
Tone	none		
Rhythm	no information		
Vowel harmony	none		
Morphology	fusional	stem-based	
Particular formation types	prefix; root-and-pattern; suffix		
Syntax			
Word order	VSO	NA NPoss	prepositions
Particular syntactic phenomena	gender; morphological aspect; nominative / accusative marking		
Points of interest			
Sources	Campbell (1991), Ruhlen (1976), Weninger (1993)		

Language name	Georgian		'dʒɔːdʒən
Autonym (if known and different)			
Language family	Caucasian	Southern Caucasian	
Spoken in	Georgia		
Approximate number of speakers	3.5m		
Writing system	Mxedruli		
Phonetics/phonology			
Stress	word-antepenultimate		
Contains following rare consonant (types)	uvular, ejective		
Said to have how many vowels?	5 + 1 overshort		
Marked vowel types			
Tone	none		
Rhythm	no information		
Vowel harmony	none		
Morphology	agglutinative	stem-based	
Particular formation types	dvandva; prefix; suffix; synaffix; apophony		
Syntax			
Word order	SOV and SVO	AN PossN	postpositions
Particular syntactic phenomena	conjugation classes		
Points of interest	allows 6-consonant clusters word-initially; tense–mood–aspect paradigms called 'screeves'		
Sources	Campbell (1991), Gordon (2002), Harris (2003), Haspelmath et al. (2005), Hewitt (1995), Maddieson (1984), Ruhlen (1976), Wälchli (2005)		

Language name	Gilyak	Nivkh
Autonym (if known and different)	Nivxgu	'gɪljæk
Language family	isolate	
Spoken in	Sakhalin Island	
Approximate number of speakers	400	
Writing system	Cyrillic, Roman	
Phonetics/phonology		
Stress	word-initial	
Contains following rare consonant (types)	uvular, pharyngeal	
Said to have how many vowels?	6 + length (4)	
Marked vowel types		
Tone	some tonal distinctions	
Rhythm	no information	
Vowel harmony	traces of vowel height disharmony	
Morphology	agglutinative	word-based
Particular formation types	prefix; full reduplication; suffix	
Syntax		
Word order	SOV	AN PossN / postpositions
Particular syntactic phenomena	inclusive / exclusive 1st plural; dual;morphological aspect	
Points of interest		
Sources	Campbell (1991), Gordon (2002), Gruzdeva (1998), Maddieson (1984)	

Gio see Dan

Language name	German	
Autonym (if known and different)	Deutsch	'dʒɜːmən
Language family	Indo-European	Germanic
Spoken in	Germany, Austria, Switzerland	
Approximate number of speakers	100m	
Writing system	Roman	
Phonetics/phonology		
Stress	word-initial	
Contains following rare consonant (types)	uvular	
Said to have how many vowels?	8 + length (7) + 3 diphthongs	
Marked vowel types	front rounded	
Tone	none	
Rhythm	stress-timed	
Vowel harmony	none	
Morphology	agglutinative and fusional	word-based
Particular formation types	prefix; suffix; synaffix; apophony	
Syntax		
Word order	V2	AN PossN / prepositions
Particular syntactic phenomena	gender; nominative /accusative marking	
Points of interest		
Sources	Campbell (1991), Maddieson (1984), Ruhlen (1976)	

Giiz see Geez

Language name	Greek (Classical)		griːk
Autonym (if known and different)			
Language family	Indo-European	Hellenic	
Spoken in	Greece		
Approximate number of speakers	extinct		
Writing system	Greek		
Phonetics/phonology			
Stress			
Contains following rare consonant (types)			
Said to have how many vowels?	7 + length (5)		
Marked vowel types			
Tone	none		
Rhythm	no information		
Vowel harmony	none		
Morphology	fusional	stem-based	
Particular formation types	prefix; suffix; partial initial reduplication		
Syntax			
Word order	Free	AN PossN and NPoss	prepositions
Particular syntactic phenomena	gender; nominative / accusative marking; morphological aspect; dual; conjugation classes		
Points of interest			
Sources	Campbell (1991), Luraghi (2005), Ruhlen (1976)		

Language name	Gothic		'goθk
Autonym (if known and different)			
Language family	Indo-European	Germanic	
Spoken in			
Approximate number of speakers	extinct		
Writing system	modified version of the Greek alphabet		
Phonetics/phonology			
Stress	word-initial		
Contains following rare consonant (types)			
Said to have how many vowels?	7 + 5 short + 3 diphthongs		
Marked vowel types			
Tone	none		
Rhythm	no information		
Vowel harmony	none		
Morphology	fusional	stem-based	
Particular formation types	prefix; reduplication; suffix; apophony		
Syntax			
Word order	SOV	NA NPoss	prepositions
Particular syntactic phenomena	gender; nominative / accusative marking; dual; conjugation classes		
Points of interest	known from a fourth-century translation of the Bible by Wulfila; persisted in the Crimea until the sixteenth century		
Sources	Jasanoff (2004)		

Language name	Guarani		'gwɑːraniː; gwærə'niː
Autonym (if known and different)			
Language family	Andean-Equatorial	Tupi-Guarani	
Spoken in	Paraguay, Argentina, Brazil		
Approximate number of speakers	4m		
Writing system	Roman		
Phonetics/phonology			
Stress	word-final		
Contains following rare consonant (types)			
Said to have how many vowels?	6 + nasalisation		
Marked vowel types			
Tone	none		
Rhythm	no information		
Vowel harmony	none		
Morphology	agglutinative	stem-based	
Particular formation types	incorporation; prefix; suffix		
Syntax			
Word order	SVO	NA PossN	postpositions
Particular syntactic phenomena	inclusive / exclusive 1st plural		
Points of interest			
Sources	Campbell (1991), Gordon (2002), Jensen (1999), Maddieson (1984), Ruhlen (1976)		

Language name	Greek (Modern)		griːk
Autonym (if known and different)	Neoelleniki (Dimotiki)		
Language family	Indo-European	Hellenic	
Spoken in	Greece, Cyprus		
Approximate number of speakers	12m		
Writing system	Greek		
Phonetics/phonology			
Stress	variable		
Contains following rare consonant (types)			
Said to have how many vowels?	5		
Marked vowel types			
Tone	none		
Rhythm	stress-timed		
Vowel harmony	none		
Morphology	fusional	stem-based	
Particular formation types	dvandva; prefix; suffix		
Syntax			
Word order	SVO	AN PossN	prepositions
Particular syntactic phenomena	gender; morphological aspect; nominative / accusative marking; conjugation classes		
Points of interest	a diglossic situation between *dimotiki* and the more conservative *katharevousa* is gradually being resolved, largely in favour of the former		
Sources	Campbell (1991), Mackridge (1985), Ruhlen (1976), Wälchli (2005)		

Gros Ventre see Hidatsa

Language name	Guugu Yimidhirr		
Autonym (if known and different)	guːguː ˈjimidʒiə		
Language family	Australian	Pama-Maric	
Spoken in	Queensland (Australia)		
Approximate number of speakers	600		
Writing system			
Phonetics/phonology			
Stress	word-initial		
Contains following rare consonant (types)	retroflex		
Said to have how many vowels?	3 + length		
Marked vowel types			
Tone	none		
Rhythm	no information		
Vowel harmony	none		
Morphology	agglutinative	word-based	
Particular formation types	incorporation; partial prefixed reduplication; suffix		
Syntax			
Word order	SOV	NA PossN and NPoss	postpositions
Particular syntactic phenomena	absolute / ergative marking; nominative / accusative marking; inclusive / exclusive 1st plural; dual		
Points of interest	provided English with the word *kangaroo* < *gangurru*		
Sources	Haspelmath et al (2005), Haviland (1979)		

Language name	Gujarati		
Autonym (if known and different)	gudʒəˈrɑːti		
Language family	Indo-European	Indic	
Spoken in	Gujarat, Maharashtra (India)		
Approximate number of speakers	43m		
Writing system	its own Devanagari-based script		
Phonetics/phonology			
Stress	irrelevant		
Contains following rare consonant (types)	retroflex; voiced aspirated plosives		
Said to have how many vowels?	8 + nasalisation (6)		
Marked vowel types			
Tone	none		
Rhythm	no information		
Vowel harmony	none		
Morphology	agglutinative	stem-based verbs; word-based nouns	
Particular formation types	(prefix); suffix		
Syntax			
Word order	SOV	AN PossN	postpositions
Particular syntactic phenomena	gender; morphological aspect; nominative /accusative marking and ergative / absolute marking		
Points of interest			
Sources	Campbell (1991), Mistry (2003)		

Gunavidji see Ndjébbana

Language name	Haida	'haidə
Autonym (if known and different)		
Language family	isolate	
Spoken in	Queen Charlotte Island (Canada)	
Approximate number of speakers	100	
Writing system		
Phonetics/phonology		
Stress		
Contains following rare consonant (types)	uvular, ejective	
Said to have how many vowels?	3	
Marked vowel types		
Tone	tonal accent	
Rhythm	no information	
Vowel harmony	none	
Morphology	agglutinative	
Particular formation types	prefix; suffix	
Syntax		
Word order	SVO	NA PossN	postpositions
Particular syntactic phenomena	classifiers; collective as well as plural; morphological aspect	
Points of interest		
Sources	Haspelmath et al. (2005), Maddieson (1984), Mithun (1999), Ruhlen (1976)	

Language name	Hakka	'hakə
Autonym (if known and different)	Hak-fa	
Language family	Sino-Tibetan	Sinitic
Spoken in	SE China	
Approximate number of speakers	40m	
Writing system	Chinese characters	
Phonetics/phonology		
Stress		
Contains following rare consonant (types)		
Said to have how many vowels?	6 + many diphthongs	
Marked vowel types		
Tone	contour	
Rhythm	no information	
Vowel harmony	none	
Morphology	isolating	word-based
Particular formation types	prefix; full reduplication; suffix	
Syntax		
Word order	SVO	AN PossN	prepositions
Particular syntactic phenomena	classifier	
Points of interest		
Sources	Campbell (1991), Maddieson (1984), Ramsey (1987), Ruhlen (1976)	

Halh see Mongolian

Language name	Halkomelem		
Autonym (if known and different)	hɔlkəʼmeiləm		
Language family	Salishan		
Spoken in	British Columbia (Canada)		
Approximate number of speakers	50		
Writing system	Roman		
Phonetics/phonology			
Stress	variable		
Contains following rare consonant (types)	uvular, lateral affricate, labialised uvular		
Said to have how many vowels?	6		
Marked vowel types			
Tone	tonal accent		
Rhythm	no information		
Vowel harmony	none		
Morphology	agglutinative	word-based	
Particular formation types	infix; prefix; partial prefixed and suffixed reduplication; suffix; metathesis		
Syntax			
Word order	VOS	AN NPoss	prepositions
Particular syntactic phenomena	morphological aspect		
Points of interest			
Sources	Galloway (1993)		

Language name	Hausa		
Autonym (if known and different)	ʼhausə		
Language family	Afro-Asiatic	Chadic	
Spoken in	Nigeria		
Approximate number of speakers	30m		
Writing system	Roman		
Phonetics/phonology			
Stress			
Contains following rare consonant (types)	ejective, implosive		
Said to have how many vowels?	5 + length + 2 diphthongs		
Marked vowel types			
Tone	register		
Rhythm	no information		
Vowel harmony	none		
Morphology	agglutinative and fusional	stem-based	
Particular formation types	infix; prefix; partial prefixed and full reduplication; suffix		
Syntax			
Word order	SVO	AN and NA NPoss	prepositions
Particular syntactic phenomena	gender; morphological aspect		
Points of interest			
Sources	Campbell (1991), Maddieson (1984), Newman (2003), Ruhlen (1976)		

Language name	Hebrew	ʼhiːbruː
Autonym (if known and different)		
Language family	Afro-Asiatic	Semitic
Spoken in	Israel	
Approximate number of speakers	3m	
Writing system	Hebrew	
Phonetics/phonology		
Stress	word-final	
Contains following rare consonant (types)	uvular	
Said to have how many vowels?	5	
Marked vowel types		
Tone	none	
Rhythm	no information	
Vowel harmony	none	
Morphology	fusional	stem-based
Particular formation types	prefix; root-and-pattern; partial suffixed reduplication; suffix	
Syntax		
Word order	SVO	NA / NPoss / prepositions
Particular syntactic phenomena	gender; dual; case-marked prepositions	
Points of interest	pronouns as suffixes on prepositions; the best-known case of successful language revival, Hebrew survived as a liturgical language for 1,700 years before being revived as a national language	
Sources	Berman (2003), Campbell (1991), Glinert (1989), Gordon (2002), Maddieson (1984)	

Language name	Hawaiian	həˈwaɪən
Autonym (if known and different)		
Language family	Austronesian	Polynesian
Spoken in	Hawaii (USA)	
Approximate number of speakers	15k	
Writing system	Roman	
Phonetics/phonology		
Stress	quantity-based, else word–penultimate	
Contains following rare consonant (types)		
Said to have how many vowels?	5	
Marked vowel types		
Tone	none	
Rhythm	no information	
Vowel harmony	none	
Morphology	isolating and agglutinative	word–based
Particular formation types	prefix; partial prefixed, partial suffixed and full reduplication; suffix	
Syntax		
Word order	VSO	NA / PossN / prepositions
Particular syntactic phenomena	inclusive / exclusive 1st plural; dual	
Points of interest		
Sources	Campbell (1991), Elbert (1970), Maddieson (1984)	

Language name	Hindi		ʰɪndi
Autonym (if known and different)			ʰɪndi
Language family	Indo-European	Indic	
Spoken in	India		
Approximate number of speakers	225m		
Writing system	Devanagari		
Phonetics/phonology			
Stress	weight-based		
Contains following rare consonant (types)	retroflex, voiced aspirated plosives		
Said to have how many vowels?	5 + length + nasalisation + 4 diphthongs		
Marked vowel types			
Tone	none		
Rhythm	syllable-timed		
Vowel harmony	none		
Morphology	fusional	word-based	
Particular formation types	dvandva; suffix		
Syntax			
Word order	SOV	AN PossN	postpositions
Particular syntactic phenomena	gender; morphological aspect; nominative /accusative marking; serial verbs		
Points of interest	basically the same language as Urdu, though written with a different script, and several vocabulary differences; the name Hindustani was once used for Hindi and/or Urdu		
Sources	Bhatia (2005), Campbell (1991), Kachru (2003), Katzner (1977), Maddieson (1984), Masica (1991), McGregor (1977), Wälchli (2005)		

Language name	Hidatsa	Gros Ventre	hɪˈdætsə
Autonym (if known and different)			hɪˈdætsə
Language family	Siouan		
Spoken in	North Dakota (USA)		
Approximate number of speakers	450		
Writing system			
Phonetics/phonology			
Stress			
Contains following rare consonant (types)			
Said to have how many vowels?			
Marked vowel types			
Tone	none		
Rhythm	no information		
Vowel harmony	none		
Morphology	polysynthetic	word-based	
Particular formation types	prefix; suffix; apophony		
Syntax			
Word order	SOV	NA PossN	postpositions
Particular syntactic phenomena	evidentials		
Points of interest			
Sources	Haspelmath et al. (2005), Wesley-Jones (1992)		

Language name	Hixkaryana		'hɪʃkæˈrjuːnə
Autonym (if known and different)			
Language family	Ge-Pano-Carib	Macro-Carib	
Spoken in	Northern Brazil		
Approximate number of speakers	120		
Writing system	Roman		
Phonetics/phonology			
Stress	word-final		
Contains following rare consonant (types)	retroflex		
Said to have how many vowels?	5		
Marked vowel types	back unrounded		
Tone	none		
Rhythm	no information		
Vowel harmony	front–back		
Morphology	agglutinative and fusional	stem-based	
Particular formation types	incorporation; prefix; suffix; synaffix		
Syntax			
Word order	OVS	NA (see 'points of interest') PossN	postpositions
Particular syntactic phenomena	inclusive / exclusive 1st plural; morphological aspect; conjugation classes; present vs. past possession		
Points of interest	the first OVS language described; although this language does not have adjectives as a class, modifiers follow the nouns		
Sources	Derbyshire (1979)		

Language name	Hittite		'hɪtatt
Autonym (if known and different)			
Language family	Indo-European	Anatolian	
Spoken in	second century BCE round modern Kültepe in Turkey		
Approximate number of speakers			
Writing system	cuneiform syllabary and hieroglyphics		
Phonetics/phonology			
Stress	variable, probably quality-based		
Contains following rare consonant (types)	'laryngeals' whose precise quality is unknown		
Said to have how many vowels?	4 + length		
Marked vowel types			
Tone	none		
Rhythm	no information		
Vowel harmony	none		
Morphology	fusional	word-based	
Particular formation types	infix; prefix; partial prefixed reduplication; suffix; apophony		
Syntax			
Word order	SOV	AN PossN	postpositions
Particular syntactic phenomena	gender; morphological aspect; nominative / accusative marking but with some ergativity; conjugation class; serial verbs		
Points of interest			
Sources	Luraghi (1990, 1997), Watkins (2004)		

Language name	Hopi	ˈhoʊpi	
Autonym (if known and different)			
Language family	Aztec-Tanoan	Uto-Aztecan	
Spoken in	Arizona (USA)		
Approximate number of speakers	2k		
Writing system			
Phonetics/phonology			
Stress	word-initial		
Contains following rare consonant (types)	retroflex, uvular (voiceless sonorants in some dialects)		
Said to have how many vowels?	5 + 1 diphthong		
Marked vowel types	front rounded; back unrounded		
Tone	none		
Rhythm	no information		
Vowel harmony	none		
Morphology	agglutinative	word-based	
Particular formation types	prefix; partial prefixed and partial suffixed reduplication; suffix		
Syntax			
Word order	SOV	AN PossN	postpositions
Particular syntactic phenomena	morphological aspect; dual		
Points of interest			
Sources	Campbell (1991), Kalectaca (1982), Katzner (1977), Maddieson (1984), Whorf (1946)		

Hottentot see Nama

Language name	Hungarian	hʌŋˈɡeəriən	
Autonym (if known and different)	Magyar		
Language family	Uralic	Finno-Ugric	
Spoken in	Hungary, Romania		
Approximate number of speakers	14m		
Writing system	Roman (with diacritics)		
Phonetics/phonology			
Stress	word-initial		
Contains following rare consonant (types)			
Said to have how many vowels?	7 + length		
Marked vowel types	front rounded		
Tone	none		
Rhythm	no information		
Vowel harmony	front–back and rounded–unrounded		
Morphology	agglutinative	word-based	
Particular formation types	prefix; suffix; metathesis		
Syntax			
Word order	(SOV) and SVO	AN PossN	postpositions
Particular syntactic phenomena	morphological aspect; nominative / accusative marking		
Points of interest			
Sources	Campbell (1991), Gordon (2002), Katzner (1977), Maddieson (1984), Rounds (2001)		

Ibo see Igbo

Language name	Igbo	Ibo
Autonym (if known and different)	ibo	'igbəu, 'i:bəu
Language family	Niger-Congo	Benue-Congo
Spoken in	Nigeria	
Approximate number of speakers	10m	
Writing system	Roman	
Phonetics/phonology		
Stress		
Contains following rare consonant (types)	implosive	
Said to have how many vowels?	8 + nasalisation	
Marked vowel types		
Tone	register, terrace-level	
Rhythm	no information	
Vowel harmony	ATR	
Morphology	agglutinative	word-based
Particular formation types	prefix; suffix; tone used morphologically	
Syntax		
Word order	SVO	NA NPoss	prepositions
Particular syntactic phenomena	noun classes; serial verbs	
Points of interest		
Sources	Campbell (1991), Carrell (1970), Givon (1975), Maddieson (1984), Ruhlen (1976), Williamson (1969a), Williamson & Emenanjo (2003)	

Ijaw see Ijo

Language name	Icelandic	
Autonym (if known and different)	islenzka	ais'lændik
Language family	Indo-European	Germanic
Spoken in	Iceland	
Approximate number of speakers	250k	
Writing system	Roman (with extra letters)	
Phonetics/phonology		
Stress	word-initial	
Contains following rare consonant (types)	pre-aspirated plosives; voiceless sonorants	
Said to have how many vowels?	9 + length	
Marked vowel types	front rounded	
Tone	none	
Rhythm	no information	
Vowel harmony	none	
Morphology	fusional	stem-based
Particular formation types	prefix; suffix	
Syntax		
Word order	SVO	AN NPoss	prepositions
Particular syntactic phenomena	gender; nominative / accusative marking; conjugation classes	
Points of interest		
Sources	Campbell (1991), Einarsson (1945), Katzner (1977), Maddieson (1984), Ruhlen (1976)	

Language name	Ijo	Ijaw	'iidʒəu, 'iidʒɔː
Autonym (if known and different)			
Language family	Niger-Congo	Benue-Congo	
Spoken in	Nigeria		
Approximate number of speakers	500k		
Writing system	Roman		
Phonetics/phonology			
Stress			
Contains following rare consonant (types)	implosive		
Said to have how many vowels?	9 + nasalisation (8)		
Marked vowel types			
Tone	register, terrace-level		
Rhythm	tone-group-based		
Vowel harmony	ATR		
Morphology	isolating and agglutinative	word-based	
Particular formation types	prefix; suffix; reduplication; tone used morphologically		
Syntax			
Word order	SOV	AN PossN	postpositions
Particular syntactic phenomena	serial verbs; gender		
Points of interest			
Sources	Givon (1975), Jenewari (1989), Katzner (1977), Ruhlen (1976), Westermann & Bryan (1970), Williamson (1969b), Williamson & Blench (2000)		

Language name	Ilocano, Ilokano	Iloko	iːlɒʊˈkɑːnəu
Autonym (if known and different)			
Language family	Austronesian		
Spoken in	Philippines		
Approximate number of speakers	5m		
Writing system	Roman		
Phonetics/phonology			
Stress	one of the last two syllables		
Contains following rare consonant (types)			
Said to have how many vowels?	4		
Marked vowel types			
Tone	none		
Rhythm	no information		
Vowel harmony	none		
Morphology	agglutinative	stem-based	
Particular formation types	infix; prefix; partial prefixed and partial infixed and full reduplication; suffix		
Syntax			
Word order	VSO	AN NPoss	prepositions
Particular syntactic phenomena	inclusive / exclusive 1st plural; ergative / absolutive marking; dual; morphological aspect		
Points of interest	different reduplication patterns have different meanings		
Sources	Campbell (1991), Rubino (2005)		

Ilokano, Iloko see Ilocano

Language name	Irish	Erse
Autonym (if known and different)		'aɪərʃ
Language family	Indo-European	Celtic
Spoken in	Ireland	
Approximate number of speakers	30k	
Writing system	Roman	
Phonetics/phonology		
Stress	word-initial	
Contains following rare consonant (types)	contrasting palatalised and velarised consonants	
Said to have how many vowels?	6 + length + nasalisation + ə in unstressed syllables	
Marked vowel types	back unrounded	
Tone	none	
Rhythm	no information	
Vowel harmony	some height harmony	
Morphology	fusional	stem-based
Particular formation types	prefix; suffix; internal modification	
Syntax		
Word order	VSO / NA NPoss	prepositions
Particular syntactic phenomena	gender; inflecting prepositions; morphological aspect; conjugation classes	
Points of interest	initial mutation; the term 'Erse' seems to be avoided in technical descriptions because it is ambiguous between the Scottish and Irish languages	
Sources	Campbell (1991), Katzner (1977), Gordon (2002), Mac Eoin (1993), Ó Siadhail (1989)	

isiXhosa see Xhosa
isiZulu see Zulu

Language name	Indonesian	Bahasa Indonesia	ndʌʊˈniːʒɛn
Autonym (if known and different)			
Language family	Austronesian		
Spoken in	Indonesia		
Approximate number of speakers	190m		
Writing system	Roman		
Phonetics/phonology			
Stress	word-penultimate		
Contains following rare consonant (types)			
Said to have how many vowels?	6 + 3 diphthongs		
Marked vowel types			
Tone	none		
Rhythm	syllable-timing		
Vowel harmony	none		
Morphology	agglutinative	word-based	
Particular formation types	dvandva; infix; prefix; partial prefixed and partial suffixed and full reduplication; suffix; synaffix		
Syntax			
Word order	SVO / NA NPoss	prepositions	
Particular syntactic phenomena	classifier; inclusive / exclusive 1st plural		
Points of interest	3 degrees of formality in pronouns		
Sources	Campbell (1991), Katzner (1977), Kwee (1976), Macdonald & Darjowidjojo (1967), Ruhlen (1976)		

Language name	Jacaltec		haːkaltʔek
Autonym (if known and different)			
Language family	Penutian	Mayan	
Spoken in	Guatemala		
Approximate number of speakers	12k		
Writing system			
Phonetics/phonology			
Stress	word-initial		
Contains following rare consonant (types)	retroflex, uvular, ejective, implosive		
Said to have how many vowels?	5		
Marked vowel types			
Tone	none		
Rhythm	no information		
Vowel harmony	none		
Morphology	agglutinative	stem-based for verbs; word-based for nouns	
Particular formation types	prefix; suffix		
Syntax			
Word order	VSO	NA NPoss	prepositions
Particular syntactic phenomena	morphological aspect; gender; classifiers; ergative / absolutive marking; pronouns inflect for aspect; serial verbs; noun classes		
Points of interest			
Sources	Craig (1987), Haspelmath et al. (2005), Ruhlen (1976)		

Language name	Italian		ɪˈtaelɪən
Autonym (if known and different)	italiano		
Language family	Indo-European	Romance	
Spoken in	Italy, Switzerland		
Approximate number of speakers	55m		
Writing system	Roman		
Phonetics/phonology			
Stress	variable in the last three syllables of the word		
Contains following rare consonant (types)			
Said to have how many vowels?	7		
Marked vowel types			
Tone	none		
Rhythm	no information		
Vowel harmony	none		
Morphology	fusional	stem-based	
Particular formation types	prefix; suffix		
Syntax			
Word order	SVO	(AN) NA NPoss	prepositions
Particular syntactic phenomena	gender; conjugation classes		
Points of interest			
Sources	Campbell (1991), Katzner (1977), Maiden & Robustelli (2000)		

Language name	Javanese		dʒɑːvəˈniːz
Autonym (if known and different)			
Language family	Austronesian	West Indonesian	
Spoken in	Java		
Approximate number of speakers	55m		
Writing system	Javanese script; Roman		
Phonetics/phonology			
Stress	no word stress		
Contains following rare consonant (types)	retroflex		
Said to have how many vowels?	8		
Marked vowel types			
Tone	none		
Rhythm	no information		
Vowel harmony	some height harmony		
Morphology	agglutinative		word-based
Particular formation types	infix; prefix; partial prefixed and full reduplication; suffix; synaffix		
Syntax			
Word order	SVO	NA NPoss	prepositions
Particular syntactic phenomena	inclusive / exclusive 1st plural		
Points of interest	well-developed 'elevated' register		
Sources	Campbell (1991), Horne (1961), Katzner (1977), Maddieson (1984), Oglobin (2005)		

Jicaque see Tol
Jieng see Dinka

Language name	Japanese		dʒæpəˈniːz
Autonym (if known and different)	Nihongo		
Language family	Disputed; possibly Altaic		
Spoken in	Japan		
Approximate number of speakers	120m		
Writing system	Japanese kana; Chinese characters		
Phonetics/phonology			
Stress			
Contains following rare consonant (types)			
Said to have how many vowels?	5		
Marked vowel types	back unrounded (in Tokyo)		
Tone	tonal accent		
Rhythm	mora-timing		
Vowel harmony	none		
Morphology	agglutinative		stem-based
Particular formation types	dvandva; prefix; suffix		
Syntax			
Word order	SOV	AN PossN	postpositions
Particular syntactic phenomena	classifiers; evidentials		
Points of interest			
Sources	Campbell (1991), Haspelmath et al. (2005), Katzner (1977), Maddieson (1984), Shibatani (1990), Yip (2002)		

Language name	Kamba		'kæmba
Autonym (if known and different)	KiKamba		
Language family	Niger-Congo		
Spoken in	Kenya		
Approximate number of speakers	750k		
Writing system			
Phonetics/phonology			
Stress	root-initial		
Contains following rare consonant (types)			
Said to have how many vowels?	7		
Marked vowel types			
Tone	register tone		
Rhythm	no information		
Vowel harmony	none		
Morphology	agglutinative	stem-based	
Particular formation types	infix; prefix; suffix		
Syntax			
Word order	SVO	NA / NPoss	prepositions
Particular syntactic phenomena	noun classes; negative tenses		
Points of interest	4 vowel lengths		
Sources	Whitely & Muli (1962)		

Language name	Kabardian	Circassian	kə'bɑːdɪən
Autonym (if known and different)			
Language family	NW Caucasian	Abkhaz-Adyge	
Spoken in	Northern Caucasus		
Approximate number of speakers	350k		
Writing system	Cyrillic		
Phonetics/phonology			
Stress	root-final		
Contains following rare consonant (types)	uvular; pharyngeal; ejective		
Said to have how many vowels?	7		
Marked vowel types			
Tone	none		
Rhythm	no information		
Vowel harmony	none		
Morphology	agglutinative and fusional	stem-based	
Particular formation types	infix; prefix; suffix		
Syntax			
Word order	SOV	NA / PossN	postpositions
Particular syntactic phenomena	absolute / ergative marking; nominative / accusative marking; morphological aspect; conjugation classes		
Points of interest			
Sources	Campbell (1991), Gordon (2002), Katzner (1977), Maddieson (1984)		

Language name	Kannada		'kaːnədə, 'kænədə
Autonym (if known and different)			
Language family	Dravidian		
Spoken in	Karnataka (India)		
Approximate number of speakers	30m		
Writing system	Devanagari		
Phonetics/phonology			
Stress	word-initial		
Contains following rare consonant (types)	retroflex		
Said to have how many vowels?	5 + length + 2 diphthongs		
Marked vowel types			
Tone	none		
Rhythm	no information		
Vowel harmony	none		
Morphology	agglutinative	word-based	
Particular formation types	dvandva; full reduplication; suffix		
Syntax			
Word order	SOV	AN PossN	postpositions
Particular syntactic phenomena	classifiers; semantically based gender; nominative / accusative marking; conjugation classes; evidentials		
Points of interest			
Sources	Campbell (1991), Haspelmath et al. (2005), Katzner (1977), Ruhlen (1976), Sridhar (1990)		

Language name	Kambera		'kæmberə
Autonym (if known and different)	Hilu Humba		
Language family	Austronesian	Malayo-Polynesian	
Spoken in	Sumba (Indonesia)		
Approximate number of speakers	150k		
Writing system	Roman		
Phonetics/phonology			
Stress	root-initial		
Contains following rare consonant (types)	implosive		
Said to have how many vowels?	5 + length (3) + 2 diphthongs		
Marked vowel types			
Tone	none		
Rhythm	no information		
Vowel harmony	some height harmony		
Morphology	polysynthetic	word-based	
Particular formation types	incorporation; prefix; partial prefixed and full reduplication; suffix; synaffix		
Syntax			
Word order	SVO	NA (see 'points of interest') NPoss	prepositions
Particular syntactic phenomena	classifiers; inclusive / exclusive 1st plural; nominative / accusative marking; morphological aspect; serial verbs		
Points of interest	argued not to have adjectives but postnominal modifying verbs		
Sources	Gordon (2002), Klamer (1994, 2005)		

Language name	Karen		kəˈren
Autonym (if known and different)	kəjɛ̃ lì ŋò		
Language family	Tibeto-Burman		
Spoken in	Thailand, Myanmar		
Approximate number of speakers	2m		
Writing system	Roman; there is also a local script of recent invention		
Phonetics/phonology			
Stress			
Contains following rare consonant (types)	retroflex; implosive		
Said to have how many vowels?	11 + 2 diphthongs		
Marked vowel types	back unrounded		
Tone	register		
Rhythm	no information		
Vowel harmony	none		
Morphology	isolating	word-based	
Particular formation types	dvandva; prefix; partial suffixed and full reduplication; suffix		
Syntax			
Word order	SVO	NA PossN	prepositions
Particular syntactic phenomena	classifier; serial verbs		
Points of interest	Karen is a group of languages rather than a single language		
Sources	Campbell (1991), Kato (2003), Katzner (1977), Maddieson (1984), Solnit (1997), Wälchli (2005)		

Language name	Kanuri		kəˈnuːri
Autonym (if known and different)			
Language family	Nilo-Saharan	Saharan	
Spoken in	Chad, Nigeria		
Approximate number of speakers	2m		
Writing system			
Phonetics/phonology			
Stress			
Contains following rare consonant (types)	retroflex		
Said to have how many vowels?	6 + 13 diphthongs		
Marked vowel types			
Tone	register tone		
Rhythm	no information		
Vowel harmony	none		
Morphology	agglutinative and fusional	word-based	
Particular formation types	prefix; reduplication; suffix		
Syntax			
Word order	SOV	NA NPoss	prepositions and postpositions
Particular syntactic phenomena	morphological aspect; nominative / accusative marking; conjugation classes		
Points of interest	case marked on the adjective rather than on the noun		
Sources	Lukas (1967), Maddieson (1984), Ruhlen (1976)		

Language name	Ket	Yenisey Ostyak	
Autonym (if known and different)		ket	
Language family	Paleo-Asiatic		
Spoken in	Siberia		
Approximate number of speakers	500		
Writing system	Cyrillic		
Phonetics/phonology			
Stress	word–initial		
Contains following rare consonant (types)	uvular		
Said to have how many vowels?	7		
Marked vowel types			
Tone	yes		
Rhythm	no information		
Vowel harmony	none		
Morphology	agglutinative and fusional	stem–based	
Particular formation types	infix; prefix; suffix		
Syntax			
Word order	SOV	AN PossN	postpositions
Particular syntactic phenomena	gender; conjugation classes		
Points of interest			
Sources	Campbell (1991), Gordon (2002), Haspelmath et al. (2005), Katzner (1977), Maddieson (1984), Ruhlen (1976), Vajda (2004)		

Khalkha see Mongolian
Khanty see Ostyak

Language name	Kashmiri		kəʃ'miəri
Autonym (if known and different)	kaːʃur, kaʃir zabaːn		
Language family	Indo-European	Indic	
Spoken in	Kashmir, India, Pakistan		
Approximate number of speakers	3m		
Writing system	various, including a version of Devanagari and Sharada for religious purposes		
Phonetics/phonology			
Stress	no word stress		
Contains following rare consonant (types)	retroflex		
Said to have how many vowels?	8 + length + nasalisation		
Marked vowel types			
Tone	none		
Rhythm	syllable–timing		
Vowel harmony	none		
Morphology	fusional	stem–based	
Particular formation types	dvandva; prefix; full reduplication; suffix		
Syntax			
Word order	SVO (rather free)	AN PossN	postpositions
Particular syntactic phenomena	absolutive / ergative marking; nominative / accusative marking; gender; morphological aspect; conjugation classes		
Points of interest			
Sources	Campbell (1991), Katzner (1977), Wali & Koul (1997)		

Kilivila

Language name	Kilivila		
Autonym (if known and different)			
Language family	Austronesian	Malayo-Polynesian	
Spoken in	Trobriand Islands		
Approximate number of speakers	22k		
Writing system			
Phonetics/phonology			
Stress	word-penultimate		
Contains following rare consonant (types)			
Said to have how many vowels?	5 + 5 diphthongs		
Marked vowel types			
Tone	none		
Rhythm	no information		
Vowel harmony	none		
Morphology	agglutinative	stem-based	
Particular formation types	prefix; full and partial reduplication; suffix		
Syntax			
Word order	VOS	NA PossN	prepositions
Particular syntactic phenomena	classifiers; inclusive / exclusive 1st plural/ dual; morphological aspect; noun class; dual		
Points of interest			
Sources	Haspelmath et al. (2005), Senft (1986)		

Khmer

Language name	Khmer	Cambodian	kmeə, kaʔmeə
Autonym (if known and different)			
Language family	Mon-Khmer		
Spoken in	Cambodia, Vietnam, Thailand		
Approximate number of speakers	7m		
Writing system	Khmer		
Phonetics/phonology			
Stress	word-final		
Contains following rare consonant (types)	retroflex; implosive		
Said to have how many vowels?	7 + length (5) + 15 diphthongs		
Marked vowel types	back unrounded		
Tone	none		
Rhythm	no information		
Vowel harmony	none		
Morphology	isolating (agglutinative)	word-based	
Particular formation types	dvandva; infix; prefix; partial prefixed and full reduplication; suffix (only in loans)		
Syntax			
Word order	SVO	NA NPoss	prepositions
Particular syntactic phenomena	classifiers		
Points of interest			
Sources	Campbell (1991), Diffloth (2003), Ehrman (1972), Katzner (1977), Maddieson (1984), Wälchli (2005)		

Language name	Kirghiz		kɯˈgiːz
Autonym (if known and different)			
Language family	Altaic	Northern Turkic	
Spoken in	Kirghizistan, Uzbekistan, Kazakhstan, Tadzhikistan, Mongolia		
Approximate number of speakers	1.5m		
Writing system	Cyrillic, Roman		
Phonetics/phonology			
Stress	word-final		
Contains following rare consonant (types)	uvular		
Said to have how many vowels?	8 + length (6)		
Marked vowel types	front rounded		
Tone	none		
Rhythm	no information		
Vowel harmony	front-back and rounded-unrounded		
Morphology	agglutinative	stem-based	
Particular formation types	dvandva; suffix		
Syntax			
Word order	SOV	AN NPoss	postpositions
Particular syntactic phenomena	morphological aspect; nominative / accusative marking		
Points of interest			
Sources	Campbell (1991), Kirchner (1998), Maddieson (1984), Ruhlen (1976), Wälchli (2005)		

KiSwahili see Swahili

Language name	Kiowa		ˈkiːəwə
Autonym (if known and different)			
Language family	Uto-Aztecan	Kiowa-Tanoan	
Spoken in	Oklahoma (USA)		
Approximate number of speakers	200		
Writing system	Roman		
Phonetics/phonology			
Stress			
Contains following rare consonant (types)	ejective		
Said to have how many vowels?	6 + 4 diphthongs + length + nasalisation		
Marked vowel types			
Tone	register		
Rhythm	no information		
Vowel harmony	none		
Morphology	agglutinative	word-based	
Particular formation types	incorporation; prefix; suffix		
Syntax			
Word order	SOV	NA PossN	postpositions
Particular syntactic phenomena	morphological aspect; noun classes; dual; conjugation classes; switch-reference; evidentials		
Points of interest	some noun classes are inherently singular or dual and a marker makes them plural; others are inherently plural and the same marker makes them singular		
Sources	Haspelmath et al. (2005), Mithun (1999), Watkins (1984)		

Language name	Klamath	'klæmǝθ	
Autonym (if known and different)			
Language family	Penutian		
Spoken in	Oregon (USA)		
Approximate number of speakers	50		
Writing system			
Phonetics/phonology			
Stress	quantity-based		
Contains following rare consonant (types)	uvular; ejective; implosive		
Said to have how many vowels?	4 + length		
Marked vowel types			
Tone	none		
Rhythm	no information		
Vowel harmony	none		
Morphology	agglutinative	word-based	
Particular formation types	prefix; partial prefixed and full reduplication; suffix		
Syntax			
Word order	Free	AN PossN	postpositions
Particular syntactic phenomena	morphological aspect		
Points of interest			
Sources	De Lancey (1991), Haspelmath et al. (2005), Katzner (1977), Maddieson (1984), Mithun (1999), Ruhlen (1976)		

Language name	Kobon		
Autonym (if known and different)			
Language family	Trans-New-Guinea	East New Guinea Highlands	
Spoken in	Papua New Guinea		
Approximate number of speakers	6k		
Writing system			
Phonetics/phonology			
Stress	word-penultimate		
Contains following rare consonant (types)			
Said to have how many vowels?	7		
Marked vowel types	front rounded		
Tone	none		
Rhythm	no information		
Vowel harmony	none		
Morphology	agglutinative and fusional	word-based	
Particular formation types	dvandva; incorporation; full reduplication; suffix		
Syntax			
Word order	SOV	NA PossN	postpositions
Particular syntactic phenomena	morphological aspect; dual; conjugation classes		
Points of interest			
Sources	Davies (1981)		

Language name	Kolyma Yukaghir		
Autonym (if known and different)			
Language family	Uralic	Isolate	
Spoken in	Yakutia Republic (Russia)		
Approximate number of speakers	50		
Writing system	Cyrillic		
Phonetics/phonology			
Stress	weight-based, tending to word-final		
Contains following rare consonant (types)	uvular		
Said to have how many vowels?	6 + length		
Marked vowel types	front rounded		
Tone	none		
Rhythm	no information		
Vowel harmony	front–back, some rounding		
Morphology	agglutinative	word-based	
Particular formation types	(prefixation); (reduplication); suffixation		
Syntax			
Word order	SOV	AN PossN	postpositions
Particular syntactic phenomena	morphological aspect; nominative / accusative marking		
Points of interest			
Sources	Maslova (2003)		

Language name	Koiari		kɔrˈɑːri
Autonym (if known and different)			
Language family	Trans–New–Guinea		
Spoken in	Papua New Guinea		
Approximate number of speakers	2k		
Writing system	Roman		
Phonetics/phonology			
Stress	variable but with a word-initial bias		
Contains following rare consonant (types)			
Said to have how many vowels?	5		
Marked vowel types			
Tone	none		
Rhythm	no information		
Vowel harmony	none		
Morphology	agglutinative	stem-based verbs and word-based nouns	
Particular formation types	partial prefixed and full reduplication; suffix		
Syntax			
Word order	SOV	AN (NA) PossN	postpositions
Particular syntactic phenomena	absolutive / ergative marking; nominative / accusative marking; morphological aspect; noun classes; verb classes		
Points of interest	verbs inflect for tense/aspect etc. only when sentence-final, not when sentence-medial; no /p/ in native words, but /b/		
Sources	Dutton (1996)		

Language name	Koromfe	
Autonym (if known and different)		
Language family	Niger-Congo	Volta-Congo
Spoken in	Burkina Faso (W Africa)	
Approximate number of speakers		
Writing system		
Phonetics/phonology		
Stress	none	
Contains following rare consonant (types)		
Said to have how many vowels?	6	
Marked vowel types		
Tone	none	
Rhythm	no information	
Vowel harmony	ATR	
Morphology	isolating and fusional	stem-based
Particular formation types	full reduplication; suffix	
Syntax		
Word order	SVO	NA
		PossN
		prepositions and postpositions
Particular syntactic phenomena	classifiers; morphological aspect; noun classes	
Points of interest		
Sources	Rennison (1997)	

Language name	Korean	kə'riːan
Autonym (if known and different)		
Language family	Disputed: possibly Altaic	
Spoken in	Korea	
Approximate number of speakers	70m	
Writing system	Korean (Hangul and Chinese characters)	
Phonetics/phonology		
Stress	phrase-initial	
Contains following rare consonant (types)		
Said to have how many vowels?	10 + length (8)	
Marked vowel types	front rounded, back unrounded	
Tone	none in standard varieties	
Rhythm	no information	
Vowel harmony	some traces remain	
Morphology	agglutinative	stem-based for verbs; word-based for nouns
Particular formation types	dvandva; partial suffixed and full reduplication; suffix	
Syntax		
Word order	SOV	AN
		PossN
		postpositions
Particular syntactic phenomena	morphological aspect; nominative / accusative marking; evidentials	
Points of interest		
Sources	Campbell (1991), Haspelmath et al. (2005), Katzner (1977), Kim (2003), Maddieson (1984), Sohn (1994), Wälchli (2005)	

Language name	Kurdish		'kɜːdɪʃ
Autonym (if known and different)			
Language family	Indo-European	Iranian	
Spoken in	Turkey, Syria, Iraq, Iran		
Approximate number of speakers	10m		
Writing system	Arabic, Cyrillic, depending on the country where it is spoken		
Phonetics/phonology			
Stress	word-final		
Contains following rare consonant (types)	uvular; pharyngeal		
Said to have how many vowels?	4 + 5 long + 8 diphthongs		
Marked vowel types			
Tone	none		
Rhythm	no information		
Vowel harmony	none		
Morphology	fusional	stem-based	
Particular formation types	dvandva; suffix		
Syntax			
Word order	SOV	NA NPoss	prepositions
Particular syntactic phenomena	conjugation classes		
Points of interest			
Sources	Campbell (1991), Gordon (2002), Katzner (1977), Maddieson (1984), Ruhlen (1976), Wälchii (2005)		

Language name	Kpelle		kɔʔpelə
Autonym (if known and different)	kpɛlɛɛ-woo		
Language family	Niger-Congo	Mande	
Spoken in	Liberia		
Approximate number of speakers	700k		
Writing system			
Phonetics/phonology			
Stress			
Contains following rare consonant (types)	implosive		
Said to have how many vowels?	7 + length + nasalisation (6)		
Marked vowel types			
Tone	register		
Rhythm	no information		
Vowel harmony	none		
Morphology	agglutinative and fusional	stem-based	
Particular formation types	suffix; suprasegmentals used morphologically		
Syntax			
Word order	SOV	NA PossN	postpositions
Particular syntactic phenomena			
Points of interest			
Sources	Campbell (1991), Katzner (1977), Maddieson (1984), Ruhlen (1976), Westermann & Bryan (1970)		

Kunavidji see **Ndjébbana**
!Kung see **!Xũ**, p. 367

Language name	Kwakwala	Kwakiutl	kwɑ'kwɑːlə
Autonym (if known and different)			
Language family	Wakashan		
Spoken in	British Columbia, Vancouver Island (Canada)		
Approximate number of speakers	250		
Writing system			
Phonetics/phonology			
Stress			
Contains following rare consonant (types)	uvular; ejective		
Said to have how many vowels?	6		
Marked vowel types			
Tone	none		
Rhythm	no information		
Vowel harmony	none		
Morphology	polysynthetic	stem-based for verbs; word-based for nouns	
Particular formation types	suffix		
Syntax			
Word order	SVO	AN NPoss	postpositions
Particular syntactic phenomena	evidentials		
Points of interest			
Sources	Haspelmath et al. (2005), Maddieson (1984)		

Lao see **Laotian**

Language name	Kusaiean		
Autonym (if known and different)			
Language family	Austronesian	Malayo-Polynesian	
Spoken in	Caroline Islands		
Approximate number of speakers			
Writing system			
Phonetics/phonology			
Stress	word-penultimate		
Contains following rare consonant (types)			
Said to have how many vowels?	12 + 9 short		
Marked vowel types			
Tone	none		
Rhythm	no information		
Vowel harmony	none		
Morphology	isolating and agglutinative	word-based	
Particular formation types	incorporation; prefix; partial prefixed and full reduplication; suffix		
Syntax			
Word order	SVO	NA NPoss	prepositions
Particular syntactic phenomena	noun classes; alienable / inalienable possession		
Points of interest			
Sources	Lee (1975)		

Kwakiutl see **Kwakwala**

Language name	Latin		'lætɪn
Autonym (if known and different)			
Language family	Indo-European	Italic	
Spoken in	Italy (and throughout the Roman Empire)		
Approximate number of speakers	0		
Writing system	Roman		
Phonetics/phonology			
Stress	word-penultimate or antepenultimate		
Contains following rare consonant (types)			
Said to have how many vowels?	5 + length		
Marked vowel types			
Tone	none		
Rhythm	no information		
Vowel harmony	none		
Morphology	fusional		
Particular formation types	suffix	stem-based	
Syntax			
Word order	SOV (but variable)	NA PossN	prepositions
Particular syntactic phenomena	gender; morphological aspect; nominative / accusative marking; conjugation classes		
Points of interest			
Sources	Campbell (1991), Vincent (1988)		

Language name	Lao	Laotian	'lauʃən
Autonym (if known and different)			
Language family	Tai	Kam–Tai	
Spoken in	Laos, Thailand		
Approximate number of speakers	10m		
Writing system	Tua Lao		
Phonetics/phonology			
Stress			
Contains following rare consonant (types)			
Said to have how many vowels?	9 + length + 3 diphthongs (long and short)		
Marked vowel types	back unrounded		
Tone	contour		
Rhythm	no information		
Vowel harmony	none		
Morphology	isolating	word-based	
Particular formation types	full reduplication		
Syntax			
Word order	SVO	NA NPoss	prepositions
Particular syntactic phenomena	classifiers; alienable / inalienable possession		
Points of interest			
Sources	Campbell (1991), Haspelmath et al. (2005), Ruhlen (1976)		

Language name	Lenakel		
Autonym (if known and different)			
Language family	Austronesian	Malayo-Polynesian	
Spoken in	Vanuatu		
Approximate number of speakers	6.5k		
Writing system			
Phonetics/phonology			
Stress	word-penultimate		
Contains following rare consonant (types)			
Said to have how many vowels?	6		
Marked vowel types			
Tone	none		
Rhythm	no information		
Vowel harmony	none		
Morphology	agglutinative	stem-based for verbs; word-based for nouns	
Particular formation types	prefix; full reduplication; suffix; synaffix		
Syntax			
Word order	SVO	NA NPoss	prepositions
Particular syntactic phenomena	morphological aspect; noun classes; dual and trial; conjugation classes		
Points of interest			
Sources	Lynch (1978)		

Lettish see Latvian

Language name	Latvian	Lettish	ˈlætviən
Autonym (if known and different)			
Language family	Indo-European	Baltic	
Spoken in	Latvia		
Approximate number of speakers	2.5m		
Writing system	Roman (with diacritics)		
Phonetics/phonology			
Stress	word-initial		
Contains following rare consonant (types)			
Said to have how many vowels?	6 + length (5)		
Marked vowel types			
Tone	tonal accent		
Rhythm	no information		
Vowel harmony	none		
Morphology	fusional	stem-based	
Particular formation types	dvandva; prefix; suffix		
Syntax			
Word order	SVO	AN PossN	postpositions (postpositions)
Particular syntactic phenomena	gender; nominative / accusative marking; conjugation classes		
Points of interest			
Sources	Campbell (1991), Gordon (2002), Katzner (1977), Nau (1998), Ruhlen (1976), Wälchli (2005)		

Language name	Lithuanian		lɪθˈjuːˈɛnɪən
Autonym (if known and different)	Lietuvos		
Language family	Indo-European	Baltic	
Spoken in	Lithuania		
Approximate number of speakers	3m		
Writing system	Roman		
Phonetics/phonology			
Stress			
Contains following rare consonant (types)			
Said to have how many vowels?	6 + length (5)		
Marked vowel types			
Tone	tonal accent		
Rhythm	no information		
Vowel harmony	none		
Morphology	fusional	stem-based	
Particular formation types	dvandva; prefix; suffix		
Syntax			
Word order	SVO	AN PossN	prepositions
Particular syntactic phenomena	gender; nominative / accusative marking; conjugation classes; evidentials		
Points of interest	definiteness marked on adjectives		
Sources	Campbell (1991), Haspelmath et al. (2005), Katzner (1977), Maddieson (1984), Ruhlen (1976), Wälchli (2005)		

Language name	Lezgian		ˈlezgiən
Autonym (if known and different)	lezgi		
Language family	Nakho-Daghestanian		
Spoken in	Daghestan, Azerbaijan		
Approximate number of speakers	400k		
Writing system	Cyrillic		
Phonetics/phonology			
Stress	second syllable of the root		
Contains following rare consonant (types)	uvular; ejective; contrastive labialisation		
Said to have how many vowels?	6		
Marked vowel types			
Tone	none		
Rhythm	no information		
Vowel harmony	front–back and rounding		
Morphology	agglutinative	word-based	
Particular formation types	dvandva; prefixation; suffixation		
Syntax			
Word order	SOV	AN PossN	prepositions
Particular syntactic phenomena	morphological aspect; ergative / absolutive marking conjugation classes;		
Points of interest	has 18 case forms for nouns		
Sources	Haspelmath (1993)		

Luganda see **Ganda**
Lusatian see **Sorbian**

Language name	Macedonian		mæsə'dəʊnɪən
Autonym (if known and different)			
Language family	Indo-European	Slavic	
Spoken in	Macedonia, Bulgaria, Greece		
Approximate number of speakers	2.5m		
Writing system	Cyrillic		
Phonetics/phonology			
Stress	word-antepenultimate		
Contains following rare consonant (types)			
Said to have how many vowels?	5		
Marked vowel types			
Tone	none		
Rhythm	no information		
Vowel harmony	none		
Morphology	fusional	stem-based in verbs; word-based in nouns	
Particular formation types	prefixation; suffixation		
Syntax			
Word order	SVO	AN / PossN and NPoss	prepositions
Particular syntactic phenomena	morphological aspect; nominative / accusative marking		
Points of interest	there was an ancient Indo-European language with the same name		
Sources	Friedman (1993)		

Language name	Maasai	Masai	'mɑːsai
Autonym (if known and different)			
Language family	Nilo-Saharan	Lotuxo-Teso	
Spoken in	Kenya, Tanzania		
Approximate number of speakers	400k		
Writing system	Roman		
Phonetics/phonology			
Stress	word-penultimate		
Contains following rare consonant (types)	implosive		
Said to have how many vowels?	5 + length		
Marked vowel types			
Tone	register		
Rhythm	no information		
Vowel harmony	none		
Morphology	agglutinative	stem-based	
Particular formation types	prefix; partial suffixed reduplication; suffix		
Syntax			
Word order	VSO	NA / NPoss	prepositions
Particular syntactic phenomena	classifier; gender; nominative / accusative marking		
Points of interest			
Sources	Campbell (1991), Hollis (1970), Maddieson (1984)		

Language name	Madi		
Autonym (if known and different)	mà̰dì		
Language family	Nilo-Saharan	Central Sudanic	
Spoken in	Uganda, Sudan		
Approximate number of speakers	250k		
Writing system	Roman		
Phonetics/phonology			
Stress	none		
Contains following rare consonant (types)	implosive; prenasalised fricative		
Said to have how many vowels?	9		
Marked vowel types			
Tone	register		
Rhythm	no information		
Vowel harmony	ATR		
Morphology	isolating and agglutinative	word-based	
Particular formation types	prefix; full reduplication; suffix; tone used morphologically		
Syntax			
Word order	(SOV) SVO	NA PossN	postpositions
Particular syntactic phenomena	inclusive / exclusive 1st plural		
Points of interest	suffixes do not combine		
Sources	Blackings & Fabb (2003), Katzner (1977)		

Language name	Macushi		
Autonym (if known and different)			
Language family	Cariban		
Spoken in	Brazil, Guyana, Venezuela		
Approximate number of speakers	10k		
Writing system	Roman		
Phonetics/phonology			
Stress	phrase-final		
Contains following rare consonant (types)			
Said to have how many vowels?	6 + length		
Marked vowel types			
Tone	none		
Rhythm	no information		
Vowel harmony	none		
Morphology	agglutinative	word-based in nouns, stem-based in verbs	
Particular formation types	prefix; suffix		
Syntax			
Word order	OVS and SOV	NA (see 'points of interest') PossN	postpositions
Particular syntactic phenomena	absolutive / ergative marking; inclusive / exclusive 1st plural; morphological aspect; conjugation classes; alienable / inalienable possession; collective as well as plural; noun classes		
Points of interest	no adjectives, but modifiers (usually nouns) follow the nouns they modify		
Sources	Abbott (1991), Haspelmath et al. (2005)		

Malagasy

Language name	Malagasy			mælə'gæsi
Autonym (if known and different)				
Language family	Austronesian	Western Austronesian		
Spoken in	Madagascar, Seychelles			
Approximate number of speakers	14m			
Writing system	Roman			
Phonetics/phonology				
Stress	word–penultimate			
Contains following rare consonant (types)	retroflex			
Said to have how many vowels?	4 + 4 diphthongs			
Marked vowel types				
Tone	none			
Rhythm	no information			
Vowel harmony	none			
Morphology	agglutinative		word-based	
Particular formation types	dvandva; incorporation; infix; prefix; full and partial suffixed reduplication; suffix; synaffix; stress used morphologically			
Syntax				
Word order	VOS	NA NPoss		prepositions
Particular syntactic phenomena	inclusive / exclusive 1st plural			
Points of interest	tensed prepositions; deictics distinguish visible from invisible			
Sources	Campbell (1991), Katzner (1977), Keenan & Polinsky (1998), Maddieson (1984), Rasoloson & Rubino (2005), Ruhlen (1976), Wälchli (2005)			

Maidu

Language name	Maidu			'maidu:
Autonym (if known and different)	Májdy			
Language family	Penutian			
Spoken in	California (USA)			
Approximate number of speakers	<10			
Writing system				
Phonetics/phonology				
Stress	weight-based			
Contains following rare consonant (types)	ejective; implosive			
Said to have how many vowels?	5			
Marked vowel types				
Tone	none			
Rhythm	no information			
Vowel harmony	some traces			
Morphology	polysynthetic		stem-based	
Particular formation types	apophony; incorporation; prefix; suffix; reduplication			
Syntax				
Word order	SOV	AN PossN		neither
Particular syntactic phenomena	evidentials; inclusive / exclusive 1st plural; dual; nominative / accusative marking; alienable / inalienable possession; switch reference			
Points of interest				
Sources	Haspelmath et al. (2005), Maddieson (1984), Mithun (1999), Ruhlen (1976)			

Language name	Malayalam		mæləˈjɑːləm
Autonym (if known and different)			
Language family	Dravidian		
Spoken in	Kerala (India)		
Approximate number of speakers	30m		
Writing system	a form of Devanagari		
Phonetics/phonology			
Stress	quantity-sensitive, but largely word-initial		
Contains following rare consonant (types)	retroflex		
Said to have how many vowels?	5 + length		
Marked vowel types			
Tone	none		
Rhythm	some tendency to stress timing		
Vowel harmony	none		
Morphology	agglutinative	word-based	
Particular formation types	dvandva; incorporation; suffix		
Syntax			
Word order	SOV	AN PossN	postpositions
Particular syntactic phenomena	gender; inclusive / exclusive 1st plural; morphological aspect; nominative / accusative marking		
Points of interest			
Sources	Asher & Kumari (1997), Baker (1988), Campbell (1991), Katzner (1977), Maddieson (1984), Ruhlen (1976)		

Language name	Malay		məˈleɪ
Autonym (if known and different)			
Language family	Austronesian	Western Austronesian	
Spoken in	Malaysia		
Approximate number of speakers	10m		
Writing system	Jawi, Roman		
Phonetics/phonology			
Stress	word-penultimate		
Contains following rare consonant (types)			
Said to have how many vowels?	6 + length + 3 diphthongs		
Marked vowel types			
Tone	none		
Rhythm	syllable-timing		
Vowel harmony	none		
Morphology	isolating and agglutinative	word-based	
Particular formation types	dvandva; prefix; full reduplication; suffix; synaffix		
Syntax			
Word order	SVO	NA NPoss	prepositions
Particular syntactic phenomena	classifiers; inclusive / exclusive 1st plural; noun classes		
Points of interest			
Sources	Katzner (1977), Maddieson (1984), Mintz (1994), Ruhlen (1976), Wälchli (2005)		

Language name	Mam	
Autonym (if known and different)		
Language family	Penutian	Mayan
Spoken in	Guatemala	
Approximate number of speakers	440k	
Writing system	Roman	
Phonetics/phonology		
Stress	weight-based	
Contains following rare consonant (types)	retroflex; uvular; ejective; implosive	
Said to have how many vowels?	5 + length	
Marked vowel types		
Tone	none	
Rhythm	no information	
Vowel harmony	some marginal semi-productive vowel harmony	
Morphology	agglutinative	stem-based verbs and word-based nouns and adjectives
Particular formation types	incorporation; prefix; partial suffixed reduplication; suffix; synaffix	
Syntax		
Word order	VSO	AN / NPoss / prepositions and postpositions
Particular syntactic phenomena	absolutive / ergative marking; classifier; inclusive / exclusive 1st plural; morphological aspect; inflecting adpositions; noun classes; evidentials	
Points of interest		
Sources	Campbell (1991), England (1983), Haspelmath et al. (2005), Katzner (1977), Mithun (1984), Ruhlen (1976)	

Language name	Maltese	mɔlˈtiz, mɒlˈtiiz
Autonym (if known and different)		
Language family	Afro–Asiatic	Semitic
Spoken in	Malta	
Approximate number of speakers	400k	
Writing system	Roman	
Phonetics/phonology		
Stress	word-penultimate	
Contains following rare consonant (types)	pharyngeal (variably)	
Said to have how many vowels?	5 + length + 7 diphthongs	
Marked vowel types		
Tone	none	
Rhythm	no information	
Vowel harmony	very restricted, affects only 1 vowel	
Morphology	fusional	stem-based
Particular formation types	prefix; root-and-pattern; suffix	
Syntax		
Word order	SVO	NA / NPoss / prepositions
Particular syntactic phenomena	gender; dual; conjugation classes	
Points of interest		
Sources	Borg & Azzopardi-Alexander (1997), Campbell (1991), Katzner (1977)	

Language name	Mangarayi		
Autonym (if known and different)			
Language family	Australian	Gunwingguan	
Spoken in	Australia		
Approximate number of speakers	50		
Writing system			
Phonetics/phonology			
Stress	tendency to word-penultimate		
Contains following rare consonant (types)	retroflex		
Said to have how many vowels?	5		
Marked vowel types			
Tone	none		
Rhythm	no information		
Vowel harmony	some height harmony caused by particular affixes		
Morphology	agglutinative	word-based	
Particular formation types	prefix; suffix; synaffix		
Syntax			
Word order	OVS	NA / PossN and NPoss	neither
Particular syntactic phenomena	gender; nominative / accusative and ergative / absolutive marking; dual		
Points of interest	most of its verbs have an idiosyncratic inflection pattern		
Sources	Dixon (1980), Merlan (1982)		

Language name	Mandarin (Chinese)		'mændərɪn, mendə'rɪn
Autonym (if known and different)	Pǔtōnghuà (PRC); Guóyǔ (Taiwan)		
Language family	Sino–Tibetan	North Sinitic	
Spoken in	People's Republic of China, Singapore, Taiwan		
Approximate number of speakers	387m		
Writing system	Chinese characters		
Phonetics/phonology			
Stress			
Contains following rare consonant (types)	retroflex; uvular		
Said to have how many vowels?	9		
Marked vowel types	front rounded; back unrounded		
Tone	contour		
Rhythm	no information		
Vowel harmony	none		
Morphology	isolating	word-based	
Particular formation types	dvandva; (infix); (prefix); full reduplication; suffix		
Syntax			
Word order	topic prominent	AN / PossN	prepositions and postpositions
Particular syntactic phenomena	classifiers		
Points of interest			
Sources	Li & Thompson (1981), Maddieson (1984), Ruhlen (1976), Wälchli (2005), Yip (2002)		

Language name	Marathi		mə'raːti
Autonym (if known and different)			
Language family	Indo-European	Indic	
Spoken in	Maharashtra (India)		
Approximate number of speakers	60m		
Writing system	Devanagari (baḷbodh 'understood by children')		
Phonetics/phonology			
Stress	weight-based		
Contains following rare consonant (types)	retroflex		
Said to have how many vowels?	8 + length (2) + 2 diphthongs		
Marked vowel types			
Tone	none		
Rhythm	no information		
Vowel harmony	none		
Morphology	fusional	stem-based for verbs; word-based for nouns	
Particular formation types	dvandva; prefix; partial suffixed and full reduplication; suffix; apophony		
Syntax			
Word order	SOV	AN PossN	postpositions
Particular syntactic phenomena	absolutive / ergative marking; nominative / accusative marking; gender; inclusive / exclusive 1st plural; conjugation classes		
Points of interest			
Sources	Campbell (1991), Katzner (1977), Pandharipande (1997, 2003), Ruhlen (1976)		

Language name	Maori		'mauri
Autonym (if known and different)	Te Reo Māori		
Language family	Austronesian	Polynesian	
Spoken in	New Zealand		
Approximate number of speakers	100k		
Writing system	Roman		
Phonetics/phonology			
Stress	weight-based		
Contains following rare consonant (types)			
Said to have how many vowels?	5 + length		
Marked vowel types			
Tone	none		
Rhythm	mora-timing		
Vowel harmony	none		
Morphology	isolating	word-based	
Particular formation types	incorporation; prefix; partial prefixed and full reduplication; suffix		
Syntax			
Word order	VSO	NA PossN and NPoss	prepositions
Particular syntactic phenomena	dual; inclusive / exclusive 1st plural and dual; possessive categories similar to alienable / inalienable		
Points of interest	agreement between certain adverbials and passive and nominalisation		
Sources	Bauer (1993), Campbell (1991), Katzner (1977), Maddieson (1984), Ruhlen (1976)		

Language name	Mari	Cheremis
Autonym (if known and different)		
Language family	Uralic	Finno–Ugric
Spoken in	Russia	
Approximate number of speakers	500k	
Writing system	Cyrillic	
Phonetics/phonology		
Stress	quantity-based	
Contains following rare consonant (types)		
Said to have how many vowels?	8	
Marked vowel types	front rounded	
Tone	none	
Rhythm	no information	
Vowel harmony	front-back	
Morphology	agglutinative	word-based
Particular formation types	dvandva; suffix	
Syntax		
Word order	SOV	AN PossN
Particular syntactic phenomena	nominative / accusative marking	
Points of interest		
Sources	Campbell (1991), Katzner (1977), Ruhlen (1976), Wälchli (2005)	

Masai see Maasai
Mazatec see Mazateco

Language name	Margi	
Autonym (if known and different)	Mārgyi	
Language family	Afro–Asiatic	Chadic
Spoken in	Nigeria	
Approximate number of speakers	150k	
Writing system	Roman	
Phonetics/phonology		
Stress		
Contains following rare consonant (types)	implosive; voiced labio-dental flap in ideophones	
Said to have how many vowels?	6	
Marked vowel types		
Tone	register	
Rhythm	no information	
Vowel harmony	none	
Morphology	agglutinative	word-based
Particular formation types	prefix; full reduplication; suffix; tone used morphologically	
Syntax		
Word order	SVO	NA NPoss	prepositions
Particular syntactic phenomena	inclusive / exclusive 1st dual and plural; morphological aspect	
Points of interest		
Sources	Campbell (1991), Hoffmann (1963), Maddieson (1984), Ruhlen (1976)	

Meithei

Language name	Meithei		'mettei
Autonym (if known and different)	Meitheirón		
Language family	Sino–Tibetan	Tibeto-Burman	
Spoken in	India, Bangladesh, Myanmar		
Approximate number of speakers	1.3m		
Writing system	Meithei Mayek (a syllabary) or Bengali script		
Phonetics/phonology			
Stress			
Contains following rare consonant (types)			
Said to have how many vowels?	6		
Marked vowel types			
Tone	tonal accent		
Rhythm	no information		
Vowel harmony	none		
Morphology	agglutinative	stem-based	
Particular formation types	prefix; suffix		
Syntax			
Word order	variable	AN (NA) PossN	postpositions
Particular syntactic phenomena	morphological aspect; dual; evidentials		
Points of interest			
Sources	Chelliah (1997), Haspelmath et al. (2005), Katzner (1977)		

Mazatec

Language name	Mazateco	Mazatec	mæzəˈtekəʊ
Autonym (if known and different)			
Language family	Oto-Manguean	Popolocan	
Spoken in	Mexico		
Approximate number of speakers	85k		
Writing system			
Phonetics/phonology			
Stress	word-final		
Contains following rare consonant (types)	retroflex		
Said to have how many vowels?	4 + nasalisation		
Marked vowel types			
Tone	register		
Rhythm	no information		
Vowel harmony	none		
Morphology	polysynthetic	word-based for nouns	
Particular formation types	incorporation; prefix		
Syntax			
Word order	VOS	NA	prepositions
Particular syntactic phenomena	classifiers		
Points of interest			
Sources	Gordon (2002), Haspelmath et al. (2005), Katzner (1977), Maddieson (1984), Ruhlen (1976), Yip (2002)		

Language name	Menomini		mɔ'nɔmini
Autonym (if known and different)			
Language family	Macro-Algonkian	Central Algonkian	
Spoken in	Wisconsin (USA)		
Approximate number of speakers	0		
Writing system			
Phonetics/phonology			
Stress	quantity-based		
Contains following rare consonant (types)			
Said to have how many vowels?	6 + length + 2 diphthongs		
Marked vowel types			
Tone	none		
Rhythm	no information		
Vowel harmony	none		
Morphology	agglutinative	word-based	
Particular formation types	prefix; suffix; synaffix		
Syntax			
Word order	free	free PossN	neither
Particular syntactic phenomena			
Points of interest	inclusive / exclusive 1st plural; noun classes; conjugation classes		
Sources	Bloomfield (1946), Campbell (1991), Haspelmath et al. (2005), Ruhlen (1976)		

Language name	Mende		'mendi
Autonym (if known and different)	mɛ́ndɛ jia		
Language family	Niger-Congo	Mande	
Spoken in	Sierra Leone, Liberia		
Approximate number of speakers	1.5m		
Writing system	Roman		
Phonetics/phonology			
Stress			
Contains following rare consonant (types)			
Said to have how many vowels?	7 + length		
Marked vowel types			
Tone	register		
Rhythm	no information		
Vowel harmony	none		
Morphology	agglutinative		
Particular formation types	suffix; tone used morphologically		
Syntax			
Word order	SOV	NA PossN	postpositions
Particular syntactic phenomena			
Points of interest			
Sources	Campbell (1991), Katzner (1977), Westermann & Bryan (1970)		

Language name	Miwok	'mi:wok	
Autonym (if known and different)			
Language family	Penutian	Miwok-Costanoan	
Spoken in	California (USA)		
Approximate number of speakers	<30		
Writing system			
Phonetics/phonology			
Stress	first long syllable		
Contains following rare consonant (types)	ejective		
Said to have how many vowels?	5 + length		
Marked vowel types			
Tone	none		
Rhythm	no information		
Vowel harmony	none		
Morphology	polysynthetic	stem-based	
Particular formation types	incorporation; full and partial reduplication; suffix		
Syntax			
Word order	SOV	free	neither
Particular syntactic phenomena	inclusive / exclusive 1st plural; nominative / accusative marking; evidentials		
Points of interest			
Sources	Callaghan (1984, 1987), Haspelmath et al. (2005), Ruhlen (1976)		

Language name	Mixtec	Mixteco	'mi:kstek
Autonym (if known and different)			
Language family	Otomanguean		
Spoken in	Mexico		
Approximate number of speakers	250k		
Writing system			
Phonetics/phonology			
Stress			
Contains following rare consonant (types)			
Said to have how many vowels?	5 + nasalisation		
Marked vowel types			
Tone	register		
Rhythm	no information		
Vowel harmony	none		
Morphology	isolating and agglutinative	stem-based for verbs; word-based for nouns	
Particular formation types	prefix; suffix; tone used morphologically		
Syntax			
Word order	VSO	NA NPoss	prepositions
Particular syntactic phenomena	gender; inflecting adpositions; morphological aspect		
Points of interest			
Sources	Campbell (1991), Haspelmath et al. (2005), Maddieson (1984)		

Mixteco see **Mixtec**

Language name	Mohawk	
Autonym (if known and different)	'mɑʊhɔːk	
Language family	Iroquoian	Mohawk-Oneida
Spoken in	Quebec, Ontario (Canada)	
Approximate number of speakers	350	
Writing system		
Phonetics/phonology		
Stress	word-penultimate	
Contains following rare consonant (types)		
Said to have how many vowels?	6	
Marked vowel types		
Tone	tonal accent	
Rhythm	no information	
Vowel harmony	none	
Morphology	polysynthetic	stem-based
Particular formation types	prefix; suffix; incorporation	
Syntax		
Word order	free	NA (see 'points of interest') PossN	postpositions
Particular syntactic phenomena	gender; morphological aspect; alienable / inalienable possession	
Points of interest	no labial consonants, though has labial-velars; no separate class of adjectives	
Sources	Baker (1996), Campbell (1991), Gordon (2002), Katzner (1977), Mithun (1999), Yip (2002)	

Language name	Miya	
Autonym (if known and different)	vèna mij	
Language family	Chadic	North Bauchi
Spoken in	Bauchi State (Nigeria)	
Approximate number of speakers	5k	
Writing system		
Phonetics/phonology		
Stress		
Contains following rare consonant (types)		
Said to have how many vowels?	3	
Marked vowel types		
Tone	register	
Rhythm	no information	
Vowel harmony	none	
Morphology	agglutinative	stem-based
Particular formation types	infix; prefix; partial prefixed and partial suffixed and full reduplication; suffix	
Syntax		
Word order	SVO (VOS)	NA NPoss	prepositions
Particular syntactic phenomena	gender; morphological aspect; conjugation classes	
Points of interest		
Sources	Schuh (1998)	

Language name	Mongolian	Halh, Khalkha	
Autonym (if known and different)			mɔŋˈɢɔɬɪɑn
Language family	Altaic	Mongolic	
Spoken in	Mongolia		
Approximate number of speakers	5m		
Writing system	Cyrillic		
Phonetics/phonology			
Stress	word-initial		
Contains following rare consonant (types)			
Said to have how many vowels?	7 + length		
Marked vowel types	front rounded		
Tone	none		
Rhythm	no information		
Vowel harmony	front–back and rounding		
Morphology	agglutinative	word-based	
Particular formation types	prefix; suffix		
Syntax			
Word order	SOV	AN PossN	postpositions
Particular syntactic phenomena	nominative / accusative marking		
Points of interest			
Sources	Bosson (1964), Campbell (1991), Katzner (1977)		

Múra-Pirahã see Pirahã

Language name	Nahuatl		
Autonym (if known and different)			ˈnaːwaːtɛl
Language family	Aztecan	Uto-Aztecan	
Spoken in	Mexico		
Approximate number of speakers	1m		
Writing system	Roman		
Phonetics/phonology			
Stress	word-penultimate		
Contains following rare consonant (types)			
Said to have how many vowels?	4 + length		
Marked vowel types			
Tone	none		
Rhythm	no information		
Vowel harmony	none		
Morphology	polysynthetic	stem-based	
Particular formation types	incorporation; prefix; partial prefixed reduplication; suffix		
Syntax			
Word order	Free	AN PossN	postpositions
Particular syntactic phenomena	morphological aspect; nominative / accusative marking; evidentials		
Points of interest			
Sources	Campbell (1991), Gordon (2002), Haspelmath et al. (2005), Mithun (1984)		

Language name	Navajo		'nævəhɑʊ
Autonym (if known and different)	diné bizaad		
Language family	Na-Dene	Athabaskan	
Spoken in	New Mexico, Arizona, Utah, Colorado (USA)		
Approximate number of speakers	130k		
Writing system	Roman		
Phonetics/phonology			
Stress			
Contains following rare consonant (types)	ejective		
Said to have how many vowels?	4 + length + nasalisation		
Marked vowel types			
Tone	register		
Rhythm	no information		
Vowel harmony	none		
Morphology	agglutinative	stem-based	
Particular formation types	prefix; suffix; tone used morphologically		
Syntax			
Word order	SOV	NA PossN	postpositions
Particular syntactic phenomena	classifier; morphological aspect; noun class; dual		
Points of interest			
Sources	Campbell (1991), Katzner (1977), Maddieson (1984), Ruhlen (1976), Speas (1990), Yip (2002)		

Language name	Nama	Hottentot	'nɑːmə
Autonym (if known and different)			
Language family	Khoisan		
Spoken in	SW Africa		
Approximate number of speakers	90k		
Writing system	Roman		
Phonetics/phonology			
Stress	word-initial mora		
Contains following rare consonant (types)	clicks		
Said to have how many vowels?	6 + nasalisation (3)		
Marked vowel types			
Tone	register		
Rhythm	mora timing		
Vowel harmony	none		
Morphology	isolating and agglutinative	stem-based	
Particular formation types	suffix		
Syntax			
Word order	focus-based	AN PossN	postpositions
Particular syntactic phenomena	gender; inclusive / exclusive 1st plural; dual		
Points of interest			
Sources	Campbell (1991), Gordon (2002), Hagman (1973), Katzner (1977), Maddieson (1984)		

Language name	Ndyuka		
Autonym (if known and different)			
Language family	English superstrate pidgin		
Spoken in	Surinam		
Approximate number of speakers	few native speakers		
Writing system	Roman		
Phonetics/phonology			
Stress	weight-based system		
Contains following rare consonant (types)			
Said to have how many vowels?	5 + length		
Marked vowel types			
Tone	register		
Rhythm	no information		
Vowel harmony	none		
Morphology	isolating		
Particular formation types	partial prefixed and full reduplication		
Syntax			
Word order	SVO	AN PossN	prepositions
Particular syntactic phenomena			
Points of interest			
Sources	Huttar & Huttar (1994)		

Language name	Ndjébbana	Gunavidji, Kunavidji	
Autonym (if known and different)			
Language family	Australian	Burarran	
Spoken in	Northern Territory (Australia)		
Approximate number of speakers	150		
Writing system	Roman		
Phonetics/phonology			
Stress	variable but not word-final		
Contains following rare consonant (types)			
Said to have how many vowels?	5		
Marked vowel types			
Tone	none		
Rhythm	no information		
Vowel harmony	limited high-vowel		
Morphology	polysynthetic	stem-based	
Particular formation types	prefix; suffix		
Syntax			
Word order	focus-based	NA PossN and NPoss	neither
Particular syntactic phenomena	gender; inclusive / exclusive 1st plural; dual and trial; conjugation classes		
Points of interest	case marking only for ablative and purposive; because the names of the recently deceased are taboo, the books of recently deceased authors have had to be withdrawn from bookshop shelves in some instances		
Sources	McKay (2000)		

Language name	Ngiti	Southern Lendu	əŋˈgɪːti
Autonym (if known and different)			
Language family	Nilo-Saharan	Central Sudanic	
Spoken in	Zaire		
Approximate number of speakers	90k		
Writing system	Roman		
Phonetics/phonology			
Stress			
Contains following rare consonant (types)	retroflex; implosive (voiced and voiceless)		
Said to have how many vowels?	9		
Marked vowel types			
Tone	register		
Rhythm	no information		
Vowel harmony	ATR		
Morphology	agglutinative	word-based nouns, stem-based verbs	
Particular formation types	prefix; partial prefixed, partial suffixed and full reduplication; suffix; tone used morphologically		
Syntax			
Word order	SVO	AN PossN	postpositions
Particular syntactic phenomena	conjugation classes; alienable / inalienable possession; inclusive / exclusive 1st plural		
Points of interest			
Sources	Lojenga (1994)		

Language name	Nez Perce		nez ˈpɜːset
Autonym (if known and different)	numíːpuː		
Language family	Penutian	Sahaptian	
Spoken in	Idaho (USA)		
Approximate number of speakers	1k		
Writing system			
Phonetics/phonology			
Stress	variable		
Contains following rare consonant (types)	uvular; ejective		
Said to have how many vowels?	5 + length		
Marked vowel types			
Tone	none		
Rhythm	no information		
Vowel harmony	dominant-recessive		
Morphology	agglutinative	word-based	
Particular formation types	prefix; suffix; partial prefixed reduplication		
Syntax			
Word order	OVS	NA and AN PossN	postpositions
Particular syntactic phenomena	morphological aspect		
Points of interest			
Sources	Aoki (1970), Katzner (1977), Maddieson (1984), Mithun (1999), Ruhlen (1976)		

Language name	Nias		
Autonym (if known and different)			
Language family	Austronesian		
Spoken in	Indonesia		
Approximate number of speakers			
Writing system			
Phonetics/phonology			
Stress	word-penultimate		
Contains following rare consonant (types)	voiced bilabial trill		
Said to have how many vowels?	6		
Marked vowel types	back unrounded		
Tone	none		
Rhythm	no information		
Vowel harmony	none		
Morphology	agglutinative		word-based
Particular formation types	infix; prefix; partial prefixed reduplication; suffix; apophony		
Syntax			
Word order	VOS	NA NPoss	prepositions
Particular syntactic phenomena	inclusive / exclusive 1st plural; absolutive / ergative marking; classifier		
Points of interest	one of the few languages to allow a voiced bilabial trill before any vowel		
Sources	Brown (2005)		

Language name	Niuean			nju'eɔn
Autonym (if known and different)				
Language family	Austronesian	Polynesian		
Spoken in	Niue, New Zealand			
Approximate number of speakers	11k			
Writing system	Roman			
Phonetics/phonology				
Stress	quantity-based system, with antepenultimate default			
Contains following rare consonant (types)				
Said to have how many vowels?	5 + length			
Marked vowel types				
Tone	none			
Rhythm	no information			
Vowel harmony	none			
Morphology	agglutinative		word-based	
Particular formation types	prefix; partial prefixed, partial suffixed and full reduplication; suffix			
Syntax				
Word order	VSO	NA PossN and NPoss	prepositions	
Particular syntactic phenomena	absolutive / ergative marking; inclusive / exclusive 1st plural			
Points of interest				
Sources	McEwen (1970), Seiter (1980)			

Nivkh see **Gilyak**

Language name	Nootka		'nuːtka
Autonym (if known and different)	Nuu-chah-nulth		
Language family	Wakashan		
Spoken in	British Columbia, Vancouver Island (Canada)		
Approximate number of speakers	2k		
Writing system			
Phonetics/phonology			
Stress			
Contains following rare consonant (types)	uvular; pharyngeal / epiglottal; ejective		
Said to have how many vowels?	3 + length + 2 extra long vowels in loans		
Marked vowel types			
Tone	none		
Rhythm	no information		
Vowel harmony	none		
Morphology	polysynthetic	word-based	
Particular formation types	suffix; infix; partly prefixed reduplication; incorporation		
Syntax			
Word order	VSO	AN	neither
		NPoss	
Particular syntactic phenomena	morphological aspect		
Points of interest	*Nootka!* means 'circle about' and was an instruction given to Captain Cook when he first arrived		
Sources	Howe (2005), Katzner (1977), Maddieson (1984), Mithun (1999), Nakayama (2001), Ruhlen (1976)		

Language name	Nkore Kiga		
Autonym (if known and different)			
Language family	Niger-Congo	Bantu	
Spoken in	Uganda		
Approximate number of speakers	1m		
Writing system	Roman		
Phonetics/phonology			
Stress	not relevant		
Contains following rare consonant (types)			
Said to have how many vowels?	5 + length		
Marked vowel types			
Tone	register		
Rhythm	no information		
Vowel harmony	front–back		
Morphology	agglutinative	stem-based for verbs; word-based for nouns	
Particular formation types	infix; prefix; suffix		
Syntax			
Word order	SVO	NA	prepositions
		NPoss	
Particular syntactic phenomena	morphological aspect; noun classes		
Points of interest			
Sources	Taylor (1985)		

Language name	Norwegian		nɔːˈwiːdʒən
Autonym (if known and different)	Norsk; Bokmål and Nynorsk are two distinct Norwegian languages, sometimes called by the older names Riksmål and Landsmål respectively; Bokmål/Riksmål is sometimes called Dano-Norwegian, because of its origins		
Language family	Indo-European	Germanic	
Spoken in	Norway		
Approximate number of speakers	4m		
Writing system	Roman + extra letters		
Phonetics/phonology			
Stress	word-initial		
Contains following rare consonant (types)	retroflex		
Said to have how many vowels?	10 + length + 5 diphthongs		
Marked vowel types	front rounded		
Tone	tonal accent		
Rhythm	no information		
Vowel harmony	none		
Morphology	agglutinative	word-based	
Particular formation types	prefix; suffix		
Syntax			
Word order	V2	AN PossN	prepositions
Particular syntactic phenomena	gender		
Points of interest			
Sources	Campbell (1991), Haugen (1938), Katzner (1977), Maddieson (1984), Ruhlen (1976)		

Occitan see Provençal

Language name	Norn		nɔːn
Autonym (if known and different)			
Language family	Indo-European	Germanic	
Spoken in	Orkney and Shetland, c. 800–1800 CE		
Approximate number of speakers	0		
Writing system	runes, Roman		
Phonetics/phonology			
Stress	probably word-initial		
Contains following rare consonant (types)			
Said to have how many vowels?			
Marked vowel types	front rounded		
Tone	none		
Rhythm	no information		
Vowel harmony	none		
Morphology	fusional	stem-based	
Particular formation types	suffix; apophony		
Syntax			
Word order	SVO	AN PossN	prepositions
Particular syntactic phenomena			
Points of interest	to the extent that Norn survives, it is in dialect words of the Orkneys and Shetlands		
Sources	Barnes (1998), Jakobsen (1985)		

Language name	Ojibwa	Chippewa	əˈdʒɪbweɪ
Autonym (if known and different)			
Language family	Algonkian		
Spoken in	Ontario (Canada)		
Approximate number of speakers	40k		
Writing system	Cree syllabary		
Phonetics/phonology			
Stress			
Contains following rare consonant (types)			
Said to have how many vowels?	4 + short (3) + nasalisation		
Marked vowel types			
Tone	none		
Rhythm	no information		
Vowel harmony	none		
Morphology	polysynthetic	stem-based for verbs; word-based for nouns	
Particular formation types	full and partial reduplication; suffix		
Syntax			
Word order	free	free PossN	prepositions and postpositions
Particular syntactic phenomena	noun classes		
Points of interest			
Sources	Bailin & Grafstein (1991), Haspelmath et al. (2005), Katzner (1977), Maddieson (1984), Mithun (1999), Ruhlen (1976)		

Language name	Old Church Slavonic		ɔld tʃɜːtʃ sləˈvɒnɪk
Autonym (if known and different)			
Language family	Indo-European	Slavic	
Spoken in	Moravia		
Approximate number of speakers	0		
Writing system	Cyrillic; Glagolitic		
Phonetics/phonology			
Stress			
Contains following rare consonant (types)			
Said to have how many vowels?	9		
Marked vowel types			
Tone	none		
Rhythm	no information		
Vowel harmony	none		
Morphology	fusional	stem-based	
Particular formation types	prefix; suffix		
Syntax			
Word order	free	free / free	prepositions
Particular syntactic phenomena	gender; morphological aspect; nominative / accusative marking; dual; conjugation classes		
Points of interest			
Sources	Campbell (1991), Huntley (1993)		

Old Ethiopic see **Geez**

Language name	Oromo	Galla, Gallinya	ɔɔˈbrɑmˈɔu
Autonym (if known and different)			
Language family	Afro-Asiatic	Cushitic	
Spoken in	Somalia, Ethiopia, Kenya		
Approximate number of speakers	9m		
Writing system	Roman; Ethiopic syllabary		
Phonetics/phonology			
Stress			
Contains following rare consonant (types)	ejective; implosive		
Said to have how many vowels?	5		
Marked vowel types			
Tone	register		
Rhythm	no information		
Vowel harmony	none		
Morphology	agglutinative	stem-based	
Particular formation types	prefix; partial prefixed reduplication; suffix		
Syntax			
Word order	SOV	NA NPoss	postpositions
Particular syntactic phenomena	gender; nominative / accusative marking; alienable / inalienable possession		
Points of interest			
Sources	Campbell (1991), Katzner (1977), Sprouse (2000)		

Language name	Oneida		oʊˈnaɪdə
Autonym (if known and different)			
Language family	Macro-Siouan	Iroquoian	
Spoken in	Wisconsin (USA)		
Approximate number of speakers	1k		
Writing system			
Phonetics/phonology			
Stress	word-penultimate		
Contains following rare consonant (types)			
Said to have how many vowels?	4 + length		
Marked vowel types			
Tone	none		
Rhythm	no information		
Vowel harmony	none		
Morphology	polysynthetic		
Particular formation types	incorporation; prefix; suffix		
Syntax			
Word order	free	PossN	neither
Particular syntactic phenomena	gender		
Points of interest			
Sources	Katzner (1977), Mithun (1984), Ruhlen (1976)		

Language name	Pa'anci		Pa'a	
Autonym (if known and different)	fuucəka			
Language family	Afro-Asiatic		West Chadic	
Spoken in	Nigeria			
Approximate number of speakers	20k			
Writing system				
Phonetics/phonology				
Stress				
Contains following rare consonant (types)	ejective			
Said to have how many vowels?	5 + length + 2 diphthongs			
Marked vowel types				
Tone	register			
Rhythm	no information			
Vowel harmony	none			
Morphology	agglutinative		stem-based	
Particular formation types	partial prefixed and full reduplication; suffix			
Syntax				
Word order	SOV	AN (NA) NPoss		prepositions
Particular syntactic phenomena	gender; morphological aspect			
Points of interest	possessive pronouns marked for gender of possessor and of possessee			
Sources	Skinner (1979)			

Language name	Ostyak	Khanty		'ɒstɪæk
Autonym (if known and different)	Hanti			
Language family	Uralic	Finno-Ugric		
Spoken in	Former USSR			
Approximate number of speakers	15k			
Writing system				
Phonetics/phonology				
Stress	word-initial			
Contains following rare consonant (types)	retroflex			
Said to have how many vowels?	8 + 4 overshort			
Marked vowel types	back unrounded			
Tone	none			
Rhythm	stress-timing			
Vowel harmony	front–back harmony			
Morphology	agglutinative	word-based		
Particular formation types	dvandva; suffix			
Syntax				
Word order	SOV	AN PossN		postpositions
Particular syntactic phenomena	nominative / accusative marking; dual; conjugation classes			
Points of interest	Note that Ostyak is also an alternative name for Ket.			
Sources	Collinder (1957), Maddieson (1984), Rédei (1965), Ruhlen (1976), Wälchli (2005)			

Ostyak see Ket

Pa'a see Pa'anci

Language name	Panjabi	Punjabi	pʌnˈdʒuːbi
Autonym (if known and different)			
Language family	Indo-European	Indic	
Spoken in	India, Pakistan		
Approximate number of speakers	50m		
Writing system	Gurmukhi, LaNDa, Devanagari and Arabic		
Phonetics/phonology			
Stress	variable		
Contains following rare consonant (types)	retroflex; uvular (in loan-words)		
Said to have how many vowels?	10 + nasalisation		
Marked vowel types			
Tone	register		
Rhythm	no information		
Vowel harmony	none		
Morphology	fusional	stem-based	
Particular formation types	dvandva; incorporation; prefix; partial prefixed, partial suffixed and full reduplication; suffix; suprasegmentals used morphologically		
Syntax			
Word order	SOV	AN PossN	postpositions
Particular syntactic phenomena	absolutive / ergative marking; nominative / accusative marking; gender; conjugation classes		
Points of interest			
Sources	Bhatia (1993), Campbell (1991), Katzner (1977), Maddieson (1984), Ruhlen (1976)		

Language name	Paiute		'pauːt
Autonym (if known and different)			
Language family	Aztec-Tanoan	Uto-Aztecan	
Spoken in	Utah, Idaho (USA)		
Approximate number of speakers	2.5k		
Writing system			
Phonetics/phonology			
Stress	2nd mora		
Contains following rare consonant (types)			
Said to have how many vowels?	5 + length		
Marked vowel types			
Tone	none		
Rhythm	mora-timing		
Vowel harmony	none		
Morphology	polysynthetic	stem-based	
Particular formation types	infix; prefix; partial prefixed and partial suffixed reduplication; suffix		
Syntax			
Word order	SOV	AN PossN	postpositions
Particular syntactic phenomena	inclusive/exclusive 1st plural; morphological aspect; noun classes; dual; evidentials		
Points of interest			
Sources	Gordon (2002), Haspelmath et al. (2005), Katzner (1977), Ruhlen (1976), Sapir (1930)		

Language name	Pashto		ˈpæʃtəʊ
Autonym (if known and different)			
Language family	Indo-European	Iranian	
Spoken in	Afghanistan, Pakistan		
Approximate number of speakers	15m		
Writing system	Arabic		
Phonetics/phonology			
Stress	variable		
Contains following rare consonant (types)	retroflex; uvular		
Said to have how many vowels?	6		
Marked vowel types			
Tone	none		
Rhythm	no information		
Vowel harmony	none		
Morphology	fusional	stem-based	
Particular formation types	prefix; suffix		
Syntax			
Word order	SOV	AN PossN	
Particular syntactic phenomena	prepositions and postpositions		
Points of interest	gender; morphological aspect; conjugation classes		
Sources	Campbell (1991), Katzner (1977), MacKenzie (2003)		

Language name	Papiamentu		pæpjæˈmentuː pæpjæˈmentəʊ
Autonym (if known and different)			
Language family	Iberian-based creole		
Spoken in	Netherlands Antilles, Aruba, Virgin Islands		
Approximate number of speakers	300k		
Writing system	Roman		
Phonetics/phonology			
Stress	quantity-based		
Contains following rare consonant (types)			
Said to have how many vowels?	9 + 9 diphthongs		
Marked vowel types	front rounded		
Tone	register		
Rhythm	no information		
Vowel harmony	none		
Morphology	agglutinative	word-based	
Particular formation types	prefix; full reduplication; suffix; tone used morphologically		
Syntax			
Word order	SVO	NA PossN	prepositions
Particular syntactic phenomena			
Points of interest			
Sources	Katzner (1977), Kouwenberg & Murray (1994)		

Pascuense see Rapanui

Pima

Language name	Pima
Autonym (if known and different)	ʼpiːmə
Language family	Aztec-Tanoan	Uto-Aztecan
Spoken in	Arizona (USA)
Approximate number of speakers	18k
Writing system	
Phonetics/phonology	
Stress	word-initial
Contains following rare consonant (types)	
Said to have how many vowels?	5 + length
Marked vowel types	
Tone	none
Rhythm	no information
Vowel harmony	none
Morphology	polysynthetic
Particular formation types	incorporation
Syntax	
Word order	SOV	AN PossN	postpositions
Particular syntactic phenomena	
Points of interest	
Sources	Haspelmath et al. (2005), Katzner (1977), Ruhlen (1976)

Paumari

Language name	Paumari
Autonym (if known and different)	
Language family	Aruan
Spoken in	Brazil
Approximate number of speakers	500
Writing system	Roman
Phonetics/phonology	
Stress	word-antepenultimate
Contains following rare consonant (types)	implosive
Said to have how many vowels?	3
Marked vowel types	
Tone	none
Rhythm	no information
Vowel harmony	none
Morphology	polysynthetic	stem-based
Particular formation types	incorporation; prefix; partial prefixed reduplication; suffix
Syntax	
Word order	(OVS SOV) SVO	NA PossN	postpositions
Particular syntactic phenomena	absolutive / ergative marking; classifiers; gender; morphological aspect; nominative / accusative marking; noun classes; conjugation classes
Points of interest	absolutive/ergative or nominative/accusative depends on word order
Sources	Chapman & Derbyshire (1991)

Persian see Farsi
Pilipino see Tagalog

Language name	Pitjantjatjara	Western Desert
Autonym (if known and different)		pɪtʃʌntʃəˈtʃɑːɾɑ
Language family	Pama-Nyungan	
Spoken in	South Australia	
Approximate number of speakers	3k	
Writing system		
Phonetics/phonology		
Stress	word-initial	
Contains following rare consonant (types)	retroflex	
Said to have how many vowels?	3 + length	
Marked vowel types		
Tone	none	
Rhythm	no information	
Vowel harmony	none	
Morphology	agglutinative	stem-based
Particular formation types	suffix; partial prefixed reduplication	
Syntax		
Word order	SOV	NA / PossN / postpositions
Particular syntactic phenomena	morphological aspect; dual; inclusive / exclusive 1st plural; conjugation classes	
Points of interest		
Sources	Glass & Hackett (1970)	

Language name	Pirahã	Múra-Pirahã
Autonym (if known and different)	xapaitíiso	
Language family	Chibchan	Mura
Spoken in	Brazil	
Approximate number of speakers	100	
Writing system	Roman	
Phonetics/phonology		
Stress	weight-based	
Contains following rare consonant (types)		
Said to have how many vowels?	3	
Marked vowel types		
Tone	register	
Rhythm	no information	
Vowel harmony	none	
Morphology	agglutinative	word-based for nouns, stem-based for verbs
Particular formation types	incorporation; prefix; partial suffixed reduplication; suffix	
Syntax		
Word order	SOV	NA / PossN / postpositions
Particular syntactic phenomena	morphological aspect; gender; evidentials	
Points of interest	no plural forms of pronouns	
Sources	Asher (1994), Everett (1986), Haspelmath et al. (2005)	

Language name	Polish		'paʊltʃ
Autonym (if known and different)			
Language family	Indo-European	Slavic	
Spoken in	Poland		
Approximate number of speakers	46m		
Writing system	Roman		
Phonetics/phonology			
Stress	word-penultimate		
Contains following rare consonant (types)			
Said to have how many vowels?	5 + nasalisation (2)		
Marked vowel types			
Tone	none		
Rhythm	stress-timed		
Vowel harmony	none		
Morphology	fusional	stem-based	
Particular formation types	prefix; suffix		
Syntax			
Word order	SOV	AN PossN	prepositions
Particular syntactic phenomena	gender; morphological aspect; nominative / accusative marking; conjugation classes		
Points of interest			
Sources	Campbell (1991), Gordon (2002), Katzner (1977), Richter (1987), Rothstein (1993), Ruhlen (1976)		

Language name	Pomo		'pɔmɔu
Autonym (if known and different)			
Language family	Hokan	Northern Pomo	
Spoken in	California (USA)		
Approximate number of speakers	100		
Writing system			
Phonetics/phonology			
Stress	word-initial		
Contains following rare consonant (types)	uvular; ejective		
Said to have how many vowels?	5		
Marked vowel types			
Tone	none		
Rhythm	no information		
Vowel harmony	none		
Morphology	agglutinative	stem-based for verbs; word-based for nouns	
Particular formation types	prefix; suffix; full reduplication		
Syntax			
Word order	SOV	NA PossN	neither
Particular syntactic phenomena	evidentials; ergative / absolutive marking; morphological aspect; serial verbs; switch reference		
Points of interest			
Sources	Gordon (2002), Maddieson (1984), McLendon (1975), Mithun (1998, 1999), Ruhlen (1976)		

Language name	Provençal	Occitan	provon'sæl
Autonym (if known and different)			
Language family	Indo-European	Romance	
Spoken in	France		
Approximate number of speakers	2m		
Writing system	Roman		
Phonetics/phonology			
Stress			
Contains following rare consonant (types)			
Said to have how many vowels?	8		
Marked vowel types	front rounded		
Tone	none		
Rhythm	no information		
Vowel harmony	none		
Morphology	fusional	stem-based	
Particular formation types			
Syntax			
Word order	SVO VSO	NA / PossN	prepositions
Particular syntactic phenomena	gender; conjugation classes		
Points of interest			
Sources	Campbell (1991), Katzner (1977)		

Language name	Portuguese		pɔːtju'giz
Autonym (if known and different)			
Language family	Indo-European	Romance	
Spoken in	Portugal, Brazil, Angola, Mozambique, Cape Verde		
Approximate number of speakers	134m		
Writing system	Roman		
Phonetics/phonology			
Stress	stem-final		
Contains following rare consonant (types)			
Said to have how many vowels?	9 + nasalisation (5) + many diphthongs		
Marked vowel types			
Tone	none		
Rhythm	stress-timed (European); syllable-timed (Brazilian)		
Vowel harmony	none		
Morphology	agglutinative	stem-based	
Particular formation types	suffix		
Syntax			
Word order	SVO	NA / NPoss	prepositions
Particular syntactic phenomena	gender; conjugation classes		
Points of interest			
Sources	Camara (1972), Campbell (1991), Katzner (1977), Parkinson (2003), Ruhlen (1976)		

Pulaar see Fula
Punjabi see **Panjabi**

Language name	Quiché		kiːtʃeɪ
Autonym (if known and different)			
Language family	Penutian	Mayan	
Spoken in	Guatemala, Mexico		
Approximate number of speakers	500k		
Writing system	Roman		
Phonetics/phonology			
Stress	word-final		
Contains following rare consonant (types)	uvular; ejective		
Said to have how many vowels?	5		
Marked vowel types			
Tone	none		
Rhythm	no information		
Vowel harmony	none		
Morphology	agglutinative and fusional	word-based	
Particular formation types	suffix		
Syntax			
Word order	SOV	NA PossN	prepositions
Particular syntactic phenomena	conjugation classes		
Points of interest			
Sources	Campbell (1991), Katzner (1977)		

Language name	Quechua		ˈketʃwə
Autonym (if known and different)			
Language family	Andean-Equatorial	Andean	
Spoken in	Peru, Ecuador, Bolivia, Argentina		
Approximate number of speakers	8m		
Writing system	Roman		
Phonetics/phonology			
Stress	word-penultimate		
Contains following rare consonant (types)	uvular; ejective		
Said to have how many vowels?	5		
Marked vowel types			
Tone	none		
Rhythm	no information		
Vowel harmony	none		
Morphology	agglutinative	stem-based verbs, word-based nouns	
Particular formation types	incorporation; full and partial reduplication; suffix		
Syntax			
Word order	SOV	AN PossN	postpositions
Particular syntactic phenomena	inclusive / exclusive 1st plural; nominative / accusative marking; evidentials		
Points of interest			
Sources	Campbell (1991), Haspelmath et al. (2005), Katzner (1977), Maddieson (1984), Mithun (1984)		

Language name	Quileute		ˈkwɪləjuːt
Autonym (if known and different)			
Language family	isolate		
Spoken in	Washington State (USA)		
Approximate number of speakers	20		
Writing system			
Phonetics/phonology			
Stress	word-penultimate		
Contains following rare consonant (types)	uvular; ejective		
Said to have how many vowels?	4		
Marked vowel types			
Tone	none		
Rhythm	no information		
Vowel harmony	none		
Morphology	polysynthetic	stem-based for verbs; word-based for nouns	
Particular formation types	prefix; infix; infixed reduplication; suffix		
Syntax			
Word order	VSO	AN NPoss	
Particular syntactic phenomena	evidentials		
Points of interest	no nasal consonants		
Sources	Gordon (2002), Haspelmath et al. (2005), Hoard (1979), Maddieson (1984), Ruhlen (1976)		

Language name	Rapanui	Pascuense	ræpəˈnuːi
Autonym (if known and different)			
Language family	Malayo-Polynesian	Polynesian	
Spoken in	Easter Island		
Approximate number of speakers	1.5k		
Writing system	Rongorongo, Roman		
Phonetics/phonology			
Stress	word-penultimate		
Contains following rare consonant (types)			
Said to have how many vowels?	5 + length		
Marked vowel types			
Tone	none		
Rhythm	no information		
Vowel harmony	none		
Morphology	isolating agglutinative	word-based	
Particular formation types	partial prefixed, partial suffixed and full reduplication; suffix		
Syntax			
Word order	VSO	NA NPoss	prepositions
Particular syntactic phenomena	absolutive / ergative marking; inclusive / exclusive 1st plural; dual		
Points of interest			
Sources	Campbell (1991), Du Feu (1996), Gordon (2002), Katzner (1977)		

Romani see **Romany**

Language name	Romanian	Rumanian	raʊˈmeɪnɪən
Autonym (if known and different)			
Language family	Indo-European	Romance	
Spoken in	Romania, Hungary, Bulgaria		
Approximate number of speakers	20m		
Writing system	Roman		
Phonetics/phonology			
Stress	variable		
Contains following rare consonant (types)			
Said to have how many vowels?	7 + 3 diphthongs		
Marked vowel types			
Tone	none		
Rhythm	no information		
Vowel harmony	none		
Morphology	fusional	stem-based	
Particular formation types	prefix; suffix		
Syntax			
Word order	SVO	AN / NPoss	prepositions
Particular syntactic phenomena	gender; conjugation classes		
Points of interest			
Sources	Campbell (1991), Katzner (1977), Maddieson (1984), Mallinson (1986)		

Language name	Romany	Romani	ˈraʊmənɪ
Autonym (if known and different)	romani chib		
Language family	Indo-European	Indic	
Spoken in	Across central and eastern Europe, including Estonia, Lithuania, Ukraine, Hungary, Poland, Slovakia, Romania, Czech Republic		
Approximate number of speakers	3.5m		
Writing system	Roman		
Phonetics/phonology			
Stress	word-final		
Contains following rare consonant (types)	retroflex; uvular; ejective		
Said to have how many vowels?	5		
Marked vowel types			
Tone	none		
Rhythm	no information		
Vowel harmony	none		
Morphology	agglutinative and fusional	word-based	
Particular formation types	partial suffixed reduplication; suffix		
Syntax			
Word order	SVO	AN / PossN	prepositions
Particular syntactic phenomena	gender; nominative / accusative marking; conjugation classes		
Points of interest	the language of the Rom or the gypsies, this does not have a standard form because it is spoken across so many countries		
Sources	Campbell (1991), Matras (2002), Ruhlen (1976)		

Language name	Russian		'rʌʃən
Autonym (if known and different)			
Language family	Indo-European	Slavic	
Spoken in	Russia		
Approximate number of speakers	160m		
Writing system	Cyrillic		
Phonetics/phonology			
Stress	variable		
Contains following rare consonant (types)			
Said to have how many vowels?	5		
Marked vowel types			
Tone	none		
Rhythm	no information		
Vowel harmony	none		
Morphology	fusional	stem-based	
Particular formation types	prefix; suffix		
Syntax			
Word order	SVO	AN PossN	prepositions
Particular syntactic phenomena	gender; morphological aspect; nominative / accusative marking; conjugation classes		
Points of interest			
Sources	Campbell (1991), Katzner (1977), Maddieson (1984), Timberlake (1993)		

Language name	Rotuman		
Autonym (if known and different)			
Language family	Austronesian	Eastern Oceanic	
Spoken in	Rotuma		
Approximate number of speakers	7k		
Writing system	Roman		
Phonetics/phonology			
Stress	quantity-based		
Contains following rare consonant (types)			
Said to have how many vowels?	10		
Marked vowel types	front rounded		
Tone	none		
Rhythm	no information		
Vowel harmony	none		
Morphology	agglutinative	word-based	
Particular formation types	prefix; partial prefixed and full reduplication; suffix; synaffix		
Syntax			
Word order	SVO	NA PossN	prepositions
Particular syntactic phenomena	inclusive / exclusive 1st plural; dual; nominative / accusative marking		
Points of interest			
Sources	Ruhlen (1976), Schmidt (2002)		

Rumanian see Romanian

Samoan

Language name	Samoan		sə'moʊən
Autonym (if known and different)			
Language family	Austronesian	Polynesian	
Spoken in	Samoa, New Zealand		
Approximate number of speakers	200k		
Writing system	Roman		
Phonetics/phonology			
Stress	penultimate mora of the word		
Contains following rare consonant (types)			
Said to have how many vowels?	5 + length		
Marked vowel types			
Tone	none		
Rhythm	no information		
Vowel harmony	none		
Morphology	agglutinative	word-based	
Particular formation types	incorporation; prefix; partial prefixed, partial suffixed, partial infixed and full reduplication; suffix		
Syntax			
Word order	VSO	NA PossN	prepositions
Particular syntactic phenomena	inclusive / exclusive 1st plural; nominative / accusative marking; dual		
Points of interest			
Sources	Campbell (1991), Katzner (1977), Marsack (1962), Mithun (1984), Ruhlen (1976)		

Saami

Language name	Saami, Sami	Lappish, Lapp	'saːmi
Autonym (if known and different)			
Language family	Uralic	Finno-Ugric	
Spoken in	Norway, Sweden, Finland, Russia		
Approximate number of speakers	30k		
Writing system	Roman, Cyrillic		
Phonetics/phonology			
Stress	word-initial		
Contains following rare consonant (types)			
Said to have how many vowels?	6 + 4 diphthongs		
Marked vowel types			
Tone	none		
Rhythm	no information		
Vowel harmony	none		
Morphology	agglutinative (and fusional)	stem-based in verbs, word-based in nouns	
Particular formation types	dvandva; suffix		
Syntax			
Word order	SVO	AN NPoss	prepositions and postpositions
Particular syntactic phenomena	nominative / accusative marking; dual		
Points of interest			
Sources	Campbell (1991), Gordon (2002), Katzner (1977), Maddieson (1984), Nickel (1994), Ruhlen (1976), Wälchli (2005)		

Sami see Saami

Language name	Sanuma		'sɨnɨma
Autonym (if known and different)	'sɨnɨma		
Language family	Yanomami		
Spoken in	Venezuela, Brazil		
Approximate number of speakers	2k		
Writing system	Roman		
Phonetics/phonology			
Stress	word–penultimate		
Contains following rare consonant (types)			
Said to have how many vowels?	7 + nasalisation (6)		
Marked vowel types			
Tone	none		
Rhythm	no information		
Vowel harmony	nasality		
Morphology	isolating and agglutinative	word–based	
Particular formation types	suffix		
Syntax			
Word order	SOV	NA PossN	postpositions
Particular syntactic phenomena	absolutive / ergative marking; classifiers; inclusive / exclusive 1st plural; morphological aspect; conjugation classes; alienable / inalienable possession; evidentials		
Points of interest	no overt coordination markers		
Sources	Borgman (1990)		

Language name	Sanskrit		'sænskrɪt
Autonym (if known and different)	saṃskṛta 'correct, formed for sacred use'		
Language family	Indo-European	Indic	
Spoken in	India		
Approximate number of speakers	2k		
Writing system	Devanagari		
Phonetics/phonology			
Stress	quantity–based		
Contains following rare consonant (types)	retroflex		
Said to have how many vowels?	5 + length (4) + 4 diphthongs		
Marked vowel types			
Tone	none		
Rhythm	no information		
Vowel harmony	none		
Morphology	fusional	stem-based	
Particular formation types	dvandva; partial prefixed reduplication; suffix		
Syntax			
Word order	free	AN NPoss	prepositions and postpositions
Particular syntactic phenomena	gender; nominative / accusative marking; dual; conjugation classes		
Points of interest			
Sources	Campbell (1991), Gonda (1966), Katzner (1977), Mayrhofer (1972)		

Scottish Gaelic see Gaelic

Serbian

Language name	Serbian	Serbo-Croat	'sɜːbiən
Autonym (if known and different)			
Language family	Indo-European	Slavic	
Spoken in	Serbia		
Approximate number of speakers	18m		
Writing system	Cyrillic		
Phonetics/phonology			
Stress			
Contains following rare consonant (types)			
Said to have how many vowels?	5 + length		
Marked vowel types			
Tone	tonal accent		
Rhythm	no information		
Vowel harmony	none		
Morphology	fusional	stem-based	
Particular formation types	prefix; suffix		
Syntax			
Word order	free	AN / PossN	prepositions
Particular syntactic phenomena	gender; morphological aspect; nominative / accusative marking; conjugation classes		
Points of interest	see also Croatian		
Sources	Campbell (1991), Ruhlen (1976)		

Serbo-Croat see Croatian; Serbian
Sesotho see Sotho
Setswana see Tswana

Seneca

Language name	Seneca		'senɪkə
Autonym (if known and different)			
Language family	Macro-Siouan	Iroquoian	
Spoken in	New York State (USA)		
Approximate number of speakers	150		
Writing system	Roman		
Phonetics/phonology			
Stress	second-syllable		
Contains following rare consonant (types)			
Said to have how many vowels?	6 + nasalisation (2) + 9 diphthongs		
Marked vowel types			
Tone	none		
Rhythm	no information		
Vowel harmony	none		
Morphology	polysynthetic	stem-based verbs; word-based nouns	
Particular formation types	incorporation; infix; prefix; suffix		
Syntax			
Word order	VSO	NA / PossN	postpositions
Particular syntactic phenomena	gender; dual; morphological aspect; alienable / inalienable possession; inclusive / exclusive 1st plural		
Points of interest			
Sources	Campbell (1991), Holmer (1954), Katzner (1977), Maddieson (1984), Mithun (1984, 1999)		

Language name	Shona		'ʃɔunə
Autonym (if known and different)			
Language family	Niger-Congo	Bantu	
Spoken in	Zambia, Zimbabwe		
Approximate number of speakers	118k		
Writing system	Roman		
Phonetics/phonology			
Stress	word-penultimate		
Contains following rare consonant (types)	retroflex; implosive; 'whistling' labial-alveolar fricatives		
Said to have how many vowels?	5		
Marked vowel types			
Tone	register		
Rhythm	no information		
Vowel harmony	none		
Morphology	agglutinative		
Particular formation types	prefix; reduplication; suffix		
Syntax			
Word order	SVO	NA NPoss	prepositions and postpositions
Particular syntactic phenomena	noun classes		
Points of interest			
Sources	Doke (1954), Gordon (2002), Katzner (1977), Ruhlen (1976)		

Language name	Shelta	Cant	'ʃeltə
Autonym (if known and different)			
Language family	Indo-European	Celtic	
Spoken in	Ireland, United Kingdom, USA		
Approximate number of speakers	6k		
Writing system			
Phonetics/phonology			
Stress			
Contains following rare consonant (types)			
Said to have how many vowels?	7 + length (5) + 3 diphthongs		
Marked vowel types			
Tone	none		
Rhythm	no information		
Vowel harmony	none		
Morphology			
Particular formation types	prefix; suffix		
Syntax			
Word order			
Particular syntactic phenomena			
Points of interest	largely a cryptic jargon used by tinkers, etc., with English syntax predominating		
Sources	Hancock (1984), Macalister (1974)		

Language name	Sindhi		'sindi
Autonym (if known and different)			
Language family	Indo-European	Indic	
Spoken in	Pakistan, Baluchistan, India		
Approximate number of speakers	6m		
Writing system	its own Arabic-based script		
Phonetics/phonology			
Stress			
Contains following rare consonant (types)	retroflex; implosive		
Said to have how many vowels?	5 + length		
Marked vowel types			
Tone	none		
Rhythm	no information		
Vowel harmony	none		
Morphology	fusional	stem-based	
Particular formation types	suffix		
Syntax			
Word order	SOV	AN NPoss	postpositions
Particular syntactic phenomena	gender; conjugation classes		
Points of interest			
Sources	Campbell (1991), Katzner (1977)		

Sinhala see Sinhalese

Language name	Shoshone		ʃoʊˈ ʃouni
Autonym (if known and different)	sosoni, nümü		
Language family	Aztec–Tanoan	Uto–Aztecan	
Spoken in	Oklahoma, California, Nevada (USA)		
Approximate number of speakers	5k		
Writing system			
Phonetics/phonology			
Stress	word-initial		
Contains following rare consonant (types)			
Said to have how many vowels?	6 + length + 1 diphthong		
Marked vowel types	back unrounded		
Tone	none		
Rhythm	mora-timing		
Vowel harmony	rounding		
Morphology	polysynthetic	stem-based for verbs; word–based for nouns	
Particular formation types	incorporation; prefix; partial prefixed reduplication; suffix		
Syntax			
Word order	SOV	AN PossN	postpositions
Particular syntactic phenomena	inclusive / exclusive 1st plural; morphological aspect; nominative / accusative marking; dual;		
Points of interest			
Sources	Dayley (1989), Gordon (2002), Katzner (1977), Ruhlen (1976)		

Siamese see Thai

Language name	Sinhalese	Sinhala	sinə'liːz
Autonym (if known and different)			
Language family	Indo-European	Indic	
Spoken in	Sri Lanka		
Approximate number of speakers	17m		
Writing system	its own syllabary		
Phonetics/phonology			
Stress			
Contains following rare consonant (types)	retroflex		
Said to have how many vowels?	7 + length		
Marked vowel types			
Tone	none		
Rhythm	no information		
Vowel harmony	none		
Morphology	agglutinative	stem-based	
Particular formation types	infix; full reduplication; suffix		
Syntax			
Word order	SOV	AN PossN	postpositions
Particular syntactic phenomena	gender; nominative / accusative marking; conjugation classes		
Points of interest	plural unmarked for inanimates		
Sources	Campbell (1991), Gair (2003), Gair & Paolillo (1997), Katzner (1977), Maddieson (1984), Ruhlen (1976)		

Language name	Slave	Slavey	'slevi
Autonym (if known and different)			
Language family	Na-Dene	Athabaskan	
Spoken in	North-West Territories (Canada)		
Approximate number of speakers	250		
Writing system			
Phonetics/phonology			
Stress			
Contains following rare consonant (types)	ejective		
Said to have how many vowels?	6 + nasalisation		
Marked vowel types			
Tone	register		
Rhythm	no information		
Vowel harmony	none		
Morphology	polysynthetic	stem-based for verbs; word-based for nouns	
Particular formation types	incorporation; prefix; (suffix)		
Syntax			
Word order	SOV	NA PossN	postpositions
Particular syntactic phenomena	morphological aspect; gender		
Points of interest			
Sources	Haspelmath et al. (2005), Rice (1998), Yip (2002)		

Slavey see **Slave**
Slovak see **Slovakian**

Language name	Slovenian	Slovene	sləʊˈviːnɪən
Autonym (if known and different)	slovénščina		
Language family	Indo-European	Slavic	
Spoken in	Slovenia, Austria, Italy		
Approximate number of speakers	2.5m		
Writing system	Roman		
Phonetics/phonology			
Stress	quantity-based system		
Contains following rare consonant (types)			
Said to have how many vowels?	8 distinct qualities, 7 long and 6 short		
Marked vowel types			
Tone	tonal accent		
Rhythm	no information		
Vowel harmony	none		
Morphology	fusional	stem-based	
Particular formation types	suffix		
Syntax			
Word order	SVO	AN PossN	prepositions
Particular syntactic phenomena	gender; morphological aspect; nominative / accusative marking; dual; conjugation classes		
Points of interest			
Sources	Campbell (1991), Katzner (1977), Priestly (1993)		

Language name	Slovakian	Slovak	slaʊˈvækɪən
Autonym (if known and different)			
Language family	Indo-European	Slavic	
Spoken in	Slovakia, Slovenia, Hungary		
Approximate number of speakers	5m		
Writing system	Roman		
Phonetics/phonology			
Stress	word-initial		
Contains following rare consonant (types)			
Said to have how many vowels?	6 + length + 4 diphthongs		
Marked vowel types			
Tone	none		
Rhythm	stress-timing		
Vowel harmony	none		
Morphology	fusional	stem-based	
Particular formation types	infix; prefix; suffix		
Syntax			
Word order	SVO	AN NPoss	prepositions
Particular syntactic phenomena	gender; morphological aspect; nominative / accusative marking; conjugation classes		
Points of interest	mutually intelligible with Czech		
Sources	Campbell (1991), Ruhlen (1976), Short (1993b)		

Slovene see Slovenian

Language name	Sorbian	Lusatian, Wendish	ˈsɔːbɪən
Autonym (if known and different)	wendisch, sorbisch, serbski		
Language family	Indo-European	Slavic	
Spoken in	Saxony (Germany)		
Approximate number of speakers	70k		
Writing system	Roman		
Phonetics/phonology			
Stress	word-initial		
Contains following rare consonant (types)			
Said to have how many vowels?	7		
Marked vowel types			
Tone	none		
Rhythm	no information		
Vowel harmony	none		
Morphology	fusional	stem-based	
Particular formation types	prefix; suffix		
Syntax			
Word order	SOV	AN PossN	prepositions
Particular syntactic phenomena	gender; morphological aspect; nominative / accusative marking; dual; conjugation classes		
Points of interest			
Sources	Gordon (2002), Katzner (1977), Stone (1993)		

Language name	Somali		sɔʊˈmɑːli
Autonym (if known and different)	afka Soomaaliga		
Language family	Afro-Asiatic	Cushitic	
Spoken in	Somalia, Kenya, Ethiopia		
Approximate number of speakers	10m		
Writing system	Roman		
Phonetics/phonology			
Stress			
Contains following rare consonant (types)	uvular; pharyngeal		
Said to have how many vowels?	5 + length		
Marked vowel types			
Tone	tonal accent		
Rhythm	no information		
Vowel harmony	ATR		
Morphology	agglutinative	stem-based	
Particular formation types	prefix; partial suffixed reduplication; suffix; apophony		
Syntax			
Word order	SOV	NA PossN	prepositions
Particular syntactic phenomena	gender; conjugation classes		
Points of interest			
Sources	Biber & Saeed (2003), Campbell (1991), Katzner (1977), Maddieson (1984), Ruhlen (1976)		

Language name	Sotho	Sesotho	'suːtuː
Autonym (if known and different)			
Language family	Niger-Congo	Bantu	
Spoken in	Botswana, South Africa		
Approximate number of speakers	4m		
Writing system	Roman		
Phonetics/phonology			
Stress	word-penultimate		
Contains following rare consonant (types)	retroflex; click; ejective		
Said to have how many vowels?	9 + length		
Marked vowel types			
Tone	register		
Rhythm	no information		
Vowel harmony	some height		
Morphology	agglutinative	word-based	
Particular formation types	prefix; partial suffixed and full reduplication; suffix		
Syntax			
Word order	SVO	NA NPoss	prepositions
Particular syntactic phenomena	morphological aspect; noun classes		
Points of interest			
Sources	Doke (1954), Doke & Mofokeng (1957), Katzner (1977), Gordon (2002)		

Southern Lendu see Ngiti

Language name	Spanish		'spaniʃ
Autonym (if known and different)	español		
Language family	Indo-European	Romance	
Spoken in	Spain, Mexico, Argentina, Chile, Colombia, Venezuela, Paraguay, Uruguay, Puerto Rico, etc.		
Approximate number of speakers	300m		
Writing system	Roman		
Phonetics/phonology			
Stress	word-penultimate		
Contains following rare consonant (types)			
Said to have how many vowels?	5 + 5 diphthongs		
Marked vowel types			
Tone	none		
Rhythm	usually classified as syllable-timed		
Vowel harmony	none		
Morphology	fusional	word-based	
Particular formation types	suffix		
Syntax			
Word order	SVO	NA NPoss	prepositions
Particular syntactic phenomena	gender; conjugation classes		
Points of interest			
Sources	Campbell (1991), Katzner (1977), Maddieson (1984)		

Language name	Sumerian		suːˈmɛrɪən
Autonym (if known and different)			
Language family	isolate		
Spoken in	extinct, but spoken in modern Iraq from c. 3200 BCE to 1600 BCE		
Approximate number of speakers	0		
Writing system	cuneiform		
Phonetics/phonology			
Stress			
Contains following rare consonant (types)			
Said to have how many vowels?	4		
Marked vowel types			
Tone	none		
Rhythm	no information		
Vowel harmony	some apparent		
Morphology	agglutinative	word-based	
Particular formation types	apophony; incorporation; prefixation; reduplication; suffixation		
Syntax			
Word order	SOV	NA PossN	postpositions
Particular syntactic phenomena	ergative / absolutive and nominative / accusative marking; morphological aspect		
Points of interest	some of the oldest written texts still extant are in Sumerian		
Sources	Michalowski (2004)		

Language name	Squamish		ˈskwɔːmɪʃ
Autonym (if known and different)			
Language family	Salishan	Central Coast	
Spoken in	British Columbia (Canada)		
Approximate number of speakers	0		
Writing system			
Phonetics/phonology			
Stress	variable		
Contains following rare consonant (types)	uvular; ejective		
Said to have how many vowels?	4		
Marked vowel types			
Tone	none		
Rhythm	no information		
Vowel harmony	none		
Morphology	polysynthetic	stem-based	
Particular formation types	incorporation; prefix; partial prefixed and partial suffixed and full reduplication; suffix; synaffix		
Syntax			
Word order	VSO	AN NPoss	prepositions
Particular syntactic phenomena	ergative / absolutive marking; classifiers		
Points of interest			
Sources	Campbell (1991), Kuipers (1967), Maddieson (1984), Ruhlen (1976)		

Language name	Swahili	KiSwahili	swɑˈhiːli
Autonym (if known and different)			
Language family	Niger-Congo	Bantu	
Spoken in	Tanzania, Kenya, Zaire, Congo, Somalia, Mozambique, Uganda, etc.		
Approximate number of speakers	60m		
Writing system	Roman		
Phonetics/phonology			
Stress	word-penultimate		
Contains following rare consonant (types)	implosive		
Said to have how many vowels?	5		
Marked vowel types			
Tone	none		
Rhythm	no information		
Vowel harmony	some height		
Morphology	agglutinative	stem-based	
Particular formation types	prefix; suffix		
Syntax			
Word order	SVO	NA NPoss	prepositions
Particular syntactic phenomena	noun classes		
Points of interest			
Sources	Ashton (1947), Campbell (1991), Hinnebusch (2003), Katzner (1977), Maddieson (1984)		

Language name	Sundanese		sʌndəˈniːz
Autonym (if known and different)	basa gumung		
Language family	Austronesian	Malayo-Polynesian	
Spoken in	Java, Sumatra (Indonesia)		
Approximate number of speakers	25m		
Writing system	Roman		
Phonetics/phonology			
Stress	word-penultimate		
Contains following rare consonant (types)			
Said to have how many vowels?	7		
Marked vowel types			
Tone	none		
Rhythm	no information		
Vowel harmony	none		
Morphology	isolating and agglutinative	word-based	
Particular formation types	dvandva; infix; prefix; partial prefixed and full reduplication; suffix; synaffix		
Syntax			
Word order	SVO	NA NPoss	prepositions
Particular syntactic phenomena			
Points of interest	well-developed vocabulary for showing respect		
Sources	Campbell (1991), Katzner (1977), Maddieson (1984), Müller-Gotama (2001), Wälchli (2005)		

Language name	Tagalog	Pilipino	tə'gɑːlɒg
Autonym (if known and different)			
Language family	Austronesian	Philippine	
Spoken in	Philippines		
Approximate number of speakers	40m		
Writing system	Roman		
Phonetics/phonology			
Stress	quantity-based		
Contains following rare consonant (types)			
Said to have how many vowels?	5 + length		
Marked vowel types			
Tone	none		
Rhythm	no information		
Vowel harmony	none		
Morphology	agglutinative	word-based	
Particular formation types	infix; prefix; partial infixed, partial prefixed and full reduplication; suffix		
Syntax			
Word order	VSO	AN and NA NPoss	prepositions
Particular syntactic phenomena	inclusive / exclusive 1st plural; morphological aspect; gender; nominative / accusative marking		
Points of interest			
Sources	Blake (1925), Campbell (1991), Haspelmath et al. (2005), Maddieson (1984), Ruhlen (1976)		

Language name	Swedish		'swiːdʃ
Autonym (if known and different)	svenska		
Language family	Indo-European	Germanic	
Spoken in	Sweden, Finland		
Approximate number of speakers	8m		
Writing system	Roman		
Phonetics/phonology			
Stress	root-initial		
Contains following rare consonant (types)	retroflex		
Said to have how many vowels?	10 + length		
Marked vowel types	front rounded		
Tone	tonal accent		
Rhythm	no information		
Vowel harmony	none		
Morphology	agglutinative	word-based	
Particular formation types	prefix; suffix		
Syntax			
Word order	V2	AN PossN	prepositions
Particular syntactic phenomena	gender; conjugation classes		
Points of interest			
Sources	Campbell (1991), Holmes & Hinchcliffe (1994), Katzner (1977)		

Sye see Erromangan

Language name	Tahitian		tɑˈhiːʃən
Autonym (if known and different)			
Language family	Austronesian	Polynesian	
Spoken in	Tahiti		
Approximate number of speakers	60k		
Writing system	Roman		
Phonetics/phonology			
Stress	quantity-based		
Contains following rare consonant (types)			
Said to have how many vowels?	5 + length		
Marked vowel types			
Tone	none		
Rhythm	no information		
Vowel harmony	none		
Morphology	agglutinative	word-based	
Particular formation types	prefix; partial prefixed and full reduplication; suffix		
Syntax			
Word order	VSO	NA PossN	prepositions
Particular syntactic phenomena	inclusive / exclusive 1st plural; dual		
Points of interest			
Sources	Campbell (1991), Katzner (1977), Ruhlen (1976), Tryon (1970)		

Language name	Takelma		tɐˈkɛlmə
Autonym (if known and different)			
Language family	Penutian		
Spoken in	Oregon (USA)		
Approximate number of speakers	0		
Writing system			
Phonetics/phonology			
Stress			
Contains following rare consonant (types)	ejective		
Said to have how many vowels?	6 + length		
Marked vowel types			
Tone	tonal accent		
Rhythm	no information		
Vowel harmony	none		
Morphology	fusional and polysynthetic	word-based	
Particular formation types	apophony; suffix; partial suffixed reduplication; incorporation		
Syntax			
Word order	SVO	AN PossN	postpositions
Particular syntactic phenomena	evidentials		
Points of interest			
Sources	Haspelmath et al. (2005), Mithun (1999), Ruhlen (1976)		

Language name	Telugu		'telugu:
Autonym (if known and different)			
Language family	Dravidian		
Spoken in	Andhra Pradesh (India)		
Approximate number of speakers	54m		
Writing system	its own system		
Phonetics/phonology			
Stress	quantity-based		
Contains following rare consonant (types)	retroflex		
Said to have how many vowels?	5 + length + 2 diphthongs		
Marked vowel types			
Tone	none		
Rhythm	no information		
Vowel harmony	some complete assimilation		
Morphology	agglutinative	word-based	
Particular formation types	suffix		
Syntax			
Word order	SOV	AN PossN	postpositions
Particular syntactic phenomena	gender; inclusive / exclusive 1st plural; nominative / accusative marking; conjugation classes		
Points of interest	the speech of the educated uses 33 consonant phonemes, while uneducated users have only 17 consonant phonemes, the difference being largely in aspirated consonants		
Sources	Krishnamurti (2003), Krishnamurti & Gwynn (1985), Prakasam (2005)		

Tetun see Tetun

Language name	Tamil		'tæml
Autonym (if known and different)	tamic		
Language family	Dravidian	Tamil-Kannada	
Spoken in	Tamil Nadu (India), Sri Lanka, Malaysia, Singapore		
Approximate number of speakers	66m		
Writing system	its own alphabet		
Phonetics/phonology			
Stress	weight-based, usually word-initial		
Contains following rare consonant (types)	retroflex		
Said to have how many vowels?	5 + length + 2 diphthongs		
Marked vowel types	back unrounded (in borrowed words)		
Tone	none		
Rhythm	syllable-timed		
Vowel harmony	none		
Morphology	agglutinative	word-based	
Particular formation types	dvandva; partial suffixed and full reduplication; suffix		
Syntax			
Word order	SOV	AN PossN	postpositions
Particular syntactic phenomena	gender; inclusive / exclusive 1st plural; nominative / accusative marking; evidentials		
Points of interest			
Sources	Annamali & Steever (1998), Asher (1982), Campbell (1991), Haspelmath et al. (2005), Katzner (1977), Krishnamurti (2003), Ruhlen (1976)		

Language name	Thai	Siamese	tai
Autonym (if known and different)			
Language family	Tai	Kam-Tai	
Spoken in	Thailand		
Approximate number of speakers	40m		
Writing system	Thai script (originally based on Southern Indian script)		
Phonetics/phonology			
Stress	word-final		
Contains following rare consonant (types)			
Said to have how many vowels?	9 + length + 16 diphthongs		
Marked vowel types	back unrounded		
Tone	contour		
Rhythm	no information		
Vowel harmony	none		
Morphology	isolating	word-based	
Particular formation types	dvandva; infix; prefix; partial prefixed, partial suffixed and full reduplication; (suffix); tone used morphologically; apophony		
Syntax			
Word order	SVO	NA NPoss	prepositions
Particular syntactic phenomena	classifiers; serial verbs		
Points of interest			
Sources	Campbell (1991), Diller (2003), Gordon (2002), Hudak (1990), Katzner (1977), Maddieson (1984), Ruhlen (1976), Yip (2002)		

Language name	Tetum	Tetum, Tetung	'tetum
Autonym (if known and different)			
Language family	Austronesian	Malayo-Polynesian	
Spoken in	Timor (Indonesia)		
Approximate number of speakers	300k		
Writing system	Roman		
Phonetics/phonology			
Stress	word-penultimate		
Contains following rare consonant (types)			
Said to have how many vowels?	5		
Marked vowel types			
Tone	none		
Rhythm	no information		
Vowel harmony	only in the restricted sense that a mid vowel cannot follow a syllable with a close vowel		
Morphology	isolating and agglutinative	word-based	
Particular formation types	dvandva; prefix; partial prefixed and full reduplication; synaffix		
Syntax			
Word order	SVO	NA NPoss	prepositions
Particular syntactic phenomena	classifiers; inclusive / exclusive 1st plural; noun classes; serial verbs		
Points of interest	no productive suffixes. The word for 'three' is a taboo word because it is homophonous with the word for 'egg' or 'testicle'; it is even impolite to photograph three people together		
Sources	Van Engelenhoven & Williams-van Klinken (2005), Van Klinken (1999)		

Tetung see Tetum

Language name	Tigrinya		tɪˈɡrɪnjə
Autonym (if known and different)			
Language family	Afro-Asiatic	Semitic	
Spoken in	Eritrea		
Approximate number of speakers	3m		
Writing system	Amharic syllabary		
Phonetics/phonology			
Stress	word-final		
Contains following rare consonant (types)	pharyngeal; ejective		
Said to have how many vowels?	7		
Marked vowel types			
Tone	none		
Rhythm	no information		
Vowel harmony	some limited		
Morphology	fusional		stem-based
Particular formation types	prefix; root-and-pattern; suffix		
Syntax			
Word order	SOV	AN PossN	prepositions
Particular syntactic phenomena	gender; morphological aspect; conjugation classes		
Points of interest			
Sources	Bender et al. (1976), Campbell (1991), Katzner (1977), Maddieson (1984), Ruhlen (1976)		

Language name	Tibetan		tɪˈbetən
Autonym (if known and different)			
Language family	Sino-Tibetan	Tibeto-Burman	
Spoken in	Tibet, India, Nepal, China		
Approximate number of speakers	4m		
Writing system	its own syllabary		
Phonetics/phonology			
Stress			
Contains following rare consonant (types)	retroflex, uvular		
Said to have how many vowels?	5 + nasalisation (3)		
Marked vowel types	front rounded		
Tone	register		
Rhythm	no information		
Vowel harmony	dominant/recessive		
Morphology	agglutinative		word-based
Particular formation types	apophony; dvandva; prefix; full reduplication; suffix		
Syntax			
Word order	SOV	NA and AN PossN	postpositions
Particular syntactic phenomena	absolutive / ergative marking; inclusive / exclusive 1st plural; dual		
Points of interest			
Sources	Chang (2003), Chang & Shefts (1964), Delancey (2003), Wälchli (2005)		

Language name	Tiwi		'ti:wi
Autonym (if known and different)			
Language family	Australian		
Spoken in	Bathurst and Melville Islands, Northern Territory (Australia)		
Approximate number of speakers	1k		
Writing system			
Phonetics/phonology			
Stress	word–penultimate		
Contains following rare consonant (types)	retroflex		
Said to have how many vowels?	4		
Marked vowel types			
Tone	none		
Rhythm	no information		
Vowel harmony	none		
Morphology	polysynthetic	stem–based	
Particular formation types	incorporation; prefix; partial prefixed reduplication; suffix		
Syntax			
Word order	SVO	AN PossN	prepositions
Particular syntactic phenomena	gender; inclusive / exclusive 1st plural; morphological aspect		
Points of interest			
Sources	Gordon (2002), Maddieson (1984), Osborne (1974)		

Language name	Tiwa		'ti:wa
Autonym (if known and different)			
Language family	Aztec–Tanoan	Tanoan	
Spoken in	New Mexico (USA)		
Approximate number of speakers	3k		
Writing system			
Phonetics/phonology			
Stress			
Contains following rare consonant (types)	ejective		
Said to have how many vowels?	6 + nasalisation		
Marked vowel types			
Tone	none		
Rhythm	no information		
Vowel harmony	none		
Morphology	polysynthetic		
Particular formation types	incorporation		
Syntax			
Word order	variable		postpositions
Particular syntactic phenomena	evidentials; dual		
Points of interest			
Sources	Haspelmath et al. (2005), Katzner (1977), Maddieson (1984), Mithun (1999), Ruhlen (1976)		

Language name	Toba Batak	Batak	'taʊba 'bætak
Autonym (if known and different)			
Language family	Austronesian	West-Indonesian	
Spoken in	Northern Sumatra (Indonesia)		
Approximate number of speakers	3m		
Writing system	Roman and Devanagari-based script		
Phonetics/phonology			
Stress	word–penultimate		
Contains following rare consonant (types)			
Said to have how many vowels?	7		
Marked vowel types			
Tone	none		
Rhythm	no information		
Vowel harmony	none		
Morphology	agglutinative	word-based	
Particular formation types	prefix; partial prefixed and full reduplication; suffix; synaffix		
Syntax			
Word order	VOS and VSO	AN / NPoss	prepositions
Particular syntactic phenomena	inclusive / exclusive 1st plural; noun classes		
Points of interest			
Sources	Campbell (1991), Katzner (1977), Nababan (1981), Percival (1981)		

Language name	Tlingit	'klɪŋɪt, 'tlɪŋɪt	
Autonym (if known and different)			
Language family	Na-Dene		
Spoken in	Alaska (USA), Canada		
Approximate number of speakers	800		
Writing system			
Phonetics/phonology			
Stress			
Contains following rare consonant (types)	uvular; ejective		
Said to have how many vowels?	5		
Marked vowel types			
Tone	register		
Rhythm	no information		
Vowel harmony	none		
Morphology	polysynthetic	stem-based	
Particular formation types	prefix; suffix; incorporation		
Syntax			
Word order	SVO	AN / PossN	postpositions
Particular syntactic phenomena	morphological aspect		
Points of interest			
Sources	Campbell (1991), Katzner (1977), Maddieson (1984)		

Language name	Tokelauan		tɔʊkɔˈlauən
Autonym (if known and different)			
Language family	Austronesian	Polynesian	
Spoken in	Tokelau, Samoa, New Zealand, USA		
Approximate number of speakers	5k		
Writing system	Roman		
Phonetics/phonology			
Stress	quantity-based		
Contains following rare consonant (types)			
Said to have how many vowels?	5 + length		
Marked vowel types			
Tone	none		
Rhythm	no information		
Vowel harmony	none		
Morphology	isolating	word based	
Particular formation types	incorporation; prefix; partial prefixed, partial suffixed and full reduplication; suffix; synaffix		
Syntax			
Word order	VSO	NA PossN and NPoss	prepositions
Particular syntactic phenomena	absolutive / ergative marking; inclusive / exclusive 1st plural; dual		
Points of interest	several number systems, depending on what is being counted		
Sources	Hooper (1996)		

Language name	Tok Pisin		tok ˈpɪsɪn
Autonym (if known and different)			
Language family	English-based creole		
Spoken in	Papua New Guinea		
Approximate number of speakers	50k (L1), 2m (L2)		
Writing system	Roman		
Phonetics/phonology			
Stress	word-initial		
Contains following rare consonant (types)			
Said to have how many vowels?	5 + 8 diphthongs		
Marked vowel types			
Tone	none		
Rhythm	no information		
Vowel harmony	none		
Morphology	isolating and agglutinative	word-based	
Particular formation types	dvandva; prefix; full reduplication; suffix		
Syntax			
Word order	SVO	AN and NA NPoss	prepositions
Particular syntactic phenomena	inclusive / exclusive 1st plural; dual and trial; serial verbs		
Points of interest			
Sources	Givón (1991), Wälchli (2005), Woolford (1979), Wurm & Mühlhäusler (1985)		

Language name	Tol	Jicaque	
Autonym (if known and different)			
Language family	Hokan	isolate	
Spoken in	Honduras		
Approximate number of speakers	200		
Writing system			
Phonetics/phonology			
Stress	weight-based system; last two syllables of the word		
Contains following rare consonant (types)	ejective		
Said to have how many vowels?	6		
Marked vowel types	back unrounded		
Tone	none		
Rhythm	no information		
Vowel harmony	vowel height		
Morphology	agglutinative	stem-based	
Particular formation types	apophony; infix; prefix; partial prefixed and full reduplication; suffix; suprasegmentals used morphologically		
Syntax			
Word order	SOV	NA NPoss	postpositions
Particular syntactic phenomena	conjugation classes		
Points of interest			
Sources	Holt (1999)		

Language name	Tondano		
Autonym (if known and different)			
Language family	Austronesian	Malayo-Polynesian	
Spoken in	Sulawesi (Indonesia)		
Approximate number of speakers	92k		
Writing system	Roman, but not standardised		
Phonetics/phonology			
Stress	word-penultimate		
Contains following rare consonant (types)			
Said to have how many vowels?	6		
Marked vowel types			
Tone	register		
Rhythm	no information		
Vowel harmony	none		
Morphology	agglutinative	word-based	
Particular formation types	infix; prefix; suffix; synaffix		
Syntax			
Word order	SVO	NA NPoss	prepositions
Particular syntactic phenomena	classifiers; morphological aspect; conjugation classes		
Points of interest			
Sources	Sneddon (1975)		

Language name	Trukese		trʌˈkiːz
Autonym (if known and different)	Chuuk		
Language family	Austronesian	Micronesian	
Spoken in	Micronesia		
Approximate number of speakers	25k		
Writing system	Roman		
Phonetics/phonology			
Stress			
Contains following rare consonant (types)	retroflex		
Said to have how many vowels?	9		
Marked vowel types			
Tone	none		
Rhythm	no information		
Vowel harmony	some vowel-height		
Morphology	agglutinative	word-based	
Particular formation types	prefix; partial prefixed and full reduplication; suffix		
Syntax			
Word order	SVO	NA NPoss	prepositions
Particular syntactic phenomena	inclusive / exclusive 1st plural		
Points of interest			
Sources	Campbell (1991), Goodenough & Sugita (1980), Katzner (1977)		

Language name	Tongan		ˈtɒŋən
Autonym (if known and different)			
Language family	Austronesian	Polynesian	
Spoken in	Tonga, New Zealand		
Approximate number of speakers	120k		
Writing system	Roman		
Phonetics/phonology			
Stress	word-penultimate		
Contains following rare consonant (types)			
Said to have how many vowels?	5 + length		
Marked vowel types			
Tone	none		
Rhythm	no information		
Vowel harmony	none		
Morphology	isolating and agglutinative	word-based	
Particular formation types	incorporation; prefix; partial prefixed and full reduplication; suffix		
Syntax			
Word order	VSO	NA NPoss	prepositions
Particular syntactic phenomena	absolutive / ergative marking; inclusive / exclusive 1st plural; dual		
Points of interest			
Sources	Campbell (1991), Churchward (1953), Mithun (1984)		

Language name	Tswana	Setswana	ˈtswɑːnə
Autonym (if known and different)			
Language family	Niger-Congo	Bantu	
Spoken in	Botswana, Namibia, Zimbabwe, South Africa		
Approximate number of speakers	4m		
Writing system	Roman		
Phonetics/phonology			
Stress	word–penultimate		
Contains following rare consonant (types)	clicks in ideophones		
Said to have how many vowels?	8		
Marked vowel types			
Tone	register		
Rhythm	no information		
Vowel harmony	none		
Morphology	agglutinative	stem-based	
Particular formation types	prefix; suffix		
Syntax			
Word order	SVO	NA NPoss	neither
Particular syntactic phenomena	morphological aspect; noun classes		
Points of interest			
Sources	Cole (1955), Gordon (2002)		

Language name	Tukang Besi	
Autonym (if known and different)		
Language family	Austronesian	Malayo-Polynesian
Spoken in	Tukang Besi (Indonesia)	
Approximate number of speakers	90k	
Writing system	Roman	
Phonetics/phonology		
Stress	word–penultimate	
Contains following rare consonant (types)	implosive	
Said to have how many vowels?	5	
Marked vowel types	back unrounded	
Tone	none	
Rhythm	no information	
Vowel harmony	none	
Morphology	agglutinative	word-based
Particular formation types	prefix; partial prefixed, partial infixed and partial suffixed reduplication; suffix	
Syntax		
Word order	verb-initial	NA NPoss
Particular syntactic phenomena	classifiers; dual; paucal	
Points of interest		
Sources	Donohue (1999)	

Tungus see Evenki

Language name	Turkish		'tɜːkɪʃ
Autonym (if known and different)	Türkçe		
Language family	Altaic	Turkic	
Spoken in	Turkey, Cyprus, Bulgaria, Greece		
Approximate number of speakers	50m		
Writing system	Roman (since 1929)		
Phonetics/phonology			
Stress	word-final		
Contains following rare consonant (types)			
Said to have how many vowels?	8		
Marked vowel types	front rounded		
Tone	none		
Rhythm	no information		
Vowel harmony	front–back and rounding		
Morphology	agglutinative	word-based	
Particular formation types	dvandva; incorporation; partial suffixed reduplication; suffix		
Syntax			
Word order	SOV	AN NPoss	postpositions
Particular syntactic phenomena	morphological aspect; nominative / accusative marking		
Points of interest			
Sources	Campbell (1991), Katzner (1977), Kornfilt (1997), Wälchli (2005)		

Language name	Turkana		tɜːˈkɑːnə
Autonym (if known and different)			
Language family	Nilo–Saharan	Eastern Sudanic	
Spoken in	Kenya		
Approximate number of speakers	340k		
Writing system			
Phonetics/phonology			
Stress			
Contains following rare consonant (types)			
Said to have how many vowels?	9 + voicelessness		
Marked vowel types			
Tone	register		
Rhythm	no information		
Vowel harmony	ATR		
Morphology	agglutinative	stem-based	
Particular formation types	prefix; suffix		
Syntax			
Word order	VSO	NA NPoss	prepositions
Particular syntactic phenomena	noun classes		
Points of interest			
Sources	Dimmendaal (1983), Haspelmath et al. (2005), Katzner (1977)		

Language name	Tzeltal		'tseltaːl
Autonym (if known and different)			
Language family	Penutian	Mayan	
Spoken in	Mexico		
Approximate number of speakers	100k		
Writing system			
Phonetics/phonology			
Stress			
Contains following rare consonant (types)	ejective		
Said to have how many vowels?	5		
Marked vowel types			
Tone	none		
Rhythm	no information		
Vowel harmony	none		
Morphology	polysynthetic	stem-based for verbs; word-based for nouns	
Particular formation types	dvandva; prefix; suffix; full and partial reduplication		
Syntax			
Word order	VOS		
Particular syntactic phenomena	classifiers; ergative / absolutive marking		
Points of interest			
Sources	Katzner (1977), Maddieson (1984), Ruhlen (1976), Wälchli (2005)		

Language name	Tuvaluan		tuːvəˈluːən
Autonym (if known and different)			
Language family	Austronesian	Polynesian	
Spoken in	Tuvalu		
Approximate number of speakers	11k		
Writing system	Roman		
Phonetics/phonology			
Stress	word-penultimate		
Contains following rare consonant (types)			
Said to have how many vowels?	5 + length		
Marked vowel types			
Tone	none		
Rhythm	no information		
Vowel harmony	none		
Morphology	isolating and agglutinative	word-based	
Particular formation types	prefix; partial suffixed, internal and full reduplication; suffix		
Syntax			
Word order	verb-initial	NA NPoss	prepositions
Particular syntactic phenomena	absolutive / ergative marking; inclusive / exclusive 1st plural; dual		
Points of interest			
Sources	Besnier (2000), Katzner (1977)		

Twi see Akan

Language name	Tzutujil		'(t)suːtʼɛwiːl
Autonym (if known and different)			
Language family	Mayan	Greater Quichean	
Spoken in	Guatemala		
Approximate number of speakers	50k		
Writing system	Roman		
Phonetics/phonology			
Stress	word-final		
Contains following rare consonant (types)	ejective; implosive		
Said to have how many vowels?	5 + length + 2 diphthongs		
Marked vowel types			
Tone	none		
Rhythm	no information		
Vowel harmony	none		
Morphology	agglutinative	word-based	
Particular formation types	prefix; partial prefixed and partial suffixed reduplication; suffix; synaffix		
Syntax			
Word order	VOS	AN and NA NPoss	prepositions
Particular syntactic phenomena	ergative / absolutive marking; morphological aspect		
Points of interest			
Sources	Dayley (1985)		

Language name	Tzotzil		'tsʌotsil
Autonym (if known and different)			
Language family	Penutian	Mayan	
Spoken in	Mexico		
Approximate number of speakers	65k		
Writing system			
Phonetics/phonology			
Stress	word-final		
Contains following rare consonant (types)	ejective		
Said to have how many vowels?	5		
Marked vowel types			
Tone	none		
Rhythm	no information		
Vowel harmony	none		
Morphology	agglutinative	stem-based	
Particular formation types	dvandva; prefix; suffix		
Syntax			
Word order	VOS	AN NPoss	prepositions
Particular syntactic phenomena	ergative / absolutive marking; inclusive / exclusive 1st plural; morphological aspect; classifiers		
Points of interest			
Sources	Aissen (1987), Katzner (1977), Ruhlen (1976), Wälchli (2005)		

Uighur see Uyghur

Language name	Ulithian		jiu'kreɪnən
Autonym (if known and different)			
Language family	Austronesian	Malayo-Polynesian	
Spoken in	Caroline Islands		
Approximate number of speakers	1k		
Writing system	Roman		
Phonetics/phonology			
Stress	variable		
Contains following rare consonant (types)			
Said to have how many vowels?	8 + length		
Marked vowel types			
Tone	none		
Rhythm	no information		
Vowel harmony	none		
Morphology	agglutinative	word–based	
Particular formation types	prefix; partial prefixed reduplication; suffix		
Syntax			
Word order	SVO	NA NPoss	prepositions
Particular syntactic phenomena	classifiers; inclusive / exclusive 1st plural		
Points of interest			
Sources	Lynch (2002b), Ruhlen (1976), Sohn & Bender (1973)		

Language name	Ukrainian		jiu'kreɪnən
Autonym (if known and different)			
Language family	Indo–European	Slavic	
Spoken in	Ukraine		
Approximate number of speakers	60m		
Writing system	Cyrillic		
Phonetics/phonology			
Stress	variable		
Contains following rare consonant (types)			
Said to have how many vowels?	6		
Marked vowel types			
Tone	none		
Rhythm	no information		
Vowel harmony	none		
Morphology	fusional	stem–based	
Particular formation types	prefix; suffix		
Syntax			
Word order	SVO	AN NPoss	prepositions
Particular syntactic phenomena	gender; nominative / accusative marking; conjugation classes; morphological aspect		
Points of interest			
Sources	Campbell (1991), Ruhlen (1976), Shevelov (1993)		

Language name	Urdu		'ʊəduː, 'ɜːduː
Autonym (if known and different)			
Language family	Indo-European	Indic	
Spoken in	Pakistan, India		
Approximate number of speakers	50m		
Writing system	Urdu script, modified from Perso-Arabic		
Phonetics/phonology			
Stress			
Contains following rare consonant (types)	retroflex; voiced aspirated plosive		
Said to have how many vowels?	5 + length + nasalisation + 4 diphthongs		
Marked vowel types			
Tone	none		
Rhythm	no information		
Vowel harmony	none		
Morphology	fusional	stem-based	
Particular formation types	suffix		
Syntax			
Word order	SOV	AN / PossN	postpositions
Particular syntactic phenomena	gender; morphological aspect; nominative / accusative marking; conjugation classes		
Points of interest	basically the same language as Hindi, though written with a different script, and several vocabulary differences		
Sources	Barz (1977), Campbell (1991), Maddieson (1984), Ruhlen (1976)		

Language name	Urubu-Kaapor		
Autonym (if known and different)			
Language family	Tupí-Guaraní		
Spoken in	Brazil		
Approximate number of speakers	500		
Writing system	Roman		
Phonetics/phonology			
Stress	word-final		
Contains following rare consonant (types)			
Said to have how many vowels?	6 + nasalisation		
Marked vowel types			
Tone	none		
Rhythm	no information		
Vowel harmony	none		
Morphology	agglutinative	stem-based	
Particular formation types	(incorporation); prefix; full reduplication; suffix		
Syntax			
Word order	SOV	NA / NPoss	postpositions
Particular syntactic phenomena	morphological aspect		
Points of interest			
Sources	Kakumasu (1986)		

Language name	Vietnamese	Annamite	
Autonym (if known and different)	tiếng Việt	viːetnəˈmiːz	
Language family	Austro–Asiatic	Mon–Khmer	
Spoken in	Vietnam		
Approximate number of speakers	66m		
Writing system	Roman		
Phonetics/phonology			
Stress			
Contains following rare consonant (types)	retroflex; implosive		
Said to have how many vowels?	11 + 20 diphthongs		
Marked vowel types	back unrounded		
Tone	contour		
Rhythm	no information		
Vowel harmony	none		
Morphology	isolating	word–based	
Particular formation types	dvanda; prefix; partial suffixed and full reduplication; suffix		
Syntax			
Word order	SVO	NA / NPoss	prepositions
Particular syntactic phenomena	classifier		
Points of interest	usually cited as the best example of an isolating language		
Sources	Campbell (1991), Maddieson (1984), Nguyễn (1990), Ruhlen (1976), Thompson (1965), Yip (2002)		

Language name	Uyghur	Uighur	ˈwɨiguə
Autonym (if known and different)			
Language family	Altaic	Turkic	
Spoken in	China		
Approximate number of speakers	4.7m		
Writing system	Arabic, Roman and Cyrillic		
Phonetics/phonology			
Stress	word–final		
Contains following rare consonant (types)	uvular		
Said to have how many vowels?	9		
Marked vowel types	front rounded		
Tone	none		
Rhythm	no information		
Vowel harmony	front–back and rounding		
Morphology	agglutinative	word–based	
Particular formation types	suffix		
Syntax			
Word order	SOV	AN / PossN	postpositions
Particular syntactic phenomena	nominative / accusative marking		
Points of interest	very similar to Uzbek		
Sources	Hahn (1998)		

Language name	Warekena	wæleˈkenə
Autonym (if known and different)		
Language family	Arawakan	North Maipuran
Spoken in	Brazil, Venezuela	
Approximate number of speakers	300	
Writing system	Roman	
Phonetics/phonology		
Stress	variable	
Contains following rare consonant (types)		
Said to have how many vowels?	4 + length + nasalisation	
Marked vowel types		
Tone	none	
Rhythm	no information	
Vowel harmony	none	
Morphology	agglutinative	word-based
Particular formation types	prefix; partial suffixed and full reduplication; suffix	
Syntax		
Word order	SVO	NA (PossN) NPoss
Particular syntactic phenomena	classifiers; gender; morphological aspect	
Points of interest	no coordinating conjunctions; no underived adjectives	prepositions and postpositions
Sources	Aikhenvald (1998), Asher (1994)	

Language name	Wai Wai	ˈwaɪwaɪ
Autonym (if known and different)		
Language family	Cariban	
Spoken in	Guyana, Brazil, Surinam	
Approximate number of speakers	2k	
Writing system	Roman	
Phonetics/phonology		
Stress	word-final	
Contains following rare consonant (types)		
Said to have how many vowels?	6 + length	
Marked vowel types		
Tone	none	
Rhythm	no information	
Vowel harmony	none	
Morphology	agglutinative	stem-based for verbs; word-based for nouns
Particular formation types	prefix; suffix; synaffix	
Syntax		
Word order	OV	NModifier PossN	postpositions
Particular syntactic phenomena	absolutive / ergative marking; inclusive / exclusive 1st plural; collectives rather than plurals	
Points of interest		
Sources	Hawkins (1998)	

Language name	Warlpiri	Warlbiri	'waɪlbri
Autonym (if known and different)			
Language family	Pama-Nyungan		
Spoken in	Central Australia		
Approximate number of speakers	3k		
Writing system			
Phonetics/phonology			
Stress	word-inital		
Contains following rare consonant (types)	retroflex		
Said to have how many vowels?	3 + length		
Marked vowel types			
Tone	none		
Rhythm	stress-timing		
Vowel harmony	front–back (which also involves rounding)		
Morphology	agglutinative	word-based	
Particular formation types	partial suffixed and full reduplication; suffix		
Syntax			
Word order	free	NA / NPoss	postpositions
Particular syntactic phenomena	absolutive / ergative marking; inclusive / exclusive 1st plural; morphological aspect; nominative / accusative marking; dual; conjugation classes		
Points of interest			
Sources	Nash (1985), Simpson (1991)		

Language name	Wari'		
Autonym (if known and different)			
Language family	Chapakuran		
Spoken in	Brazil		
Approximate number of speakers	2k		
Writing system			
Phonetics/phonology			
Stress	word-final		
Contains following rare consonant (types)	simultaneous apico-dental plosive and bilabial trills		
Said to have how many vowels?	6		
Marked vowel types	front rounded		
Tone	none		
Rhythm	no information		
Vowel harmony	vowel identity; also some disharmony		
Morphology	isolating	word-based	
Particular formation types	conversion; prefix; partial suffixed, partial infixed and full reduplication; suffix		
Syntax			
Word order	VOS	no adjectives / NPoss	prepositions
Particular syntactic phenomena	gender; inclusive / exclusive 1st plural; inflecting preposition		
Points of interest			
Sources	Everett & Kern (1997), Gordon (2002)		

Warlbiri see **Warlpiri**

Language name	Welsh		welʃ
Autonym (if known and different)			
Language family	Indo-European	Celtic	
Spoken in	Wales		
Approximate number of speakers	750k		
Writing system	Roman		
Phonetics/phonology			
Stress	word-final or penultimate		
Contains following rare consonant (types)			
Said to have how many vowels?	13		
Marked vowel types			
Tone	none		
Rhythm	no information		
Vowel harmony	none		
Morphology	fusional	stem-based	
Particular formation types	apophony; prefix; partial prefixed reduplication; suffix; synaffix		
Syntax			
Word order	VSO	NA / NPoss	prepositions
Particular syntactic phenomena	gender; inflecting prepositions; conjugation classes		
Points of interest	mutation of word-initial consonants		
Sources	Campbell (1991), Thorne (1993)		

Wendish see **Sorbian**

Language name	Washoe, Washo		'woʃəu
Autonym (if known and different)			
Language family	Hokan		
Spoken in	California, Nevada (USA)		
Approximate number of speakers	100		
Writing system			
Phonetics/phonology			
Stress	ejective		
Contains following rare consonant (types)			
Said to have how many vowels?	6 + length + nasalisation		
Marked vowel types			
Tone	none		
Rhythm	no information		
Vowel harmony	some		
Morphology	agglutinative	stem-based	
Particular formation types	prefix; suffix; partial prefixed and partial suffixed and full reduplication		
Syntax			
Word order	SOV	AN / PossN	postpositions
Particular syntactic phenomena	inclusive / exclusive 1st plural; switch reference		
Points of interest			
Sources	Haspelmath et al. (2005), Mithun (1999), Ruhlen (1976)		

Language name	Wintu	win'tu:
Autonym (if known and different)		
Language family	Penutian	
Spoken in	California (USA)	
Approximate number of speakers	10	
Writing system		
Phonetics/phonology		
Stress	word-initial	
Contains following rare consonant (types)	uvular; ejective	
Said to have how many vowels?	5 + length	
Marked vowel types		
Tone	none	
Rhythm	no information	
Vowel harmony	some	
Morphology	agglutinative	word-based
Particular formation types	prefix; full reduplication; suffix	
Syntax		
Word order	Free	AN / NPoss / prepositions
Particular syntactic phenomena	classifiers; noun class; inclusive / exclusive 1st plural; evidentials; nominative / accusative marking; dual; morphological aspect	
Points of interest		
Sources	Maddieson (1984), Mithun (1999), Pitkin (1984), Shepherd (1989)	

Language name	West Greenlandic	Inuit	west grin'laendik
Autonym (if known and different)	kalaallit oqaasii		
Language family	Eskimo-Aleut		
Spoken in	Greenland, Denmark		
Approximate number of speakers	40k		
Writing system	Roman		
Phonetics/phonology			
Stress	word-final		
Contains following rare consonant (types)	uvular		
Said to have how many vowels?	3 + length		
Marked vowel types			
Tone	none		
Rhythm	no information		
Vowel harmony	none		
Morphology	polysynthetic	stem-based	
Particular formation types	incorporation; suffix		
Syntax			
Word order	SOV	NA / PossN	postpositions
Particular syntactic phenomena	absolutive / ergative marking; inclusive / exclusive 1st plural; morphological aspect		
Points of interest			
Sources	Fortescue (1984)		

Western Desert see Pitjantjatjara

Wolof

Language name	Wolof		'wolɔf
Autonym (if known and different)			
Language family	Niger-Congo	Atlantic	
Spoken in	Senegal, Gambia		
Approximate number of speakers	10m		
Writing system	Arabic and Roman		
Phonetics/phonology			
Stress			
Contains following rare consonant (types)	uvular; ejective, implosive		
Said to have how many vowels?	7 + length		
Marked vowel types	front rounded		
Tone	none		
Rhythm	no information		
Vowel harmony	none		
Morphology	isolating and agglutinative		
Particular formation types	reduplication; suffix; apophony		
Syntax			
Word order	SVO	NA PossN	prepositions
Particular syntactic phenomena	morphological aspect; classifiers; noun classes		
Points of interest			
Sources	Campbell (1991), Maddieson (1984), Robert (2003), Ruhlen (1976)		

Woleaian

Language name	Woleaian		
Autonym (if known and different)			
Language family	Austronesian	Micronesian	
Spoken in	Caroline Islands		
Approximate number of speakers	1.5k		
Writing system	Roman (recently introduced)		
Phonetics/phonology			
Stress			
Contains following rare consonant (types)			
Said to have how many vowels?	14 (8 long, 6 short)		
Marked vowel types			
Tone	none		
Rhythm	no information		
Vowel harmony	none		
Morphology	agglutinative and fusional	word-based	
Particular formation types	prefix; partial prefixed, partial suffixed and full reduplication; suffix		
Syntax			
Word order	SVO	AN NPoss	prepositions
Particular syntactic phenomena	classifiers; inclusive / exclusive 1st plural		
Points of interest			
Sources	Sohn (1975)		

Language name	Xhosa		'kauso, 'kɔːsə
Autonym (if known and different)	isiXhosa		
Language family	Niger-Congo	Bantu	
Spoken in	South Africa, Botswana		
Approximate number of speakers	7m		
Writing system			
Phonetics/phonology			
Stress	word-penultimate		
Contains following rare consonant (types)	click; ejective; implosive		
Said to have how many vowels?	5 + 4 diphthongs		
Marked vowel types			
Tone	register		
Rhythm	no information		
Vowel harmony	none		
Morphology	agglutinative	stem-based in nouns, word-based in verbs	
Particular formation types	prefix; suffix		
Syntax			
Word order	SVO	NA NPoss	prepositions
Particular syntactic phenomena	nominative / accusative marking; noun classes		
Points of interest			
Sources	Boyce (1844), Doke (1954)		

!Xũ see p. 367

Language name	Yagua		postpositions
Autonym (if known and different)	'jaːgwə		
Language family	Peba-Yaguan		
Spoken in	Peru, Brazil		
Approximate number of speakers	3k		
Writing system	Roman		
Phonetics/phonology			
Stress			
Contains following rare consonant (types)	retroflex		
Said to have how many vowels?	6 + nasalisation		
Marked vowel types			
Tone	register		
Rhythm	no information		
Vowel harmony	none		
Morphology	agglutinative	stem-based	
Particular formation types	prefix; suffix		
Syntax			
Word order	(VSO) SVO	NA PossN	
Particular syntactic phenomena	classifiers; noun class; dual		
Points of interest			
Sources	Payne (1986), Payne & Payne (1990)		

Yakuba see Dan

Language name	Yawelmani	jɑːwelˈmɑːni	
Autonym (if known and different)			
Language family	Yokutsan		
Spoken in	California (USA)		
Approximate number of speakers			
Writing system			
Phonetics/phonology			
Stress	word-penultimate		
Contains following rare consonant (types)	ejective		
Said to have how many vowels?	5 + length		
Marked vowel types			
Tone	none		
Rhythm	no information		
Vowel harmony	rounding		
Morphology	agglutinative	stem-based	
Particular formation types	apophony; suffix; full and partial reduplication		
Syntax			
Word order	variable	neither	
Particular syntactic phenomena	morphological aspect; dual; nominative / accusative marking		
Points of interest			
Sources	Haspelmath et al. (2005), Mithun (1999)		

Language name	Yiddish		ˈjɪdɪʃ
Autonym (if known and different)			
Language family	Indo-European	Germanic	
Spoken in	USA, Israel, Eastern Europe		
Approximate number of speakers	3m		
Writing system	Hebrew		
Phonetics/phonology			
Stress	word-initial		
Contains following rare consonant (types)			
Said to have how many vowels?	6 + 3 diphthongs		
Marked vowel types			
Tone	none		
Rhythm	stress-timing		
Vowel harmony	none		
Morphology	fusional	word-based	
Particular formation types	apophony; prefix; suffix; synaffix		
Syntax			
Word order	SVO	AN PossN	prepositions
Particular syntactic phenomena	gender; nominative / accusative marking; conjugation classes		
Points of interest	Jewish lingua franca with elements from Hebrew, Aramaic and Slavic as well as Germanic		
Sources	Birnbaum (1979), Campbell (1991), Katz (1987)		

Language name	Yoruba		
Autonym (if known and different)	'jọrụba		
Language family	Niger-Congo	Kwa	
Spoken in	Nigeria, Dahomey, Benin		
Approximate number of speakers	20m		
Writing system	Roman		
Phonetics/phonology			
Stress			
Contains following rare consonant (types)			
Said to have how many vowels?	7 + nasalisation (4)		
Marked vowel types			
Tone	register		
Rhythm	syllable-timing		
Vowel harmony	some height		
Morphology	isolating and agglutinative	word-based	
Particular formation types	prefix; full reduplication		
Syntax			
Word order	SVO	NA NPoss	prepositions
Particular syntactic phenomena	morphological aspect; serial verbs		
Points of interest			
Sources	Bamgbose (1969), Campbell (1991), Pulleyblank (2003), Rowlands (1969), Ruhlen (1976)		

Language name	Yimas		
Autonym (if known and different)			
Language family	Papuan	Lower Sepik	
Spoken in	Papua New Guinea		
Approximate number of speakers	250		
Writing system			
Phonetics/phonology			
Stress	word-initial		
Contains following rare consonant (types)			
Said to have how many vowels?	4		
Marked vowel types			
Tone	none		
Rhythm	no information		
Vowel harmony	none		
Morphology	polysynthetic	stem-based for verbs; word-based for nouns	
Particular formation types	incorporation; partial prefixed and full reduplication; suffix		
Syntax			
Word order	verb-final	AN and NA PossN and NPoss	neither
Particular syntactic phenomena	morphological aspect; noun class; dual and paucal; serial verbs		
Points of interest			
Sources	Foley (1986, 1991)		

Yinisey see Ket

Language name	Zapotec		'zæpatek
Autonym (if known and different)			
Language family	Oto-Manguean		
Spoken in	Mexico		
Approximate number of speakers	300k		
Writing system	Roman		
Phonetics/phonology			
Stress	root-final		
Contains following rare consonant (types)	retroflex		
Said to have how many vowels?	7		
Marked vowel types			
Tone	register		
Rhythm	no information		
Vowel harmony	none		
Morphology	agglutinative		
Particular formation types	prefix; suffix		
Syntax			
Word order	VSO	NA NPoss	prepositions
Particular syntactic phenomena	inclusive / exclusive 1st plural; morphological aspect; noun classes		
Points of interest			
Sources	Campbell (1991), Gordon (2002), Ruhlen (1976)		

Language name	Yupik		'juːpɪk
Autonym (if known and different)			
Language family	Eskimo-Aleut		
Spoken in	Alaska (USA), Siberia, Aleutian Islands		
Approximate number of speakers	21k		
Writing system			
Phonetics/phonology			
Stress	2nd vowel		
Contains following rare consonant (types)	uvular		
Said to have how many vowels?	3 + length		
Marked vowel types			
Tone	tonal accent		
Rhythm	no information		
Vowel harmony	none		
Morphology	polysynthetic		
Particular formation types	incorporation; suffix		
Syntax			
Word order	SVO	NA	neither
Particular syntactic phenomena	absolutive / ergative marking; dual; evidentials		
Points of interest	over 450 derivational affixes		
Sources	Gordon (2002), Haspelmath et al. (2005), Mithun (1999), Ruhlen (1976), Yip (2002)		

Language name	Zoque		'soʊkeɪ
Autonym (if known and different)			
Language family	Penutian	Mixe-Zoque	
Spoken in	Mexico		
Approximate number of speakers	20k		
Writing system			
Phonetics/phonology			
Stress	word-penultimate		
Contains following rare consonant (types)			
Said to have how many vowels?	6		
Marked vowel types			
Tone	none		
Rhythm	no information		
Vowel harmony	none		
Morphology	agglutinative	word-based	
Particular formation types	prefix; suffix		
Syntax			
Word order	SVO	AN PossN	prepositions and/or postpositions
Particular syntactic phenomena	evidentials; dual		
Points of interest			
Sources	Gordon (2002), Haspelmath et al. (2005), Maddieson (1984), Ruhlen (1976)		

Language name	Zulu	isiZulu	'zuːlu:
Autonym (if known and different)			
Language family	Niger-Congo	Bantu	
Spoken in	South Africa		
Approximate number of speakers	8m		
Writing system			
Phonetics/phonology			
Stress	word-penultimate		
Contains following rare consonant (types)	click; ejective; implosive		
Said to have how many vowels?	5 + length		
Marked vowel types			
Tone	register		
Rhythm	no information		
Vowel harmony	some height		
Morphology	agglutinative	stem-based	
Particular formation types	prefix; suffix; tone used morphologically		
Syntax			
Word order	SVO	NA NPoss	prepositions
Particular syntactic phenomena	noun classes		
Points of interest			
Sources	Doke (1927, 1954), Haspelmath et al. (2005), Maddieson (1984), Poulos & Bosch (1997), Ruhlen (1976)		

Language name	!Xũ	!Kung
Autonym (if known and different)		
Language family	Khoisan	
Spoken in	Botswana, Angola, Namibia	
Approximate number of speakers	10k	
Writing system		
Phonetics/phonology		
Stress		
Contains following rare consonant (types)	click; ejective; contrastive breathy voicing	
Said to have how many vowels?	5 + length + nasalisation + pharygealisation (24 in all) + 22 diphthongs	
Marked vowel types		
Tone		
Rhythm	no information	
Vowel harmony	none	
Morphology	isolating	
Particular formation types	suffix	
Syntax		
Word order	SVO	NA postpositions PossN
Particular syntactic phenomena		
Points of interest	48 contrastive click consonants and another 47 non-click consonants gives this language one of the largest consonant inventories known	
Sources	Campbell (1991), Maddieson (1984)	

Language name	Zuñi	'zunji
Autonym (if known and different)		
Language family	isolate	
Spoken in	New Mexico (USA)	
Approximate number of speakers	3k	
Writing system		
Phonetics/phonology		
Stress	word-initial	
Contains following rare consonant (types)	ejective	
Said to have how many vowels?	5 + length	
Marked vowel types		
Tone	none	
Rhythm	no information	
Vowel harmony	none	
Morphology	polysynthetic	stem-based
Particular formation types	prefix; suffix; incorporation; partial prefixed reduplication	
Syntax		
Word order	SOV	NA postpositions PossN
Particular syntactic phenomena	conjugation classes; dual; morphological aspect; nominative / accusative marking; noun classes; switch reference	
Points of interest		
Sources	Campbell (1991), Maddieson (1984), Mithun (1999), Ruhlen (1976)	

Sources for language file

Abbott, Miriam (1991). Macushi. In Desmond C. Derbyshire & Geoffrey K. Pullum (eds), *Handbook of Amazonian Languages*, Vol. III. Berlin and New York: Mouton de Gruyter, 23–160.

Aikhenvald, Alexandra Y. (1998). Warekena. In Desmond C. Derbyshire & Geoffrey K. Pullum (eds), *Handbook of Amazonian Languages*, Vol. IV. Berlin and New York: Mouton de Gruyter, 225–440.

Aikhenvald, Alexandra Y. & R. M .W. Dixon (1999). Other small families and isolates. In R. M. W. Dixon & Alexandra Y. Aikhenvald (eds), *Amazonian Languages*. Cambridge: Cambridge University Press, 341–84.

Aissen, Judith L. (1987). *Tzotzil Clause Structure*. Dordrecht: Reidel.

Amith, Jonathan D. & Thomas C. Smith-Stark (1994). Predicate nominal and transitive verbal expressions of interpersonal relations. *Linguistics* 32: 511–47.

Annamalai, E. & Stanford B. Steever (1998). Modern Tamil. In Stanford B. Steever (ed.), *The Dravidian Languages*. London and New York: Routledge, 100–28.

Aoki, Haruo (1970). *Nez Perce Grammar*. Berkeley: University of California Press.

Arnott, D. W. (1970). *The Nominal and Verbal Systems of Fula*. London: Oxford University Press.

Asher, R. E. (1982). *Tamil*. Amsterdam: North-Holland.

Asher, R. E. (ed.) (1994). *The Encyclopedia of Language and Linguistics*. 10 vols. Oxford: Pergamon.

Asher, R. E. & T. C. Kumari (1997). *Malayalam*. London and New York: Routledge.

Ashton, E. O. (1947). *Swahili Grammar*. 2nd edn. Harlow: Longman.

Austin, Peter (1981). *A Grammar of Diyari, South Australia*. Cambridge: Cambridge University Press.

Bailin, Alan & Ann Grafstein (1991). The assignment of thematic roles in Ojibwa. *Linguistics* 29: 397–422.

Baker, Mark C. (1988). *Incorporation*. Chicago: University of Chicago Press.

Baker, Mark (1996). *The Polysynthesis Parameter*. New York: Oxford University Press.

Bamgbose, Ayo (1969). Yoruba. In Elizabeth Dunstan (ed.), *Twelve Nigerian Languages*. New York: Africana, 163–72.

Barnes, Michael P. (1998). *The Norn Language of Orkney and Shetland*. Lerwick: The Shetland Times.

Barz, R. K. (1977). *An Introduction to Hindi and Urdu*. Canberra: Australian National University.

Bashir, Elena (2005). Burushaski. In Philipp Strazny (ed.), *Encyclopedia of Linguistics*. New York: Fitzroy Dearborn, 163–7.

Bauer, Laurie (1988). A descriptive gap in morphology. *Yearbook of Morphology* 1: 17–27.

Bauer, Robert S. & Stephen Matthews (2003). Cantonese. In Graham Thurgood & Randy A. LaPolla (eds), *The Sino-Tibetan Languages*. London and New York: Routledge, 146–55.

Bauer, Winifred (1993). *Maori*. London and New York: Routledge.

Bender, M. Lionel (2003). Amharic. In W. Frawley (ed.), *The International Encyclopedia of Linguistics*, Vol. I. 2nd edn. Oxford: Oxford University Press, 72–7.

Bender, Marvin L., Hailu Fulass & Roger Cowley (1976). Two Ethio-Semitic languages. In M. L. Bender, J. D. Bower, B. L. Cooper and C. A. Ferguson (eds), *Language in Ethiopia*. London: Oxford University Press, 107–19.

Bendor-Samuel, John (1989). *The Niger-Congo Languages*. Lanham MD: University Press of America.

Berman, Ruth (2003). Hebrew. In W. Frawley (ed.), *The International Encyclopedia of Linguistics*, Vol. II. 2nd edn. Oxford: Oxford University Press, 145–50.

Besnier, Niko (2000). *Tuvaluan*. London and New York: Routledge.

Bhatia, Tej K. (1993). *Punjabi*. London and New York: Routledge.

Bhatia, Tej K. (2005). Hindi-Urdu. In Philipp Strazny (ed.), *Encyclopedia of Linguistics*. New York: Fitzroy Dearborn, 455–9.

Biber, Douglas & John Saeed (2003). Somali. In W. Frawley (ed.), *The International Encyclopedia of Linguistics*, Vol. IV. 2nd end. Oxford: Oxford University Press, 106–9.

Birnbaum, Solomon (1979). *Yiddish*. Toronto and Buffalo NY: University of Toronto Press.

Blackings, Mairi & Nigel Fabb (2003). *A Grammar of Ma'di*. Berlin and New York: Mouton de Gruyter.

Blake, Barry (2003). *The Bunganditj (Buwandik) Language of the Mount Gambier Region*. Canberra: Pacific Linguistics.

Blake, Frank R. (1925). *A Grammar of the Tagalog Language*. New Haven CT: American Oriental Society.

Bloomfield, Leonard (1946). Algonquian. In Harry Hoijer (ed.), *Linguistic Structures of Native America*. New York: Johnson Reprint, 85–129.

Bonfante, Giuliano & Larissa Bonfante (2002). *The Etruscan Language*. 2nd edn. Manchester and New York: Manchester University Press.

Borg, Albert & Marie Azzopardi-Alexander (1997). *Maltese*. London and New York: Routledge.

Borgman, Donald M. (1990). Sanuma. In Desmond C. Derbyshire & Geoffrey K. Pullum (eds), *Handbook of Amazonian Languages*, Vol. II. Berlin and New York: Mouton de Gruyter, 17–248.

Bosson, James E. (1964). *Modern Mongolian*. Bloomington: Indiana University Press.

Boyce, William B. (1844). *A Grammar of the Kaffir Language*. 2nd edn, augmented and improved by J. Davis. London: Wesleyan Missionary Society.

Bray, R. G. A. de (1980). *A Guide to the South Slavonic Languages*. Columbus OH: Slavica.

Bredsdorff, Elias (1956). *Danish*. Cambridge: Cambridge University Press.

Bright, William (ed.) (1992). *International Encyclopedia of Linguistics*. 4 vols. New York and Oxford: Oxford University Press.

Bromley, H. Myron (1981). *A Grammar of Lower Grand Valley Dani*. Canberra: Pacific Linguistics.

Brown, Lea (2005). Nias. In Alexander Adelaar & Nikolaus P. Himmelmann (eds), *The Austronesian Languages of Asia and Madagascar*. London and New York: Routledge, 562–89.

Browne, Wayles (1993). Serbo-Croat. In Bernard Comrie & Greville G. Corbett (eds), *The Slavonic Languages*. London and New York: Routledge, 306–87.

Buchholz, Oda & Wilfried Fiedler (1987). *Albanische Grammatik*. Leipzig: VEB.

Byrne, L. S. R. & E. L. Churchill (1993). *A Comprehensive Grammar of French*. 4th edn. Oxford and Cambridge MA: Blackwell.

Callaghan, Catherine A. (1984). *Plains Miwok Dictionary*. Berkeley: University of California Press.

Callaghan, Catherine A. (1987). *Northern Sierra Miwok Dictionary*. Berkeley: University of California Press.

Camara, J. Mattoso Jr. (1972). *The Portuguese Language*. Chicago and London: University of Chicago Press.

Campbell, George L. (1991). *Compendium of the World's Languages*. London and New York: Longman.

Carrell, Patricia L. (1970). *A Transformational Grammar of Igbo*. Cambridge: Cambridge University Press.

Chang, Kun (2003). Tibetan. In W. Frawley (ed.), *The International Encyclopedia of Linguistics*, Vol. IV. 2nd edn. Oxford: Oxford University Press, 246–50.

Chang, Kun & Betty Shefts (1964). *A Manual of Spoken Tibetan*. Seattle: University of Washington Press.

Chapman, Shirley & Desmond C. Derbyshire (1991). Paumarí. In Desmond C. Derbyshire & Geoffrey K. Pullum (eds), *Handbook of Amazonian Languages*, Vol. III. Berlin and New York: Mouton de Gruyter, 161–352.

Chelliah, Shobhana L. (1997). *A Grammar of Meithei*. Berlin and New York: Mouton de Gruyter.

Churchward, C. M. (1953). *Tongan Grammar*. Nuku'alofa: Vava'u Press.

Clements, G. N. (2000). Phonology. In Bernd Heine & Derek Nurse (eds), *African Languages*. Cambridge: Cambridge University Press, 123–60.

Cole, Desmond T. (1955). *An Introduction to Tswana Grammar*. Cape Town: Longman Penguin.

Collinder, Björn (1957). *Survey of the Uralic Languages*. Stockholm: Almquist & Wiksell.

Cook, Thomas L. (1969). Efik. In Elizabeth Dunstan (ed.), *Twelve Nigerian Languages*. New York: Africana, 35–46.

Cook, William H. (1979). A grammar of North Carolina Cherokee. Unpublished PhD dissertation, Yale University.

Craig, Colette Grinevald (1987). Jacaltec. In Timothy Shopen (ed.), *Languages and their Speakers*. Cambridge MA: Winthrop, 3–57.

Crazzolara, J. P. (1955). *A Study of the Acooli Language*. London: Oxford University Press.

Crowley, Terry (1998). *An Erromangan (Sye) Grammar*. Honolulu: University of Hawaii Press.

Davies, John (1981). *Kobon*. Amsterdam: North-Holland.

Dayley, Jon P. (1985). *Tzutujil Grammar*. Berkeley: University of California Press.

Dayley, Jon P. (1989). *Tümpisa (Panamint) Shoshone Grammar*. Berkeley: University of California Press.

De Lancey, Scott (1991). Chronological strata of suffix classes in the Klamath verb. *International Journal of American Linguistics* 57: 426–45.

Delancey, Scott (2003). Lhasa Tibetan. In Graham Thurgood & Randy J. LaPolla (eds), *The Sino-Tibetan Languages*. London and New York: Routledge, 270–88.

Derbyshire, Desmond C. (1979). *Hixkaryana*. Amsterdam: North-Holland.

Diderichsen, Paul (1972). *Essentials of Danish Grammar*. Copenhagen: Akademisk.

Diffloth, Gérard (2003). Khmer. In W. Frawley (ed.), *The International Encyclopedia of Linguistics*, Vol. II. 2nd edn. Oxford: Oxford University Press, 355–9.

Diller, Anthony (2003). Thai. In W. Frawley (ed.), *The International Encyclopedia of Linguistics*, Vol. IV. 2nd edn. Oxford: Oxford University Press, 239–46.

Dimmendaal, Gerrit Jan (1983). *The Turkana Language*. Dordrecht : Foris.

Dixon, R. M. W. (1972). *The Dyirbal Language of North Queensland*. London: Cambridge University Press.

Dixon, Robert (1980). *The Languages of Australia*. Cambridge: Cambridge University Press.

Doak, Ivy Grace (1997). Coeur d'Alene grammatical relations. Unpublished PhD dissertation, University of Texas at Austin.

Doke, Clement M. (1927). *Textbook of Zulu Grammar*. Cape Town: Maskew Miller Longman.

Doke, C. M. (1954). *The Southern Bantu Languages*. London: Oxford University Press.

Doke, C. M. & S. M. Mofokeng (1957). *Textbook of Southern Sotho Grammar*. Cape Town: Maskew Miller Longman.

Donaldson, Bruce C. (1993). *A Grammar of Afrikaans*. Berlin and New York: Mouton de Gruyter.

Donohue, Mark (1999). *A Grammar of Tukang Besi*. Berlin and New York: Mouton de Gruyter.

Driem, George van (1993). *A Grammar of Dumi*. Berlin and New York: Mouton de Gruyter.

Du Feu, Veronica (1996). *Rapanui*. London and New York: Routledge.

Dunstan, Elizabeth (1969). *Twelve Nigerian Languages*. New York: Africana.

Dutton, Tom E. (1996). *Koiari*. Munich and Newcastle: Lincom Europa.

Ehrman, Madeleine E. (1972). *Contemporary Cambodian*. Washington DC: Department of State.

Einarsson, Stefán (1945). *Icelandic*. Baltimore MD: Johns Hopkins University Press.

Elbert, Samuel H. (1970). *Spoken Hawaiian*. Honolulu: University of Hawaii Press.

Engelenhoven, Aone van & Catharina Williams-van Klinken (2005). Tetun and Leti. In Alexander Adelaar & Nikolaus P. Himmelmann (eds), *The Austronesian Languages of Asia and Madagascar*. London and New York: Routledge, 735–68.

England, Nora C. (1983). *A Grammar of Mam, a Mayan Language*. Austin: University of Texas Press.

Everett, Daniel (1986). Pirahã. In Desmond C. Derbyshire & Geoffrey K. Pullum (eds), *Handbook of Amazonian Languages*, Vol. I. Berlin and New York: Mouton de Gruyter, 200–325.

Everett, Dan & Barbara Kern (1997). *Wari*. London and New York: Routledge.

Foley, William A. (1986). *The Papuan Languages of New Guinea*. Cambridge: Cambridge University Press.

Foley, William A. (1991). *The Yimas Language of New Guinea*. Stanford CA: Stanford University Press.

Fortescue, Michael (1984). *West Greenlandic*. London: Croom Helm.

Friedman, Victor A. (1993). Macedonian. In Bernard Comrie & Greville G. Corbett (eds), *The Slavonic Languages*. London and New York: Routledge, 249–305.

Gair, James W. (2003). Sinhala. In W. Frawley (ed.), *The International Encyclopedia of Linguistics*, Vol. IV. 2nd edn. Oxford: Oxford University Press, 67–73.

Gair, James W. & John C. Paolillo (1997). *Sinhala*. Munich and Newcastle: Lincom Europa.

Galloway, Brent D. (1993). *A Grammar of Upriver Halkomelem*. Berkeley: University of California Press.

George, Ken (1993). Cornish. In Martin J. Ball (ed.), *The Celtic Languages*. London and New York: Routledge, 410–68.

Gillies, William (1993). Scottish Gaelic. In Martin J. Ball (ed.), *The Celtic Languages*. London and New York: Routledge, 145–227.

Givon, Tom (1975). Serial verbs and syntactic change: Niger-Congo. In Charles Li (ed.), *Word Order and Word Order Change*. Austin: University of Texas Press, 47–112.

Givon, Tom (1991). Serial verbs and the mental reality of event: grammatical vs cognitive packaging. In Elizabeth Closs Traugott & Bernd Heine (eds), *Approaches to Grammaticalization*. Amsterdam and Philadelphia: Benjamins, 81–128.

Glass, Amee & Dorothy Hackett (1970). *Pitjantjatjara Grammar*. Canberra: Australian Institute of Aboriginal Studies.

Glinert, Lewis (1989). *The Grammar of Modern Hebrew*. Cambridge: Cambridge University Press.

Gonda, Jan (1966). *A Concise Elementary Grammar of the Sanskrit Language*. University AL: University of Alabama Press.

Goodenough, Ward H. & Hiroshi Sugita (1980). *Trukese-English Dictionary*. Philadelphia PA: American Philosophical Society.

Gordon, Matthew (2002). A factorial typology of quantity-insensitive stress. *Natural Language and Linguistic Theory* 20: 491–522.

Gruzdeva, Ekatarina (1998). *Nivkh*. Munich and Newcastle: Lincom Europa.

Guy, J. B. M. (1974). *Handbook of Bichelamar*. Canberra: Pacific Linguistics.

Hagman, Roy Stephen (1973). *Nama Hottentot Grammar*. Ann Arbor MI: UMI Dissertation Services.

Hahn, Reinhard F. (1998). Uyghur. In Lars Johanson & Éva Ágnes Csató (eds), *The Turkic Languages*. London and New York: Routledge, 379–96.

Hancock, Ian (1984). Shelta and Polari. In Peter Trudgill (ed.), *Language in the British Isles*. Cambridge: Cambridge University Press, 384–403.

Harms, Robert T. (1962). *Estonian Grammar*. Bloomington: Indiana University Press.

Harris, Alice C. (2003). Georgian. In W. Frawley (ed.), *The International Encyclopedia of Linguistics*, Vol. II. 2nd edn. Oxford: Oxford University Press, 72–6.

Haspelmath, Martin (1993). *A Grammar of Lezgian*. Berlin and New York: Mouton de Gruyter.

Haspelmath, Martin, Hans-Jorg Bibiko, Hagen Jung & Claudia Schmidt (eds) (2005). *The World Atlas of Language Structures*. Oxford: Oxford University Press.

Haugen, Einar (1938). *Beginning Norwegian*. London: Harrap.

Haviland, John (1979). Guugu Yimidhirr. In R. M. W. Dixon & B. J. Blake (eds), *Handbook of Australian Languages*. Canberra: Australian National University Press, 26–180.

Hawkins, Robert E. (1998). Wai Wai. In Desmond C. Derbyshire & Geoffrey K. Pullum (eds), *Handbook of Amazonian Languages*, Vol. IV. Berlin and New York: Mouton de Gruyter, 25–224.

Hercus, Luise A. (1994). *A Grammar of the Arbana-Wangkanguru Language*. Canberra: Pacific Linguistics.

Hewitt, B. G. (1995). *Georgian*. Amsterdam and Philadelphia: Benjamins.

Hewitt, B. G. & Z. K. Khiba (1979). *Abkhaz*. Amsterdam: North-Holland.

Hinnebusch, Thomas J. (2003). Swahili. In W. Frawley (ed.), *The International Encyclopedia of Linguistics*, Vol. IV. 2nd edn. Oxford: Oxford University Press, 181–8.

Hoard, James E. (1979). On the semantic representation of oblique complements. *Language* 55: 319–32.

Hoffmann, Carl (1963). *A Grammar of the Margi Language*. London: Oxford University Press.

Hollis, A. C. (1970 [1905]). *The Masai: Their Language and Folklore*. Westport CT: Negro Universities Press.

Holmer, Nils M. (1954). *The Seneca Language*. Uppsala: Lundequist.

Holmes, Philip & Ian Hinchcliffe (1994). *Swedish*. London and New York: Routledge.

Holmes, Ruth Bradley & Betty Sharp Smith (1977). *Beginning Cherokee*. 2nd edn. Norman: Oklahoma University Press.

Holt, Dennis (1999). *Tol (Jicaque)*. Munich and Newcastle: Lincom Europa.

Hooper, Robin (1996). *Tokelauan*. Munich and Newcastle: Lincom Europa.

Horne, Elinor C. (1961). *Beginning Javanese*. New Haven and London: Yale University Press.

Howe, Darin (2005). Nootka and Wakashan languages. In Philipp Strazny (ed.), *Encyclopedia of Linguistics*. New York : Fitzroy Dearborn, 753–6.

Hualdo, Jose Ignacio (1992). *Catalan*. London and New York: Routledge.

Hudak, Thomas John (1990). Thai. In Bernard Comrie (ed.), *The Major Languages of East and South-East Asia*. London: Routledge, 29–48.

Huntley, David (1993). Old Church Slavonic. In Bernard Comrie & Greville G. Corbett (eds), *The Slavonic Languages*. London and New York: Routledge, 125–87.

Huttar, George L. & Mary L. Huttar (1994). *Ndyuka*. London and New York: Routledge.

Jakobsen, Jakob (1985 [1928]) *An Etymological Dictionary of the Norn Language in Shetland*. Lerwick: Shetland Folk Society.

Jasanoff, Jay H. (2004). Gothic. In Roger D. Woodard (ed.), *The Cambridge Encyclopedia of the World's Ancient Languages*. Cambridge: Cambridge University Press, 881–906.

Jenewari, Charles E. W. (1989). Ijoid. In John Bendor-Samuels (ed.), *The Niger-Congo Languages*. Lanham MD: University Press of America.

Jensen, Cheryl (1999). Tupí-Guaraní. In R. M. W. Dixon & Alexandra Y. Aikhenvald, *The Amazonian Languages*. Cambridge: Cambridge University Press, 125–63.

Kachru, Yamuna (2003). Hindi. In W. Frawley (ed.), *The International Encyclopedia of Linguistics*, Vol. II. 2nd edn. Oxford: Oxford University Press, 152–6.

Kakumasu, James (1986). Urubu-Kaapor. In Desmond C. Derbyshire and Geoffrey K. Pullum (eds), *Handbook of Amazonian Languages*, Vol. I. Berlin and New York: Mouton de Gruyter, 326–403.

Kalectaca, Milo (1982). *Lessons in Hopi*. Tucson AZ: University of Arizona Press.

Kato, Atsuhiko (2003). Pwo Karen. In Graham Thurgood & Randy La Polla (eds), *Sino-Tibetan Languages*. London and New York: Routledge, 632–48.

Katz, David (1987). *Grammar of the Yiddish Language*. London: Duckworth.

Katzner, Kenneth (1977). *The Languages of the World*. London and New York: Routledge.

Keenan, Edward L. & Maria Polinsky (1998). Malagasy (Austronesian). In Andrew Spencer & Arnold M. Zwicky (eds), *The Handbook of Morphology*. Oxford and Malden MA: Blackwell, 563–623.

Key, Harold H. (1967). *The Morphology of Cayuvava*. The Hague and Paris: Mouton.

Kibrik, Aleksandr E. (1998). Archi (Caucasian – Daghestanian). In Andrew Spencer & Arnold M. Zwicky (eds), *The Handbook of Morphology*. Oxford and Malden MA: Blackwell, 455–76.

Kim, Nam-Kil (2003). Korean. In W. Frawley (ed.), *The International Encyclopedia of Linguistics*, Vol. II. 2nd edn. Oxford: Oxford University Press, 366–70.

Kirchner, Mark (1998). Kirghiz. In Lars Johansson & Éva Ágnes Csató, *The Turkic Languages*. London and New York: Routledge, 344–56.

Klamer, Marian (1994). *Kambera: A Language of Eastern Indonesia*. The Hague: Holland Institute of Generative Linguistics.

Klamer, Marian (2005). Kambera. In Alexander Adelaar & Nikolaus P. Himmelmann (eds), *The Austronesian Languages of Asia and Madagascar*. London and New York: Routledge, 709–34.

Klinken, Catharina Lumien van (1999). *A Grammar of the Fehan Dialect of Tetun*. Canberra: Pacific Linguistics.

Koehn, Edward & Sally Koehn (1986). Apalai. In Desmond C. Derbyshire and Geoffrey K. Pullum (eds), *Handbook of Amazonian Languages*, Vol. 1. Berlin and New York: Mouton de Gruyter, 33–127.

Koolhoven, H. (1949). *Teach Yourself Dutch*. London: English Universities Press.

Kornfilt, Jaklin (1997). *Turkish*. London and New York: Routledge.

Kossmann, Marten (2003). Berber Languages. In W. Frawley (ed.), *The International Encyclopedia of Linguistics*, Vol. I. 2nd edn. Oxford: Oxford University Press, 218–20.

Kouwenberg, Silvia & Eric Murray (1994). *Papiamentu*. Munich and Newcastle: Lincom Europa.

Kraft, C. H. & A. H. M. Kirk-Greene (1973). *Hausa*. London: English Universities Press.

Krishnamurti, Bhadriraju (2003). *The Dravidian Languages*. Cambridge: Cambridge University Press.

Krishnamurti, Bhadriraju & J. P. L. Gwynn (1985). *A Grammar of Modern Telugu*. Delhi: Oxford University Press.

Kuipers, Aert H. (1967). *The Squamish Language*. The Hague and Paris: Mouton.

Kwee, John B. (1976). *Indonesian*. New York: Hodder and Stoughton.

Lee, Kee-dong (1975). *Kusaiean Reference Grammar*. Honolulu: University of Hawaii Press.

Li, Charles N. & Sandra A. Thompson (1981). *Mandarin Chinese*. Berkeley: University of California Press.

Lockwood, W. B. (1964). *An Introduction to Modern Faroese*. Copenhagen: Munksgaard.

Lojena, Constance Kutsch (1994). *Ngiti*. Köln: Koppe.

Lukas, Johannes (1967). *A Study of the Kanuri Language*. London: Dawsons.

Luraghi, Silvia (1990). *Old Hittite Sentence Structure*. London and New York: Routledge.

Luraghi, Silvia (1997). *Hittite*. Munich and Newcastle: Lincom Europa.

Luraghi, Silvia (2005). Ancient Greek. In Philipp Strazny (ed.), *Encyclopedia of Linguistics*. New York: Fitzroy Dearborn, 58–62.

Lynch, John (1978). *A Grammar of Lenakel*. Canberra: Pacific Linguistics.

Lynch, John (2000). *A Grammar of Anejom*. Canberra: Pacific Linguistics.

Lynch, John (2002a). Anejom. In John Lynch, Malcolm Ross & Terry Crowley (eds), *The Oceanic Languages*. Richmond: Curzon, 723–52.

Lynch, John (2002b). Ulithian. In John Lynch, Malcolm Ross & Terry Crowley (eds), *The Oceanic Languages*. Richmond: Curzon, 792–803.

Lyovin, Anatole V. (1997). *An Introduction to the Languages of the World*. Oxford and New York: Oxford University Press.

Mac Eoin, Gearoid (1993). Irish. In Martin J. Ball (ed.), *The Celtic Languages*. London and New York: Routledge, 101–44.

Macalister, R. A. Stewart (1974). *The Secret Languages of Ireland*. London: Cambridge University Press.

Macdonald, R. R. & S. Darjowidjojo (1967). *A Student's Reference Grammar of Modern Formal Indonesian*. Washington DC: Georgetown University Press.

MacKenzie, D. N. (2003). Pashto. In W. Frawley (ed.), *The International Encyclopedia of Linguistics*, Vol. III. 2nd edn. Oxford: Oxford University Press, 251–7.

Mackridge, Peter (1985). *The Modern Greek Language*. Oxford: Oxford University Press.

Maddieson, Ian (1984). *Patterns of Sound*. Cambridge: Cambridge University Press.

Mahootran, Shahrzad (1997). *Persian*. London and New York: Routledge.

Maiden, Martin & Cecilia Robustelli (2000). *A Reference Grammar of Modern Italian*. London: Arnold.

Mallinson, Graham (1986). *Rumanian*. Dover and Sydney: Croom Helm.

Marsack, C. C. (1962). *Teach Yourself Samoan*. London: English Universities Press.

Masica, Colin P. (1991). *The Indo-Aryan Languages*. Cambridge: Cambridge University Press.

Maslova, Elena (2003). *A Grammar of Kolyma Yukaghir*. Berlin and New York: Mouton de Gruyter.

Matras, Yaron (2002). *Romani*. Cambridge: Cambridge University Press.

Matthews, Stephen & Virginia Yip (1994). *Cantonese*. London and New York: Routledge.

Mayrhofer, Manfred (1972). *A Sanskrit Grammar*. University: University of Alabama Press.

McEwen, J. M. (1970). *Niue Dictionary*. Wellington: Department of Maori and Island Affairs.

McGregor, R. S. (1977). *Outline of Hindi Grammar*. Delhi: Oxford University Press.

McKay, Graham (2000). Ndjébanna. In R. M. W. Dixon and B. J. Blake (eds), *The Handbook of Australian Languages*, Vol. V. Melbourne: Oxford University Press, 155–354.

McLendon, Sally (1975). *A Grammar of Eastern Pomo*. Berkeley: University of California Press.

Merlan, Francesca (1982). *Mangarayi*. Amsterdam: North-Holland.

Merrifield, William R. (1968). *Palantla Chinatec Grammar*. Corobda: Instituto Nacional de Antopologia.

Michalowski, Piotr (2004). Sumerian. In Roger D. Woodward (ed.), *The Cambridge Encyclopedia of the World's Ancient Languages*. Cambridge: Cambridge University Press, 19–59.

Milner, G. B. (1972). *Fijian Grammar*. Suva: Government Press.

Mintz, Malcolm W. (1994). *A Student's Grammar of Malay and Indonesian*. Singapore: EPB.

Mistry, P. J. (2003). Gujarati. In W. Frawley (ed.), *The International Encyclopedia of Linguistics*, Vol. II. 2nd edn. Oxford: Oxford University Press, 115–18.

Mithun, Marianne (1984). The evolution of noun incorporation. *Language* 60: 847–94.

Mithun, Marianne (1998). Fluid aspects of negation in central Pomo. In Leanne Hinton & Pamela Munro (eds), *Studies in American Indian Languages*. Berkeley: University of California Press, 77–86.

Mithun, Marianne (1999). *The Languages of Native North America*. Cambridge: Cambridge University Press.

Morice, A. G. (1932). *The Carrier Language*. Wien: Anthropos.

Müller-Gotama, Franz (2001). *Sundanese*. Munich and Newcastle: Lincom Europa.

Nababan, P. W. J. (1981). *A Grammar of Toba-Batak*. Canberra: Pacific Linguistics.

Nakayama, Toshide (2001). *Nuuchahnulth (Nootka) Morphosyntax*. Berkeley: University of California Press.

Nash, David (1985). *Topics in Warlpiri Grammar*. New York and London: Garland.

Nasr, Raja T. (1967). *The Structure of Arabic*. Beirut: Librairie du Liban.

Nau, Nicole (1998). *Latvian*. Munich and Newcastle: Lincom Europa.

Nedjalkov, Igor (1997). *Evenki*. London and New York: Routledge.

Newman, Paul (2003). Hausa. In W. Frawley (ed.), *The International Encyclopedia of Linguistics*, Vol. II. 2nd edn. Oxford: Oxford University Press, 130–7.

Nguyễn, Đinh-Hoa (1990). Vietnamese. In Bernard Comrie (ed.), *The Major Languages of East and South-East Asia*. London: Routledge, 49–68.

Nickel, Klaus Peter (1994). *Samisk Gramatikk. 2. utgave*. Karasjok: Girji.

Ó Siadhail, Micheál (1989). *Modern Irish*. Cambridge: Cambridge University Press.

Oglobin, Alexander K. (2005). Javanese. In Alexander Adelaar & Nikolaus P. Himmelmann (eds), *The Austronesian Languages of Asia and Madagascar*. London and New York: Routledge, 590–624.

Osborne, C. R. (1974). *The Tiwi Language*. Canberra: Australian Institute of Aboriginal Studies.

Pandharipande, Rajeshwari V. (1997). *Marathi*. London and New York: Routledge.

Pandharipande, Rajeshwari V. (2003). Marathi. In W. Frawley (ed.), *The International Encyclopedia of Linguistics*, Vol. III. 2nd edn. Oxford: Oxford University Press, 8–11.

Parkinson, Stephen (2003). Portuguese. In W. Frawley (ed.), *The International Encyclopedia of Linguistics*, Vol. III. 2nd edn. Oxford: Oxford University Press, 371–5.

Payne, Doris L. (1986). Basic constituent order in Yagua clauses. In Desmond C. Derbyshire & Geoffrey K. Pullum (eds), *Handbook of Amazonian Languages*, Vol. I. Berlin and New York: Mouton de Gruyter, 440–65.

Payne, Thomas & Doris Payne (1990). Yagua. In Desmond C. Derbyshire & Geoffrey K. Pullum (eds), *Handbook of Amazonian Languages*, Vol. II. Berlin and New York: Mouton de Gruyter, 249–474.

Percival, W. K. (1981). *A Grammar of the Urbanised Toba-Batak of Medan*. Canberra: Pacific Linguistics.

Pitkin, Harvey (1984). *Wintu Grammar*. Berkeley: University of California Press.

Popjes, Jack & Jo Popjes (1986). Canela-Krahô. In Desmond C. Derbyshire & Geoffrey K. Pullum (eds), *Handbook of Amazonian Languages*, Vol. I. Berlin: Mouton de Gruyter, 128–99.

Poulos, George & Sonja E. Bosch (1997). *Zulu*. Munich and Newcastle: Lincom Europa.

Prakasam, Vennelakanti (2005). Telugu. In Philipp Strazny (ed.), *Encyclopedia of Linguistics*. New York: Fitzroy Dearborn, 1086–8.

Press, Ian (1986). *A Grammar of Modern Breton*. Berlin and New York: Mouton de Gruyter.

Priestly, T. M. S. (1993). Slovenian. In Bernard Comrie & Greville G. Corbett (eds), *The Slavonic Languages*. London and New York: Routledge, 388–454.

Pulleyblank, Douglas (2003). Yoruba. In W. Frawley (ed.), *The International Encyclopedia of Linguistics*, Vol. IV. 2nd edn. Oxford: Oxford University Press, 402–7.

Ramsey, S. Robert (1987). *The Languages of China*. Princeton: Princeton University Press.

Rasoloson, Janie & Carl Rubino (2005). Malagasy. In Alexander Adelaar & Nikolaus P. Himmelmann (eds), *The Austronesian Languages of Asia and Madagascar*. London and New York: Routledge, 456–88.

Rédei, Károly (1965). *Northern Ostyak Chrestomathy*. Bloomington: Indiana University Publications.

Reid, Lawrence A. (1976). *Bontok-English Dictionary*. Canberra: Pacific Linguistics.

Rennison, John R. (1997). *Koromfe*. London and New York: Routledge.

Rice, Keren (1998). Slave (Northern Athapaskan). In Andrew Spencer & Arnold M. Zwicky (eds), *The Handbook of Morphology*. Oxford and Malden MA: Blackwell, 648–9.

Richter, Lutoslawa (1987). Modelling the rhythmic structure of utterances in Polish. *Studia Phonetica Posnaniensia* 1: 91–126.

Rijk, Rudolf P. G. de (2003). Basque. In W. Frawley (ed.), *The International Encyclopedia of Linguistics*, Vol. I. 2nd edn. Oxford: Oxford University Press, 206–13.

Rix, Helmut (2004). Etruscan. In Roger D. Woodard (ed.), *The Cambridge Encyclopedia of the World's Ancient Languages*. Cambridge: Cambridge University Press, 943–66.

Robert, Stéphane (2003). Wolof. In W. Frawley (ed.), *The International Encyclopedia of Linguistics*, Vol. IV. 2nd edn. Oxford: Oxford University Press, 372–4.

Roberts, John R. (1987). *Amele*. London and New York: Croom Helm.

Rood, David S. (1979). Siouan. In Lyle Campbell & Marianne Mithun (eds), *The Languages of Native America*. Austin and London: University of Texas Press, 236–98.

Rothstein, Robert A. (1993). Polish. In Bernard Comrie & Greville G. Corbett (eds), *The Slavonic Languages*. London and New York: Routledge, 686–758.

Rounds, Carol (2001). *Hungarian*. London and New York: Routledge.

Rowlands, E. C. (1969). *Yoruba*. London: Hodder and Stoughton.

Rubino, Carl (2005). Iloko. In Alexander Adelaar & Nikolaus P. Himmelmann (eds), *The Austronesian Languages of Asia and Madagascar*. London and New York: Routledge, 326–49.

Ruhlen, M. (1976). *A Guide to the Languages of the World*. Stanford CA: Stanford University.

Saltarelli, Mario (1988). *Basque*. London: Croom Helm.

Sapir, Edward (1930). Southern Paiute, a Shoshonean language. In William Bright (ed.) (1992), *The Collected Works of Edward Sapir*, Vol. X. Berlin and New York: Mouton de Gruyter, 17–314.

Scatton, Ernest A. (1993). Bulgarian. In Bernard Comrie & Greville G. Corbett (eds), *The Slavonic Languages*. London and New York: Routledge, 188–248.

Schaub, Willi (1985). *Babungo*. London: Croom Helm.

Schmidt, Hans (2002). Rotuman. In John Lynch, Malcolm Ross & Terry Crowley (eds), *The Oceanic Languages*. Richmond: Curzon, 815–32.

Schuh, Russell G. (1998). *A Grammar of Miya*. Berkeley: University of California Press.

Scott, Graham (1978). *The Fore Language of Papua New Guinea*. Canberra: Pacific Linguistics.

Seiler, Hans-Jakob (1977). *Cahuilla Grammar*. Banning CA: Malki Museum Press.

Seiter, William J. (1980). *Studies in Niuean Syntax*. New York and London: Garland.

Senft, Gunter (1986). *Kilivila*. Berlin and New York: Mouton de Gruyter.

Shepherd, Alice (1989). *Wintu Texts*. Berkeley: University of California Press.

Shevelov, George Y. (1993). Ukrainian. In Bernard Comrie & Greville G. Corbett (eds), *The Slavonic Languages*. London and New York: Routledge, 947–98.

Shibatani, Masayoshi (1990). *The Languages of Japan*. Cambridge: Cambridge University Press.

Short, David (1993a). Czech. In Bernard Comrie & Greville G. Corbett (eds), *The Slavonic Languages*. London and New York: Routledge, 455–532.

Short, David (1993b). Slovak. In Bernard Comrie & Greville G. Corbett (eds), *The Slavonic Languages*. London and New York: Routledge, 533–92.

Short, David (2003). Czech and Slovak. In W. Frawley (ed.), *The International Encyclopedia of Linguistics*, Vol. I. 2nd edn. Oxford: Oxford University Press, 410–14.

Silverstein, Michael (1972a). Chinook Jargon I. *Language* 48: 378–406.

Silverstein, Michael (1972b). Chinook Jargon II. *Language* 48: 596–625.

Simpson, Jane (1991). *Warlpiri Morphosyntax*. Dordrecht: Kluwer.

Skinner, Margaret G. (1979). *Aspects of Pa'anci Grammar*. Michigan: UMI Dissertation Services.

Skribnik, Elena (2003). Buryat. In Juha Janhunen (ed.), *The Mongolic Languages*. London and New York: Routledge, 102–28.

Sneddon, J. N. (1975). *Tondano Phonology and Grammar*. Canberra: Pacific Linguistics.

Snoxall, R. A. (1967). *Luganda-English Dictionary*. Oxford: Oxford University Press.

Sohn, Ho-Min (1975). *Woleaian Reference Grammar*. Honolulu: University of Hawaii Press.

Sohn, Ho-Min (1994). *Korean*. London and New York: Routledge.

Sohn, Ho-Min & B. W. Bender (1973). *A Ulithian Gramma*r. Canberra: Pacific Linguistics.

Solnit, David B. (1997). *Eastern Kayah Li*. Honolulu: University of Hawaii Press.

Speas, Margaret J. (1990). *Phrase Structure in Natural Language*. Dordrecht: Kluwer.

Sprouse, Ronald (2000). The moraic status of /ʔ/ and /dʼ/ in Oromo. In Vicki Carstens & Frederick Parkinson (eds), *Advances in African Linguistics*. Trenton and Asmara: Africa World Press, 219–32.

Sridhar, S. N. (1990). *Kannada*. London and New York: Routledge.

Stone, Gerald (1993). Sorbian. In Bernard Comrie & Greville G. Corbett (eds), *The Slavonic Languages*. London and New York: Routledge, 593–685.

Strehlow, T. G. H. (1944). *Aranda Phonetics and Grammar*. Sydney: Australian National Research Centre.

Sulkala, Helena & Merja Karjalainen (1992). *Finnish*. London and New York: Routledge.

Taylor, Charles (1985). *Nkore-Kiga*. London: Croom Helm.

Thomas, David D. (1971). *Chrau Grammar*. Honolulu: University of Hawaii Press.

Thomason, Sarah Grey (1983). Chinook Jargon in areal and historical context. *Language* 59: 820–70.

Thompson, Laurence C. (1965). *A Vietnamese Grammar*. Seattle: University of Washington Press.

Thorne, David A. (1993). *A Comprehensive Welsh Grammar*. Oxford: Blackwell.

Tiersma, Peter Meijes (1985). *Frisian Reference Grammar*. Dordrecht: Foris.

Timberlake, Alan (1993). Russian. In Bernard Comrie & Greville G. Corbett (eds), *The Slavonic Languages*. London and New York: Routledge, 827–86.

Tovar, Antonio (1957). *The Basque Language*. Philadelphia: University of Pennsylvania Press.

Tryon, D. T. (1970). *Conversational Tahitian*. Berkeley and Los Angeles: University of California Press.

Tsumagari, Toshiro (2003). Dagur. In Juha Janhunen (ed.), *The Mongolic Languages*. London and New York: Routledge, 129–53.

Ullendorf, Edward (1965). *An Amharic Chrestomathy*. London: Oxford University Press.

Vajda, Edward (2004). *Ket*. Munich and Newcastle: Lincom Europa.

Vincent, Nigel (1988). Latin. In Martin Harris & Nigel Vincent (eds), *The Romance Languages*. London and Sydney: Croom Helm, 26–78.

Wälchli, Bernhard (2005). *Co-compounds and Natural Coordination*. Oxford: Oxford University Press.

Wali, Kashi & Omkar N. Koul (1997). *Kashmiri*. London and New York: Routledge.

Watkins, Calvert (2004). Hittite. In Roger D. Woodard (ed.), *The Cambridge Encyclopedia of the World's Ancient Languages*. Cambridge: Cambridge University Press, 551–75.

Watkins, Laurel J. (1984). *A Grammar of Kiowa*. Lincoln NE and London: University of Nebraska Press.

Weninger, Stefan (1993). Gəʿəz. Munich and Newcastle: Lincom Europa

Wesley-Jones A. (1992). The Hidatsa approximative. *Anthropological Linguistics* 34: 324–37.

Westermann, Diedrich (1967). *A Study of the Ewe Language*. London: Oxford University Press.

Westermann, Diedrich & M. A. Bryan (1970). *Handbook of African Languages. Part II*. Folkestone: Dawson.

Wheatley, Julian K. (2003). Burmese. In Graham Thurgood & Randy J. LaPolla (eds), *The Sino-Tibetan Languages*. London and New York: Routledge, 195–207.

Whiteley, W. H. & M. G. Muli (1962). *Practical Introduction to Kamba*. London: Oxford University Press.

Whorf, Benjamin Lee (1946). The Hopi language, Toreval dialect. In Harry Hoijer (ed.), *Linguistic Structures of Native America*. New York: Viking Fund, 158–83.

Williamson, Kay (1969a). Igbo. In Elizabeth Dunstan (ed.), *Twelve Nigerian Languages*. New York: Africana, 85–96.

Williamson, Kay (1969b). Ijo. In Elizabeth Dunstan (ed.), *Twelve Nigerian Languages*. New York: Africana, 97–114.

Williamson, Kay & Roger Blench (2000). Niger-Congo. In Bernd Heine & Derek Nurse (eds), *African Languages*. Cambridge: Cambridge University Press, 11–42.

Williamson, Kay & E. Nolue Emenanjo (2003). Igbo. In W. Frawley (ed.), *The International Encyclopedia of Linguistics*, Vol. II. 2nd edn. Oxford: Oxford University Press, 257–61.

Windfuhr, Gernot L. (2003). Persian. In W. Frawley (ed.), *The International Encyclopedia of Linguistics*, Vol. III. 2nd edn. Oxford: Oxford University Press, 263–8.

Wmffre, Iwan (1998a). *Central Breton*. Munich and Newcastle: Lincom Europa.

Wmffre, Iwan (1998b). *Late Cornish*. Munich and Newcastle: Lincom Europa.

Woolford, Ellen B. (1979). *Aspects of Tok Pisin*. Canberra: Pacific Linguistics.

Wu, Chaolu (1996). *Daur*. Munich and Newcastle: Lincom Europa.

Wurm, Stephen & Peter Mühlhäusler (1985). *Handbook of Tok Pisin (New Guinea Pidgin)*. Canberra: Pacific Linguistics.

Yallop, Colin (1982). *Australian Aboriginal Languages*. London: André Deutsch.

Yip, Moira (2002). *Tone*. Cambridge: Cambridge University Press.

Zenk, Henry (1988). Chinook Jargon in the speech economy of Grand Ronde Reservation, Oregon. *International Journal of the Sociology of Language* 71: 107–24.

Index